THE LEGAL STATUS OF
THE ARABIAN GULF STATES

This volume has been published with the aid of a grant made by the International Law Fund and the British Institute of International and Comparative Law.

TO
MY FATHER AND MOTHER

The Legal Status
of the
Arabian Gulf States

A STUDY OF THEIR TREATY RELATIONS AND THEIR INTERNATIONAL PROBLEMS

by

HUSAIN M. ALBAHARNA
Ph.D. (Cantab)

MANCHESTER UNIVERSITY PRESS
U.S.A.: OCEANA PUBLICATIONS INC.

© 1968 HUSAIN M. ALBAHARNA
Published by the University of Manchester
at THE UNIVERSITY PRESS
316–324 Oxford Road, Manchester 13
U.S.A.
OCEANA PUBLICATIONS INC.
75 Main Street, Dobbs Ferry, N.Y. 10522
distributed in India by
N. M. TRIPATHI PRIVATE LTD.
Booksellers and Publishers
Princess Street, Bombay-2

G.B. SBN 7190 0332 6
Library of Congress Catalog Card No. 68-57676

Printed in Great Britain by Butler & Tanner Ltd., Frome and London

Preface

An examination in systematic and comprehensive form of the international legal problems of the Arabian Gulf scarcely requires justification or introduction. The political and economic importance of the area is self-evident; while the rate of political, economic and social change is very great. The evolution into full independence of the protected State of Kuwait and the arrangements connected with it seem to indicate the future pattern of British legal relations with the remaining Shaikhdoms which are today being prepared, in varying degrees, for the assumption of greater responsibilities in their foreign relations.[1]

Moreover, as the pages of this volume will show, the range of international legal problems which arise in relation to the area is wide. It stretches from those examined in the first two parts of the book, which involve primarily questions of the legal and international status of the Arabian Gulf States, to those, examined in the last two parts which involve issues connected with territorial and boundary claims in the Gulf.

So far as I have been able to discover, no previous attempt has been made to canvass all these matters within a single volume. There are, of course, pioneer works such as Aitchison's *Collection of Treaties, Engagements and Sanads*, of which the eleventh volume relates to the Arabian Gulf, but this is no more than its title indicates, namely, a collection of treaty texts, prefaced by short, though valuable, historical notes. Lorimer's *Gazetteer of the Persian Gulf* is essentially a historical work. But in terms of analysis of the international legal problems, no effort appears previously to have been made in English or, for that matter, it would seem, in any other language, to discuss the various juridical difficulties of the whole area in a connected form.

Yet, as will be readily appreciated, even the present work has some limitations to it—of breadth as well as of depth. As regards breadth, although it may perhaps be felt that I have in any case already spread my net too wide, I have nevertheless excluded certain specific items, of which the problems of British foreign jurisdiction in the Gulf and of the relations of the Shaikhdoms with the foreign oil companies in the area are the most significant.[2] And as regards depth, I have

---

[1] It is regretted, however, that these Shaikhdoms still lack the attributes of democratic governments.

[2] Although these problems, which do not, in fact, exclusively belong to the field of public international law, were dealt with in the Ph.D. thesis, which formed

v

attempted to find a middle way through the conflicting considerations
that, on the one hand, this is not a general textbook of international
law and, on the other, that an assessment of the special problems of the
Arabian Gulf unavoidably calls for at least some description of the
general part of the law to which they are related.

The sources relied upon vary from one chapter to another. When
necessary, they are explained in full in the footnotes. In general, their
nature may be briefly summarised as follows:

In the first part of this study, containing a consideration of British
treaty relations with the Gulf States, the sources are, essentially, based
on the official records of the Government of British India kept in the
India Office (now known as the Commonwealth Office). Aitchison's
Treaties and Lorimer's *Gazetteer* are the two main publications containing these materials. Although these constitute the printed part
of the official records of the India Office, they, nevertheless, still
retain their importance as original records on the Arabian Gulf
region. Indeed, until a few years ago Lorimer's *Gazetteer* was included
among the list of books referred to by the Foreign Office as 'Secret'.

As regards the other parts of the study, the following are some of
the main original sources which have been consulted:

(*a*) Unpublished papers of the Public Record Office of the Foreign
Office, in connection with the consideration of the historical and legal
basis of the Iranian claim to Bahrain.

(*b*) Published official records of the India Office, based on the
Selections from the Records of the Bombay Government and Lorimer's
work, in relation to the consideration of the historical aspect of the
Saudi Arabian claim to Buraimi. I have also been able to see both
the British and Saudi Arabian pleadings in the abortive Buraimi
arbitration.

(*c*) Official records of the General Assembly and the Security
Council of the United Nations, in relation to the examination of the
position of the Arabian Gulf States within the framework of the
United Nations.

I am deeply grateful to Mr E. Lauterpacht, Fellow of Trinity
College, Cambridge, under whose guidance and encouragement this
work was completed. I am also grateful to Professor B. A. Wortley,
of the University of Manchester, and Dr C. Parry, Fellow of Downing
College, Cambridge, who were kind enough to criticise this work and

---

the basis of this work, it was not felt appropriate to include them in this book
which, as its title indicates, is limited to the discussion of issues connected with
the application of international law. The thesis, submitted for the Ph.D. degree in
International Law in the University of Cambridge, was entitled 'Legal Problems
of the Persian Gulf States'.

recommend it for publication. Further, I wish to express my gratitude to both the British Institute of International and Comparative Law and the International Law Fund for their generous financial assistance in the publication of this book. Thanks are also due to Mrs J. M. Sutcliffe, Assistant Secretary, Manchester University Press, for her help in seeing the book through the press. Finally, I extend my sincere thanks to all the editors, authors and writers of books, articles and other materials consulted or reproduced in this book.

H. M. A.

Bahrain, Arabian Gulf

Contents

		page
Preface		v
Table of cases		xi
Abbreviations		xiv
1	Introduction	1
	Political history of the Arabian Gulf States	2
	Constitutional structure of the Arabian Gulf Governments	10

PART ONE

British treaty relations with the Arabian Gulf States

2	Relations with the Trucial Shaikhdoms	25
3	Relations with Bahrain	31
4	Relations with Qatar	36
5	Relations with Kuwait	40
6	Treaty relations of Muscat	47
	The United Kingdom	47
	Other foreign powers	54

PART TWO

The international status of the Arabian Gulf States

7	General considerations affecting the legal position of protectorates	61
8	The present legal position of the Gulf States	67
	Their status in the light of their treaties with the United Kingdom	67
	Position within the framework of British constitutional law: comparison with British Protectorates	80
	Treaty-making capacity	84
	War	114
	Nationality	122
9	International responsibility	129
	Responsibility for the international delinquencies of the Gulf States	129
	Responsibility for protection of nationals of the Gulf States	140
10	Immunity of the rulers of the Gulf States from the jurisdiction of foreign courts	145
	The problem of jurisdictional immunities of protected states	145
	Legal basis for immunity of protected states	149

page
11 Position within the framework of the United Nations   151
   Applicability of Chapter XI of the United Nations Charter to the
      Gulf States   151
   Competence of the United Nations to settle disputes arising between
      the Gulf States and the United Kingdom   156
   Qualification for membership of the United Nations   161

PART THREE

Territorial claims

12 Iran's claim to sovereignty over Bahrain   167
13 British-Saudi controversy over the sovereignty of Buraimi   196
   Introduction   196
   Facts relating to the territory in dispute   208
   The facts in the light of relevant legal principles   220
   Conclusion   237
14 Disputes over Inner Oman and Zubarah   239
   The claim of the Imam of Oman to sovereignty over Inner Oman   239
   The Zubarah dispute   247
15 Iraqi claim to sovereignty over Kuwait   250

PART FOUR

Boundary problems

16 Disputes over land boundaries   261
17 Disputes over the determination of submarine boundaries in the
   Arabian Gulf   278
   The unsettled boundary disputes   290
   The settled boundary disputes   306

Appendices
    I Agreement of the Shaikh of Bahrain, 1880   313
   II Agreement of the Shaikh of Bahrain, 1892   313
  III Agreement of the Shaikh of Abu Dhabi, 1892   314
   IV Undertaking by the Shaikh of Sharjah for the establishment
      of a lighthouse on the Island of Tanb—1912   315
    V The Treaty of Sib, between the Sultan of Muscat and the
      Tribes of Oman, 1920   315
   VI Undertaking by the Shaikh of Sharjah regarding oil—1922   316
  VII Undertaking by the Shaikh of Dubai, regarding oil—1922   317
 VIII Kuwait-Najd Boundary Convention—1922   317
   IX Bahrain Government proclamation, 1949   318
    X Bahrain-Saudi Arabia Boundary Agreement, 1958   319
   XI Kuwait-U.K. Agreement relating to the independence of
      Kuwait, 1961   322
  XII Kuwait-Saudi Arabia Agreement relating to the partition of
      the Neutral Zone, 1965   324
 XIII English version of the Agreement of 27 February 1968, form-
      ing the 'Federation of the Arab Amirates'   328

page
XIV Land boundaries of the Trucial States, 1968 (map)   331
Select bibliography   332
Index   344

MAPS

page
1 The Arabian Gulf States   xvi
2 Buraimi boundary lines   197
3 The villages of Buraimi   209
4 The Bahrain-Saudi Arabia boundary 1958   262

Table of cases

Abdul Rahman Al-Baker v. *Robert Edmund Aldorf and Patrick Vincent Truebody*, Privy Council Appeal, No. 43, 1959.
Adolph, G. Studer (1925), Nielsen, F. K., American and British Claims Arbitration, Report 1926, p. 547.
Antoun v. *Harrison and Sons, Ltd., and others*, September 23, 1965, *The Times*, September 24, 1965, p. 15.
Brown's (R.E.) Claim, American and British Claims Arbitration Tribunal (1923), *B.Y.I.L.*, 5 (1924), p. 210.
Casablanca Case, The (1909), Scott, J. B., *The Hague Court* Reports (1916), p. 110.
Casdagli v. *Casdagli* [1919] A.C. 145.
Chamizal Arbitration, The (1911), *A.J.I.L.*, 5 (1911), p. 785.
Charkieh Case, The [1873] L.R. 4 A.E. 59.
Chief Tschekodi Khama v. *S. Ratshosa and Others* [1931] A.C. 784.
Clipperton Island Case (1932), *A.J.I.L.*, 26 (1932), p. 390; United Nations, *Reports of International Arbitral Awards*, vol. 2, p. 1108.
Competence of the General Assembly for the Admission of a State to the United Nations, *I.C.J. Reports*, 1950, p. 8.
Conditions of Admission of a State to Membership in the United Nations (Article 4 of the Charter), *I.C.J. Reports*, 1948, p. 57.
Doss v. *Secretary of State for India* [1875] 5 L.R. 19 Eq. 509.
Duff Development Co. v. *Government of Kelantan* [1924] A.C. 797.
Hoogstraten, H.C. van v. *Low Lum Seng* (1939), *Annual Digest*, 1938–1940, case No. 16.
Huttinger v. *Upper Congo—Great African Lake Railway Co., The Independent State of the Congo and the Belgian Minister for the Colonies* (1934), *Annual Digest*, 1933–1934, case No. 65.
Ionian Ships, The (1855) 2 Spinks 212.
Island of Palmas Case (1928), United Nations, *Reports of International Arbitral Awards*, vol. 2, p. 829; *A.J.I.L.*, 22 (1928), p. 873.
Joyce v. *Director of Public Prosecutions* [1946] A.C. 347.
King, The, v. *Earl of Crewe ex parte Sekgome* [1910] 2 K.B. 576.
Laurene and Societé Marseillaise de Crédit v. *Gouvernement du Maroc* (1934), *Annual Digest*, 1933–1934, case No. 64.
Legal Status of Eastern Greenland, P.C.I.J., Series A/B, No. 53 (1933), p. 22.
Mighell v. *Sultan of Johore* [1894] 1 Q.B. 149.
Minquiers and Ecrehos Case, I.C.J. Reports, 1953, p. 65.
Morocco and Maspero v. *Laurene, Societé Marseillaise de Crédit, and Others* (1929), *Annual Digest*, 1929–1930, case No. 75.
Mosul Case, The—Interpretation of Article 3 of the Treaty of Lausanne—*P.C.I.J.*, Series B, No. 12 (1925).
Muscat Dhows, The (1905), Scott, J.B., *The Hague Court Reports* (1916), p. 93.

National Bank of Egypt v. *German Government and Bank für Handel und Industrie* (1924), *Annual Digest*, 1923–1924, case No. 9.

National Bank of Egypt v. *Austro-Hungarian Bank* (1923), *Annual Digest*, 1923–1924, case No. 10.

Nationality Decrees Issued by France in Tunis and Morocco, P.C.I.J., Series B, No. 4 (1923), p. 24.

Parlement Belge, The [1880] L.R. 5 P.D. 197.

Petroleum Development (Qatar) Ltd, v. *Ruler of Qatar* (1950), *International Law Reports* (1951), case No. 38, p. 161.

Petroleum Development (Trucial Coast) Ltd v. *The Shaikh of Abu Dhabi* (1951), I.C.L.Q., 1 (1952), p. 247.

Rights of United States Nationals in Morocco, I.C.J. *Reports*, 1952, p. 176.

Ruler of Qatar v. *International Maritime Oil Company Ltd* (1953), *International Law Reports* (1953), p. 539.

Salaman v. *Secretary of State for India* [1906], 1 K.B. 613.

Sayce v. *Ameer Ruler Sadiq Mohammad Abbasi Bahawalpur State* [1952] 2 Q.B. 390.

Sobhuza II v. *Miller* [1926] A.C. 518.

Spanish Zone of Morocco Claims (Great Britain–Spain), (1924), *Annual Digest*, 1923–1924, case Nos. 85, 101, 204.

Statham v. *Statham* [1912] P. 92.

Sultan of Johore v. *Abubakar Tunku Aris Bendahara and Others* [1952] A.C. 318; *Idem, Record of Proceedings*, Privy Council, case No. 45, 1950.

Venezuela-British Guiana Boundary Arbitration, A.J.I.L., 11 (1917), p. 700.

Wiercinski v. *Seyyid Ali Ben Hamod* (1916), *Journal du Droit International*, XLIV (1917), p. 1465.

Wimbledon Case, The, P.C.I.J. Series A, No. 1 (1923).

Ziat Ben Kiran (Great Britain–Spain), (1919), *Annual Digest*, 1923–1924, case No. 87.

Abbreviations

Aitchison	Aitchison, C. U., *A Collection of Treaties, Engagements and Sanads Relating to India and Neighbouring Countries*, vol. XI (1933).
A.J.I.L.	*American Journal of International Law.*
Annual Digest	*Annual Digest and Reports of Public International Law Cases.*
Bombay Selections	*Selections from the Records of the Bombay Government*, vol. 24, New Series, The Persian Gulf, Bombay (1856).
Brierly	Brierly, J. L., *The Law of Nations*, 5th ed. (1955).
British Memorial	*Arbitration Concerning Buraimi and the Common Frontier Between Abu Dhabi and Saudi Arabia*, Memorial Submitted by the Government of the United Kingdom of Great Britain and Northern Ireland, 2 vols, 1955.
B.Y.I.L.	*British Yearbook of International Law.*
Cmd., Cmnd.	United Kingdom, Command Papers.
F.O.	Foreign Office Papers.
Hall	Hall, W. E., *A Treatise on International Law*, 8th ed., (1924), by A. Pearce Higgins.
Hyde	Hyde, C. C., *International Law, Chiefly as Interpreted and Applied by the United States, 3 vols, 2nd rev. ed.* (1945).
I.C.L.Q.	*The International and Comparative Law Quarterly.*
I.C.J.	International Court of Justice, Reports of Judgments and Advisory Opinions.
I.O.	India Office Records.
Lauterpacht	Lauterpacht, H., *Recognition in International Law* (1947).
L.N.O.J.	League of Nations, Official Journal.
Lindley	Lindley, M. F., *The Acquisition and Government of Backward Territory in International Law* (1926).
Lorimer	Lorimer, J. G., *Gazetteer of the Persian Gulf, Oman and Central Arabia, Official Records of the Government of India*, vol. I, Historical (1915).
Lorimer, II	Lorimer, J. G., *Gazetteer of the Persian Gulf, Oman and Central Arabia, Official Records of the Government of India*, vol. II, Geographical and Statistical (1908).
McNair, *Opinions*	McNair, Lord A., *International Law Opinions*, 3 vols (1956).

McNair, *Treaties*	McNair, Sir A., *The Law of Treaties, British Practice and Opinions* (1938).
MEES	*Middle East Economic Survey*, A Weekly Review of News and Views on Middle East Oil, Published by the Middle East Research and Publishing Centre, Beirut.
NSGT	United Nations, *Non Self Governing Territories*, Summaries and Analysis of Information Transmitted to the Secretary General (Under Article 73 of the United Nations Charter).
Oppenheim	Oppenheim, L., *International Law*, vol. I, 8th ed. (1955), by H. Lauterpacht.
Oppenheim, II	Oppenheim, L., *International Law*, vol. II, 7th Revised ed. (1952), by H. Lauterpacht.
P.C.I.J.	*Publications of the Permanent Court of International Justice.*
Saudi Memorial	*Arbitration for the Settlement of the Territorial Dispute Between Muscat and Abu Dhabi on one Side and Saudi Arabia on the Other*, Memorial of the Government of Saudi Arabia, 3 vols. (1955).
Schwarzenberger	Schwarzenberger, G., *International Law, International Court*, vol. I, 3rd ed. (1957).
Smith	Smith, H. A., *Great Britain and the Law of Nations, A Selection of Documents*, vol. I (1932), vol. II (1933).
S.I.	Statutory Instruments, United Kingdom.
Treaty Series (U.K.T.S.)	United Kingdom Treaty Series.
UNCIO	United Nations Conference on International Organisation, Documents, San Francisco (1945).
U.N.G.A.	United Nations, General Assembly.
U.N.S.C.	United Nations, Security Council.
U.N.L.S., High Seas	United Nations, Legislative Series, Laws and Regulations on the Regime of the High Seas, U.N. 1951.
U.N.L.S., Treaties	United Nations, Legislative Series, Laws and Practices concerning the Conclusion of Treaties, U.N. 1953.
U.N.L.S., Territorial Seas	United Nations, Legislative Series, Laws and Regulations on the Regime of the Territorial Seas, U.N. 1957.
U.N.T.S.	United Nations, Treaty Series.
Westlake	Westlake, J., *International Law*, vol. I, 2nd ed. (1910), vol. II, 2nd ed. (1913).
Y.U.N.	Yearbook of the United Nations.

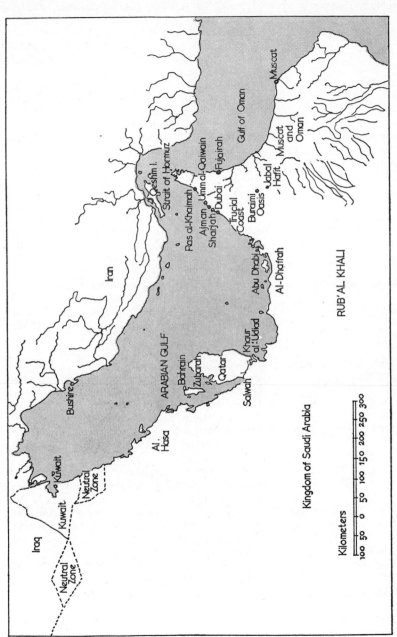

MAP 1: The Arabian Gulf States

Iraq

Kuwait

Neutral
Zone

Neutral
Zone

Kuwait

Bushire

Iran

ARABIAN GULF

Al-
Hasa

Salwah

Bahrain
Zubarah

Qatar

Khaur
al-'Udaid

Abu Dhabi

Al-Dhafrah

Qeshm I.

Strait of Hormuz

Ras al-Khaimah

Ajman
Sharjah
Dubai

Umm al-Qaiwain

Fujairah

Trucial
Coast

Buraimi
Oasis

Jabal
Hafit

Muscat and
Oman

Gulf of Oman

Muscat

RUB' AL KHALI

Kingdom of Saudi Arabia

Kilometers

100 50   0   50 100 150 200 250 300

1

Introduction

The Arabian Gulf[1] States comprise eleven countries stretching along the eastern and south-eastern coast of the Arabian Peninsula, from north to south, in the following order: Kuwait, Bahrain, Qatar, the seven Shaikhdoms of the Trucial Coast of Oman (namely, Abu Dhabi, Dubai, Sharjah, Ajman, Umm al-Qaiwain, Ras al-Khaimah, Fujairah), and the Sultanate of Muscat and Oman.[2] Between Kuwait and Saudi Arabia lies the area of the Kuwait–Saudi Arabia Neutral Zone in which both Kuwait and Saudi Arabia enjoy equal rights of sovereignty by treaty. The other side of the Arabian Gulf, the eastern, is wholly occupied by Iran whose territory extends to the Gulf of Oman below.[3]

Bahrain, Qatar and the seven Trucial Shaikhdoms are commonly known as the British Protected States,[4] or Shaikhdoms, of the Arabian

[1] The terms 'Arabian Gulf' and 'Persian Gulf' are synonyms. During the last decade or so the term 'Arabian Gulf' has become more commonly used by all the Arab States, including the countries of the Arabian Peninsula, in preference to the traditional and internationally recognised name 'Persian Gulf'. The Arab States, including the Gulf Shaikhdoms, have passed laws making the use of the term 'Arabian Gulf' compulsory in all communications with the outside world bearing reference to the area. Iran, on the other hand, is the only country in the area which objects vigorously to the use of a term other than the 'Persian Gulf'. However, despite Iran's constant objections and repeated protests, the new term 'Arabian Gulf' seems to be gradually gaining universal recognition, though on a limited scale. In line with this present Arab trend, the author has adopted the name Arabian Gulf throughout this book whose topic is limited to the Arab States of the Gulf. In order to avoid confusion, however, all uses of the term 'Persian Gulf' in various quotations from sources relied upon in this book will remain unchanged.

[2] See Map 1.

[3] For general geographical and other information on the Arabian Gulf, see: Wilson, Sir A. T., *The Persian Gulf* (1928, reprinted 1954), Part XV; Great Britain, British Admiralty, *A Handbook of Arabia*, vol. I (1916); Bent, J. T., 'The Bahrain Islands in the Persian Gulf', *Proceedings of Royal Geographical Society*, vol. 12 (1890), pp. 1–19; Buss, K. C., 'Persian Gulf', *Encyclopaedia Britannica*, vol. 17, ed. (1963), pp. 595–9. Describing the Arabian Gulf waters, Buss states at p. 595: 'The Persian Gulf is the shallow trough which extends 500 miles from the Shatt-al Arab in a southeasterly direction to the Musandam peninsula in Oman. There the Hormuz strait separates it from the Gulf of Oman. The breadth of the Persian Gulf varies from 50 miles at the entrance, the Hormuz strait, to 140 miles at the head and 200 miles at its widest part. . . . In the Persian Gulf the depth of water rarely exceeds 50 fathoms and, generally speaking, increases more rapidly from the Iranian than the Arabian shore . . .'

[4] Although the Arabian Gulf Shaikhdoms are described, in British legal parlance,

1

Gulf; they are in special treaty relations with the United Kingdom. Kuwait, which until the early part of 1961 belonged to this category, is now an independent State and a member of the United Nations. Similarly, the Sultanate of Muscat and Oman is an independent State, but she is not a member of the United Nations and still maintains very close treaty relations with the United Kingdom dating back to the eighteenth century.

In this study the expression 'the Arabian Gulf States' (or the Gulf States) refers to the eleven States altogether and 'the Shaikhdoms' refers to the Gulf Protected States, including Kuwait before 1961. The Sultanate of Muscat and Oman, which is not included in the expression 'the Gulf Protected States', will be referred to, briefly, as Muscat. Concerning Kuwait, this study deals, basically, with her former status as a British Protected State (i.e., before attaining full independence on 19 June 1961).

POLITICAL HISTORY OF THE ARABIAN GULF STATES

(a) *Evolution of the States*

The political evolution of these States into their present position within the British sphere of influence took place during the first half of the nineteenth century. However, it appears that they had achieved various degrees of political independence (in certain cases with loose Ottoman suzerainty) long before they had any contact with the British Government. The history of the gradual emergence of these States may be traced briefly below:

Muscat

The present Sultanate of Muscat and Oman was originally known as the Imamate of Oman. The Imamate was governed between A.D. 751 and 1792 by elected Imams of the Ibadi (originally the Kharijites) sect of Islam. The present reigning Sultan, Sayyid Saʿid ibn Taimur, belongs to the dynasty of Al Bu Saʿid which was originally founded in 1774, by Ahmad ibn Saʿid. The latter, having succeeded in ex-

---

as 'States'—in contradistinction to British Protectorates which are, generally, of more dependent status—they are, in fact, only quasi-sovereign States, since they do not have all the attributes of statehood in the international sense of the word. For example, they do not control their external affairs. It is agreed that protection over the Gulf States 'developed out of the needs initially to check the slave trade and to prevent regional warfare, and later to obtain and preserve special commercial interests and advantages'. See Fawcett, J. E. S., *The British Commonwealth in International Law* (1963), p. 120. However, it may be assumed that the sovereignty of the Gulf States, which has been partially suspended for the duration of protection, will revive in full when British treaties of protection are finally brought to an end. In support of this assumption, see below, p. 40 for the manner in which British protection over Kuwait was terminated.

pelling the Persians from the coast of Batinah, was elected by the Omanis as the first Imam of the dynasty of Al Bu Saʿid. He was succeeded by Saʿid ibn Sultan, the second genuinely elected Imam of Al Bu Saʿid. In 1797, Sultan ibn Ahmad, who succeeded in 'usurping the authority of his elder brother', established himself as an independent secular ruler in Muscat on the coast, under the new title of Sayyid Sultan. Consequently, Muscat has ever since continued to be governed by the hereditary rule of the dynasty of Al Bu Saʿid, instead of the old traditional rule of the elected Imams. British dealings with the rulers of Muscat, who later came to be addressed as Sultans, date back to 1798. In that year, the British Government, through the East India Company, concluded with Sayyid Sultan ibn Ahmad the first treaty of commerce and navigation.[1]

Kuwait

The modern history of Kuwait (formerly known as al-Qurain) dates back to 1716, when a combination of three Najdi tribes known as al-ʿUtub, or Bani ʿUtbah, migrated to that place. The three tribes were Al-Sabah, Al-Khalifah and Al-Jalahimah. The family of Al-Sabah took the first step towards consolidating their position as the hereditary rulers of Kuwait in 1756, when they moved, under their tribal head, Shaikh Sabah, from a place called Umm Qasr and settled permanently in Kuwait. The dynasty of Al-Sabah still rules Kuwait today.

Although the recorded history of British commercial relations with Kuwaiti Shaikhs goes back to 1775, British political contacts with them were not made before the turn of the nineteenth century. And it was in 1899 that the British Government concluded, secretly, the first political agreement with the Ruler of Kuwait, then Shaikh Mubarak Al-Sabah, while still openly acknowledging Turkish suzerainty over Kuwait.[2]

Bahrain

The Al-Khalifah branch of ʿUtub, who originally settled Kuwait, moved in 1766, under their leader Shaikh Khalifah ibn Muhammad, to a place called Zubarah, on the western shore of the Qatar peninsula,

[1] For the general history of Muscat and Oman, see *Bombay Selections*, pp. 122–3; Lorimer, pp. 397–430; Aitchison, Part III; Wilson, op. cit., pp. 231–44; Great Britain, Foreign Office, Historical Section, *Peace Handbook*, No. 76 (1920), pp. 40–2.
[2] For the history of al-ʿUtub, or Bani ʿUtbah, and their original settlement in Kuwait, see F.O. 60/118 (1945): *Chronological table of events connected with Bahrain from 1716 to 1814, extracted from records of the Presidency of the Persian Gulf by Lieutenant A. B. Hennel, Asst. Political Resident.* On the history of Kuwait, in general, see Lorimer, pp. 1002 et seq.; *Bombay Selections*, pp. 140–2; Aitchison, pp. 202 et seq.; Wilson, op. cit., pp. 249–53; Dickson, H. R. P., *Kuwait and Her Neighbours* (1956), pp. 26–8, and Chapter VI.

and established an autonomous State there. However, on 28 July 1783 the Al-Khalifah rulers of Zubarah launched an attack on the Bahrain Islands, and, having successfully conquered them, expelled their Arab Governor who then derived his authority from Persia. The dynasty of Al-Khalifah has, since that date, continued to rule Bahrain which outlived unsuccessful attempts by the Sultan of Muscat, the Persians, the Turks and the Wahhabis to extend their sovereignty over her.

British treaty relations with Bahrain were established as early as 1861, when the British Government signed a friendly Convention with Shaikh Muhammad Al-Khalifah in his capacity as the 'Independent Ruler of Bahrain'. The present British relations with Bahrain are based on the treaties of protection of 1880–92.[1]

Qatar

Shortly after 1766 the ʿUtubi branch of Al-Jalahimah left Kuwait, as a result of a quarrel with Al-Sabah, and sought the protection of 'their kinsmen' at Zubarah. The Al-Jalahimah remained in the Qatar peninsula for some time until their 'almost total destruction' in tribal quarrels.

The extension of Turkish influence to Arabia in or about 1871, brought Qatar under Turkish suzerainty, but she continued to be governed, directly, by indigenous rulers of the dynasty of Al-Thani. This same dynasty still rules Qatar today. The first British contact with Qatar was in 1868, when the Ruler of Qatar at the time, Shaikh Muhammad ibn Thani, undertook not to commit a breach of the maritime peace. However, Qatar was virtually brought under British protection by the treaty of 1916, concluded by Shaikh ʿAbd Allah ibn Jasim Al-Thani.[2]

The Trucial Shaikhdoms

The rulers of the petty Shaikhdoms established their independence at various places along the Coast of Oman, or the Trucial Coast (for-

[1] For the history of the Al-Khalifah branch of 'Utub, see F.O. 60/118 (1845), op. cit.; I.O. Bombay Secret Proceedings (Historical Sketches on the Powers of the Arabs of Muscat, the Jassimees, the Uttoobees and the Oman, by Mr Warden), No. 41, Consultn. 37, September 1819, pp. 1657–721; Saldanha, J. A., A Précis of Bahrain Affairs, 1854–1904 (1904); Al-Nabhani, Muhmmad ibn Khalifah, Tarik al-Bahrain (Arabic), Cairo, 1342 (1923). On the general history of Bahrain and her treaty relations, see Aitchison, pp. 190–7; Oestrup, J., 'Al-Bahrain', Encyclopaedia of Islam, vol. 2 (1913), pp. 584–5; Belgrave, J. H. D., Welcome to Bahrain, 5th ed. (1965), pp. 61 et seq.; Belgrave, Sir Charles D., Personal Column: Autobiography (1960).

[2] On the general history of Qatar and her treaty relations, see I.O., Bombay Secret Proceedings, op. cit.; Lorimer, pp. 787 et seq.; Saldanha, J. A., A Précis of Katar Affairs (1904); Aitchison, pp. 193, 195, 258; Admiralty Handbook, op. cit., pp. 325–32.

merly the Pirate Coast), long before they had any contact with the British Government. Formal relations between these Shaikhdoms and the British Government were established after the East India Company's expedition of 1819 against the Arab Shaikhs of Al-Qawasim at Ras al-Khaimah. Subsequently, the rulers of these Shaikhdoms concluded, in 1820, a General Treaty with the British Government in which they agreed to abstain from piratical acts and to maintain 'a lasting peace' between them and the British Government. This treaty was followed by the Perpetual Treaty of Peace of 1853 and the Exclusive Agreements of 1892 which today constitute the basis of British special treaty relations with these Shaikhdoms.

The number of the independent rulers of the Trucial Shaikhdoms varied from time to time in the past. Ras al-Khaimah, which was incorporated for some years with Sharjah, secured, from 1921, British recognition as an independent Shaikhdom. Fujairah, the smallest Shaikhdom on the Gulf of Oman, established her independence from Sharjah in 1901, but she was not recognised as an independent Shaikhdom until 1952, when her Ruler acceded to the same treaty obligations of the other Trucial Shaikhdoms with Britain.[1]

(b) *The establishment of British influence in the Gulf*

The recorded modern history of the Arabian Gulf begins with the inception of the Portuguese influence in the region during the sixteenth century. After about a hundred years of Portuguese predominance in the Gulf, they were finally driven from it by the Persians—assisted by the British—in or about 1622. In the beginning, British interest in the Gulf was of a commercial character. It started in 1763, when the British East India Company opened a Residency at Bushire, on the Persian side of the Gulf. After eliminating the influence of its rivals, the Dutch, the French and the Turks, the British Government managed, during the eighteenth century, to consolidate its political influence in the Gulf. In the beginning of the nineteenth century, the British Government assumed the task of suppressing piracy in the Gulf which had exposed British trade with India to danger. British expeditions against the Pirate Coast (now called Trucial Coast) resulted in

---

[1] On the general history of the Trucial Shaikhdoms and their treaty relations, see I.O., *Bombay Secret Proceedings*, op. cit.; *Bombay Selections* (Chronological Table of events connected with the Joasmee Tribe of Arabs and with the Debaye (Boo Felasa) Tribe of Arabs, from 1765 to 1844, by Lieutenant A. B. Kemball, Asst Political Resident in the Persian Gulf), pp. 129–39, 159–65; Saldanha, J. A., *A Précis of Correspondence Regarding the Trucial Chiefs*, 1854–1905 (1906); Aitchison, pp. 197–202; Hay, Sir Rupert, *The Persian Gulf States* (1959), pp. 122–3; Mann, C., *Abu Dhabi: Birth of an Oil Shaikhdom* (1964); Wilkinson, J. C., 'A Sketch of the Historical Geography of the Trucial Oman down to the Beginning of the Sixteenth Century', *Geographical Journal*, vol. 130, Part 3, September (1964), pp. 338–49.

the conclusion of the Treaty of Peace of 1820 with the Arab Shaikhs of the coast, as well as with the Shaikh of Bahrain. Subsequently the British Government established its influence in the Gulf by means of treaties and engagements concluded with the Shaikhdoms between 1853 and 1916.[1]

In a speech in the House of Lords on 5 March 1903, Lord Lansdowne put on record the British unrivalled position in the Gulf in these terms:

> I say it without hesitation, we should regard the establishment of a naval base or a fortified port in the Persian Gulf by any other Power as a very grave menace to British interests, and we should certainly resist it by all the means at our disposal.[2]

Similarly, while speaking about the establishment of British influence in the Gulf, it seems pertinent to refer to a famous speech made by Lord Curzon, the then Viceroy of India, on 21 November 1903. This speech was delivered by Lord Curzon in the presence of the rulers of the Trucial Coast, on the occasion of his visit to the Gulf. Lord Curzon defined British policy in the Gulf and assured the rulers of his Government's continued support for the maintenance of their independence in the following statement:

> Sometimes I think that the record of the past is in danger of being forgotten, and there are persons who ask—Why should Great Britain continue to exercise these powers? The history of your States . . . and the present conditions of the Gulf, are the answer. . . . It was our commerce as well as your security that was threatened and called for protection. . . . We have not seized or held your territory. We have not destroyed your independence, but have preserved it. . . . The peace of these waters must still be maintained; your independence will continue to be upheld; and the influence of the British Government must remain supreme.[3]

The above-mentioned statements of British politicians about Britain's unrivalled political position in the Arabian Gulf have now been overtaken by events. For, in view of the present changed con-

---

[1] For general information on the gradual establishment of British influence in the Arabian Gulf, see Mahan, A. T., 'The Persian Gulf and International Relations', *The National Review*, vol. 6, Sept.–Feb. (1902–3), pp. 27–45; 'Curzon's Analysis of British Policy and Interests in Persia and the Persian Gulf, September 21, 1899', published in Hurewitz, J. C., *Diplomacy in the Near and Middle East*, vol. 1 (1956), pp. 219–41; Saldanha, J. A., *A Précis of Correspondence Regarding the Affairs of the Persian Gulf, 1801–53* (1906); Bulletin of International News, British Interests in the Persian Gulf, vol XVIII, No. 19, 20 September (1914), pp. 1193–8; Wilson, op cit., Chapters VIII–XIII.

[2] See Gooch, G. and Temperley, H., *British Documents on the Origins of the War, 1898–1914*, vol. IV (1938), p. 371.

[3] See India, Foreign and Political Department, *Treaties and Engagements in Force in January, 1906, Between the British Government and the Trucial Chiefs of the Arab Coast, Including Lord Curzon's Address* (1906), pp. 1–4.

ditions in the Gulf, Britain's former predominant political role as the policeman of the region cannot still be maintained without a direct challenge to the national interests of the newly emerging riparian States concerned. The present economic realities of the Arabian Gulf, which has become a nucleus of international commercial activities, should provide the need for a fundamental revision in the archaic British network of relationships with the Governments of the area.

It appears that the British Government has realised these facts recently, and a major change in British policy towards the Arabian Gulf Shaikhdoms can now be seen in the British Government's announcement in January 1968 that it had decided to withdraw all its forces from the Gulf area by the end of 1971. It is not clear, however, whether this announcement can be interpreted to mean that Britain's special treaty relations with the Gulf Rulers would also come to an end after the British withdrawal. It may be assumed, in the light of the present trend of British policy in the Gulf, that British withdrawal from the region would necessarily entail the total abrogation of this anachronistic protectorate system which has since the middle of the nineteenth century subjugated the foreign policies of the various Rulers to the unrivalled control of the British Government. At any rate, it is taken for granted in the Rulers' circles that even if the withdrawal of British forces from the Gulf does not affect British treaty commitments to the Rulers, these commitments will practically be worthless without a military force to support them on the spot.

Following this abrupt change of British policy in the Arabian Gulf, the Rulers, seemingly shocked and worried about their own future without British support, decided, therefore, with dramatic pledges of solidarity, to form a 'Federation of Arab Amirates'. The agreement forming this Federation was quickly drafted and agreed upon by the Rulers at their summit conference held in Dubai on 27 February 1968. This agreement, which was signed by the Rulers of Bahrain, Qatar and the seven Trucial States, came into force at the beginning of the Muslim Hijrah year 1388 (corresponding to 30 March 1968).[1]

[1] The Agreement of 27 February provides, *inter alia*, for the establishment of a 'Supreme Council' which shall be formed of the nine Rulers in the Federation. This Supreme Council, constituting the highest authority in the Federation, shall draw up a comprehensive and permanent charter for the Federation and represent the foreign relations of the federated States. It shall have sole authority to formulate the high policy of the Federation in respect of all international, political, defence, economic and cultural matters. In the internal sphere, it has the right to legislate the necessary federal laws.

It is clear from the provisions of this agreement that the real intention of the conferring Rulers was to create some sort of 'Personal Union' among themselves for the purpose of co-ordinating and unifying their foreign, defence and economic policies *vis-à-vis* foreign States which shall, in turn, recognise the Federation (or the Union) as one single independent and sovereign State. This type of federation does not, however, interfere in the internal affairs of each member State which shall

The East India Company

A word must now be said about the East India Company which was responsible for the formulation of British policy in the Arabian Gulf and the conclusion of the original treaties of the nineteenth century with the Gulf Rulers. The British East India Company was empowered under the Charter of Charles II of 1661—which confirmed the Charter of 1660 granted by Queen Elizabeth—'to make war or peace with any Prince not Christian' and to conclude treaties in the name of the Crown. When in 1858, the powers of the Company were brought to an end by the Act of 1858, it was provided in this Act that 'all treaties made by the said Company shall be binding on Her Majesty's Government' in the United Kingdom. Consequently, the Government of the United Kingdom succeeded to all the treaties between the East India Company and the Eastern countries.[1]

The East India Company was responsible for the conclusion of the various treaties, agreements and engagements with the Rulers and Shaikhs of the Arabian Gulf coast prior to 1858, in its capacity as the Agent in the area for the British Crown. But following the passing of the 1858 Act, which in effect transferred the powers of the East India Company to the British Government of India, British Government's relations with the Gulf Rulers came to be conducted through the British Government of India. However, from 1 April 1947 the British Foreign Office assumed full responsibility for the conduct of their foreign relations.[2] It is generally assumed that obligations arising from all the treaties, agreements and engagements concluded with the Rulers of the Arabian Gulf States during the nineteenth century devolved upon Her Majesty's Government in the United Kingdom rather than the Government of India. Accordingly, Sir Rupert Hay, a former British Political Resident in the Arabian Gulf, points out that

---

continue to be controlled by its respective Sovereign.

One important criticism against this Federation is the emphasis in the agreement on the sovereignty and independence of each member country. Moreover, the important provision of Article 4 that 'the decisions of the Supreme Council shall be made unanimously' could in effect cripple the authority of this council, because it gives the right to any of the Rulers to veto the decisions approved by all the other eight Rulers. Finally, it is regretted that the Federation agreement purposely fails to provide for the establishment of a democratic parliamentary system, or any kind of representative institutions, within the Federation. Consequently, there appears to be a danger of the Federation becoming a symbol of the absolute authority of the various Rulers, governing through a Supreme Council composed of themselves. See Appendix XIII.

[1] Lindley, pp. 31, 94; Lee Warner, Sir W., *The Native States of India* (1910), pp. 37–8, 46.

[2] Great Britain, Central Office of Information, *The Arab States of the Persian Gulf*, August (1956), p. 2; Hay, op. cit., pp. 11–18.

all the treaties and engagements entered into by the various Rulers, including the Sultan of Muscat, were with the central British Government—though in some of them the Government of India is also mentioned. When the British decided to transfer power in India it would clearly have been inappropriate to hand over responsibility for dealing with the Gulf Arabs to Indians or Pakistanis.[1]

British political residency in the Arabian Gulf

The British Resident in the Gulf to whose name the word 'Political' was added in 1862, has, since 1 April 1947, been responsible directly to the British Foreign Office. In 1946, the British Residency was removed from its former place at Bushire, on the Iranian coast, to Bahrain. The British Resident is 'graded' Ambassador in the Gulf region. He attends to his responsibilities towards the Gulf States by maintaining a number of representatives, referred to as 'Political Agents', in Bahrain, Qatar, Dubai and Abu Dhabi. In the other Trucial Shaikhdoms he has political officers who are attached to the British Agency at Dubai. British relations with Muscat are conducted through a British Consul-General who is also, administratively, responsible to the British Resident in Bahrain.[2] The duties of the British Political Resident are, *inter alia*, to maintain, through his Political Agents, close contact with the rulers and governments of the Shaikhdoms and safeguard their political and economic interests and the interests of the British Government 'on the basis of the treaties and agreements' governing British relations with these Shaikhdoms. According to Rupert Hay, the Shaikhdoms have independent control over their internal affairs, but the British Government 'ordinarily only exercises control in matters involving negotiations or the possibility of complications with foreign powers, such as civil aviation and posts and telegraphs'. However, he continues, 'constant advice and encouragement are . . . offered to the various Rulers regarding the improvement of their administrations and the development of their resources, mostly in an informal manner.'[3]

[1] Hay, op cit., p. 18. And see U.N., General Assembly, 19th Session, *Question of Oman, Report of the Ad Hoc Committee on Oman* (A/5846), 22 January 1965, pp. 116–17.

[2] Hay, op cit., pp. 11–18.

[3] Ibid., pp. 18–19. For a lucid description of the various important duties of the British Resident in the Gulf, see ibid., pp. 19–27. To mention only one aspect of the Resident's duties, namely his role in the conclusion of oil concession agreements between the Rulers and foreign oil companies, Sir Rupert Hay says: 'The oil companies naturally bulk largely in the Political Resident's portfolio. He has closely to watch all negotiations for new agreements or the amendment of existing agreements and to make sure that nothing is decided which will seriously affect the position or the Rulers of the British Government. . . .' The same author also refers to what he terms the 'Political Agreements' to which, he says, the oil companies' are all bound . . . with the British Government, . . . in addition to their concession agreements with the Rulers. . . .' 'One of the main objects of these', he

Furthermore, the British Resident is entrusted with the duty of administering the British extra-territorial jurisdiction which has, since 1925, been exercised by the British Crown in the various territories of the Rulers concerned. This extra-territorial jurisdiction, which is being gradually relinquished today, was ceded to the British Crown from the beginning of this century by virtue of informal agreements with the Rulers of the Shaikhdoms. In the case of Muscat it is based on formal agreements which are being renewed periodically. This British extra-territorial jurisdiction, which was generally applied to all classes of persons residing in the Gulf States, with the exception of nationals of the Rulers concerned, is now limited to British subjects, Commonwealth nationals and non-Muslim foreigners residing in the Shaikhdoms. In the case of Muscat, it is even more limited; it applies to cases involving non-Muslim United Kingdom or (with certain exceptions) Commonwealth citizens only. British extra-territorial jurisdiction in Kuwait was formally relinquished on 4 May 1961. Consequently, jurisdiction over all classes of foreigners has been transferred to the Kuwaiti national courts. British extra-territorial jurisdiction in the Gulf has been exercised under the authority of the British Foreign Jurisdiction Acts of 1890–1913, which empower the Crown to establish courts of justice and legislate for the categories of persons subject to the jurisdiction by means of Orders in Council.[1]

CONSTITUTIONAL STRUCTURE OF THE ARABIAN GULF GOVERNMENTS

(a) *The protected States*

The protected States of the Gulf, comprising Bahrain, Qatar and the seven Trucial Shaikhdoms, are, internally, independent governments ruled by indigenous Rulers or Shaikhs who are usually chosen by the agreement and consent of senior members of their families. Generally, succession to rulership has been handed down from father to son, on the death of the former or on his abdication. In 1958, for example, the Shaikh of Bahrain appointed his son, Shaikh Isa ibn Salman Al-Khalifah, as heir apparent to the Shaikhdom.[2] Also on 24 October

---

continues, 'is to ensure that their relations with the Rulers in all matters of importance are conducted through, or with, the knowledge of the British political officers.' See ibid., pp. 66–7.

[1] Hay, op. cit., pp. 19–22. And see *Persian Gulf Gazette* (Containing Orders in Council, Laws and Regulations), published by Her Majesty's Political Resident in the Arabian Gulf by Authority, *Supplements*, Nos 1–32 (1952–61).

[2] Shaikh Isa ibn Salman Al-Khalifah, who is now the Ruler of Bahrain, succeeded to the rulership on 16 December 1961, following the death of his father. The pre-

1960 the Ruler of Qatar, Shaikh Ali ibn ʿAbd Allah, who succeeded to the rulership in 1947, abdicated in favour of his eldest son, Shaikh Ahmad ibn Ali Al-Thani. However, there is now a real tendency in some of the Shaikhdoms to choose any suitable successor to the rulership from amongst the senior members of the ruling family without necessarily this new successor being the son of the dead or retiring Ruler.[1] It is customary for the British Government, after the settlement of the question of succession of a new Ruler in any of the Shaikhdoms, to announce its recognition of the chosen Ruler at an official ceremony held in the Shaikhdom concerned. At this ceremony, which is usually attended by the Political Resident, or any of his representatives, the new Ruler formally announces his intention to respect and carry out in good faith the treaties and engagements of his predecessor with the British Government.[2]

The system of government in these Shaikhdoms does not appear to be based on any written constitution. Nor do there exist such institutions as representative or elective legislatures of a kind normally associated with the operation of non-autocratic governments. Legally speaking, therefore, the Rulers possess exclusive legislative, executive and judiciary powers in their own rights.

---

sent Ruler has, in turn, appointed his elder son, Shaikh Hamad, as heir apparent. For the manner of succession to rulership in Kuwait in the past, see Political Agency, Kuwait, *Administrative Report for the Year 1921*, by Major More, J. C., Political Agent (1922). For the Proclamation of the late Ruler of Bahrain appointing his elder son, the present Ruler, as heir apparent, see *Al-Jaridah al-Rasmiyah* (Bahrain Official Gazette), No. 242, 6 February (1958). For the Ruler of Qatar's abdication in favour of his elder son, presently the Ruler, see *The Times*, 26 October 1960.

[1] This tendency is clear in Kuwait which has become a constitutional Amirate. According to the constitution, succession to the throne is limited to the ruling family of Al-Sabah in the line of Shaikh Mubarak, the founder of the present Amirate. Similarly, in Qatar, Abu Dhabi and Sharjah the tendency appears to be against restricting the succession to rulership to the sons of the dead or retiring Rulers. Accordingly, in Qatar the heir apparent, Shaikh Khalifah, is a cousin of the Ruler; in Sharjah, the former Ruler, Shaikh Saqr ibn Sultan, was deposed in July 1965 by the council of the ruling family, with the express support and blessing of the British Government, and his cousin Shaikh Khalid al-Qasimi, was appointed as the succeeding Ruler; while in Abu Dhabi, the former notorious Ruler, Shaikh Shakhbut ibn Sultan, was replaced on 6 August 1966 by his brother, Shaikh Zayid, who was elected as the new Ruler by the unanimous decision of the ruling family of the Shaikhdom. This decision had full British backing because Shaikh Shakhbut had always obstructed the introduction of certain reforms in his very wealthy country. For such developments, see The Economist Intelligence Unit Limited, London, *Quarterly Economic Review*, No. 22, July (1965), p. 22; *The Observer*, London, 14 August 1966; *The Times*, 8 August 1966.

[2] For an account of British recognition of the succession of Shaikh Rashid ibn Saʿid al-Maktum who became Ruler of Dubai in 1958, see *The Times*, 6 October 1958. And for an interesting description of ceremonies on the occasion of the succession of a new Arabian Gulf Ruler, see Hay, op. cit., pp. 29–30.

The internal administration in these Shaikhdoms will now be described:

Bahrain and Qatar

Modern systems of administration have been developed in Bahrain and Qatar, where a number of government departments, such as customs, education, electricity, finance, health, justice, passports, police and public works, have been organised. Most of these departments have Arab directors, usually members of the ruling families, but some of the technical departments have British experts as directors. In Bahrain the Government is represented by a head office known as the Secretariat which is in turn administered by a Secretary to the Government. The latter is a British subject but he reports directly to the Ruler, Shaikh Isa ibn Salman Al-Khalifah, who is responsible for his appointment and dismissal. The Secretary acts as a co-ordinator between the various departments of the State and issues a regular State budget each year.[1] In addition, he acts as a liaison officer between the Ruler's Government and the local office of the British Political Agent which protects the foreign interests of the Ruler.[2] As regards Qatar, there was practically no administration before 1949. But since 1950, there has been rapid evolution of proper administration on departmental level. Also in that year a British financial adviser was appointed. Subsequently, a regular budget was prepared.[3] Recently, the finance department has been converted into a Ministry of Finance, with Shaikh Khalifah ibn Hamad Al-Thani, the Deputy Ruler and Heir to the throne, becoming the Minister of Finance. Shaikh Khalifah, who now has effective control over the finance of the State, has employed an Egyptian lawyer, Dr Hassan Kamel, as the Director-General of the Government of Qatar. Dr Kamel has helped Shaikh Khalifah in introducing some important fiscal and legal reforms in

[1] The office of the Secretariat was known before 1957, as the Adviserate. Sir Charles Belgrave, to whom goes the credit of establishing an orderly and workable administration in Bahrain, served in this office between 1926 and 1957, in his capacity as the Adviser to the Government. The present Secretary to the Government has followed in the steps of the former Adviser in continuing the practice of issuing annual Administration Reports. However, it appears that the present Reports are inferior, in quality and style, to the pre-1957 Reports. Also budget accounts tend to be much summarised today. For a good comparison, see Bahrain Government, *Annual Reports*, Years 1950–65.

[2] It is noteworthy that Bahrain appears to be the only Shaikhdom which has retained the services of a British subject, first as an 'Adviser' and later as a 'Secretary', for such a long period of time going back to 1926. In comparison, the Shaikhdom of Qatar does not, at present, maintain a British Secretary to the Government. The former British Adviser, whose service was terminated some years ago, has now been replaced by an Arab Director-General. Similarly, in Kuwait there was an Arab Secretary to the Government until her independence in 1961, when the office of the Secretariat was converted into a Ministry of Foreign Affairs.

[3] Hay, op. cit., pp. 109–10.

the administration. The Ruler, Shaikh Ahmad ibn 'Ali Al-Thani, has very recently formed an Advisory Council of his own choice to assist him in supervising the affairs of his administration.[1] However, substantial reforms of a democratic nature have not yet been introduced in the autocratic machinery of Government.[2]

Concerning Bahrain, an organisation called the Council of Administration has been formed, since March 1956, for the purpose of supervising the affairs of the various government departments as well as considering 'topics of general interest' which formerly used to be handled by the Ruler personally.[3] The members of this Council, who have all been hand-picked by the Ruler himself, number ten, seven of whom, including the President, are members of the ruling family and the remaining three are government officials. The President of the Council, Shaikh Khalifah ibn Salman, is also the President of the Department of Finance and the members are heads of some of the government departments. In addition, there are Education and Health Councils which regularly discuss the affairs of their respective departments.[4] Although the Ruler's decrees forming these Councils in 1956 provided, in deference to popular demands at the time, for the election of half the members of each council and the nomination by the Government of the other half, this principle has never been adhered to in practice.[5] Instead the procedure which has been followed allows for nominating five of the eight members of each council by the four urban Municipal Councils in the country, the remaining three members being selected by the Ruler himself.[6] The President of the Education Council is Shaikh Muhammad ibn Salman, the youngest brother

[1] Europa Publications Limited, London, *The Middle East and North Africa, 1966–1967*, 13th ed. (1966), pp. 536–8.

[2] It is clear that the ruling family of Qatar has shown no inclination whatsoever towards encouraging the establishment of any kind of representative institutions in the country, in disregard of pressing public demands.

[3] See Bahrain Government, *Annual Report*, Bahrain, 1956; Belgrave, J. H. D., *Welcome to Bahrain*, 5th ed. (1965), p. 13.

[4] Ibid.

[5] See Notice (or Decree) No. 19, dated 9 Sha'ban, 1375 (corresponding to 21 March 1956), and Notice No. 20, dated 28 Jumada I, 1376 (31 December 1956). For Sir Charles Belgrave's own account about the political movement in Bahrain, later known as the Committee of National Union, which precipitated the forming of these Councils as part of general demands for reforms, see Bahrain Government, *Annual Report*, 1956. For an enlightening description of the Bahrain national movement between 1954–6, see Owen, R., *The Golden Bubble*, London (1957).

[6] Europa Publications, op. cit., p. 533; Belgrave, J., op. cit. It is noteworthy that although, in principle, half of the members of the Municipal Councils, from which members are nominated for the Education and Health Councils, should be elected by the people, no municipal elections have been held in Bahrain for many years. Consequently, the elected members of the municipal councils continue to serve in their positions despite the expiry of the terms of their mandate. The attempt made by the Government to hold municipal elections in early 1966 failed, due to the people's boycott of, or apathy to, the elections. In a leading article the Bahrain

of the Ruler, who is also the Chief of Police and Public Security Department. The President of the Health Council is Shaikh Mubarak, one of the Ruler's uncles. It is clear that none of these councils, which have been established since 1956, could be considered as a representative body in a real democratic sense.[1] Moreover, judged by their performance during the last decade or so, the contribution of such councils towards the welfare and progressive development of the country has been negligible.

The Judicial system: in Bahrain and Qatar the local courts exercise jurisdiction over Bahraini and Qatari subjects and nationals of all Arab and Muslim States, with the exception of Muslim nationals of Commonwealth countries. British subjects and nationals of non-Muslim and Commonwealth States are subject to the British system of jurisdiction which is exercised by the British courts established in

---

al-Adhwa', the only recently licensed newspaper, criticises the Government's decision to extend, for an unspecified period of time, the term of service of the members of municipal councils, despite the recommendations of the 'specialised British experts' who were hired by the Government to advise it on implementing administrative reforms. See *al-Adhwa'* (Bahrain), No. 14, 9 December 1965.

[1] The educated and politically conscious class, which has, since 1954, been agitating, both overtly and covertly, for fundamental constitutional reforms in the country, is far from satisfied with the present 'autocratic' institutions which, in its view, do not represent the true will of the people. There was between 1954–6 a mature, reasonable and moderate political movement, the Committee of National Union, which called on the late Ruler, Shaikh Salman Al-Khalifah, to implement certain political and legal reforms in the archaic administration of the country. However, in consequence of the riots which infested the city during the Suez war in 1956, the Ruler succeeded, with the assistance of the locally based British troops, in ruthlessly suppressing the C.N.U., whose leaders were brought to trial in December 1956 on charges of treason, before a special tribunal composed of the Ruler's relatives. Although throughout the trial the accused pleaded their innocence and refused to defend themselves against the 'unproven' charges unless they were allowed to be represented by counsel, they were convicted on 23 December 1956. Three of the leaders, 'Abd al-Rahman al-Baker and his friends, were five days later transferred, with British assistance, to the British colony of St Helena to serve their terms of fourteen-year imprisonment. During the four and a half years of their detention in the colony the Bahraini prisoners contested the legality of their imprisonment by applying for a writ of *habeas corpus* before British courts. After at least one unsuccessful attempt, they finally succeeded in June 1961, in their case before the Supreme Court of St Helena, when the presiding Judge, Mr Justice Abbott, ruled that the Bahraini prisoners were 'unlawfully detained'. Subsequently, on their release they were issued with special British passports, since their Government had already deprived them of their Bahraini passports.

For detailed information on the political movement in Bahrain and the legal consequences ensuing from the confinement of the Bahrainis in St Helena, see the following: Bahrain Government, *Annual Report*, 1956; Owen, R., *The Golden Bubble* (1957); *The Spectator*, London, 1 July 1960, 17 February, 16 June 1961; *House of Commons, Parliamentary Debates*, col. 669, 7 March 1957; *Persian Gulf Gazette*, Suppl. No. 16, 1 April 1957; *Abdul Rahman Al Baker v. Robert Edmund Alford and Patrick Vincent Truebody, Privy Council Appeal*, No. 43 of 1959. Judg-

Bahrain and Qatar.[1] Justice in the national courts of the two Shaikhdoms is administered on the directions of the Rulers who generally
promulgate laws by means of proclamations, decrees or notices which
have the force of law in courts. In addition, the Rulers have, in recent
years, agreed to adopt and apply in their own courts certain modern
ordinances and regulations which have been brought into force for the
British courts in both Shaikhdoms by means of British Orders in
Council, or Queen's Regulations, as the case may be.[2]

Until 1956, codified criminal or civil laws were non-existent in the
two Shaikhdoms. In November 1956 a penal code, or a limited portion of it, was put into operation in Bahrain. This was followed by a
labour code which was applied in 1957. Apart from the technical and
legal deficiencies involved in these codes, they are, in any case, only
partially applied.[3] Concerning Qatar, legal reforms did not start until
1962–3, when progress towards the promulgation of a number of
criminal and civil codes was made. Consequently, there are now a
labour law and criminal and civil codes with civil and criminal procedure regulations. For the application of the labour law a labour
court has been established to try disputes regulated by the labour law,
irrespective of the nationality of the parties to such disputes.[4]

The local courts in Bahrain and Qatar are usually staffed by judges
from the ruling families, with no legal qualifications whatsoever. They

---

ment delivered on 1 June 1960; *The Times*, 14 June 1961; *The Guardian*, London,
14 June 1961; *The Observer*, 18 June 1961; Thornburg, Max Weston, *People and
Policy in the Middle East*, New York (1964), p. 104; Marlowe, J., *The Persian Gulf
in the Twentieth Century*, London (1962), p. 199. And see 'Abd al-Rahman al-
Baker's own account of the episode in his book *Min al-Bahrain Ela al-Manfa*
(From Bahrain to Exile), Beirut (1965).

[1] See above, p. 10.
[2] For clear examples of such ordinances and regulations, see *Persian Gulf
Gazette*, op. cit., Suppls. 1–32 (1952–61).
[3] According to Sir Charles Belgrave, 'until 1956, no criminal or civil codes had
been formally adopted, but the Senior Bahrain Court moulded its procedure on
the Sudan Penal Code, which was based on the Indian Penal Code. In November,
1956, portions of the Criminal Code which had been drafted for use in Bahrain
became law.' See Bahrain Government, *Annual Report*, 1956.
The following are the main body of codified laws existing in Bahrain: *The
Bahrain Penal Code*, June 1955; *The Bahrain Labour Ordinance*, November 1957;
The Bahrain Employed Persons Compensation Ordinance, November 1957; *The
Bahrain Patents, Designs and Trade Marks Ordinance*, July 1955. There is even
today no civil law in Bahrain. Civil law is, therefore, dependent on the collection
of proclamations, ordinances and notices issued by the Ruler over the last 35 years.
The collection, which deals with various civil matters, suffers greatly from incon-
sistencies, anachronism and bad drafting. See *Majmu'at Al-Qawanin Wal-E'lanaat*
(Collection of Laws and Notices), dated 19 Thu al-Q'adah, 1377 (7 June 1958).
[4] Europa Publications, op. cit., pp. 536–8; *Statement of the Chairman of The
British Bank of the Middle East for the year 1963*, *The Times*, 11 March 1964;
Hay, op. cit., 109–10.

have no regular procedure laws in the modern sense and their conditions are generally unsatisfactory. The courts apply the laws and regulations passed by the Rulers from time to time, when occasion arises. In commercial disputes, which constitute the bulk of civil cases, the judges are assisted by specially appointed committees of merchants, called *Majlis al-Tijarah*, which settle disputes according to commercial custom and local tradition.[1] Although in Qatar Shariʿah law has been followed rather strictly in various disputes, the very harsh punishments like chopping off hands for stealing have long been replaced by prison terms.[2] However, in recent years the promulgation of some modern civil and criminal codes, usually administered by civil judges, has restricted the application of Shariʿah law to matters of family and personal status. Similarly, in Bahrain Shariʿah law is more strictly administered in disputes relating to family and personal status.

The Trucial Shaikhdoms

In the seven Shaikhdoms of Trucial Oman there is very little in the way of modern or organised administration. Generally, these Shaikhdoms still remain backward and the people's nomadic life seems to have changed very little.[3] The Rulers' administration is patriarchal; they adjudicate in disputes among their peoples and dispose of their governmental functions on a personal basis. However, exception must be made in the case of the Shaikhdom of Dubai, lying to the east of Abu Dhabi, which has developed, in recent years, an administrative machinery. Accordingly, there are today departments for customs,

---

[1] In October 1954 a British Judicial Adviser, Mr G. L. Peace, was appointed by the Ruler of Bahrain to assist the lay judges of the courts on legal matters, especially on the interpretation and application of the newly promulgated laws which aspire to British legal principles. Mr Peace was succeeded after some years by a British barrister, Mr D. Humphreys, who, in turn, left the post sometime in 1962, as a result of differences with the Government over the extent of his authority in the courts. He has been succeeded by his Assistant who appears to have been able to accommodate himself to the generally static conditions of the courts. In addition to the Judicial Adviser, the Government has recently appointed a number of experienced Jordanian judges to assist the lay judges in entertaining cases in courts. For a fuller account of the historical development of the courts, see Belgrave's Report on the Judiciary in the Bahrain Government *Annual Report*, 1956.

[2] Information about the administration of justice in Qatar was supplied by Sayyid Ahmad al-Mulla, then Assistant Adviser to the Government of Qatar, in May 1959. And see Hay, op. cit., p. 110. In recent years, an Egyptian lawyer, Dr H. Kamel, has been appointed a Legal Adviser. He has helped greatly in the codification of new laws, though they are rarely applied in practice.

[3] It may be of interest to note, in this connection, Lord Asquith's observation in the *Abu Dhabi Award* that 'it would be fanciful to suggest that in this very primitive region there is any settled body of legal principles . . .' See *Petroleum Development (Trucial Coast) Ltd.* v. *The Shaikh of Abu Dhabi* (1951), *I.C.L.Q.*, 1 (1952), p. 247. And see Marlowe, J., op cit., p. 121.

police, health, education, finance, etc. There is also a municipal committee and a chamber of commerce. Moreover, there is a court of
law in Dubai, administered by a qualified *qadi*. However, except in
certain cases covered by local custom and tradition, most of the legal
disputes are settled in accordance with the principles of Shari'ah law.
Similarly, in the rest of the Shaikhdoms the Rulers administer justice
in accordance with a loose system of Shari'ah law which is interpreted
arbitrarily by the Rulers or their religious *qadis*.[1]

As in the case of Bahrain and Qatar, the Rulers of these Shaikhdoms
exercise jurisdiction only over their own nationals and nationals of
neighbouring Arab and Muslim countries. All other foreigners, including Europeans and Commonwealth citizens over whom jurisdiction has not been transferred to the Rulers, are subject to the British
extra-territorial jurisdiction exercised by the British territorial court
(The Court for the Trucial States), with appeals lying to the 'Chief
Court for the Persian Gulf'. In Abu Dhabi, however, all matters
regulated by the Abu Dhabi Traffic Ordinance, 1963, have been
transferred to the Ruler's court.[2]

The Trucial States Council: this Council, on which all the seven
Rulers of the Trucial Shaikhdoms are represented, was set up some
years ago by the British Government to discuss problems of mutual
interest. It meets once or twice a year, with the British Political Agent
at Dubai presiding. For some years past this council constituted the
only symbol of administrative co-operation among these autonomous Rulers. But, due to British encouragement, the Rulers have
recently shown more interest in co-operation on both the administrative and economic levels. Accordingly, a new 'deliberative council',
consisting of one or two representatives from each State, has taken
shape. This council, which is subordinate to the Trucial States Council,
is supposed to implement the decisions taken by the latter. Also in
1965, the seven Trucial Rulers held a British-sponsored conference in
Dubai during which they agreed to establish the Trucial States
Development Office. The Rulers agreed on a programme of mutual
co-operation 'whereby aid from the richer States, including Qatar,
Abu Dhabi and Bahrain, would be channelled through this office to
assist in the economic and social development of the poorer States'.
At present, only Abu Dhabi is an oil producing country in the whole
Trucial Coast.[3]

[1] See Hay, op. cit., pp. 114, 116, 120; Europa Publications, op. cit., pp. 539–42.
According to Hay, op. cit., the Rulers 'mostly administer "palm tree justice"
personally in cases which are not referred to a Qadhi for settlement according to
Muslim law . . .'
[2] See the Trucial States Order, 1959, in *Persian Gulf Gazette*, Suppl. No. 25,
1 August 1959; The Trucial States (Amendment) Order, 1963, in *Persian Gulf
Gazette*, Suppl. No. 43, January 1964. And see Europa Publications, op. cit.
[3] According to Hay, op. cit., p. 115, the Trucial States Council was formed in

c

The British Government has dealt with the affairs of the Trucial Shaikhdoms collectively, through its Political Agency at Dubai. But today Abu Dhabi has a separate Political Agent of her own who reports directly to the British Political Resident in Bahrain. Moreover, a British legal adviser was appointed in 1964 for the six Trucial States, with the exception of Abu Dhabi, to assist them in their local administration.[1]

Muscat

The system of government in the Sultanate of Muscat and Oman is autocratic. There is no organised system of administration and the Sultan's rule in Muscat is maintained through a number of officials of various nationalities. These include a British Personal Adviser to the Sultan, British Military and Development Secretaries, a Pakistani Secretary for Finance and Foreign Affairs and an Egyptian Director-General of Customs. In addition, there is an Arab Minister of the Interior, Sayyid Ahmad ibn Ibrahim. The latter exercises his authority in towns through governors, known as *walis*, while authority in the interior of Oman is exercised by tribal shaikhs and religious leaders over whom the Sultan has only a nominal control. The duties of the *walis* are, *inter alia*, to collect taxes from the people and administer justice, with the help of Muslim *qadis*. Justice is exercised in accordance with the uncodified tenets and laws of the *Ibadi* sect of Islam. In addition to these Shari'ah laws applied by the *qadis* in their own courts, the Sultan, in order to keep pace with events, issues, from time to time, decrees, taking the form of legislation, to regulate emergent civil and commercial matters. These decrees, or ordinances, have the force of law in courts. There are local courts in the various districts of the Sultanate and a Chief Court in Muscat. From the latter appeals lie to the Sultan personally.[2]

1951 'with the object of inducing them to adopt a common policy in administrative matters'. And see 'Problems of the Trucial States—II', *The Times*, 4 February 1964; The Economist Intelligence Unit, *Quarterly Economic Review, Middle East Oil and the Arabian Peninsula*, Annual Supplement (1966), pp. 60–2, 18–19. For background information on the development of British-sponsored institutions on the Trucial Coast, see Marlowe, op. cit., pp. 197–8.

[1] See Hay, op. cit., p. 115; Mann, C., *Abu Dhabi*, op. cit., pp. 111–12; Europa Publications, op. cit. Shaikh Zayid ibn Sultan of Abu Dhabi, who replaced his 'reactionary' brother, Shakhbut, in August 1966, has been reported to have approved the formation of 'a board to supervise investment of state revenue'. He has also established a Finance Department which has a British Director. The latter has been instructed to set up 'a budgetary system' for the tiny Shaikhdom whose oil revenues have reached £30 million a year. See *Arab Report and Record*, London, No. 3, 23 February 1967; *The Observer*, London, 14 August 1966; *The Observer*, 11 April 1965, Patrick Seale's article on Shaikh Shakhbut, Abu Dhabi.

[2] See Hay, op. cit., pp. 140–1; *The Statesman's Year-Book*, 103rd ed., 1966–7 (1966), pp. 1266–8: Europa Publications, op. cit., pp. 515–16; *The Times*, 'Problems of the Trucial States—II', 4 February 1964.

The British Court for Muscat, established under the provisions of
the British foreign jurisdiction in the Gulf, exercises a very limited
type of jurisdiction which extends only to non-Muslim citizens of the
United Kingdom and some Commonwealth countries. Appeals from
the Court for Muscat, which applies British enactments, lie to the
British Chief Court in Bahrain.[1]

The Sultan, Sa'id ibn Taimur, conducts his country's affairs through
a radio-telephone from his palace at Salala which is 600 miles south
of Muscat. He has constantly procrastinated over the introduction of
modern reforms in his anachronistic administration. However, recent
reports indicate that the Sultan, whose Sultanate is now on the verge
of becoming an oil exporting country, is seeking expert advice on
re-organising his administration and introducing some development
projects.[2]

Kuwait

During the years preceding her independence on 19 June 1961
Kuwait lacked an organised government. Describing the administra-
tive machinery in Kuwait in early 1959, Sir Rupert Hay, once the
British Political Resident in the Gulf, states:

The system of Government is patriarchal and the high offices of State are
held by members of the ruling family, each of whom conducts the affairs
of the department entrusted to him with the minimum of financial or any
other control by any central authority. In fact, each of these Shaikhs is a
law unto himself, and there is much in the administration which depends on
their relations with each other, their presence or absence from the State or
the willingness of the Ruler to control their activities . . .

The formation, at the time, of a Supreme Council for the State, comprising these Shaikhs, showed, according to the author, 'signs of
leading to more coordination' in the administration. In the field of
justice, Sir Rupert Hay says, the Ruler's courts administered justice
'on somewhat primitive lines and the principles of Muslim law'
were usually applied in both civil and criminal cases, although

[1] See the Muscat Orders in Council, 1955 to 1962, in *Persian Gulf Gazette*,
Suppl. Nos. 25–36, 1959–62; Europa Publications, op. cit., p. 516. It is noteworthy
that British jurisdiction in Muscat has been relinquished as of 1 January 1967.
This has been provided by the Muscat (Revoking) Order 1966 (S.I. No. 1598 of
1966), the Explanatory Note of which states: 'This Order revokes the Muscat
Orders 1955 to 1962 which provided for the exercise of Her Majesty's jurisdiction
in the territories of the Sultan of Muscat and Oman . . .' Consequently, jurisdiction
over persons subject to the Muscat Orders 1955 to 1962 has been transferred to the
Sultan's Courts. See *Persian Gulf Gazette*, Suppl. No. 53, January 1967.

[2] See *The Times*, 4 February 1964; The Economist Intelligence Unit, *Quarterly
Economic Review, Annual Supplement on Middle East Oil and the Arabian Peninsula*
(1966), pp. 62–3; *MEES*, No. 22, 31 March 1967, p. 3; *Arab Report and Record*,
No. 3, 23 February 1967.

the most severe punishments prescribed by Shari'ah law were suspended.[1]

This gloomy picture of the Kuwait system of government has become quite irrelevant to Kuwait after attaining her full independence on 19 June 1961. Since that date Kuwait has moved rapidly towards a constitutional system of government, with an elected parliament, a strong council of ministers and an organised administrative machine. Under a new constitution, which was drafted by Egyptian experts, a National Assembly of fifty members was elected in January 1963, 'for a four-year term, by all natural-born literate Kuwaiti males over the age of 21'. The executive authority has been vested in a Council of Ministers, the membership of which includes both Shaikhs and commoners. The Prime Minister and his Ministers need not be members of the National Assembly which itself has no power to force the resignation of the Prime Minister by a vote of no confidence against his government. However, if, in this case, the Assembly approaches the Amir, the supreme executive power, he could either dismiss the Prime Minister and his cabinet or dissolve the National Assembly. Since the Constitution does not sanction the establishment of political parties in Kuwait, the candidates for the National Assembly are required to stand as individuals.[2]

In December 1965 a constitutional crisis reflecting the tension between the traditional ruling family, which is strongly represented in the Council of Ministers, and the only opposition group in the National Assembly, representing eight Kuwaiti-born members of the Arab Nationalist Movement, resulted in the voluntary resignation of these members from the Assembly, in protest against what they regarded as non-Arab measures adopted by the pro-government Assembly. On completing its four-year term of office, the National Assembly was dissolved by the Ruler and on 25 January 1967 a new fifty-member Assembly was elected. But this time the opposition group

---

[1] Hay, op. cit., p. 101. And see Marlowe, op. cit., pp. 135-6, where he, pertinently, states: 'In Kuwait, as in Bahrain, the British Protectorate status was later to prove embarrassing to the British Government in that it involved support for the ruling House without any provision for influencing its domestic policies which, as in Bahrain, were uncompromisingly autocratic, without being scandalously tyrannical.'

[2] See Europa Publications, op. cit., p. 389: The E.I.U., *Quarterly Economic Review*, op. cit., p. 47; The International Bank of Reconstruction and Development, Report of Missions Organised by the Bank, *The Economic Development of Kuwait*, Baltimore (1965), p. 12. For an interesting comment on the Kuwaiti constitutional experiment, see Kelly, J. B., 'The Future in Arabia', *International Affairs*, 42 (1966), p. 633. Here the writer says: 'The constitution and the assembly simply function to provide some of the native Kuwaitis with a more-or-less harmless outlet for their political energies. Real power still resides with the Ruler and his Council of Ministers, which is composed of members or adherents of the Al-Sabah.'

representing the Kuwaiti branch of the Arab Nationalist Movement won, to the surprise of many optimistic observers, only four of the seats of the new National Assembly. This was a great setback to this group of Kuwaiti intellectuals, headed by their leader, Dr Ahmad al-Khatib, who himself was defeated by his less popular opponent. These election results, which were, obviously, unfavourable to the Kuwaiti educated and progressive class, prompted 'a group of 38 candidates, including six successful ones, backed up by five of Kuwait's seven newspapers and a number of other organisations', to accuse the government of flagrant interference in the elections. In protest against these alleged irregularities, the six successful candidates, who would have represented the only opposition group in the new parliament, submitted their resignations. The Government, on the other hand, denied allegations of interference in the elections. At the same time, it took 'disciplinary measures' against a number of newspapers which criticised the Government for its improper conduct in the election. The Government, however, promised to submit all the election complaints for review by the special electoral committee, but it refused the demands for declaring the elections null and void.[1]

The present row for political power in Kuwait underlies the great strains through which the new democratic experiment is passing in this small, but fabulously rich, country, where the temporary intermarriage of 1963, between the traditional ruling family and their supporters from the aristocratic merchant and bedouin families and the new Kuwaiti educated middle class, has already collapsed. The absence of a badly needed 'intelligent opposition' in the present Kuwaiti parliament is, of course, much regretted by many admirers of Kuwait's democratic system. The Al-Sabah rulers, who are credited by the *Economist* with having 'marvellously handled the problems of their co-existence with democracy', are, nevertheless, criticised for having 'shown themselves followers rather than leaders, too ready to shelter behind an assembly which some suspect was created for this very purpose'.[2]

The Judicial System: since 1960, a codified system of law, based largely upon the Egyptian judicial system, has been established. The organisation of the judicial system was initiated some years before independence when a judicial committee was appointed, under the chairmanship of a well-known Egyptian jurist, Dr 'Abd al-Razzaq al-Sanhuri, for the purpose of promulgating modern civil and criminal laws.[3]

[1] See Europa Publications, op. cit., p. 380; *MEES*, No. 12, 20 January and No. 14, 3 February 1967; *The Economist*, 21 January 1967, p. 217; *The Times*, 3 February 1967.

[2] *The Economist*, 21 January 1967, p. 217.

[3] From 1960, Shari'ah courts were successfully replaced by modern civil courts. The modern laws promulgated at that period included the following: *The Law for*

British extra-territorial jurisdiction, which had been exercised in Kuwait over British subjects and foreigners since 1925, was finally relinquished in early 1961. Consequently, Kuwait national courts assumed jurisdiction over foreigners in all civil and criminal matters.[1]

The new Constitution of November 1962 declares the independence of the Judiciary which used to be in the past a monopoly of the ruling family. The Judiciary, which is, administratively, subject to the authority of the Minister of Justice, has recruited legally qualified judges from some Arab countries. The new national courts, which are classified into civil and criminal courts and courts of appeal, apply the Western-inspired laws, promulgated for Kuwait during the last few years. Concerning Shari'ah law, its application has been confined to matters of family and personal status.[2]

---

the Organisation of Justice, issued under Decree No. 19, 1959, al-Kuwait al-Yawm, Suppl. No. 255, 28 December 1959; Company Law, issued under Decree No. 15, 1960, al-Kuwait al-Yawm, Suppl. No. 276, 23 May 1960; Criminal Law, issued under Decree No. 16, 1960, al-Kuwait al-Yawm, Suppl. No. 278, 11 June 1960; Law of Criminal Procedure, issued under Decree No. 17, 1960, al-Kuwait al-Yawm, Suppl. No. 279, 13 June 1960; Labour Law, issued under Decree No. 18, 1960, al-Kuwait al-Yawm, Suppl. No. 280, 20 June 1960; Civil and Commercial Law of Procedure, issued under Decree No. 6, 1960, al-Kuwait al-Yawm, Suppl. No. 267, 21 March 1960.

[1] For British extra-territorial jurisdiction in Kuwait, see Kuwait Order in Council, 1959, Persian Gulf Gazette, Suppl. No. 25, August 1959. For the transfer of this jurisdiction to Kuwaiti courts, see Kuwait al-Yawm, No. 262, 14 February 1960. And see Persian Gulf Gazette, Suppl. Nos 28–30, April, July, October 1960.

[2] See Europa Publications, op. cit., p. 391.

PART ONE

BRITISH TREATY RELATIONS WITH THE ARABIAN GULF STATES

2

Relations with the Trucial Shaikhdoms

ABU DHABI, DUBAI, SHARJAH, AJMAN, UMM AL-QAIWAIN, RAS AL-KHAIMAH AND FUJAIRAH

Until the end of the eighteenth century, very little was known of the international conditions of the region which now comprises these States. However, it appears that in the past the influence of the Qawasim (Jawasim) tribe predominated over the whole coast which was then called the 'Pirate Coast'. The present seven Trucial States were then no more than small towns inhabited by various Arab tribes acknowledging the lordship of the biggest tribe, al-Qawasim, with their capital at Ras al-Khaimah.[1]

After the year 1800, the Qawasim Arabs were known to have succumbed to the influence of the Wahhabi Arabs of the mainland of Arabia. During this period the Qawasim were in the habit of carrying out piratical raids against British ships in the Arabian Gulf. Late in 1805, the British Government in India sent an expedition to the Arabian Gulf in order to put an end to the Qawasim's raids. As a result, an agreement was concluded on 6 February 1806 between Sultan ibn Saqr, Shaikh of the Qawasim, and the East India Company.[2]

The agreement dealt generally with measures concerning the restoration of peace in the waters of the Gulf and the protection of British vessels and property in the ports of the Qawasim. Two points call for special mention. First, the two parties reciprocally agreed to respect the flag and property of the subjects of each other 'wherever and in whatever it may be', thus placing no restrictions upon the Qawasim in their relations with non-British subjects (Art. 1). Secondly, the Qawasim were given the right to disregard the agreement if they were compelled to do so by the Islamic rite of 'Jihad', provided that they gave 'three months previous notice in all places' to the British authorities.

Nevertheless, the Qawasim failed to comply with the agreement, and in 1809 and 1819, the East India Company was obliged to dispatch two more expeditions. The expedition of 1809 failed to produce useful results. However, that of 1819 inflicted severe damage to the stronghold

---

[1] Lorimer, p. 631; Saldanha, *A Précis of Correspondence Regarding the Trucial Chiefs* (1906); Aitchison, pp. 196–8.
[2] Aitchison, pp. 197–8, 239–40.

of the Qawasim, and induced them to negotiate a further treaty with the East India Company.[1]

The General Treaty of Peace, 8 January 1820[2]

The object of the General Treaty of 1820 was stated to be the 'pacification of the Gulf'. The first Article provided for the 'cessation of plunder and piracy by land and sea' on the part of the parties to the Agreement. The second Article defined 'piracy' and 'acknowledged war', distinguishing between them as follows:

> An acknowledged war is that which is proclaimed, avowed and ordered by government against government, and the killing of men and taking of goods without proclamation, avowal, and the order of a government, is plunder and piracy.

This Article also confined the application of the conditions of the treaty only to those hostile acts committed by land or sea in the way of plunder and piracy:

> If any individual of the people of the Arabs contracting shall attack any that pass by land or sea of any nation whatsoever in the way of plunder and piracy and not of acknowledged war, he shall be accounted an enemy of all mankind and shall be held to have forfeited both money and goods.

It appears that the distinction drawn by this Article left the door open to the parties to declare or carry on war with each other by sea provided that this was 'proclaimed or avowed by government'.

Unfortunately, therefore, this distinction did not serve its purpose and under the guise of 'acknowledged war' many piratical acts were committed, especially during the pearl-fishing season.[3]

In order to understand Article 2 fully, it must be read in conjunction with Articles 8 and 9 which provide further examples of acts con-

---

[1] Aitchison, pp. 197–8; Lorimer, pp. 360–1.

[2] For an English translation of the original Arabic copy of the Treaty of Peace of 1820, signed by Major-General W. Grant Keir with the Arab tribes of Ras al-Khaimah, see F.O. 60/17, January 1820. For the text of the Treaty, see also Aitchison, pp. 245–8.

This Treaty was adhered to by all the tribes of the Trucial Coast which now form the seven Trucial Shaikhdoms.

[3] Aitchison, p. 199. To bring an end to this confusion, the British Government induced the Shaikhs concerned to conclude, in 1835, a maritime truce, the object of which was the cessation of all hostile activities, piratical or warlike, by sea for a fixed period. This Truce of 1835 was renewed in 1837 and 1843 until finally on 4 May 1853 it was replaced by a permanent treaty known as the Treaty of Peace of 24 August 1853. This new treaty provided for the complete cessation of hostile acts by sea on the part of the parties subscribing to it. It also provided that in the event of any aggression being inflicted 'by sea' by one party to the treaty on the other, the injured party should not retaliate, but refer the matter for the arbitration of the British Resident in the Arabian Gulf, who would cause reparation to be made to the victim. For this treaty, see ibid., pp. 252–3.

stituting piracy. These include 'the putting of men to death after they have given up their arms', and 'the carrying off of slaves, men, women, or children from the coasts of Africa or elsewhere, and the transporting them in vessels'. In practice, Article 9 was interpreted as prohibiting no more than the kidnapping of slaves, and was regarded as stopping short of prohibiting the slave traffic in general. Indeed the selling and buying of slaves was carried on with impunity even after the signing of the treaty of 1820.[1]

Article 3 prescribed a particular flag to be carried by the friendly Arabs by land and sea as a symbol of their adherence to the treaty.

Article 4 dealt with the status of the Shaikhs in the following terms:

The pacificated tribes shall all of them continue in their former relation with the exception that they shall not fight with each other, and the flag shall be a symbol of this only and nothing further.

It is clear that the object of this provision was to assure the signatories that the British Government did not entertain any designs to annex the territories of the Shaikhs.

Article 5 referred to procedural matters connected with the observance of the treaty, such as the carrying of a register by each Arab vessel containing the necessary information regarding the ship, its owner, size, destination, etc. Articles 6 and 10 authorised the British Residency in the Gulf to act as a maritime police in the waters of the Gulf for the purpose of administration and observance of the conditions of the treaty, and to settle all matters of dispute arising between the friendly Arabs adhering to the treaty. Article 7 referred to measures which should be taken by the friendly tribes in conjunction with the British authorities in order to prevent the other tribes, not being parties to the treaty, from committing piracy. Finally Article 11 enjoined the other tribes who were not originally parties to the treaty to subscribe to it.[2]

The enforcement of this treaty gave rise to a number of problems:

(a) *The attitude of the Government of Bombay towards the Treaty*

When the British authorities in India received a copy of the treaty, which was signed on behalf of the East India Company by Major-General Grant Keir, they expressed their dissatisfaction with its

---

[1] In 1839, a further treaty was concluded between the British Government and the Trucial Shaikhs in order to cover the defects arising from the treaty of 1820. The first and the second articles of the treaty of 1839 allowed the British authorities in the Gulf to seize and confiscate any vessel found 'engaged in the slave trade'. The third article prohibited the sale of 'males and females whether young or old', of the Somali tribes, and considered such dealing as piracy. See Aitchison, pp. 249–50.

[2] For the adherence in 1820 of Bahrain to the General Treaty of Peace, see p. 31 below.

terms which, they said, were very lenient. They advocated instead the imposition of more strenuous conditions on the 'pacificated' Arab Shaikhs. In their opinion, the guilty Shaikhs 'should have been removed from possession of authority and those who had actually fallen in the hands of the British expedition should have been detained in custody'. In addition, they criticised the provisions of the treaty on the grounds that

the treaty ought to have interdicted the fitting out of armed vessels at ports hitherto piratical; to have limited the size of the vessels employed in commerce; to have stipulated for powers of search by the British authorities in order to enforce these conditions; to have provided for a restriction of the export of timber from India; and to have forbidden the construction of fortifications in certain circumstances, at the same time empowering the British Government to enter on and destroy any that might be built in disregard of the prohibition.

Further, objection was taken to the treaty because it 'afforded no guarantee against the renewal of piracy'. Article 5, they said, did not give such a guarantee since it 'was so drafted that breach of its conditions would not render the culprits liable to any punishment'.[1]

In reply to these 'strictures' Major-General Grant Keir assured the Government that he was satisfied with the practicability of his treaty and that the 'minor stipulations' suggested by the Government might be

enforced at any time when necessity for them should arise for they would be in harmony with the general spirit and objects of the treaty, which were perfectly understood by the Arabs.[2]

(b) The interpretation of the Treaty

In 1823, the British Resident in the Gulf asked for the decision of Government on a number of questions relating to the interpretation of the treaty of 1820. These were: (1) Whether the British authorities had the right to inquire into the building of new vessels in the piratical ports and to destroy them if the explanation given was unsatisfactory? (2) Whether the authorities could detain the vessels of signatory states 'if not possessed of the papers or flying the flag required by Articles 3 and 5 of the Treaty?' The Government's decision on both questions was in the negative. The Government was also asked to say: (1) Whether, according to the terms of the treaty, the British authorities could forbid the building or rebuilding of fortifications by the Shaikhs? (2) What was the scope of Article 9 relating to the slave trade? (3) To what extent the British Government was under obligation, according to Article 10, to protect the 'pacificated' Arabs against the attacks of non-signatory Arabs?

---

[1] Lorimer, pp. 672–3; Saldanha, *Précis*, op. cit.   [2] Ibid.

In reply, the Government stated:

That the terms of the treaty did not warrant any prohibition of the building of forts; that the article in which slaves were mentioned referred not to the buying and selling of persons already enslaved but to raids on the coast of Africa for the purpose of making slaves which alone could be correctly described as plunder and piracy, and that the promise of protection against non-signatories only covered the Indian ports to which by the same article access was guaranteed to signatories.[1]

(c) *British attitude to the Trucial States between 1820–92*

After the signing of the General Treaty of 1820, with the Trucial States the policy of the British Government was restricted to securing the maintaining of peace and the suppression of piracy and the slave trade in the Arabian Gulf. When, therefore, a request was made by the 'petty chief states' for the establishment of a system of 'protectorship or arbitral authority over them', the United Kingdom declined to accede to it.[2] Although she regarded herself as no more than 'the head of naval confederacy for the suppression of piracy', she nevertheless interpreted the term 'piracy' in a broad manner as covering all acts of aggression or fighting between Arab tribes at sea. The stringency of British policy in this respect manifested itself also in the insistence of the British Government in applying the conditions of the Treaty of Peace of 1820 even to tribes which had not signed it.[3]

Exclusive Agreement of 6 March 1892[4]

In 1892, the British policy of non-involvement in the affairs of the Trucial Shaikhdoms seemed to have been abandoned by the conclusion, in March 1892, of the 'Exclusive Agreement' with these Shaikhdoms. This Agreement for the first time conferred on the British Government 'preferential rights' in connection with the internal affairs of the Trucial Shaikhdoms—a grant which later became a factor of importance in questions arising between them and foreign powers.[5] It also limited the authority of the Trucial Shaikhs within their territories in dealing directly with matters which might expose them to the influence of foreign powers. The Trucial Shaikhs undertook to observe the following obligations: (*a*) not to enter into any agreement or correspondence, save through the British Government; and

[1] Lorimer, pp. 678–9.   [2] Ibid., p. 694
[3] Ibid., pp. 694–719; Saldanha, *Précis*, op. cit.
[4] For the text of this Agreement, see Appendix III. For original English and Arabic texts, see India, *Foreign and Political Department*, Part I, 'Treaties and Engagements in force between the British Government and the Trucial Chiefs of the Arab Coast', 1820–1912, p. 19.
[5] Lorimer, pp. 726–9. The Agreement of 1892 was originally concluded with the Shaikh of Abu Dhabi. Then on 7 and 8 March 1892 agreements, identical in form, were signed by the other Trucial Shaikhs. See Aitchison, p. 257. The Shaikh of Bahrain also signed a similar agreement on 13 March 1892. See p. 35 below.

(b) not to allow the residence within their territories of any foreign agent without the consent of the British Government.[1]

In 1902, the question of establishing a formal British protectorate over the Trucial States was mooted by the British Government but it finally decided simply to maintain the existing loose system.[2]

In 1903 the principle of British representation of the Trucial Shaikhdoms in external affairs was affirmed by the Government of India as a result of the *Dubai Boat* incident of February 1901. In that year a boat belonging to the Trucial State of Dubai had been obliged by stress of weather to shelter in a Persian port and was detained by Persian customs. Subsequently, the boat and its cargo were released in virtue of representation made by the British Political Resident. Later, the Persian and the French Governments were officially made aware, for the first time, of the Exclusive Agreements of 1892, between the British Government and the Trucial Shaikhs. It appears that following this incident the British Government continued the practice of representing the Trucial Shaikhdoms in the international sphere.[3]

Other agreements with the British Government signed by the Trucial Shaikhdoms were: (1) An agreement in 1902, prohibiting the importation or the exportation of arms. (2) An Agreement in 1911, concerning pearling and sponge concessions. (3) An undertaking in February 1922 in which they pledged themselves not to allow the exploitation of oil resources in their territories except by 'persons appointed by the High British Government'.[4]

There is nothing in the above agreements, signed by the Trucial Shaikhdoms, which either formally extends a system of British protectorate over these Shaikhdoms or delegates to the British Government the right of representing the Shaikhdoms in their relations with foreign powers.

---

[1] Aitchison, pp. 256–7.   [2] Lorimer, p. 742.   [3] Ibid. pp. 744–5.
[4] See Appendices VI and VII. For Arabic and English texts, see India, *Foreign and Political Department*, Part I, op. cit.

3

Relations with Bahrain

The British Government appears to have established its first official contact with the Shaikhs of Al-Khalifah of Bahrain in 1816. In that year Captain Bruce, the British Resident at Bushire, paid an official visit to the Shaikhs of Al-Khalifah. This resulted in the conclusion of a draft treaty of friendship, Treaty of 31 July 1816, with the Ruler of the island, Shaikh ʿAbd Allah ibn Ahmad. But this treaty, which was apparently concluded without the authority of the Indian Government, did not come into force.[1] However, four years later, Bahrain became a party to the Treaty of Peace of 1820, concluded by the British Government with the Shaikhs of Ras al-Khaimah. This treaty was signed by an agent of the Shaikh of Bahrain on 5 February 1820. And in a supplementary agreement of the same date aimed at implementing the provisions of this treaty the Shaikh of Bahrain agreed not to allow in his country 'the sale of any commodities' obtained 'by means of plunder and piracy', nor to permit his people 'to sell anything of any kind whatsoever' to persons identified with the practice of plunder and piracy (Art. 1).[2] In addition, in 1856 the Ruler of Bahrain entered into another agreement with the same object. In this, he bound himself to seize and deliver over to the British vessels of war 'whatsoever' slaves were brought to his country. He further undertook that if any slaves were carried in his vessels or in those of any of his subjects, he would 'place an embargo on the delinquent boat' and submit this boat to the decision of the British Resident.[3]

These agreements dealt exclusively with the ways and means of suppressing piracy and slave traffic, in connection with which the Government required the assistance and co-operation of the Shaikh of Bahrain. The Shaikh was also treated in these agreements as an independent ruler, while Britain appeared to be exercising merely a 'beneficial' supervision over matters generally concerning the peace of the Gulf.

Later, however, the agreement of 1856 was followed by a 'Friendly Convention with Independent Ruler of Bahrain' of 31 May 1861.[4] This Convention restricted all the warlike activities of the Ruler of

[1] I.O. *Bombay Secret Proceedings*, vol. 41, *Secret Consultation*, 28, 20–21 July 1819, p. 1413. Dispatch from the Resident at Bushire, Captain Bruce, to the Bombay Government, 31 July 1816.

[2] Aitchison, p. 233. During this time two Rulers conjointly ruled Bahrain. See ibid., p. 191.   [3] Ibid., p. 234.

[4] Great Britain, *British Foreign and State Papers*, vol. 56 (1864–5), pp. 1402–3.

Bahrain at sea and entrusted to the British Government the right to supervise such activities. The Shaikh agreed to establish a 'perpetual Treaty of peace and friendship with the British Government', for the purposes of 'the advancement of trade and the security of all classes of people navigating etc.' (Art. 1). He then undertook to

abstain from all maritime aggressions of every description, from the pro-secution of war, piracy and slavery by sea, so long as I receive the support of the British Government in the maintenance of the security of my own possessions against similar aggressions directed against them by the Chiefs and tribes of this Gulf (Art. 2).

The importance of this article is that it prohibited the Shaikh from prosecuting even a non-piratical war. This prohibition was not con-tained in the Treaty of Peace of 1820. On the other hand, while this article prohibited the carriage of slaves by sea, it made no reference to the problem of slavery on land. This may mean that slavery on land was considered by the contracting parties as an internal matter which concerned the Shaikh alone.

In Article 3, the Shaikh agreed to make known all aggressions against himself, territories, or subjects, to the British Resident in the Arabian Gulf, 'as the arbitrator in such cases'. He also promised that 'no act of aggression or retaliation shall be committed at sea by Bahreinis, or in the name of Bahrein', by himself or any of his sub-jects, on other tribes without the consent of the British Resident. The British Resident, on the other hand, promised, on behalf of the British Government, that

he will forthwith take the necessary steps for obtaining reparation of every injury proved to have been inflicted, or in the course of infliction by sea upon Bahrein or upon its dependencies in the Gulf.

It appears that the Shaikh was committed by this article so strongly that it was doubtful whether he was allowed to exercise the right of self-defence in face of aggression directed against his territory by another country. For example, he was required to inform the British Resident or the British Government of any aggression against his country and to get the Resident's consent before taking any step on his own initiative.

Moreover, Articles 2 and 3, discussed above, followed the same pattern of the agreements of 1839 and 1853 made by Great Britain with the rulers of the Trucial Coast, and, like these earlier agree-ments, prohibited the commission of hostilities on the part of the Arab rulers at sea only.[1]

---

[1] It should be noted that Bahrain was not a party to the agreements of 1839 and 1853 concluded with the Trucial States. See Aitchison, p. 191.

Finally, in Article 4 the Shaikh promised to allow British subjects to 'reside in, and carry on their lawful trade in the territories of Bahrein, their goods being subject only to an *ad valorem* duty of 5 per cent, in cash or in kind'.

He also agreed to treat the British subjects and dependents residing in Bahrain as 'subjects and dependents of the most favoured people'. This article further conferred upon the British Government an extra-territorial jurisdiction to be exercised in respect of British subjects only. The British Resident, for his part, agreed to

use his good offices for the welfare of the subjects of Bahrein in the ports of the maritime Arab tribes of the Gulf in alliance with the British Government.

Rivalries among the ruling family of Bahrain on the one hand, and between them and the other local Shaikhs of the Gulf, on the other, continued during this period. This caused the British Government to take military and diplomatic measures designed to bring tranquillity to the Gulf and to prevent any potential conflict with Turkey and Persia, both of which appeared to be working behind the scene of tribal quarrels in attempts to establish their influence in the Island.[1] When in 1867, the Shaikh of Bahrain, Muhammad Al-Khalifah, prepared an attack against Qatar and asked for military help from Persia, the British Government's action was two-fold. First, it prevented Persian intervention in Bahrain. Secondly, it frustrated the Shaikh's military action against Qatar—an action which the British Government held to be contrary to the Agreement of 1861. Finally, after a British military action against the Shaikh and his supporters in Bahrain, the British Government denounced him as a 'pirate' and deposed him as a punishment for his violation of the Convention of 1861. Thereafter, the rulership of the island was taken over, with the agreement of members of the Al-Khalifah family, by Shaikh ʿAli, a brother of the deposed Shaikh.[2] However, Shaikh ʿAli was killed a

[1] Aitchison, pp. 193–4; Lorimer, pp. 836 et seq.

It should be noted that Persia and Ottoman Turkey continuously advanced claims to sovereignty over Bahrain. These claims were vigorously resisted by the British Government.

There is little doubt that both Turkey and Persia were encouraged by the friendly attitude of the Ruler of Bahrain during this time, Shaikh Muhammad, to press their claims to the island. It appears that the Ruler invited in 1859, and in the years following, the protection of these states simultaneously. See for a further explanation of these events, Lorimer, pp. 888–90.

[2] Aitchison, pp. 193–4. For a discussion of British policy towards these events, see Lorimer, pp. 888, et seq.

The British Government regarded the policy of Shaikh Muhammad, who continuously and in face of British objections solicited aid and assistance from both Persia and Turkey as a great menace to its position in the Gulf. 'No form of words . . . or signature could bind the crafty old fox . . .' says Lord Curzon about

D

year after he took office,[1] and was succeeded by his son, Shaikh Isa.[2]

During the period following these developments, between 1870 and 1900, both the Ottoman Government and Persia continued with great vigour to interest themselves in the affairs of Bahrain to whose sovereignty they both laid claims.[3]

The new ruler of Bahrain, Shaikh Isa, who unlike his predecessor showed no sympathy with either Turkey or Persia, signed two further Agreements of 1880 and 1892, with the British Government.[4] These two agreements, which associated the British Government more closely with the affairs of Bahrain, also strengthened the former's position in speaking, internationally, in the name of Bahrain. The provisions of these agreements are considered below:

The Agreement of 22 December 1880[5]

In this agreement, the Shaikh of Bahrain bound himself and his successors in the Government of Bahrain to the British Government to abstain from entering into negotiations or making treaties of any sort with

---

Shaikh Muhammad. See Curzon, G. N., *Persia and the Persian Question*, vol. II (1892), p. 458.

For an agreement of 6 September 1868, concluded with Shaikh 'Ali, see Aitchison, pp. 236–7.

[1] Shaikh Muhammad, who earlier escaped to the mainland of Arabia, managed, with the support of his tribe and relatives, to launch an attack against Bahrain. He killed his brother, Shaikh 'Ali, and took control over the island. However, owing to British military intervention, he was captured with some of his supporters. He and his supporters were then exiled to Bombay. See Aitchison, pp. 194–5.   [2] Ibid.

[3] Aitchison, pp. 195–6; Lorimer, pp. 919–20. The British Government had always regarded these claims as untenable. Turkey's claim was based on her territorial acquisition of the eastern coast of Arabia during the period 1870 to 1913, but it was finally relinquished by the provisions of the draft Convention of 29 July 1913. Article 13 of this Convention stated:

'The Ottoman Imperial Government renounces all its claims to the Bahrain Islands . . . and recognizes the independence of the country. Britain, for her part, declared that she "has no intention of annexing the islands of Bahrain" to her territories'. This Convention remained unratified. (See Hurewitz, vol. 1, pp. 269–272.) But by article 16 of the Treaty of Lausanne, 24 July 1923, Turkey has given up all her claims to 'the territories situated outside the frontiers laid down in the present Treaty'. This article applies also to Turkish claims over territories in the Arabian Gulf. See *Treaty Series*, No. 16 (1923), *Cmd.* 1929.

[4] The British Government had for a long time before the conclusion of these agreements declined many requests made on the part of the Shaikhs of Bahrain— including the deposed Shaikh, Muhammad, for the extension of British protection to Bahrain. For Shaikh Muhammad's letter of 19 February 1849, to the British Resident, Major Hannell, asking for British protection over Bahrain, see F.O. 60/145, 1849, cited below, p. 172.

[5] For text, see India, *Foreign and Political Department*, Treaties between the British Government and the Rulers of Bahrain (1820–1914), part 4, pp. 1–17, and see Appendix I.

any State or Government other than the British without the consent of the said British Government, and to refuse permission to any other government than the British to establish diplomatic or consular agencies or coal depots in our territory, unless with the consent of the British Government.

The effect of this agreement was to deprive the Shaikh of the power to conduct relations of any sort with foreign powers without the intervention of the British Government. The Agreement, however, did not impair the absolute authority of the Shaikh to conduct 'customary friendly correspondence with the local authorities of neighbouring States on business of minor importance'.

The Agreement of 13 March 1892[1]

This agreement supplemented the 1880 agreement and reaffirmed the alienation by the Shaikh of his right to conduct his own foreign policy contrary to the wishes of the British Government. The Shaikh undertook (a) not to 'enter into any agreement or correspondence with any power other than the British Government', (b) not to 'consent to the residence within my territory of the agent of any other Government' without the assent of the British Government, and (c) not to 'cede, sell, mortgage or otherwise give for occupation any part of my territory save to the British Government'.

The Shaikhs of Bahrain also entered into a number of other subsidiary agreements:

1. In 1898, the ruling Shaikh bound himself that he would 'absolutely prohibit the importation of arms to Bahrein territory or exportation therefrom'.[2]

2. In 1909 and in 1912,[3] the Shaikh gave an undertaking to allow the establishment of a British post office and 'Wireless Telegraph Installations' in Bahrain.

3. In a letter, dated 14 May 1914, the Shaikh undertook not to 'embark on the exploitation' of oil in his country himself nor to 'entertain overtures from any quarter regarding that without consulting the Political Agent in Bahrain and without the approval of the High Government'.[4]

The Shaikh thus limited his absolute right to control and dispose of what came to be the most important source of national income in his country.

---

[1] India, *Foreign and Political Department*, part 4, op. cit., and see Appendix II.
[2] Aitchison, p. 238.   [3] Ibid., p. 239.
[4] Ibid., *Foreign and Political Department*, part 4, op. cit.

4

Relations with Qatar

Qatar was originally (1766–83) a settlement of the Bani 'Utbah ('Utubi Arabs) who immigrated from Kuwait. After the conquest of Bahrain in 1783, the 'Utubis moved their seat of Government to Bahrain and became known by the name of Al-Khalifah. Later the Jalahimah Arabs, an off-shoot of the 'Utubis, settled in the town of Zubarah on the coast of Qatar and established their sovereignty over the whole peninsula of Qatar in spite of the objection of Al-Khalifah, the Rulers of Bahrain, who regarded Qatar as their dependency. Qatar was for many years under the sway of the Wahhabis who had also extended their influence to Bahrain and other parts of Arabia.[1]

During the first half of the nineteenth century, Qatar was regarded by the British Government as a dependency of Bahrain and it was therefore not asked to join in the treaties of peace signed with Bahrain and the other Shaikhdoms. As a dependency of Bahrain, Qatar fell under the operation of the Maritime Truce of 1835. It was even reported as late as 1867 that the Shaikh of Bahrain paid tribute to the Wahhabis, who were in power over the coast of Qatar 'on account of his possessions in Qatar'.[2]

The British relationship with Qatar began on 12 September 1868 when the Shaikh of Qatar, Muhammad ibn Thani, signed an agreement of peace with Colonel Lewis Pelly, British Resident in the Arabian Gulf, promising 'not to commit any breach of maritime peace'.[3] The Shaikh also acknowledged the authority of the British Resident in settling any 'disputes or misunderstandings arising' from the enforcement of the 'Maritime Truce'. The agreement stated, in connection with Qatar's relationship with Bahrain, that the Shaikh of Qatar would maintain friendly relations with the Shaikh of Bahrain. It also provided for the continuance of payment to Bahrain of 'the tribute hitherto paid' on account of Qatar's allegiance to Bahrain.[4]

The British agreement with Qatar of 1868 marked a deviation from the former British position in regarding Qatar as a dependency of Bahrain. It acknowledged, although indirectly, the title of Shaikh Muhammad ibn Thani to Qatar and formed a basis for the emergence of Qatar for the first time in the history of the peninsula as an independent town owing no allegiance to Bahrain.

[1] Lorimer, pp. 787–8; Saldanha, *A Précis of Katar Affairs* (1904).
[2] Lorimer, pp. 798–800.   [3] Ibid., pp. 801–2.
[4] Ibid., pp. 801–2; Aitchison, p. 255.

In the meantime Turkey occupied Qatar several times in 1872, and on many occasions warned the British Government against interference in the affairs of the Qatar coast, which was considered by her as a Turkish possession. These warnings were usually ignored by the British Government.[1] However, on 22 September 1883, the British Government told the Turkish Ambassador in London, 'in unequivocal terms', that

they were unable to accept the views of the Porte, and that they were not prepared to waive the rights which they have exercised at intervals during a long period of years of dealing directly with the Arab chiefs of the Qatar coast, when necessary, in order to preserve the peace of the seas or to obtain redress for outrages on British subjects or persons entitled to British protection.[2]

The British relations with Qatar continued during this period 'on the same unsatisfactory footing', and the Turkish influence in Qatar remained unchanged until after 1883.[3]

In a note delivered by the Turkish Ambassador in London on 15 April 1893 to Lord Rosebery, Qatar was referred to as 'a Turkish sub-governorship' and a 'dependency of Najd'.[4] In addition, the Shaikh of Bahrain also put forward a claim in 1873 to sovereignty over Zubarah village in the Peninsula of Qatar. But the Government of India took the view that the Shaikh of Bahrain 'had no clear and important rights in Qatar and that he should be restrained, so far as possible, from raising complications on the mainland'. The Shaikh, however, although expressing his willingness to obey the advice of the British Government, did not actually relinquish his claim, which remained unsettled.[5]

In 1903, the Shaikh of Qatar was anxious to know from the British Government whether his application for British protection over his country would be met favourably. It was admitted by the British authorities that an agreement with the Shaikh of Qatar would be advantageous in that it would

increase the weight of British opinion in any international question that might arise concerning the use of the adjacent pearl banks, but it was held expedient to defer a final decision until tension at the moment prevailing between Britain and Turkey should have subsided.[6]

In the light of the above policy an understanding was reached with the Government of Constantinople that the *status quo* in Qatar should be respected by both the British and the Turkish Governments.[7]

---

[1] Lorimer, pp. 802–9.
[2] Ibid., pp. 811–12; Saldanha, *A Précis of Turkish Expansion*, op. cit., pp. 100–4.
[3] Lorimer, p. 827.   [4] Ibid.   [5] Ibid., pp. 815–16.
[6] Ibid., pp. 828–30; Saldanha, *Précis of Katar*, op. cit.
[7] Lorimer, pp. 830–1; Saldanha, *Précis*, op. cit.

The Agreement of 3 November 1916

On 3 November 1916 a new agreement which virtually extended British protection to Qatar was signed between the Shaikh and the British Government.[1]

In the preamble, the Shaikh pledged his adherence, as a successor to the Government of Qatar, to the engagement of 12 September 1868. He then undertook, in Article 1, to co-operate with the British Government 'in the suppression of the slave trade and piracy and generally in the maintenance of the Maritime Peace'. Because the Shaikh was not a party to the treaties and engagements which were previously signed by the Arab Shaikhs of the Trucial Coast concerning the Maritime Truce, he also declared in this article that he would abide 'by the spirit and obligations of the aforesaid Treaties and Engagements'.

In Article 2, the British Government undertook to confer on the Shaikh, his subjects and their vessels 'all the immunities, privileges and advantages that are conferred on the friendly Shaikhs, their subjects and their vessels'. This Article pledged the British Government to assume international responsibility for the actions of the Shaikh and his subjects abroad, and to protect the interests of the Shaikh's subjects and their vessels, and to give them facilities in British ports or in ports of Arab Shaikhs in friendly relations with the British Government.

Article 3 contained a clause prohibiting the 'import and sale of arms' into the territory of the Shaikh, who was also required to publish a proclamation to that effect. The Shaikh was, however, assured of being given facilities 'to purchase and import' arms from the 'Arms Warehouse in Muscat', or from any other place approved by the British Government for the purpose of arming his 'dependents' or for his personal use, provided that this should be arranged 'hereafter through the Political Agent, Bahrain'. This was intended to take the place of similar engagements signed by other Arab rulers in connection with the arms traffic in the Gulf.

In Article 4, the Shaikh undertook to abstain from corresponding with or receiving foreign agents in his country without the British Government's assent. He also undertook not to alienate any portion of his territories to any power without prior 'consent of the High British Government.'

In Article 5, he promised not to grant pearl-fishing concessions, or any other 'monopolies, concessions or cable landing rights to anyone whomsoever' without British approval. And in Article 6, the Shaikh agreed not to impose

customs dues on the goods of British merchants imported to Qatar more than those levied from his own subjects on their goods and that those dues should not exceed five per cent *ad valorem*.

---

[1] For the text of this agreement, see Aitchison, pp. 258–60.

He further agreed that no other taxes or dues, apart from those specified, should be imposed on British goods.

In Article 7, the Shaikh undertook to protect the lives and property of British subjects residing in his country. And in Article 8, he undertook to receive in his country a British Agent to whom should be entrusted the 'transaction of such business as the British Government may have with' Qatar, and the care of the 'interests of British traders residing' in the ports of Qatar.

In Article 9, the Shaikh agreed to establish a British post office and a telegraph installation in his territory 'whenever the British Government should hereafter desire them'. By Article 10, the British Government promised to protect the Shaikh, his subjects and his territory against 'all aggressions by sea and to do their utmost to exact reparation for all injuries' that the Shaikh or his subjects, 'may suffer when proceeding to sea upon [their] lawful occasions'. And in Article 11, the British Government promised to protect the Shaikh and his subjects against 'unprovoked' acts of aggression by anyone who is not a subject of the Shaikh.

5

Relations with Kuwait

On 19 June 1961 the United Kingdom concluded with the Ruler of
Kuwait, the late Shaikh ʿAbd Allah al-Salim Al-Sabah, a new treaty
by virtue of which the former recognised Kuwait as a sovereign independent State. The treaty, entitled 'Exchange of Notes Regarding
Relations Between the United Kingdom of Great Britain and Northern Ireland and the State of Kuwait, June 19, 1961',[1] takes 'account of
the fact' that His Highness the Ruler 'has the sole responsibility for the
conduct of Kuwait's internal and external affairs', and sets down the
conclusions reached in the course of discussions between the Ruler and
Her Majesty's Political Resident in the Arabian Gulf in the following
terms:

(a) The Agreement of the 23rd of January, 1899, shall be terminated as
being inconsistent with the sovereignty and independence of Kuwait.

(b) The relations between the two countries shall continue to be governed
by a spirit of close friendship.

(c) When appropriate the two Governments shall consult together on
matters which concern them both.

(d) Nothing in these conclusions shall affect the readiness of Her Majesty's
Government to assist the Government of Kuwait if the latter request such
assistance.

Further, a concluding paragraph states that the treaty 'shall continue in force until either party gives the other at least three years'
notice of their intention to terminate it, and that the Agreement of
the 23rd of January, 1899, shall be regarded as terminated on this
day's date'.

It is clear that Kuwait, which had in the past enjoyed certain
aspects of international personality, has become, as from June 1961,
a fully fledged member of the society of independent nations. It
may be argued, however, that provision (d) in the above treaty, which
connotes a British pledge for military defence of Kuwait, constitutes,
in effect, an impediment to the proclaimed independence of Kuwait.
But this contention appears to be groundless since it overlooks the
fact that the British pledge to 'assist' Kuwait at the latter's request
derives its basis from a freely negotiated, and an internationally
recognised, instrument between two sovereign States. The Treaty of
19 June 1961, which constituted a formal recognition by Britain of

[1] *U.K.T.S.*, No. 1 (1961), *Cmnd.* 1409. For text see Appendix XI.

the full independence of Kuwait, paved the way for the recognition of the new independent status of Kuwait by foreign States. Nearly within two years of her independence Kuwait succeeded in joining the membership of the United Nations Organisation and a number of its Specialised Agencies.[1]

At present, Kuwait is *sui juris*, and she, therefore, falls outside the *sui generis* category of the 'British Protected States' of the Arabian Gulf over which the British tutelage system still prevails in full force. As the purpose of this study is to explore and evaluate this British protectorate system that has been governing the Gulf region for the last hundred years or so, it would, therefore, seem necessary, in order to understand fully the former legal status of Kuwait, to devote this chapter to an analysis of British treaty relations with Kuwait prior to 1961. Generally, before 1961, the relationship of the United Kingdom with Kuwait was based on the Agreement of 1899, which together with a number of undertakings and engagements conferred upon the British Crown a privileged position *vis-à-vis* Kuwait. But before 1899, Kuwait was considered to be under the suzerainty of the Ottoman Porte who conferred on the ruler the title of 'Qaim-maqam' and received from him an annual tribute.[2]

As late as 1893 the British Government appeared to have regarded Kuwait as a Turkish vassal or 'fief'. In a statement made by Sir C. Ford, the British Ambassador at Constantinople, in April 1893, the Turkish Government was officially informed that the British Government 'admitted the existence of a Turkish sovereignty along the coast from Basra to Qatif'.[3] This statement impliedly included Kuwait within the Turkish sphere of influence. A few years later, however, the British Government changed its attitude with regard to the status of Kuwait and adopted a different line. Thus in reply to inquiries made by P. Currie about the views of Her Majesty's Government regarding Kuwait, the British Government made it known that it had never admitted Kuwait to be under Turkish protection, but that it did not, however, deny the existence of Turkish influence in Kuwait.[4] Commander Baker on his visit to Kuwait in July 1896 formed the impression that Kuwait although in theory an independent principality had fallen greatly under Turkish influence.[5]

Shaikh Mubarak, then ruler of Kuwait, made overtures in August 1897 to the British authorities in the Arabian Gulf, expressing his wish to place his country under British protection in order to prevent annexation by Turkey. The Shaikh's request was refused by the

---

[1] See below, pp. 112–14, 251.   [2] Lorimer, pp. 1002–12.
[3] Ibid., pp. 1016–17; Saldanha, *A Précis of Turkish expansion on the Arab Littoral of the Persian Gulf and Hasa and Katif Affairs* (1904), pp. 135–42.
[4] Lorimer, pp. 1017–19; Saldanha, *Précis*, op. cit.
[5] Lorimer, pp. 1019–20; Saldanha, *Précis*, op. cit.

British Government, on the ground that it did not favour more interference in Kuwait's affairs than was necessary for the maintenance of peace in the Gulf.[1]

Soon afterwards, circumstances arose which compelled the British Government to have second thoughts over its attitude to Kuwait. The immediate danger which prompted the change in British policy took the form of a threat of Russian intrusion in Kuwait. It was believed that Russia obtained from the Porte a concession for the construction of a railway from the Mediterranean to the Arabian Gulf. The British Government feared in this scheme the establishment of a bridge for the 'creation of Russian territorial rights at Kuwait.'[2]

In order to forestall the Russian action in Kuwait, the British Government considered signing a treaty with the Shaikh of Kuwait on the same model as that concluded in 1891 with the Sultan of Muscat. The sole object of such an agreement was to prevent the Shaikh from alienating any portion of his territory to any foreign government. It was decided not to pursue the question of British protection over Kuwait for the time being.[3]

In consideration of this agreement the Shaikh was to receive 'a single payment of £5,000 or less, or an annual subsidy not exceeding £200'.

The Agreement of 23 January 1899[4]

This agreement was signed between Malcolm John Meade, the British Political Resident, and Shaikh Mubarak ibn Sabah Al-Sabah, Shaikh of Kuwait. The Shaikh pledged 'himself, his heirs and successors not to receive the Agent or Representative of any Power or Government at Kuwait, or at any other place within the limits of his territory, without the previous sanction of the British Government'.

Other provisions of the Treaty bound the Shaikh, his heirs and successors, 'not to cede, sell, lease, mortgage or give for occupation or for any other purpose any portion of his territory to the Government or the subjects of any other Power without the previous consent of Her Majesty's Government for these purposes'. Stipulations were also made against the alienation of 'any portion of the territory . . . which may now be in the possession of the subjects of any other Government'.

In a letter from Colonel Meade to the Shaikh, attached to this agreement, Colonel Meade assured the Shaikh of the good offices of

---

[1] Lorimer, pp. 1021–2.   [2] Ibid.
[3] Ibid., pp. 1022–4; Aitchison, p. 202.
[4] For the text of the Agreement, see Appendix XI. For the original Arabic and English texts see India, *Foreign and Political Departments*, Part 5, 'Treaties and undertakings in force between the British Government and Rulers of Kuwait', 1884–1913, pp. 1–14.

the British Government and emphasised 'the secret character of the Agreement'.[1]

The Agreement of 1899 was, it would appear, signed without the knowledge of Turkey. The latter would obviously have objected to it had it been made in public. What is even more striking in this agreement is that it assigned to the British Government more authority in Kuwait than was originally intended by the instructions of the home Government in London. This appears from the proceedings reported to the Government in London by Col Meade, in which he explained the reasons for his insertion of conditions in the agreement without the prior knowledge of his Government.[2]

The agreement was later published in reply to Turkish threats to assert authority in Kuwait. In September 1899, the British Ambassador at Constantinople conveyed a warning to the Porte, laying emphasis on British relations with Kuwait.[3] He stated that

the British Government, while they entertained no designs on Kuwait, had friendly relations with the Shaikh and that if any attempt were made to establish Turkish authority or customs control at Kuwait without previous agreement with Her Majesty's Government a very inconvenient and disagreeable question would be raised.[4]

The Agreement of 1899 proved to be a useful weapon for preventing the Shaikh from embarking on any designs calculated to allow foreigners to exploit his territory. In September 1899, the British Government delivered a warning to the Shaikh, through the Commander of H.M.S. *Melpomene*, not to make arrangements with the German Commission, which was understood to have visited Kuwait for the purpose of projecting the Baghdad Railway, without its approval.[5]

Again, on 15 April 1900, the British position in Kuwait was explicitly made known to the German Ambassador in London, who was told that the Shaikh 'was not at liberty to cede or in any way to alienate to the Baghdad Railway Company either Kadhama' or any part of his territory, without the assent of Her Majesty's Government.[6]

The Shaikh's request in May 1901 for British protection over his country was again refused by the British Resident who, nevertheless, assured the Shaikh of his Government's intention to 'prevent by force, if necessary, the landing of Turkish troops at Kuwait'. This was conditional on the continued observance of the Agreement of 1899.[7]

Soon after that, however, the controversy between the Porte and the British Government over Kuwait was brought to a close as a result of a preliminary agreement signed on 9 September 1901 between the two Governments. By this agreement Turkey agreed to respect the

[1] Lorimer, pp. 1023–4.   [2] Ibid.   [3] Ibid., p. 1025.   [4] Ibid.
[5] Ibid., pp. 1025–6.   [6] Ibid., p. 1027.   [7] Ibid., pp. 1027–30.

status quo in Kuwait provided that the British Government did not annex, or establish a protectorate over, Kuwait.[1]

Two further agreements were later signed by the Shaikh of Kuwait. The first, of 24 May 1900, was concerned with the suppression of 'Arms Trade'. This agreement, similar to those agreements signed by the other Gulf Shaikhdoms, was in line with the policy of the British Government at that period to halt the alarming intrusions of arms traffic in the Arabian Gulf. The agreement pledged the Shaikh to the prevention of 'the importation of arms into Kuwait or exportation therefrom'.[2]

Under the second Agreement of 28 February 1904 the Shaikh agreed to allow the establishment of a British Post Office at Kuwait, and to disallow the establishment of any post office belonging to a foreign government.[3]

The postal agreement was followed, on 26 July 1912,[4] by an acceptance by the Shaikh of Kuwait of the British Government's offer to establish a 'Wireless Telegraph Installation' at Kuwait.[5]

In 1911 and in 1913, the Shaikh gave two undertakings restricting his power in respect of exploitation of the natural resources of his territories without obtaining the prior consent of the British Government. The first undertaking, in the form of a letter of 1911, dealt specifically with 'Pearling concessions'. It was written by the Shaikh to Captain W. H. I. Shakespeare, the British Political Agent at Ku-

[1] Lorimer, pp. 1030–1. This agreement did not come into force.

[2] Aitchison, pp. 262–3.

[3] Ibid., p. 263. It is to be noted that the Agreement of 1904 came to an end on 1 February 1959 by the agreement of both the British Government and Kuwait. On this date, the London General Post Office which administered the Kuwait postal service in the past, handed over the services to the Government of Kuwait. See *The (Bahrain) Gulf Daily Times*, 3 February 1959.

[4] Aitchison, p. 264. The Agreement of 1912 also came to an end on 1 February 1959. On this date the service was handed over to the Kuwait Government's Cable and Wireless Department. See *The (Bahrain) Gulf Daily Times*, loc. cit.

[5] In 1907, the Shaikh made a perpetual lease to the British Government of a Portion of land in the south of Bandar Shuwaikh for Rs. 60,000 per annum, leaving to them the right to relinquish the lease at any time they wished to do so.

It may be argued that the lease of Bandar Shuwaikh constituted a derogation of the British Government's pledge with Turkey, according to the Agreement of 1901, to respect the *status quo* in Kuwait.

Generally speaking, however, the lease of Bandar Shuwaikh, although it conferred on the British Government some privileges with regard to the administration of a portion of the territory of Kuwait, did not amount to annexation of the leased land. Moreover the Shaikh was explicitly assured that the British Government recognised his sovereignty over Kuwait and her boundaries, including the leased land.

The Shaikh's rights in collecting 'customs duties in the Shuwaikh lands or any other lands' that the British Government 'might thereafter lease from him or his heirs after him' were also left undiminished. See Aitchison, p. 204; India, *Foreign and Political Department*, Part 5, op. cit.

wait, as a reply to the latter's letter of 29 July 1911, in which he advised
the Shaikh not to respond to any request for obtaining sponge concessions by foreigners without seeking the advice of the British Resident.[1] The Shaikh in his reply confirmed compliance with the British
Resident's advice. The second undertaking was given on 27 October
1913, in relation to the future exploitation of oil in the territories of
Kuwait. In this letter the Shaikh assured the Political Resident in the
Gulf that 'if . . . there seems hope of obtaining oil therefrom we shall
never give a concession in this matter to anyone except a person
appointed from the British Government'.[2]

On 3 November 1914 the British Political Resident gave the following assurances to the Shaikh with regard to his boundaries and his
possessions, and fruit gardens in Basrah: (1) The Shaikh was to keep
in his possession his date garden 'situated between Fao and Qumah
without being subject to the payment of revenue or taxes'; and (2)
the Shaikh was to rely on the protection of the British Government
against any consequences if he attacked 'Safwan, Um Qasr and Buzan'
and occupied them. As these places were actually under the control
of Turkey, the Shaikh was in effect encouraged to make war with
Turkey.

In addition, Kuwait was recognised by the British Government as
'an independent Government under British protection'.[3]

Successive rulers of Kuwait had pledged their adherence to the
above agreements with the British Government. So far as Kuwait's
relations with Turkey were concerned, it is worth mentioning that as
a result of a series of negotiations between the British Government
and Turkey, the latter, by the Convention of 29 July 1913, acknowledged, *inter alia*, the 'Independence' of Kuwait and the special
treaty relationship between her and the British Government. But as a
result of the outbreak of war between Turkey and the British Government in 1914, the said Convention was not ratified.[4]

In addition to the above agreements governing the relationship
between the British Government and Kuwait, there are further agreements concerning the adjustments of the boundaries of Kuwait with
neighbouring countries, such as Iraq and Saudi Arabia. These agreements, which will be discussed in a separate chapter below, were concluded by the British Government on behalf of Kuwait with both
Saudi Arabia and Iraq, in 1922 and 1923.[5] Later, the British Government enacted the first Kuwait Order in Council of May 1925, which

---

[1] Aitchison, p. 263. The letter bears the Arabic date 2 Sha'ban 1329.
[2] For original Arabic text see India, *Foreign and Political Department*, Part 5,
op. cit. For English text see Aitchison, pp. 264–5.
[3] Aitchison, pp. 265–6. India, *Foreign and Political Department*, Part 5, op. cit.
[4] Aitchison, pp. 266–7. But, as in the case of Bahrain, Turkey relinquished her
claim to Kuwait by Article 16 of the Treaty of Lausanne, 24 July 1923. See above,
p. 34.   [5] Aitchison, pp. 213, 266.

conferred on the British Government jurisdiction over British subjects and foreigners residing in Kuwait.[1]

There is no doubt that consequent to the express termination in 1961 of the principal Agreement of 1899, all the above-mentioned undertakings and engagements of the Shaikhdom have become null and void.[2]

---

[1] See above, p. 22.

[2] However, as a precautionary measure, the abrogation of these subsidiary undertakings and engagements, including those relating to the exploitation of natural resources, was formally achieved in 1962, by virtue of exchange of letters between the Kuwaiti Ministry of Foreign Affairs and the British Embassy in Kuwait.

6

Treaty relations of Muscat

The Sultanate of Muscat and Oman maintains treaty relations with the United Kingdom as well as with a number of other foreign Powers.

THE UNITED KINGDOM

Although regarded as a fully independent State, the Sultanate of Muscat maintains unusually close treaty relationship with the United Kingdom dating back to 12 October 1798,[1] when the first treaty of friendship was concluded between the Sultan (then Imam) of Muscat and the British Government of India. Although the principal treaty in force at present is the Treaty of Friendship, Commerce and Navigation of 20 September 1951,[2] it may, nevertheless, be helpful to refer to some of the early agreements concluded, under which some of the provisions are still in force. Moreover, since the conclusion of these early agreements was overshadowed by an Anglo-French controversy over the establishment of spheres of influence in Muscat and Oman, it will be convenient to divide this discussion into separate heads as follows:

Early British agreements with Muscat

(i) *Agreements of 1822 and 1845*[3]

Both of these agreements dealt with the suppression by the Sultan of the slave trade in his dominions. The Agreement of 1822, however, provided for the suppression of slave trade by the Sultan with Christian nations only, and, accordingly, gave the Sultan a free hand to trade in slaves with Muslim countries. The Agreement of 1845 imposed further restrictions in connection with slave trade with Muslim countries. It also empowered British cruisers to

seize and confiscate any vessels, whether belonging to His Highness or to his subjects, carrying on slave trade.

However, it excluded British ships from interfering with the transport of slaves from one part of the Sultan's African territories to another.

---

[1] Aitchison, pp. 287–8.
[2] See below, p. 52.
[3] Aitchison, pp. 289–91, 300–1. For Arabic and English texts, see India, Foreign and Political Department, Part 3, *List of Principal Existing Treaties in Force between the British Government and the Sultan of Muscat and Oman*, pp. 1–30.

(ii) *Agreement regarding the cession of territory, 20 March 1891*[1]

This agreement appears to have originated in an era which was characterised by intensive French activities in Muscat. Thus, while the French Government was, during this period, busy trying to obtain from the Sultan a lease for a coaling station in Muscat, the British authorities were, for their part, considering seriously the practical measures which they ought to take in order to frustrate the French action regarding the possession of the lease in question. At one time it was believed within British official circles that the declaration of a British protectorate over Muscat would provide a solution to the situation created by the French overtures to the Sultan. This is because it was then actually thought 'that the relations between Muscat and Britain' placed the former 'within the British sphere of influence'.[2] Moreover, Lord Curzon went as far as regarding Muscat as a mere 'British dependency'. 'We subsidise its ruler; we dictate its policy; we should tolerate no alien interference . . .', he observed in 1892.[3]

However, after second thoughts, the idea of declaring Muscat a British protectorate was dropped as it was found that such an action on the part of the British Government would be contrary to the Declaration of 1862 between Britain and France regarding their obligations to maintain the independence of Muscat. Consequently, the Agreement of 10 March 1891 regarding the non-alienation of territory was concluded with the Sultan as a compromise which would, in the British authorities' view, have less repercussions than a declaration of a protectorate.[4]

In this agreement the Sultan pledged and bound himself, his heirs and successors 'never to cede, sell, to mortgage or otherwise give for occupation, save to the British Government, the dominions of Muscat and Oman or any of their dependencies'.[5]

(iii) *Agreements of 1902 and 1923*[6]

On 31 May 1902 the Sultan signed an agreement with the British Government in which he bound himself not to grant concessions for working the coal-fields in the hinterland of Sur to any foreign government or company without first communicating

with the British Government in order that they may themselves take up the matter [with him] if they feel so inclined.

---

[1] Aitchison, pp. 317–18; India, *Foreign and Political Department*, Part 3, op. cit.
[2] Lorimer, p. 534.
[3] Curzon, *Persia and the Persian Question*, op. cit., p. 443.
[4] Lorimer, pp. 534–5.
[5] Aitchison, pp. 317–18.
[6] Ibid., pp. 318–19; India, *Foreign and Political Department*, Part 3, op. cit.

On 10 January 1923 a more serious agreement, regarding the exploitation of oil, was concluded. In this agreement, the Sultan promised that he would

not exploit any petroleum which may be found anywhere within (his) territories without consulting the Political Agent at Muscat and without the approval of the High Government of India.

Declaration of 10 March 1862 between Britain and France regarding the independence of Muscat and Zanzibar[1]

As an introduction to this Declaration, it should be remarked that until the death of the Sultan of Muscat, Sayyid Saʿid, in 1856, both Muscat and Zanzibar formed part of the dominions of the Sultan of Muscat, who established his permanent residence at Zanzibar in 1840. After the death of Sayyid Saʿid one of his sons, Thuwayni, succeeded as ruler of Muscat and the other, Majid, as ruler of Zanzibar. Later, Majid, the ruler of Zanzibar, asserted his independence, and consequently a dispute arose between the two brothers as to whether Zanzibar had a right to proclaim her independence. Subsequently, the dispute between the two brothers was settled by arbitration which took place in April 1861. In his Award the Arbitrator, Lord Canning, who was appointed by the Governor-General of India, approved the right of Zanzibar to independence provided that Zanzibar paid an annual tribute to Muscat. However, he stated that the payment was

not to be understood as a recognition of the dependence of Zanzibar upon Muscat.[2]

The Declaration by Britain and France in 1862 was, therefore, a recognition of the arbitral award and a joint obligation on the part of the two Powers to respect the independence of both Muscat and Zanzibar. The Declaration of 1862 was to the following effect:

Her Majesty the Queen of the United Kingdom . . . and His Majesty the Emperor of the French, taking into consideration the importance of maintaining the independence of His Highness the Sultan of Muscat and of His Highness the Sultan of Zanzibar, have thought it right to engage reciprocally to respect the independence of these Sovereigns.[3]

Anglo-French controversy over Muscat

The French Government was one of the European Powers which concluded, during the middle of the nineteenth century, treaties of friendship with the Sultan of Muscat. The French treaty with Muscat,

[1] Great Britain, *Parliamentary Papers*, vol. 109 (1899), p. 124.
[2] See Lorimer, p. 471. Text of Award in Aitchison, p. 303. In 1890, Zanzibar was placed under British protection. For the protectorate treaty of 1890, see Hertslet, *Commercial Treaties*, vol. 18 (1890), p. 1201.
[3] See *Parliamentary Papers*, vol. 109, op. cit.

E

which was signed on 17 November 1844, contained clauses conferring on France 'most-favoured nation' rights and extra-territorial jurisdiction over French nationals residing in Muscat.[1] France was for some time represented in Muscat by a French Consul, who was withdrawn later in 1920.[2] France was also a party to the Declaration of 1862, to which reference has been made above. It was due, perhaps, to the joint obligations of both Britain and France under this Declaration that the Anglo-French controversy over Muscat arose in the past. There were at least two incidents in the past in which the Declaration of 1862 played an important role:

1. *Conflict over the coaling-station grant, 1898*

The French Government's negotiation of 1890 with the Sultan, to which reference has been made before, resulted in the conclusion in 1898 of an agreement with the Sultan, by which France was granted the right to establish a coaling-station on a strip of land in Oman.[3] When this matter was brought to the knowledge of the British Government, it took a serious view of it and ordered the Sultan, in an 'ultimatum' presented to him on 9 February 1899, to revoke the grant immediately, because it was regarded as a violation of the non-alienation of territory Agreement of 1891.[4] The Sultan, not knowing what to do, met the French Consul and, to the astonishment of the latter, disclosed to him the contents of the Agreement of 1891, which was apparently signed without the knowledge of the French Government. The Sultan was then told by the French Government that his Agreement of 1891 with Britain violated the Declaration of 1862, in which both Britain and France agreed to respect the independence of Muscat and it was thus invalid.[5] Enclosing the letter he received from the French, the Sultan desperately wrote to the British Consul saying that his 'gift' of the coaling station to the French did not violate his Agreement of 1891, and urging not to be forced to go back on his word which he had given to the French.[6] However, this did not do and the grant to the French was subsequently revoked. A compromise was later sought between the British and the French Governments regarding an agreed construction of the Declaration of 1862. This was to the effect that both parties—France and Britain—were to be excluded by the terms of this Declaration from acquiring a 'lease or cession in Oman territory'.[7]

---

[1] For the Text of this Treaty, see *Bombay Selections*, pp. 265–71; Aitchison, Appendix No. II, p. xxix.
[2] Aitchison, p. 272. An American Consulate was also maintained in Muscat until 1915. See ibid.
[3] Lorimer,pp. 556–9.   [4] Ibid., p. 559.
[5] Ibid.,   [6] Ibid.
[7] Ibid., pp. 560–1.

2. *Conflict over the Muscat dhows: the Hague arbitration, 8 August 1905*

The French Government initiated, for some years towards the end of the nineteenth century, the practice of issuing to some subjects of the Sultan of the Omani coast papers authorising them to fly the French flag over their own vessels while trading in the Indian Ocean, the Red Sea and in the Arabian Gulf.[1]

By virtue of this practice, which was held to be authorised by the French-Muscat Treaty of 17 November 1844, France claimed to exercise jurisdiction over those subjects of the Sultan to whom she extended her flag.

Acting on British advice the Sultan informed the French Vice-Consul at Muscat on 16 February 1899 that he objected to French jurisdiction over his subjects and that he considered the French action in this respect as a violation of the Convention of 1862.[2] As the French Government was not prepared to liquidate its claim, the matter was brought up in 1905 to the Hague Court of Arbitration for settlement.

In the proceedings at The Hague, the Sultan was kept in the background while the British Government assumed the role of plaintiff. This was, probably, on the ground that the dispute arose, in the British view, from the violation by France of the Convention of 1862, to which the British Government was a party.

The decision of the Court, which was given on 8 August 1905, can be summed up as follows:[3]

1. It upheld the right of France as a sovereign State to allow the subjects of another sovereign State to fly her flags and to prescribe the 'rules governing its use'. Such practice by France, it was stated, does not derogate from the independence of the Sultan.

2. But, according to Article 32 of the General Act of Brussels of 2 January 1892, France was allowed to grant authority to fly her flag only to 'native vessels owned by or fitted out by her subjects or protégés'.

3. The French treaty with Muscat of 1844 which recognised certain Omani subjects as French protégés 'applies only to persons *bona fide* in the service of French subjects, but not to persons who ask for ship papers' to carry commercial trade under the French flag.

4. However, the granting of such papers prior to the ratification of the Act of Brussels was not held to be contrary to any international obligation of France.

---

[1] Lorimer, pp. 562–7.   [2] Ibid.
[3] Scott, *The Hague Court Reports* (1916), pp. 93–100. For the Anglo-French Agreement of 13 October 1904, in which they agreed to refer the dispute for arbitration by the Hague Court of Arbitration, see ibid., pp. 101–2.

Accordingly, the tribunal held:

That persons who were authorised to fly the French flag 'are entitled in the territorial waters of Muscat to the inviolability provided by the French-Muscat treaty of 1844'. But that right cannot be extended 'to any other person or dhow, and the owner, masters and crew of such dhows or members of their families who do not enjoy any right of extra-territoriality which exempts them from the jurisdiction of the Sultan of Muscat'.

Present British treaties with Muscat

(i) *The Treaty of Friendship, Commerce and Navigation, dated 20 September 1951*[1]

This treaty forms the latest of a series of treaties of this kind concluded between Muscat and the United Kingdom in the years 1798, 1839, 1891[2] and 1939. The present treaty which replaced the treaty of 5 February 1939[3] was formally concluded between 'His Majesty the King of Great Britain and Northern Ireland and the British Dominions Beyond the Seas, and Sultan Saʿid bin Taimur, Sultan of Muscat and Oman and Dependencies'. It was signed by the British Resident in the Arabian Gulf in his capacity as the British plenipotentiary, and by the Sultan himself. It entered into force on 19 May 1952 after the exchange of its instruments of ratification.

Generally, the treaty re-affirms in its preamble the friendly relations which already subsist between the parties and provides for promoting and extending their commercial relations. Some of the significant provisions of the treaty are the following:

Article 5 provides for freedom of trade and navigation between the two parties on the basis of most-favoured nation treatment. In contrast, this most-favoured nation treatment was not reciprocal in the replaced treaty of 1939, which conferred trade privileges upon the United Kingdom's nationals alone. Article 11 provides for the exchange of consular representation between the two parties on a reciprocal basis. It states that

such consuls shall be permitted to perform such consular functions and shall enjoy privileges and immunities as in accordance with international law or practice relating to consuls as recognized in the territories which they reside.

Although similar reciprocal provisions were provided in the 1939

[1] *U.K.T.S.* No. 44 (1951), *Cmd.* 8633. Also see Muscat No. 1 (1952), *Cmd.* 8462.
[2] Aitchison, pp. 287, 292, 310.
[3] *U.K.T.S.* No. 29 (1939), *Cmd.* 6037.

treaty, the latter, moreover, included provisions regarding the exercise of British extra-territorial jurisdiction in Muscat. No such provisions are contained in the body of the present treaty itself. (The British exercise of foreign jurisdiction in Muscat is based on separate exchange of letters attached to the treaty, as will be explained below.) Article 15 contains an extension clause by virtue of which Britain may apply the treaty to any territory for the international relations of which she is responsible, with the exception of the British protected States of the Arabian Gulf to which the treaty cannot be extended. In addition, the treaty contains certain provisions imposing unilateral obligations on the Sultan regarding the lifting of restrictions on goods imported from the United Kingdom. Article 17 provides for the termination of the treaty by one year's notice after the lapse of fifteen years from the time it entered into force. The treaty was registered by the United Kingdom with the Secretariat of the United Nations, under Article 102 of the Charter.[1]

(ii) *The Exchange of Letters Agreement, attached to the treaty of 1951, concerning British extra-territorial jurisdiction in Muscat.*[2]

It vests in the British Crown for a period of ten years from 1 January 1951, extra-territorial jurisdiction, exercised by the British Consular Court for Muscat over British subjects in the following civil and criminal cases:

(i) Proceedings against non-Muslim servants of the British Crown (with certain exceptions relating to acts not on duty);
(ii) Proceedings between non-Muslim, United Kingdom or (with certain exceptions) Commonwealth citizens or corporate bodies.

As pointed out earlier,[3] this British jurisdiction, which expired on 31 December 1966, was finally relinquished on 1 January 1967.[4] Consequently, the Sultan of Muscat now retains full jurisdictional powers over all foreigners in his country.

---

[1] *U.N.T.S.* vol. 149 (1952), p. 260
[2] Ibid. This agreement is rightly seen 'as evidence of the steady shrinking of the extra-territorial jurisdiction once so widely exercised by Britain throughout the Middle East'. See Young, R., 'The United Kingdom-Muscat Treaty of 1951', *A.J.I.L.*, 46 (1952), pp. 704–8.
[3] See above, p. 19, n. 1.
[4] British jurisdiction in Muscat was renewed later in 1961, after the expiry of its first ten years. It also became far more limited in its application to British subjects after 1961. See *Report of the Ad Hoc Committee on Oman*, 22 January 1965, p. 174 (*U.N.G.A.* A/5846).

(iii) *The Exchange of Letters Agreement, dated 25 July 1958, between the United Kingdom's Secretary of State for Foreign Affairs and the Sultan of Muscat and Oman, concerning the Sultan's armed forces, civil aviation, Royal Air Force facilities and economic development in Muscat and Oman*

This agreement was released recently by the British Government in the form of a memorandum submitted to the *Ad Hoc* Committee on Oman, appointed by the United Nations General Assembly. It states, *inter alia*:

In pursuance of the common interest of Your Highness and Her Majesty's Government in furthering the progress of the Sultanate of Muscat and Oman, Her Majesty's Government in the United Kingdom have agreed to extend assistance towards the strengthening of Your Highness's Army. Her Majesty's Government will also, at Your Highness's request, make available regular officers on secondment from the British Army, who will, while serving in the Sultanate, form an integral part of Your Highness's armed forces. The terms and conditions of service of these seconded British officers have been agreed with Your Highness. Her Majesty's Government will also provide training facilities for members of Your Highness's armed forces and will make advice available on training and other matters as may be required by Your Highness . . .[1]

As is shown in the above provisions, this agreement provides for full co-operation between Britain and Muscat in the political, military and economic fields. On the military plane, it constitutes the first publicly published document which has committed Britain to provide military assistance to the Sultan. As the reader will notice later in this book, it was often argued in British parliamentary circles that since the yardstick of the British protectorate regime in the Arabian Gulf does not engulf the British-Muscati relationship, the British military action in Oman in 1955–7 was, therefore, lacking of legal support.[2]

OTHER FOREIGN POWERS

The Sultanate of Muscat and Oman maintains treaties of friendship with a number of foreign States, such as France, Holland, India and the United States.

---

[1] *Report of the Ad Hoc Committee on Oman*, 22 January 1965, p. 166. And see *U.N.T.S.*, vol. 27, p. 287, for the text of *Civil Air Agreement* between the United Kingdom and Muscat, signed on 5 April 1947.
[2] See Chapter 14 below.

The Treaty of Commerce between the King of the French and His Highness Syud Sueed bin Sultan, the Sultan of Maskat, dated 17 November 1844[1]

The treaty which was ratified by both parties on 4 February 1846 provides for (*a*) reciprocal and most-favoured nation treatment, (*b*) reciprocal rights of appointing consuls in the respective territories of both parties, and (*c*) extra-territorial jurisdiction over French nationals in Muscat. In accordance with the provisions of the treaty, a French consulate was once opened in Zanzibar, formerly a dependency of the Sultan, but the consulate was later closed and the French consul withdrawn. It appears that the Sultan had never used his right to appoint a Muscati consul in France.

The Declaration of 1877 for the development of commercial relations between the Netherlands and Muscat[2]

This treaty, described as 'Declaration', was signed on 7 April and 27 August 1877 at The Hague and Muscat, respectively. It provides, *inter alia*, for most-favoured nation treatment in commercial matters between Muscat and the Netherlands.

The Treaty of Friendship, Commerce and Navigation between India and Muscat, dated 15 March 1953[3]

This treaty entered into force on 2 March 1954, fifteen days after the exchange of the instruments of ratification which took place at Muscat on 14 February 1954. Article 4 of the treaty provides for the recognition and respect of 'the independence and rights of each other'. Article 2 provides that each of the two parties 'may appoint consuls to reside in the territories of the other, subject to the consent and approval of the other as regards the persons so appointed'. The other provisions of the treaty provide for reciprocal and most-favoured nation treatment in trade between the two countries. The treaty shall remain valid for a period of fifteen years, and thereafter until terminated by one year's notice by either party. It was registered with the United Nations under Article 102 of the Charter.

It may be interesting to point out, in connection with this treaty, that in a letter dated 30 September 1964 the Permanent Representative of India to the United Nations explained the circumstances which led to the conclusion of the treaty as follows:

India, as one of the territories of His Majesty was a signatory to the Treaty of Commerce and Navigation signed between His Britannic Majesty and the Sultan of Muscat and Oman in 1939. In March 1950, the Government of

---

[1] Aitchison, Appendix No. II, p. xxix.
[2] Ibid., Appendix No. IV, p. xxxix. [3] *U.N.T.S.*, vol. 190, p. 76.

the United Kingdom informed the Government of India that His Highness the Sultan of Muscat had given a formal notice of termination of the Treaty on the expiry of its twelve years, i.e., 11th February, 1951. In view of the constitutional changes in India, the Sultan had also expressed a desire to enter into a new separate Treaty with India. India, accordingly, entered into a Treaty with the Sultan to replace the old one.[1]

The Treaty of Amity, Economic Relations and Consular Rights between the President of the United States and the Sultan of Muscat and Oman and Dependencies, signed at Salalah on 20 December 1958[2]

This new treaty which entered into force on 11 June 1960, upon the exchange of instruments of ratification, replaced and terminated the old Treaty of Amity and Commerce of 21 September 1833.[3] The latter treaty provided, under Article IX, for extra-territorial jurisdiction to be exercised by United States' consuls in Muscat. It thus stated that American 'consuls shall be exclusive judges of all disputes or suits wherein American citizens shall be engaged with each other' within the Sultan's territories.[4] Now the Treaty of 20 December 1958 has completely abolished this extra-territorial jurisdiction for the United States in Muscat. Instead, the United States' nationals are now technically subject to the jurisdiction of the Sultan's courts. On this matter, Article III of the treaty states:

Nationals and companies of either Party shall have free access to the courts of justice and administrative agencies within the territories of the other Party, in all degrees of jurisdiction, both in defense and in pursuit of their rights. Such access shall be allowed upon terms no less favorable than those applicable to nationals and companies of such other Party or of any third country, including the terms applicable to requirements for deposit of security . . .

The other articles of the treaty deal, *inter alia*, with the maintenance of freedom of commerce and navigation and the development of economic relations between the two countries on a reciprocal basis. They also provide for a reciprocal and most-favoured nation treatment. Accordingly, Article V states:

1. Nationals and companies of either Party . . . shall in no case be accorded treatment less favourable than that accorded to nationals and companies of any third country with respect to establishing or acquiring interests in

---

[1] *Ad Hoc Committee on Oman*, op. cit., p. 130. Although there is at present an Indian consul in Muscat, the latter has not yet appointed a consul in India.

[2] United States, Department of State, *Treaties in Force: A List of Treaties and Other International Agreements of the United States*, vol. 11 (1960), pp. 1835–46.

[3] Aitchison, Appendix No. I, p. xvii.

[4] It is maintained that this 'was the only remaining instance of extra-territorial jurisdiction of the United States'. See Myers, Denys P., 'Contemporary Practice of the United States Relating to International Law', *A.J.I.L.*, 54 (1960), pp. 650–1.

enterprises for engaging in industrial and other business activities within the territories of such other Party . . .

The question of consular representation between the two countries is dealt with in Article XII which reads:

Each Party shall have the right to send consular representatives to the other Party, subject to the approval of such other Party as to the persons appointed and the places at which they reside. Such consular representatives shall be permitted to perform such consular functions and shall enjoy such privileges and immunities as are in accordance with international law and practice and as provided in the protocol to this Treaty.

The protocol to which the above article refers specifies the functions, privileges, and immunities accorded to consular officers appointed in the territories of either Party.[1] Under this protocol, the privileges and immunities enjoyed by

a consular officer or employee who is a citizen of the sending State and not a permanent resident of the receiving State and who is not engaged in any other business include:

(a) Exemption from the jurisdiction of the courts of the receiving State with respect to acts performed within the scope of his official duties;

(b) Exemption from having to produce documents from consular archives or give evidence on matters falling within the scope of official duties;

(c) Exemption from arrest or prosecution except when charged with crimes other than misdemeanors;

(d) Exemption from having him or his dependents subject to the requirements of alien registration, residence permits, and similar regulations applicable generally to aliens;

(e) Exemption from all estate, inheritance, succession, or similar taxes imposed in the receiving State with respect to movable property belonging to the estate of a deceased consular . . .

By Article XVI, the treaty 'shall remain in force for seven years and shall continue in force thereafter until terminated'. Termination of the treaty takes effect by one year's written notice to be given by either Party to the other 'at the end of the initial seven-year period or at any time thereafter'. It was registered with the United Nations under Article 102 of the Charter.[2]

As demonstrated above, the Treaty of 20 December 1958 between Muscat and the United States is significant in that it establishes a novel relationship between the two States based on such principles of international law as are normally applicable to relations of sovereign independent States.

[1] In his statement to the Committee on Oman, the Sultan said that there is at present no United States consul in Muscat, in accordance with the provisions of the above article, but that the United States consul in Aden usually visits Muscat from time to time and looks after the United States' affairs. See *Ad Hoc Committee on Oman*, op. cit., p. 127.   [2] *U.N.T.S.*, vol. 380, p. 181.

PART TWO

THE INTERNATIONAL STATUS OF
THE ARABIAN GULF STATES

7

General considerations affecting the legal
position of protectorates

Historical and legal developments of the concept of protection

The term 'protection' was used in medieval times to express the relationship between two States by which a stronger State promises to guarantee the defence of a weaker one. The agreement did not, in any respect, affect the sovereignty of the guaranteed or protected State except that it implied, according to 'feudal law', a connection of 'subordination' or homage by the so-called 'vassal' State to the 'suzerain' State.[1] This meaning of 'suzerainty' or protection, involving the full sovereignty of the State under protection, found expression in the treaties of the fourteenth and the fifteenth centuries among European countries.[2]

According to Westlake, the term 'suzerainty', which had a 'medieval origin', was 'little used' in Europe, but this term has, since 1806, been revived in connection with the gradual emancipation of the provinces of the Turkish Empire chiefly inhabited by Christians'.[3]

During the eighteenth and the nineteenth centuries protection came to be regarded as an aspect of the concept of 'sphere of influence', a doctrine which developed as a result of the territorial expansion of some European Powers in Africa and Asia.[4] The new form of protection flourished as a result of the 'formal contact' made by the European Powers with the peoples of those countries who were found to have acquired a civilisation different from that of the European pattern. This form of protection which meant, according to Baty, 'protection in the new sense which involved a certain measure of control, and a definite diminution (if not a total deprivation) of sovereignty', was found to be an appropriate form for establishing relationships between the European Powers and those countries for the sole purpose of

[1] Loewenfeld, E. H., Article on 'Protectorates', *Encyclopaedia Britannica*, vol. 18 (Ed. 1957), pp. 608–9; Westlake, p. 25.
[2] Loewenfeld, op. cit.; Baty, T., 'Protectorates and Mandates', *B.Y.I.L.*, 1 (1921–2), p. 109.
[3] Westlake, pp. 25–6. Suzerainty, says Oppenheim, 'is now of more historical importance as there are no longer any vassal States in existence. Egypt, which was for a time a vassal State of Turkey, provided the best example of this kind of protectorate.' See Oppenheim, p. 189.
[4] Rutherford, G. W., 'Spheres of Influence', *A.J.I.L.*, 20 (1926), pp. 300, et seq.; For various concepts of 'Spheres of Influence', see Lindley, p. 207.

exploiting the latter's national resources.[1] Consequently, during the nineteenth century, treaties of protection on those lines were made by European Powers with a great number of African and Asian countries. Such treaties were in fact a compromise between two courses, namely, either destroying the independence of those countries by incorporation, or treating them on the basis of equality with European States, a matter which was not acceptable to the latter owing to the fundamental differences between the civilisations of the parties concerned.[2] The technical term for the above-mentioned concept of protection came to be known later as 'protectorate'. The word 'protectorate' was used, in this sense, 'to denote those cases in which a regular government exercising a large measure of internal autonomy entrusts the control of its foreign relations to the protecting power. To the extent to which this is done the protected state is withdrawn from the direct application of international law and must be regarded as identified with the protecting state, even though it may form a distinct territory from the point of view of constitutional law.'[3]

Nature and types of protectorates

In practice there have been many types and forms of protectorates. It seems, therefore, difficult to deduce general principles applying to them all without distinction. Generally speaking, however, it may be possible to classify protectorates into two principal types. There are, in the first place, the so-called 'real' or 'bona fide' protectorates. The Ionian Islands may be cited as an example of these protectorates in Europe. Those Islands were placed under British protection between 1815 and 1863 by virtue of treaties concluded by Great Britain with Russia, Austria and Prussia respectively. Under a special constitution, the Islands had a local legislature and a commercial flag of their own. They were independent but the British Government assumed full responsibility for their international affairs. The Ionian Protectorate was abolished in 1863, when the Islands were incorporated into Greece.[4] Secondly, there are protectorates exercised over African and Asian States with or without organised governments and these can be subdivided into two divisions:

(*a*) Protectorates over Oriental States enjoying an advanced civilisation and organised governments under the authority of indigenous

---

[1] Baty, *B.Y.I.L.*, op. cit., p. 109.

[2] It should be remembered, however, that a great number of African territories were regarded by the expansionist Powers as barbarous territories possessing no symbol of sovereignty whatsoever. Consequently, arrangements between the expansionist Powers and the tribal communities of these territories took the nature of cession rather than protection. This was on the ground that those African territories were not regarded as constituting States in the international sense to which protection could be extended. See Westlake, pp. 123–4; Lindley, pp. 182–3.

[3] Smith, I., p. 67.   [4] Lindley, pp. 181–4; Westlake, pp. 23–4.

Sovereigns. (Examples of such protectorates were the former Malay States, Tunisia and Morocco.)[1] These were originally sovereign States which entered into treaty relations with other sovereign States (the protecting Powers) by virtue of which some of their sovereignty, particularly their power to conduct their foreign relations, passed to the latter.[2] (b) Protectorates exercised over backward communities without organised governments such as were commonly found in Africa. These protectorates are referred to as colonial protectorates, since the degree of administration over them does not materially differ from that exercised over colonies. Colonial protectorates, however, are, unlike colonies, considered as foreign territories by the protecting Power.[3] A colonial protectorate usually arose from conquest. But in many cases the tribal chief was required to sign a document agreeing to transfer to the protecting Power the administration of the territory in question. The protecting Power of a colonial protectorate did not regard the tribal chief as possessing the attributes of sovereignty, and it thus considered its agreement with the local chief as establishing a first claim for the possible annexation of the territory under its protection.[4] As Westlake remarks, the designation of the name 'protectorates' to the territories of the African chiefs in question

had the double advantage of giving a flavour of international law to a position intended to exclude other states before such exclusion could be placed on the ground of duly acquired sovereignty, and at the same time of allowing that position to be abandoned with less discredit than attaches to the abandonment of sovereignty, if the country should be found less valuable than had been hoped.[5]

Although, as already explained above, the degree of control over protectorates may vary from one case to another, none the less, a feature common to them all is that they neither conduct their foreign relations nor enter into direct diplomatic intercourse without the permission of the protecting Power.[6] Oppenheim distinguishes between 'a number' of British protected States in Asia of which, he says, 'their international status is not clear', and 'protectorates over African tribes, acquired through a treaty with the chiefs of these tribes'. 'These latter

[1] Lindley, pp. 188–202. The old Indian States were originally classified under this category. But the status of those States underwent, later, several changes, as will be noted below.
[2] Westlake, pp. 22–3; Wright, Quincy, *Legal Problems in the Far Eastern Conflict* (1941), p. 37.
[3] Lindley, pp. 182–8; Loewenfeld, op. cit., p. 608.
[4] Lindley, pp. 182–3.
[5] Westlake, p. 122. See, in connection with these protectorates, the rules of the African Conference of Berlin laid down in Articles 34 and 35 of its General Act, 1885, regarding the acquisition of territories on the coast of Africa, discussed by Westlake at pp. 107–8.
[6] Oppenheim, pp. 192–3; Westlake, pp. 22–3; Smith, I., pp. 67–8.

protectorates', he continues, 'possess no international status what-soever.'[1] And, according to Max Huber, a colonial protectorate 'is rather a form of internal organisation of a colonial territory on the basis of autonomy for the natives'.[2]

The following may be regarded as a proper definition of protector-ates of the international type:

A protectorate arises when a weak State surrenders itself by treaty to the protection of a strong State in such a way that it transfers the management of all its more important international affairs to the protecting State. Through such a treaty an international union is called into existence between the two States, and the relation between them is called protectorate. The protecting State is internationally the superior of the protected State; the latter has with the loss of the management of its more important inter-national affairs lost its full sovereignty, and is henceforth only a half sovereign State.[3]

The significance of Oppenheim's definition is that it draws attention to the following facts: (a) that the protected State in the 'international union' was, before the establishment of the protectorate, a sovereign State; (b) that the basis of the union between the protected and the protecting State was a formal treaty; (c) that the protected State did not lose all its sovereignty and it thus remained, for some purposes of international law, an international person.[4] There are, indeed, many other writers such as Westlake, Fenwick and Cavaré, who concur in the view that a protected State of the international type presupposes that it was, before the establishment of the protectorate, a sovereign State with full capacity to enter into treaty arrangements with other sovereign States.[5]

---

[1] Oppenheim, pp. 194–6.

[2] Arbitral Award Concerning the *Island of Palmas*, *A.J.I.L.*, 22 (1928), p. 898.

[3] Oppenheim, p. 92. Professor Cavaré defines a modern protectorate as a union based on treaty arrangement, which imposes on the participants obligations of political and economic nature: 'C'est un groupement d'allure moderne, à la fois politique et juridique, constitué par deux Etats, le Protecteur et le Protégé qui tend à assurer aux participants des advantages soit d'ordre politique, soit d'ordre économique.'

It should be remarked, in this connection, that the writer who, in line with other publicists, distinguishes between 'Le Protectorat du droit de gens, régi par le Droit international' and 'Le Protectorat colonial', places the former Protec-torates of Tunisia and Morocco in the first category. See Cavaré, Louis, *Le droit international public positif*, vol. I (1951), pp. 424, 429–30.

[4] See the decisions of the International Court below.

[5] See Westlake, pp. 21–4. The writer distinguishes between protectorates over States and protectorates over tribal communities. These which he calls 'colonial protectorates' are discussed by him at pp. 121–9; Fenwick, C. G., *International Law* (1924), p. 97. According to Fenwick 'the protectorate is a state which has by formal treaty placed itself under the protection of a stronger state'; Cavaré, op. cit., pp. 424–34.

It is clear that the international position of protectorates cannot be described by reference to a single general rule, since the circumstances of each protected State vary according to the particular arrangements stipulated by the treaty or treaties establishing the protectorate. Consequently, in each case it is necessary to examine the treaties with the protecting State.[1] The fact, however, that the protecting State represents the protected State 'internationally' does not seem to affect the sovereignty and statehood of the latter which, according to Oppenheim, 'always has, and retains, for some purposes, a position of its own as an International Person and a subject of International Law'.[2]

In a case where the protectorate was established, as in Egypt,[3] by a unilateral declaration, the position of the protectorate, says Fitzmaurice, 'would have to be inferred from the circumstances in which it had been established and the manner in which it had been exercised'.[4]

Decisions of the International Court on protectorates

The International Court[5] has given two decisions relative to the status of the former French Protectorates over Tunisia and Morocco. Those decisions are of particular interest in this discussion because of the general observations which they contain on the status of certain protectorates in the international community. The following rules may be drawn from the first case, that of the *Nationality Decrees Issued in Tunis and Morocco* (1923): The extent of power conferred on the protecting Power depends in the first place upon the treaty or 'treaties between the protecting State and the protected State establishing the protectorate', and secondly, 'upon the conditions under which the Protectorate has been recognised by third Powers as against whom there is an intention to rely on the provisions of these treaties'.[6] Further, the Court held that 'in spite of common features possessed by Protectorates under international law, they have individual characteristics resulting from the special conditions under which they were

---

[1] Schwarzenberger, pp. 92–4. See also Cavaré, op. cit., p. 424; Oppenheim, p. 192.

[2] Oppenheim, pp. 192–3.

[3] Great Britain, by a unilateral declaration of 18 December 1914, terminated Turkish suzerainty over Egypt and declared a protectorate over her. On 28 February 1922 she abolished the protectorate regime over Egypt and declared the latter to be an independent sovereign State, reserving, however, certain privileges to be exercised according to the discretion of the British Government.
For the declaration of 1922, see *Treaty Series*, No. 1 (1922), *Cmd*, 1592. For British announcement to foreign Powers on this matter, see ibid., No. 2 (1922), *Cmd*. 1617. For the declaration of 18 December 1914, establishing protectorate over Egypt, see Hertslet, *Commercial Treaties*, vol. 27, pp. 107–8.

[4] Fitzmaurice, Sir Gerald, 'The Law and Procedure of the International Court of Justice', *B.Y.I.L.*, 30 (1953), p. 4.

[5] This phrase applies to the Permanent Court of International Justice as well.

[6] *P.C.I.J.*, Series B, No. 4 (1923), p. 24.

F

created, and the stage of their developments'.[1] In the second case, that of the *Rights of the United States Nationals in Morocco* (1952), the International Court of Justice accepted the principle that 'Morocco, even under the Protectorate, has retained its personality as a State in International Law'.[2] As regards the Treaty of Fez of 1912, establishing the Protectorate over Morocco, the Court was of the opinion that this was an 'international instrument' which was internationally binding.[3] Moreover the Court held that treaties concluded by the protected State, before the establishment of the protectorate, with the other States, did not lose their binding force internationally as a result of the establishment of the protectorate.[4]

[1] *P.C.I.J.* Series B, No. 4 (1923), p. 24.   [2] *I.C.J. Reports*, 1952, pp. 185–8.
[3] Ibid.   [4] *P.C.I.J.*, op. cit., pp. 27–9.

8

The present legal position of the Gulf States

THEIR STATUS IN THE LIGHT OF THEIR TREATIES WITH THE UNITED KINGDOM

Muscat

The Sultanate of Muscat may be regarded, for all purposes of state-hood, as an independent State in close treaty relations with the British Government. An examination of the specific provisions of her treaties with the British Government, to which reference has been made above, will show that there is nothing in these treaties which subjects her, either explicitly or implicitly, to a protectorate status.[1] Moreover, there are the following factors which show that Muscat always has, and retains, for all practical purposes, her position as an independent State:

1. The independence of Muscat was affirmed by the Anglo-French Declaration of 10 March 1862. This independence was reaffirmed later by the decision of The Hague Court of Arbitration, dated 8 August 1905.[2]

2. At present, Muscat maintains treaty relations not only with the United Kingdom, but also with the United States, France and other States. In all such treaties the sovereignty and independence of the Sultan has been recognised by the foreign States concerned.[3]

3. In the international sphere, Muscat conducts her foreign policy through her 'External Affairs Department' which reports directly to the Sultan. Since, however, she does not, at present, maintain diplomatic relations with foreign States, she is being represented internationally by the British Government to which the Sultan has entrusted, through an *ad hoc* arrangement, 'certain duties in respect of external affairs'.[4] However, the British representatives in foreign States act on behalf of the Sultan 'only when specifically requested by him to do so'.[5] This shows that British representation of Muscat's foreign

---

[1] And the fact that Muscat is not a member of the United Nations should not be regarded as in any way reflecting any limitation upon her independence.

[2] See above, pp. 49, 51–2.

[3] See above, pp. 55–7.

[4] See *House of Commons Debates*, vol. 574, *Written Answers*, col. 32, 22 July 1957 (Statement made by the Foreign Secretary on the status of Muscat). And see the *Ad Hoc Committee on Oman*, op. cit., p. 172 (Statement made by the Sultan of Muscat).

[5] Ibid. And see Hay, *The Persian Gulf States* (1959), p. 140.

affairs is not based on protectorate relationship, as is the case with the Shaikhdoms.[1]

4. In British state practice Muscat has been treated as an independent State. For example, she has not been included within the category of 'British Protected States', as is the case with the Shaikhdoms, and British protection cannot, therefore, be extended to Muscati subjects abroad on the basis of the British Protectorates, Protected States and Protected Persons Order in Council, 1949.[2] However, in practice British representatives abroad may extend protection to Muscat citizens in foreign States on an informal and friendly basis. The British Government is not represented in Muscat by a British Political Agent, as is the case with the Shaikhdoms, but by a Consul-General who is for administrative purposes subject to the authority of the British Political Resident in Bahrain.[3] British treaties with Muscat are published in the British Treaty Series in the same way as are those with independent States.[4] Muscat was not mentioned among the Shaikhdoms in the Treaty of Jiddah of 1927, between Britain and Saudi Arabia.[5] Nor was it mentioned in the draft Convention of 1913, between Britain and Ottoman Turkey, regarding the definition of the respective spheres of influence of the contracting parties in the Gulf States.[6]

As against the above-mentioned illustrations of Muscat's independence, in law, reference may be made to certain limitations which the Sultan has accepted upon his sovereignty:

1. The Sultan is still bound by the Agreements of 1822 and 1845,[7] regarding the suppression of slave trade. By virtue of these Agreements the British cruisers are given the right to exercise certain limitations on Muscat flag vessels, both on the high seas and in the territorial waters of Muscat, and to confiscate the vessels and properties of the Sultan or his subjects if they are found to have violated the provisions of these Agreements. These Agreements, like other similar agreements with the Shaikhdoms, entrust rights of supervision in respect of such matters, to the British Government.

[1] In his statement to the *Ad Hoc Committee on Oman*, op. cit., p. 172, the Sultan admitted that he has no 'written agreement with the United Kingdom Government concerning its handling of the foreign relations of the Sultanate'. The said Government, he said, offers its services in this respect on the basis of its 'long standing' friendship with his country. As regards consular representation in London, he confirmed that he had none before October 1963. After that date, he said, a Muscati consul was appointed in London.
[2] For the provisions of this Order, see below, p. 123.
[3] See above, Introduction.
[4] See above, p. 52. Similarly, the treaties of Muscat with foreign States have been registered with the United Nations under Article 102 of the Charter.
[5] For this treaty, see below, p. 176.
[6] See above, p. 34, n. 3.   [7] See above, p. 47.

2. Similarly, the Sultan has deprived himself by the non-alienation Agreement of 1891,[1] of the right to dispose of his territories, by any means, to any foreign Government, save to the British Government. This Agreement, which is similar to other agreements concluded with the Shaikhdoms on such matters, places a further curtailment on the rights of the Sultan to exercise sovereign acts within his own dominions.

3. Finally, the Agreements of 1902 and 1923[2] have yet placed more limitations on the Sultan's sovereignty by requiring that he should not grant coal-fields or oil concessions in his territories to foreign companies, without consulting the British Government. Consequently, these agreements appear to restrict the Sultan's right in exploiting vital resources of his country.

It is noteworthy that in view of the criticisms recently levelled against these 'unilateral' agreements, both the Sultan and the British Government found it necessary to state their views on the legal status of the agreements in question. Consequently, the Sultan told the *Ad Hoc* Committee on Oman, which interviewed him in 1964, that these agreements 'terminated with the death of the Sultan who concluded them', unless they contained clauses making them 'binding on his heirs and successors'. However, he made an exception to this rule with respect to the 'Non-alienation Bond of 1891' which, he said, has now become 'dead' despite the fact that it 'had been binding the Sultan's heirs and successors'. As regards the 'Oil Undertaking of 1923', which was concluded by his father, he stated that it 'ceased to have effect on his father's death and had not affected his freedom of action on this matter', since it embodied no succession clause.[3] The British Government's comments on the 'Non-alienation Bond of 1891' was contained in its representative's memorandum to the Committee which stated:

The essence of this agreement was that while the Government of India sought no derogation of the Sultan's independence, the Sultan deferred to Her Majesty's Government in ensuring that no other power should derogate from that independence to British disadvantage. (As circumstances changed, this particular agreement lost its force. It was finally terminated by an exchange of letters between the present Sultan and Her Majesty's Government in 1958, after having long been regarded as a dead letter.)

Regarding the Sur 'Coal-fields Undertaking of 1902', the British representative did not allude to its termination but informed the Committee that 'the parties could make whatever agreements they chose, although agreements such as this one were less known now than they used to be'. With respect to the Sultan's Undertaking of

---

[1] See above, p. 48.   [2] See above, pp. 48–9.
[3] *The Ad Hoc Committee on Oman*, op. cit., pp. 124–5.

1923, concerning oil exploitation, the British representative informed the Committee that

> In 1923, the then Sultan had offered the British Government what was in effect a first option on any oil discovered in his territories. There had been no termination, but it was not regarded as still being in force. This had not been an agreement but was simply an undertaking given by the Sultan. It might be considered to be a one-sided Declaration, but this had been something that the Sultan had offered to do.

This Undertaking, he continued,

> had not affected the Sultan's action in the last twenty years, nor did it in any way derogate from the sovereignty of the ruler at that time who had given the option. Similar arrangements had been made by the Ottoman Empire.[1]

We may conclude that although the Sultan and the British Government maintain that the agreements in question have lost their legal force a long time ago, they, none-the-less, admit that, except for the agreement of 1891, no steps have yet been taken towards their formal termination. The 1891 agreement was not terminated until 1958, as is shown in the above-mentioned British statement.

The Shaikhdoms[2]

(i) Status prior to British protection

It may be desirable, before discussing the present legal status of the Shaikhdoms, to examine their position prior to their treaty-relations with the British Government. Were the Rulers of these Shaikhdoms regarded by the British Government, before entering into treaty relations with them in 1820, as sovereigns of independent governments who were capable of conferring rights by treaties on foreign Powers?

Leaving aside the legal nature of British treaties with the Shaikhdoms—a point which will be discussed separately—this question will now be examined by reference to the official British attitude towards the Rulers of these States during the period in which the British Government established formal treaty relations with them.

It appears that the British Government treated the Rulers of these Shaikhdoms with whom it directly established official contact as heads of independent governments. These governments existed long before the British Government established its influence in the Gulf. It is true, however, that the petty rulers of the Gulf, who, during the nineteenth century, were surrounded by 'warlike and more powerful States

---

[1] *The Ad Hoc Committee on Oman*, op. cit., pp. 100, 123–4.
[2] As previously noted, the expression 'the Shaikhdoms' covers the status of Kuwait before her independence in 1961.

which menaced their independence' professed on various occasions during this period, 'an unwilling allegiance to Persia, to Turkey, to the rulers of the Wahhabis of Arabia, even to Egypt'. And, in short, those rulers paid tributes, on this account, not only to Ottoman Turkey and to Persia, but also to any strong Power which seemed at the time to be able to offer them protection.[1] However, the British Government did not seem to have taken the Rulers' unwilling allegiance to such Powers as seriously affecting their independent status. It therefore not only proceeded, during that period, to establish direct official contacts with the Gulf Rulers, but also consistently refused to recognise Turkish and Persian claims to sovereignty over the dominions of these Rulers.[2] Moreover, an examination of British treaties with the Gulf Shaikhdoms, concluded between 1820 and 1916, would reveal the following significant facts:

(a) During the period between 1820 and 1879 all British treaties with the Rulers concerned were in the nature of agreements and engagements of military alliances and friendship, the objects of which were the suppression of piracy and slave trade and the maintenance of peace in the waters of the Gulf. Consequently the British Government was entrusted with the power of supervising the implementation of the objects for which those agreements and engagements were concluded.[3] It can be deduced from all or most of the provisions of the treaties concluded during that period that the British Government recognised as an established fact the independent authority exercised by the Rulers over their own governments.[4] It may be contended, therefore, that the British Government by negotiating such treaties with the Rulers reaffirmed their pre-existing independent status.[5] Moreover, it may be noted that the British Government made no claim, in those treaties, to rights of ownership of, or jurisdiction over, any part of the territories of the Rulers.[6]

(b) During the period between 1880 and 1916 treaties of protection, and various other agreements, were concluded by the British Government with the Rulers. Those treaties of protection established closer

[1] See Britain's statements on Bahrain at pp. 190–1 below.

[2] See Chapters 3–5.   [3] See Part One.

[4] In his Note of 18 February 1929 to the Persian Government, Sir Austen Chamberlain stated:
'When, in 1820, consequent on their suppression of the piratical activities of the independent rulers of the Trucial Coast of Oman, they found it necessary to consider the position in regard to Bahrain, nearly forty years had elapsed since the conquest of this island by the ancestor of the present Sheikh. . . . They had . . . no hesitation in entering into negotiations and concluding a treaty with the independent Ruler. . . . The British Government concluded all these treaties with the Sheikh as an independent ruler, and consistently refused throughout to admit the Turkish, Persian and other claims to sovereignty over his dominions . . .' For reference, see below, p. 180.

[5] See Chapters 1–5.   [6] See Part One.

ties between the British Government and the Shaikhdoms. However, it is clear from the history of British treaty relations with the Shaikhdoms that such treaties were not imposed on the Rulers as a result of conquests but were concluded in consequence of special requests for British protection made freely by the Rulers themselves.[1]

This British attitude towards the Shaikhdoms during the period under discussion appears to have reflected the traditional practice of governments and agents of other European Powers prevailing during the same period *vis-à-vis* rulers of Arab and Asian countries of the Far and Middle East. From such practice one may deduce that governments and agents of those Powers treated the rulers of native Arab and Asian countries as 'sovereigns' who were capable of concluding treaties with foreign Powers and of transferring rights 'in the international sense' over territories subject to their sovereignty and jurisdiction.[2] Consequently, those Powers regarded themselves precluded, by usage and custom, from acquiring titles to territories within the jurisdiction of Arab and Asian rulers as if such territories were *terra nullius*.[3]

The following explanation has been given of this practice in connection with the attitudes of governments of Portuguese, Spanish, French and British Powers towards native States of Arab, Indian and Far Eastern regions:

> Some of the native states—at least in India, Ceylon, and the Arab regions —were considered by the Portuguese [and the Spanish] as entities having something akin to sovereignty in the international sense and capacity to transfer it. Treaties were made with some native potentates . . . Some treaties have clauses dealing with customs and harbour duties, extra-territorial jurisdiction, and extradition of criminals, and the inclusion of such provisions seems to correspond with the character of true international treaties . . .[4]

The same authors have explained the exceptional attitude of French and English discoverers towards rulers of Arab regions as follows:

> It was very common usage among English and French discoverers to make agreements with native inhabitants of the lands which they explored or

---

[1] See Part One.

[2] See Keller, A. S., and others, *Creation of Rights of Sovereignty through Symbolic Acts; (1400–1800)* (1938), pp. 6–9, for a study of the practice of governments and agents of European powers regarding the acquisition of title to *terra nullius*.

[3] See ibid., p. 6. In contrast, the authors state that chiefs of other African and American communities were not regarded as possessing any sovereign status. The territories of such chiefs were therefore regarded as *terra nullius* (i.e., lands not under any sovereignty).

[4] Ibid. In contrast, the authors state, at pp. 6–9, that the Portuguese regarded the tribes of Moluccas and the East Indies as possessing no sovereignty, and their territories were therefore *terra nullius*, the acquisition of which did not depend on the acts of natives *per se.*

found. The customary phrase in the instruction to such discoverers authorised them to annex, in the name of their sovereign, any lands 'not previously possessed by any Christian prince'. For practical reasons it was impossible to apply such methods to countries found in the possession of native Arab, Chinese, and East Indian peoples who were considered in practice to possess an international status, and agreements made with such governments may be regarded in general as having had the status of international treaties, as has been brought out in the preceding section.[1]

Comparing agreements made with Arab and Asian rulers with those made with African chiefs and other semi-barbarous tribes, the same authors say:

Of an entirely different nature were those arrangements made with the native tribes, often semi-barbarous or savage peoples, which were found by the French and English discoverers and to whose lands title had been claimed by the discoverers usually through the performance of symbolic acts in such lands when convenient.[2]

In conclusion, it may be stated that by recognising the sovereignty of the Rulers of the Gulf States during the nineteenth century, the British Government had merely reaffirmed the traditional practice of European powers regarding their dealings with Arab and Asian rulers of these regions.

(ii) *Status under British protection: evolution of their international personality*

An examination of the terms of the Shaikhdom's treaties with the United Kingdom (especially those treaties concluded during the period between 1880 and 1916), shows clearly that these Shaikhdoms have surrendered to the British Government their rights of sovereignty in respect of the matters following:

1. The establishment of direct diplomatic or consular relations with foreign Powers other than the United Kingdom.
2. The negotiation or the conclusion of treaties or agreements with foreign States, other than the United Kingdom, without the sanction of the United Kingdom.
3. The cession or the disposal of their territories by means of sale, lease, mortgage, or by other means, without the agreement of the United Kingdom.
4. The grant of mineral or oil concessions to foreign Governments

---

[1] Ibid., pp. 10, 150.
[2] Ibid., pp. 10–12. Another writer, Mr Snow, draws a similar analogy of European powers' practice and usage during the eighteenth and nineteenth centuries. He deduces from that practice that while rulers of North African Arab countries were recognised as possessing 'sovereignty', chiefs of 'aborigines' of other regions of Africa were not. See Snow, A. H., *The Question of Aborigines in the Law and Practice of Nations* (1919), pp. 117–27, 122–6.

or to the subjects of such Governments, without the prior consent of the United Kingdom.[1]

It is noteworthy, however, that the Kuwait Agreement of 1899, does not contain a specific provision curtailing the power of the Ruler to negotiate or to conclude treaties with foreign States.[2] Moreover, the Bahrain Agreement of 1880, does not restrict the power of the Ruler to conduct, without the mediation of the British Government, his own 'customary relations with the local authorities of neighbouring States'.[3]

In return for the above obligations made by the Shaikhdoms, the United Kingdom has undertaken (a) to protect them against foreign aggression, (b) to safeguard their continued individual independence, (c) to look after their international political and economic interests, (d) to extend her protection to their nationals abroad, and (e) to conduct, on their own behalf, their external affairs. Most of these duties are not based on treaty provisions. They have their basis in customary state practice. The above treaties clearly prohibit the Rulers from performing certain acts of sovereignty without the consent of the British Government. Accordingly, these treaties have merely curtailed, but not eliminated, the sovereignty of the Rulers.[4]

In practice, the British Government has, in dealing with the affairs of the Shaikhdoms, proceeded to act strictly on the basis of the obligations contained in these treaties, and consequently, to object to any representation made by foreign States with the Shaikhdoms without its knowledge. During the last eighty-six years (since 1880, when the first treaty of protection was signed with Bahrain), this British practice appears to have been acquiesced in by those foreign States which have raised no objections regarding British representation of the Shaikhdoms. However, it may be pointed out that on at least two occasions the right of British representation of the foreign affairs of these Shaikhdoms has been openly violated by some foreign States:

(a) *Extradition of criminals and debtors between Turkey and Bahrain, 1880*

In 1880 and after, the Turkish authorities in al-Hasa, on the mainland of Arabia, made direct requests to the Ruler of Bahrain for extraditing criminals and debtors 'who had absconded to Bahrain', and in one instance one 'Abdullah', who was accused of murder, was actually surrendered. Consequently, according to Lorimer, the Government of India wrote to the British Political Resident in the Gulf instructing him to 'discourage' the Shaikh 'from entering into direct correspondence with the Turks'. 'In the view of the Government of India', says

---

[1] See Part One.   [2] See Chapter 5.   [3] See Chapter 3.
[4] There is nothing in these treaties to show that the Rulers have ceded their sovereignty to the British Government.

Lorimer, 'requests by the Turkish authorities for extradition ... were ... an admission of the Shaikh's independence.'[1]

(b) *Direct correspondence between Saudi Arabia and Qatar, 1935: Anglo-Saudi controversy*

On 26 September 1935 the British Government sent to Saudi Arabia a Note in which it objected to Saudi Arabia's direct correspondence with Qatar in the following terms:

His Britannic Majesty's Government learned with surprise that the Saudi Arabian Government had sent a letter to the Shaikh of Qatar on a question that affects his foreign relations. Since these relations, as the Saudi Arabian Government knows, are conducted through His Britannic Majesty's Government by virtue of the special agreement (concluded) with him, my Government hope the Saudi Arabian Government will in the future contact them, and abstain from communicating with the Shaikh whenever an occasion relating to Qatar presents itself ...

In view of the language contained in His Majesty King 'Abd al-Aziz letter to His Excellency the Shaikh of Qatar, His Britannic Majesty's Government feel it is their duty to bring up this point so as to draw the attention of the Saudi Government to the provisions of Article 6 of the Jiddah Agreement, which stipulates that His Majesty King 'Abd al-Aziz undertakes, among other things, to support friendly relations with (the Shaikh) of Qatar, with whom His Britannic Majesty's Government has special treaty relations which were explicitly recognised by (Saudi Arabia) in the article referred to.[2]

Being dissatisfied with the contents of the British Note, the Saudi Arabian Government replied to the British Government on 15 October 1935 in these terms:

The undertaking of H.M. the King of the Hijaz and Najd and its dependencies is confined to friendly and peaceful relations with the Amirs of these areas, and contains no reference to any obligation on the part of His Majesty not to write to them or to be written to by them. After the Treaty of Jiddah, therefore, there was no change in the relations which existed between His Majesty and these Amirs. On the contrary, these friendly and peaceful relations continued fully and completely, as did the continuous exchange of correspondence on various matters between them and His Majesty, since this is in support of the friendly and peaceful relations which His Majesty undertook to maintain. As to the treaties referred to in Article 6 between the British Government and these Amirs, they only concern and obligate the Amirs themselves and do not place any obligation upon our Government.[3]

---

[1] Lorimer, pp. 915–17.

[2] *Saudi Memorial*, II, Annex 15. The British Chargé d'Affaires at Jiddah to Shaikh Yusuf Yasin, 26 September 1935. (Arabic translation of the text.)

[3] *Saudi Memorial*, II, Annex 16, pp. 44–5. Shaikh Yusuf Yasin to British Chargé d'Affaires at Jiddah, 15 October 1935.

It appears that Saudi Arabia has continued the practice of dealing with the

The Saudi Arabian Government appears to have taken the view that correspondence and friendly relations between the Shaikhdoms and Saudi Arabia, without the mediation of the British Government, existed both before and after the conclusion of the Anglo-Saudi Treaty of Jiddah of 1927. Consequently there was nothing in this Treaty which prohibits Saudi Arabia from communicating directly with the Shaikhdoms on matters relating to the maintenance of the peaceful relations between the former and the latter. British treaties with the Shaikhdoms seem to have been regarded as having no binding force *vis-à-vis* Saudi Arabia.

Aspects of international personality

Meanwhile, however, it appears that the Shaikhdoms, despite their treaty obligations to the United Kingdom, have not actually remained beyond the pale of the international society of independent nations. Thus, they have not, for example, been dissuaded by the terms of their treaties from negotiating and concluding, directly, with the investors of foreign oil concerns agreements for the exploitation of their oil resources.[1] Moreover, the Rulers have, on various occasions, exercised acts of sovereignty in respect of a number of matters touching upon the heart of their international relations. For example, some of the Shaikhdoms have negotiated and concluded with neighbouring States treaties and agreements of extradition, friendly relations, commerce and boundaries.[2] One of the Shaikhdoms, namely Kuwait, acceded to international conventions and became a member of a number of Inter-Governmental Organisations long before attaining her independence in 1961.[3] Moreover, other Shaikhdoms, namely Bahrain and Qatar, have obtained associate membership in one or two International Organisations, such as UNESCO and WHO. Again, in the field of Arab international relations, some of the Shaikhdoms, in particular Kuwait, Bahrain and Qatar, have taken part, since 1956, in various social and economic activities, in conjunction with other

---

Rulers of the Gulf Shaikhdoms directly, without reference to the British Government, in various matters affecting trade relations or offshore boundaries. For example, she concluded in 1958 and 1965 offshore and onshore boundary agreements with Bahrain and Qatar, respectively, without using British Foreign Office channels.

[1] It is not suggested, however, that these concessions were given without the consent of the British Government. But the practice has shown that the Rulers have negotiated these agreements themselves with foreign companies of different nationalities. Thus, the Rulers have exercised the right of granting oil concessions to non-British companies on terms favourable to themselves. The British Government, says Sir Rupert Hay, does not interfere 'in commercial negotiations' between the Rulers and oil companies. See Hay's book, op. cit., pp. 66–7.

[2] The legal nature of these various agreements is examined below, p. 102 et seq.

[3] See below, p. 112 et seq. The same principle applies to Bahrain and Qatar.

independent States of the Arab League.[1] In the case of Kuwait, it is significant to note that she attended the first conference of Oil Producing Countries which held its first meeting at Baghdad in the summer of 1960, and which established for the first time the Organisation of Petroleum Exporting Countries (OPEC).[2] Furthermore, as early as 1952, the United States established a consulate in Kuwait. The American consul held 'an exequatur from H.M. Queen Elizabeth', as being responsible at the time for the foreign relations of Kuwait.[3] It may be interesting, in this connection, to refer to the following comment of *The Times* about the evolution of the international personality of Kuwait during the few years preceding her independence:

It may seem anomalous that Britain should still conduct the Shaikh of Kuwait's foreign relations for him, though this arrangement has never prevented him from playing his own important and enterprising role in the Arab world. . . . Besides, for all its wealth, a small territory like Kuwait may not want to be burdened with the full apparatus of foreign missions.[4]

The question now presents itself whether the Shaikhdoms may properly be described, in spite of their obligations to the British Government, as States or Subjects of International Law?

It has been noted in Chapter 7 above that the former protectorates of Tunisia and Morocco were described as States possessing international personality.[5] However, it should be admitted that, although

---

[1] Kuwait attended the Arab Social Experts Conference, held in Cairo on 10 March 1956, and the Arab Social Studies Conference held in Amman on 25 April 1956. See Government of Kuwait, *Report of Social Affairs Department* (Arabic report), 1956, pp. 69–70. Also both Kuwait and Qatar attended, as full partners, the first Arab Oil Conference which opened in Beirut on 16 October 1960. Bahrain attended the said conference as an observer. See *Financial Times*, 15–17 October 1960; United Press International, 17 October 1960. Both Bahrain and Qatar have continued to attend Arab Oil Conferences and take part in various economic and social activities sponsored by the Arab League. The Shaikhdoms also maintain separate 'Israeli Boycott Offices' which report directly to the 'Arab Committee of Israel Boycott' of the Arab League.

[2] When the OPEC held its second conference in Venezuela on 21 January 1961, both Kuwait and Qatar were represented as full members. See *The Times*, 10, 22 January 1961. And see the *Financial Times*, 30 January 1961, where it comments on the membership of Kuwait and Qatar in OPEC as follows: 'Joining the (OPEC) was a major foreign policy act because it created vitally important links with other States.'

[3] Hay, op. cit., p. 151. In January 1961 the United Arab Republic requested the Ruler of Kuwait for consular representation in Kuwait. See *The Times*, 16, 27 January 1961.

[4] *The Times*, 27 January 1961. And see the *Financial Times*, 30 January 1961, which states: 'The situation is altered by the announcement that as of January 23 Kuwait took over from Britain control of its foreign relations and is proceeding directly with training Kuwaitis for the diplomatic service. . . . Kuwait is now fully independent, although still in treaty relationship with Britain.'

[5] See above, pp. 65–6.

the international position of the former North African protectorates was defined by international tribunals, no such tribunals have ever defined the position of the Shaikhdoms. Moreover, the position of the Shaikhdoms and the exact legal nature of their relations with the British Government appears to have always remained anomalous. This is because of two reasons: in the first place, the Shaikhdoms' treaties, which are couched in rudimentary terms, do not expressly or formally declare the establishment of a British Protectorate over any of the Shaikhdoms. These treaties, moreover, do not define the legal nature of the relations between the Shaikhdoms and the British Government. They may perhaps be described as unilateral declarations made on the part of the Rulers (to which are affixed the seals of British representatives) pledging themselves not to do certain things without prior consultation with the British Government.[1] Secondly, although the United Kingdom has referred to the Shaikhdoms as 'British protected States', she has made no attempt to define, in detail, their international status and the legal nature of their relations with the Crown. However, it seems necessary to mention that the British Government has, in official statements made from time to time, described the Shaikhdoms as 'independent States under British protection' or as 'independent States in special treaty relations with' Her Majesty's Government.[2] When in 1959 the British Foreign Secretary was asked to explain 'the precise nature of' Her Majesty's Government obligations to the Government of Kuwait he replied: 'The Shaikhdom of Kuwait is an independent State which Her Majesty's Government are under an obligation to protect.'[3]

It should be observed from the above statements that the Shaikhdoms are either referred to as 'independent States' under British protection or as 'States in special treaty relations with Her Majesty's Government'. And in both cases there is a specific reference to them as 'States' or as 'independent States'.

The fact that the Shaikhdoms are very 'loosely' tied up to the Crown is described in the following remarks made by Hurewitz:

---

[1] See Chapters 2-5.

[2] See statement by Sir B. Eyres, *House of Commons Debates*, vol. 388, cols 973–4, 18 April 1934; Article 6 of the Treaty of Jiddah of 20 May 1927, *Treaty Series*, No. 25 (1927), *Cmd.* 2951.

The British Foreign Secretary, Mr Selwyn Lloyd, described his Government's existing relations with the Shaikhdoms in the following terms: 'Her Majesty's Government have a Treaty obligation to protect Kuwait, Bahrain and Qatar. A similar obligation is implicit in the Perpetual Maritime Treaties of 1853 to which all the present Rulers of the seven Trucial States . . . have adhered. There is in addition an explicit undertaking to the Ruler of Fujairah that his State is under British protection.' See *House of Commons Debates*, vol. 574, *Written Answers*, col. 107, 29 July 1957.

[3] *House of Commons Debates*, vol. 599, *Written Answers*, col. 75, 4 February 1959.

Less dependent on Britain are the . . . Persian Gulf Shaikhdoms. . . . These principalities, known in official British usage as 'independent states in special treaty relations with His Majesty's Government', are quasi-protectorates. While they retained full internal sovereignty, they nevertheless surrendered to the United Kingdom in treaties . . . all external sovereignty . . .[1]

In conclusion, it may be argued that the Shaikhdoms cannot be regarded as International Persons as long as they still lack full external sovereignty by virtue of their treaties with the United Kingdom which are still in full force. But the cogency of this argument may be doubted, since it has not been suggested by either textbook writers or by the International Court that for an entity to be regarded as a Person of international law it must have achieved a full, internal and external, sovereignty.[2]

At the same time, it may be asked whether the personality enjoyed by the Shaikhdoms is similar to that enjoyed by fully independent

---

[1] Hurewitz, J. C., 'The British Imperial System', *International Conciliation*: (Unity and Disunity in the Middle East), No. 481, May 1952, p. 217. See also for a similar view, Brinton, J. Y., 'The Arabian Peninsula, The Protectorates and Shaikhdoms', *Revue Egyptienne de Droit International*, 3 (1947), pp. 5–38. And see Fawcett, J. E. S., *The British Commonwealth in International Law* (1963) p. 120, where he cites the Gulf States as examples of protection based on treaties. 'The protection over these Shaikhdoms', he says, 'developed out of the needs to check slave trade and to prevent regional warfare. . . .'

[2] 'Independence all round', says Oppenheim, 'has two main elements: (*a*) internal sovereignty, and (*b*) external sovereignty. A not fully sovereign State (a protected State), has retained in full its internal sovereignty but has departed, by treaty, with all or some of the attributes of its external sovereignty.' See Oppenheim, pp. 118–19. See also Westlake, pp. 20–2; Wheaton, p. 27; Brierly, pp. 118–19.

According to Westlake, 'It is not necessary for a state to be independent in order to be a state of international law.' See Westlake, p. 21.

And according to Willoughby, 'The sovereign state may . . . bind itself to any extent by its own will . . . by treaties (where) it may give its undertaking to other States not to exercise certain of its powers, or to exercise them only in certain ways, but these self set limitations it may legally—if not morally—escape by an exercise of that same sovereign will in pursuance of which they were created. . . .' See Willoughby, W. W., *Fundamental Concepts of Public Law* (1924), p. 21.

The international personality of a not fully sovereign, or a protected, State of this type is, further, confirmed by Holland who states: 'The inferior state is itself recognised as an international unit, though of an imperfect type.' See Holland, Sir T. E., *Lectures on International Law* (1933), p. 69.

Moreover, see Baty, T., *The Canons of International Law* (1930), pp. 6–7. He says: 'But if its [the protected State] diplomatic relations are entirely in the hands of its protector, it does not follow that it retains no international status.' And see Svarlien, Oscar, *An Introduction to the Law of Nations* (1955), p. 86.

Finally, see the decision of the International Court regarding the *Rights of the United States Nationals in Morocco* (1952), in which it was stated that 'Morocco, even under the protectorate, has retained its personality as a State in International Law'. See above, p. 66.

States? It is clear that although the Shaikhdoms, in fact, possess the rights and duties which have been described above, they nevertheless still lack some important marks of independence, namely, they are not fully independent of external control. For example, they still have no right to go to war independently of the British Government.[1] Nor have they the right to enter, without the agreement of the British Government, into political treaties which have the effect of altering their present *status quo*. In these circumstances, it may be suggested that the Shaikhdoms do not enjoy full international personality similar, in all respects, to that enjoyed by independent sovereign States. But they, or more accurately some of them, enjoy a considerable measure of international personality.

POSITION WITHIN THE FRAMEWORK OF
BRITISH CONSTITUTIONAL LAW:
COMPARISON WITH BRITISH PROTECTORATES

Under British Constitutional Law, protectorates differ from colonies in that they do not constitute part of the British Dominions. In all British Protectorates foreign relations are controlled by the British Crown.[2] However, the extent of power reserved by each protectorate internally is the basis on which British Protectorates may be legally classified as follows:

(*a*) *Colonial Protectorates:* In protectorates falling under this group the amount of power exercised by the Crown does not very much differ from that exercised in colonies. In general, the Crown reserves in these protectorates most powers of legislation and administration. However, in contradistinction to colonies, these protectorates are regarded as foreign territories.[3] Powers of the Crown in them were acquired in the past by virtue of agreements with tribal chiefs who agreed to place themselves under the sovereignty of the Queen.[4] The

---

[1] For their position during war, see below, p. 114 et seq.

[2] Under British constitutional law, the so-called dependent territories of the Crown comprise colonies, protectorates, protected States, and trust territories (formerly known as mandated territories). Colonies, whether self-governing or not, are British possessions, while the rest are not. The United Kingdom Government is responsible for the international affairs of all of these territories. See Stewart, Robert B., *Treaty Relations of the British Commonwealth of Nations* (1939), pp. 23–6; Fawcett, J. E. S., 'Treaty-Relations of British Overseas Territories', *B.Y.I.L.*, 26 (1949), p. 88.

[3] Keith, A. B., *The Governments of the British Empire* (1935), pp. 497–500; Keith, A. B., *Constitutional Law*, 7th ed. (1935), p. 353.

[4] Keith, *Governments*, op. cit., p. 464. These agreements in fact amount to cession of sovereignty by the tribal chief. For interesting examples of such agreements, see Hertslet, Sir E., *The Map of Africa by Treaty*, 3rd ed., vol. 1 (1909), pp. 290, et seq.

Crown exercises jurisdiction in these protectorates over all subjects on the basis of the Foreign Jurisdiction Act, 1890.[1] Legislation is enacted by Orders in Council, and an act of the Crown in relation to a native individual is regarded as an act of state which cannot be questioned in English Courts.[2] However, the inhabitants of these protectorates are not British subjects. They are known as British protected persons and they are entitled to British protection abroad.[3]

(b) *Protected States:* In these States the British Government has recognised the sovereignty of the local rulers who have retained their independence at least in regard to the administration of their own governments. In regard to the external affairs of these States the powers reserved by the Crown are based on treaty obligations. In practice the extent of powers exercised by the Crown in these States varies from one State to another according to the particular circumstance of each State.[4] They are all, however, considered to be sovereign States and their rulers are granted immunities from jurisdiction in British courts.[5]

The distinction between protectorates and protected States, under constitutional law, is drawn by Keith as follows:

The essential characteristic of the Protectorate is that the Crown assumes and exercises full sovereign authority, though without annexing the territory. In the case of the Protected States the sovereign authority belongs to the sovereign of the State, and not in any sense to the British Crown, and the role of the latter is derived from treaty arrangements with the States which do not confer any sovereignty over them, but give powers and duties in respect either of both internal and external affairs, or to the latter almost exclusively.[6]

According to Professor Wade, protected States 'are internally autonomous, only their foreign relations being controlled by the United Kingdom'.[7] And according to Robbins, a protected State 'is

---

[1] Keith, *Constitutional Law*, op. cit., pp. 553–8.

[2] See *The King* v. *Earl of Crewe ex parte Sekgome* [1910] 2 K.B. 576: A writ of habeas corpus for the release of a native chief in the Bechuanaland was refused on the ground that his arrest by an Order in Council was an act of state. And see *Sobhuza II* v. *Miller* [1926] A.C. 518: the Crown's authority in a protectorate cannot be challenged even by the treaty by which authority was first acquired. See also *Rex* v. *Southern Rhodesia* [1919] A.C. 211; *Chief Tshekodi Khama* v. *Ratshosa* [1931] A.C. 784: chiefs of African colonial protectorates do not enjoy immunity from jurisdiction of British courts.

[3] Stewart, op. cit., pp. 25–6.

[4] Keith, *Governments*, op. cit., p. 508; Ridges, E. W., *Constitutional Law*, 8th ed. (1950), p. 508.

[5] See *Mighell* v. *Sultan of Johore* [1894] 1 Q.B. 149; *Duff Development Company* v. *Government of Kelantan* [1924] A.C. 797.

[6] Keith, *Governments*, op. cit., p. 508.

[7] Wade and Phillips, *Constitutional Law*, 5th ed. (1955), p. 445; and see ibid., 6th ed. (1960), pp. 400–2.

G

more advanced beyond the tribal stage', and it presupposes a formerly 'established government which can agree and accept the protection'.[1] The Federated and Unfederated States of Malay were regarded 'as the most important examples of protected States'. In their treaties with the British Government the rulers of the Malay States agreed to accept the advice of a British Resident 'in all questions other than those touching Malay religion and customs'.[2] Under the Federation Agreement of 1948, Britain had 'complete control, including powers of legislation, of the defence and the external affairs of the Federation and of Johore'.[3]

The Princely States of India were also, prior to the coming into force of the India Act of 15 August 1947, referred to as protected States. The British relations with those States were established as a result of treaties of alliances and protection signed with their rulers. Theoretically, the rulers surrendered to the Crown their external sovereignty but reserved their internal autonomy. In practice, however, the rights of the Crown in the Indian States were defined not on the basis of the treaties alone, but also 'on the conception known as Paramountcy', which meant 'the powers and obligations assumed or acquired by the Crown as it became the dominant, and ultimately the supreme, power in India'.[4] The right of the Crown as the 'Paramount Power' was again affirmed by the British Government in the *Report of the Indian States Committee* of 1928 to 1929.[5]

In connection with the Gulf States, the first official reference to them as 'British Protected States' was contained in The British Protectorates, Protected States and Protected Persons Order in Council, 1949.[6] For the purposes of this Order, the 'Persian Gulf States' (the Shaikhdoms) were, together with the States of Malay, Tonga and the Maldive Islands, classified in the Second Schedule as 'British Protected States'. The First Schedule of the Order named all the African territories under British protection, including the Aden Protectorate and Zanzibar, as Protectorates.[7] Now, after the independence of these

---

[1] Robbins, R., 'The Legal Status of Aden Colony and Aden Protectorate', *A.J.I.L.*, 33 (1939), pp. 713–14.

[2] Stewart, op. cit., p. 26. For former status, see Baty, *B.Y.I.L.*, op. cit., p. 109.

[3] Oppenheim, 196, n. (3). For the Federation Agreement of 21 January 1948, see *S.I.* 1948, No. 108.

[4] See Westlake, pp. 41–3; Lee-Warner, Sir W., *The Native States of India* (1910), pp. 37–40; Somervell, D. B., 'The Indian States', *B.Y.I.L.*, 11 (1930), pp. 58–60; Hall, p. 28.

[5] See Somervell, op. cit., pp. 58–9; Publication of the Government of Hyderabad, *The Complaint of Hyderabad against the Dominion of India* (under Article 35 (2) of the U.N. Charter) (1948) pp. 29–32.

[6] *S.I.* (1949) No. 140.

[7] The Aden Protectorate, unlike the Shaikhdoms, is regarded as a protectorate of the colonial type. According to Robbins, the Aden Protectorate has no international personality, and British treaties with the rulers of the Protectorate 'are

protected States,[1] the Gulf States are the only remaining British protected States for the purposes of this Order. Hood Phillips describes
these states as 'sovereign states leaving only their foreign affairs in
the hands of the Crown'.[2]

The fundamental difference between the Shaikhdoms and the
various British protectorates and protected States described above is
that, unlike the latter, the former remained internally independent
from British control. The governments of the Shaikhdoms are, as
explained in the Introduction, headed by absolute local Rulers who
reserve in their persons the power to make laws by proclamations
and to administer, through representatives appointed by themselves,
justice, police and other various functions of government. The
British Government, which has no representation in the local administration of the Shaikhdoms, exercises no power of legislation over
persons in the Shaikhdoms, other than those subject to the jurisdiction
of British Courts. However, the British Resident in the Gulf advises
the Rulers from time to time on certain governmental matters when
his advice is sought. But the Rulers are, in theory, free to accept or
reject his advice on matters affecting administration over their own
subjects.[3]

---

not so much the source of British power over the territory as the recognition by
the native chiefs of the authority assumed by the Crown'. Under the Aden Protectorate Order in Council, 1937, the British Governor of the Aden Colony is at the
same time Governor of the Protectorate. The Crown, according to this Order,
reserves the 'power to make laws for the peace, order and good government of the
Protectorate'. It is noteworthy that Orders in Council applying to African protectorates contain similar provisions to this Order.

On the legal status of Aden Protectorate, see Robbins, op. cit. pp. 700-7;
Liebesny, Herbert J., 'International Relations of Arabia: The Dependent Areas',
The Middle East Journal, vol. 1 (1947), pp. 153-5; Hurewitz, *International Concilia-
tion*, op. cit., p. 217; Brinton, *Revue Égyptienne*, op. cit.; The Aden Protectorate
Order in Council, 1937, *S.R. & O. and S.I.* vol. VIII (Revised to 30 December
1948), p. 148.

The former Aden Protectorate was declared on 30 November 1967 a fully
independent state under the name 'The Republic of South Yemen'. For the legal
developments of its status before independence, see the Treaty of Friendship and
Protection between the United Kingdom . . . and the Federation of Arab
Amirates of the South, 11 February 1959, *Cmnd.* No. 665. This Treaty, establishing
a Federation under the protection of the United Kingdom, provides for the
development of the States within the Federation into 'an economically and politically independent State in friendly relations with the United Kingdom'. See ibid.

[1] The independence of the Federation of Malay was declared on 15 August 1957.
See *The Federation of Malay Independence Act, 1957: Report of the Federation of
Malay Constitutional Proposals for the Federation of Malay* (1957), *Cmnd.* 210.

[2] Phillips, O. Hood, *The Constitutional Law of Great Britain and the Commonwealth*, 2nd ed. (1957), pp. 646-8.

[3] See Chapter 1.

TREATY-MAKING CAPACITY

Treaties with the United Kingdom: nature and justiciability

Should the treaties between the Gulf States and the United Kingdom be regarded as internationally binding instruments, subject to arbitration in a recognised tribunal in the event of breach by either party? As there can be little real doubt about the status of the Treaty between the United Kingdom and Muscat of 1951—a recognised international instrument registered with the United Nations—and since the British-Muscati relations are not of a protectorate character, the present discussion will be limited to the position only of the treaties with the Shaikhdoms.

Whether treaties between the protected and the protecting State are treaties in the international sense or merely contracts of no binding effect internally, is a question which is very difficult to answer. Perhaps the only decision of an international tribunal which has been given on this question is that of the International Court of Justice in the case of the *Rights of the United States Nationals in Morocco* (1952). As stated before, the Court affirmed the principle that Morocco 'even under the protectorate, has retained its personality as a State in International Law . . .' As regards the Treaty of Fez of 1912, the Court held: 'It is an international instrument' under which Morocco 'remained a sovereign State . . .'[1]

However, it seems difficult to regard the above case as establishing a general principle of law which can be safely applied to all treaties between protecting and protected States, since the status of such treaties varies. Moreover, the protecting Powers do not always regard their treaties with their protectorates as the only basis of their mutual relations. The treaties between the British Government and the former States of India are a case in point. It was stated in the Indian Official Gazette of 2 August 1881 in connection with the definition of the relationship between the protected States and the Crown that:

The principles of international law have no bearing upon the relation between the government of India as representing the queen-empress on the one hand, and the native states under the suzerainty of Her Majesty on the other. The paramount supremacy of the former presupposes and implies the subordination of the latter.

British treaties with those States were not regarded as binding on the Crown in the international sense, but, according to Hall, as

little more than statements of limitations which the Imperial Government except in very exceptional circumstances, places on its own action.

---

[1] *I.C.J. Reports*, 1952, pp. 185–8.

Consequently, the Crown had no hesitation in disregarding those treaties whenever, says Hall, 'the supreme interests of Empire (were) involved or even when the interests of the subjects of the native princes (were) gravely affected'.[1]

Treaties are normally defined as 'agreements between States, including organizations of States . . .'[2] 'The result of some such interpretation of the term "States" ', says H. Lauterpacht, 'would be, for instance, that agreements made between the protected and the protecting State, either at the time of the establishment of the Protectorate or subsequently, could not be regarded as treaties.' 'However,' he continues, such agreements 'have been so treated judicially by both international and municipal tribunals. Rules and principles of international law applicable to treaties have been applied to them.'[3]

It may be pointed out that in making this statement, H. Lauterpacht had in mind the decisions of the International Court on the status of Tunisia and Morocco to which reference has been made previously. However, as a contribution to the idea that the agreement between the protecting and the protected State cannot be deprived of its international character, the *Rapporteur* cites another case as follows:

Agreements between the protecting and the protected State are frequent and there has often been no disposition, even on the part of the protecting State, to question their international character. Thus, for instance, in the proceedings before the Permanent Court of International Justice in connection with its Advisory Opinion on the *Jurisdiction of the Courts of Danzig* Poland did not seem to question the international character of the agreement concluded between her and Danzig—a protected State.[4]

In the light of the above-mentioned decisions, he proceeds to consider the following question:

If the protecting and the protected State while disagreeing as to the interpretation of a particular provision in the agreement establishing the protectorate or of any treaty subsequently concluded between themselves were to agree to submit their dispute to an international tribunal, would the latter be entitled to consider the agreement to be a treaty and interpret it by reference to rules applicable to the interpretation of treaties?

---

[1] Westlake, p. 42; Hall, p. 28 (note).

[2] Lauterpacht, H., *Special Rapporteur*, 'Report on the Law of Treaties', *International Law Commission*, 5th session, A/CN.4/63, 24 March 1953, p. 17.

[3] Ibid.

[4] Ibid., p. 18. It is to be noted that while considering the status of agreements between the protecting and protected States, H. Lauterpacht refers, quite wrongly, to the Treaty of friendship between the United Kingdom and Muscat of 1951, as an example of 'a comprehensive treaty' concluded with a protectorate. This treaty, as pointed out before, is an international instrument, since Muscat is not a protectorate.

His answer to this question is that it is difficult to reply to it in the negative.[1]

J. Brierly, on the other hand, comments upon the phrase 'A treaty is an agreement' in the following terms:

> Not every agreement, even between entities possessing capacity to make treaties, is, however, a treaty. At least within the meaning of the present draft the use of the term 'treaty' is confined to the connotation of such agreements between international persons as to establish relations under international law (i.e., create rights or obligations in international law) between the parties.[2]

It may be deduced from Brierly's statement that he did not regard treaties between the protected and the protecting State as treaties establishing relations under international law.[3]

In connection with the treaties of the Shaikhdoms, which do not seem to differ materially from other treaties in general use establishing protectorates, one is faced with the same difficulty as to whether such treaties can be regarded as establishing relationships which are governed by international law and whether a dispute between the United Kingdom and the Shaikhdoms in respect of the revision or the interpretation of these treaties can be subject to international arbitration.

The United Kingdom has, on various occasions, laid emphasis upon her treaty relations with the Shaikhdoms. She has also referred to them as 'independent States which Her Majesty's Government are under duty to protect'.[4] It would appear from such statements that the British Government does not dismiss the binding force of its treaties with the Shaikhdoms. This does not necessarily mean, however, that it regards the treaties in question as international instruments to which international rules of treaty interpretation can be applied. The fact that these treaties are neither included in the British treaty series, nor registered with the United Nations, in accordance with Article 102 of the Charter, shows that the British Government does not attribute to them international status.[5] On British practice in respect of such treaties Lord McNair states:

> An engagement between the United Kingdom and any Protected State within the Empire possessing no international status is not international

---

[1] Lauterpacht, op. cit.

[2] Brierly, J., *Special Rapporteur*, 'Report on the Law of Treaties', *International Law Commission*, A/CN.4/23, 14 April 1950, p. 12.

[3] In the discussion on Brierly's Report, Manley O. Hudson expressed the view that 'There were certain categories of States not covered by the text; for example the Malay States, which had lost their competence to make treaties.' He also held that 'Those States should also be excluded which were members of Federal Union. See U.N. *Yearbook of International Law Commission*, I (1951), p. 139.

[4] See above, p. 78.

[5] Only British treaties with Muscat were registered with the League of Nations At present, these treaties are registered with the United Nations, and are pub-

In this category, he says, 'may be placed the Native Indian States' and the 'Federated and the unfederated Malay States, Tonga' . . . etc.[1]

As regards British practice in respect of the registration of treaties with the League of Nations, he says: Agreements 'entered into between the different self-governing members of the British Empire' were not registered under Article 18 of the League's Covenant.[2] Further, it was pointed out by the British Foreign Office in a dispatch of 27 November 1924 to the Secretariat of the League of Nations that agreements entered into with the following countries were not registered under Article 18 of the Covenant of the League of Nations:

1. Agreements between various parts of the Empire.
2. Agreements between the United Kingdom and protected States.

On the other hand, it was stated in that dispatch that Agreements made between the United Kingdom and 'states standing in close friendship to one of His Majesty's Government', like Nepal and Muscat, 'have been registered under this Article'.[3] The consequence of the non-registration of a treaty or an international agreement under Article 102 of the Charter is that 'no party to any such treaty or international agreement which has not been registered may invoke that treaty or agreement before any organ of the United Nations'.[4]

Moreover, statements by British Ministers in the House of Commons, in connection with the United Kingdom's treaties with the former Somaliland Protectorate, may also be cited as evidence of the fact that the United Kingdom does not regard such treaties as international instruments. Thus, when the Secretary of State for Colonial Affairs was asked in the House of Commons on 25 February 1955 about the distinction in the legal status between the Protectorate treaties of 1886, concluded with the Somali tribes, and the treaty of 1897, entered into between the United Kingdom and Ethiopia, he stated: ' . . . the Treaty of 1897 is an international instrument, whereas the other Agreements . . . were not. . . .'[5] When he was asked whether, since the Treaty with Ethiopia of 1897 transferred some of Somaliland territories to the latter in violation of the United Kingdom's treaties

---

lished in British treaty series. For a Civil Air Agreement on 5 April 1947, signed between the United Kingdom and Muscat, see United Nations, *Treaty Series*, No. 412, vol. 27, p. 287.

But see Agreement for Air-services, 24 May 1960, between United Kingdom and Kuwait, published in *Treaty Series*, No. 6 (1960), *Cmnd.* 1168.

[1] McNair, *Treaties*, p. 156.   [2] Ibid., p. 155.   [3] Ibid., pp. 155–6.

[4] Oppenheim, p. 922. For the question whether a non-registered treaty can be invoked before an international tribunal or an organ of the United Nations, see Brandon, M., 'The Validity of Non-Registered Treaties', *B.Y.I.L.*, 29 (1952), pp. 156–204.

[5] *House of Commons Debates*, vol. 537, col. 1686, 25 February 1955.

of 1884 and 1886 with the Somali tribes, it was possible to refer the matter to arbitration by the International Court, he replied:

> I have also been asked whether there was not a case for a reference to the International Court, because of the alleged conflict between the Treaty of 1897 and the agreement previously signed with Somali leaders. . . . In a matter of this sort the Court would be bound to base its decisions on the Treaty of 1897, which, as an international instrument, leaves no doubt as to where sovereignty lies . . .[1]

In an article on the Ethiopian-Somaliland Frontier, D. J. L. Brown comments on the above-mentioned statement by saying:

> This statement demonstrated [that the United Kingdom] did not regard the tribes of Somaliland, with which it had concluded the Agreements in 1886, as sovereign, or even as part-sovereign, entities which could be recognised as persons in international law, but that it considered them as no more than subjects of the British Crown.[2]

It may be noted that the Somaliland Protectorate controversy with the British Government arose in consequence of the conclusion by the United Kingdom of an agreement, in 1954, with Ethiopia by which the parties reaffirmed their Agreement of 1897. Under this Agreement about 25,000 square miles of British Somali territory was ceded to Ethiopia. According to Gordon Waterfield, a delegation of Somali nationalists which came to London

> failed to persuade the British Government to postpone the implementation of the Agreement (of 1954) or to find any court before which they could plead that the 1897 Treaty was null and void because of the Treaties of 1884 and 1886 between Somali tribes and the British Government. Thereupon [the writer continues] they drew up a petition in February 1955 and sent it to the Secretary-General of the United Nations.[3]

In their petition, the delegates stated that the treaties with the Somali tribes did not give the British Government the right to cede or transfer the ownership of the territories of the Protectorate, and that the action of the British Government in concluding the Treaty of 1897

---

[1] *House of Commons Debates*, vol. 537, col. 1686, 25 February 1955.

[2] Brown, D. J. L., 'The Ethiopia-Somaliland Frontier Dispute', *I.C.L.Q.*, 5 (1956), pp. 263–5.

It may be relevant to point out that in his award in the case of the *Island of Palmas* (1928) Max Huber describes agreements concluded by foreign States with tribal chiefs possessing no international status as follows: 'As contracts between a state or a company and native princes or chiefs not recognised as members of the community of nations, they are not, in international law sense, treaties or conventions capable of creating rights and obligations such as may, in international law, arise out of treaties. But, on the other hand, contracts of this nature are not wholly void of indirect effects on situations governed by international law . . .' See *Award Concerning the Island of Palmas* (1928), *A.J.I.L.*, 22 (1928), p. 897.

[3] Waterfield, G., 'Trouble in the Horn of Africa: The British Somali Case', *International Affairs*, 32 (1956), p. 57.

with Ethiopia amounted to 'a breach of trust on the part of the Protecting Power'. The British Government opposed the 'hearing of the Somali Petition because it was a domestic matter and could not be discussed by the United Nations'.[1]

Subsequently, replying to a question raised in the House of Commons on the decision of the local Government of the Somaliland Protectorate to present a claim to the United Nations for the return of the 'areas' transferred to Ethiopia under the Treaty of 1897, the under-Secretary of State for Foreign Affairs stated:

The United Nations Charter does not give representatives of British Somaliland any right to petition the United Nations, since Somaliland Protectorate is neither a member of the United Nations nor a trusteeship Territory. . . .[2]

A further indication of the British Government's view of the legal nature of treaties concluded by it with tribal chiefs under its protection may be found in an official Report on Nigeria issued in November 1958. In this Report, the Secretary of State for the Colonies explains the legal and the moral nature of the treaties concluded by the Crown with the 'Oil Rivers Chiefs' of Nigeria 'from 1884 onwards' in the following terms:

I ought at this stage to refer to the strict legal position. I am advised that the Treaties of this kind have no standing in international law and it follows from this that it would be quite inappropriate to adopt the suggestion that the question of the proper interpretation of the Treaties should be referred to the International Court. I am also advised on the highest authority that such Treaties confer no rights that are enforceable in our courts, and it seems clear therefore that the question of the interpretation of the Treaties is not one which could appropriately be referred (as has been suggested) to the Judicial Committee of the Privy Council.

In stating, gentlemen, as I must, that in the view of Her Majesty's Government these Treaties did not create obligations that could be enforced either under international law or municipal law, I do not of course wish to imply for one moment that these Treaties were merely worthless scraps of paper that created no obligations whatsoever. Her Majesty's Government has in fact both accepted and I think faithfully discharged the obligation to extend the protection of the Crown over the territories affected by the Treaties and their inhabitants . . .

So in view of what I have said, it may be asked what obligations Her Majesty's Government regards the Treaties as creating at the present time. In my view there are moral obligations on Her Majesty's Government to secure justice and fair dealing on the matters mentioned in the Treaties . . .[3]

---

[1] Ibid., p. 58. See also *The Times*, 6 and 7 October 1955; *The Times*, 8 March 1956.

[2] *House of Commons Debates*, vol. 562, *Written Answers*, col. 149, 19 December 1956.

[3] See *Report by the Resumed Nigeria Constitutional Conference*, September–October 1958, *Cmnd.* 569, November 1958, Annex II, pp. 42–3.

However, it should be noted, in connection with this Report, that the Colonial

These quotations make it abundantly clear that the British Government does not regard its 'Treaties' with the tribes in question as internationally binding. Such Treaties can neither be enforced by any international tribunal, nor be invoked before British courts, though the British Government does acknowledge that they have some moral content.[1]

However, it should be mentioned that the argument that the relation between the protecting and the protected State (not a colonial protectorate) is internal has not been accepted by some text writers. Professor Schwarzenberger, for example, is of the opinion that the

recognition by third states of the exclusive international agency of the Protecting Power does not remove the internal relations between the protecting Power and the protected State from the realm of international law.[2]

Similarly, Fawcett says:

It is perhaps more tempting to hold that the relationships between the United Kingdom and protectorates, protected states and trust territories, are determined by international law.[3]

Although the practice of the United Kingdom regarding the legal nature of her treaty relations with territories and tribes under her protection has been mentioned above in some detail, it remains an open question whether it is possible to draw an analogy from this practice in relation to the position of the treaties of the Shaikhdoms. On this basis of analogy, it may be suggested that the United Kingdom would not attribute to these treaties an international status on the same footing as treaties concluded with fully independent States. It also follows that she would, in cases of disputes arising between her

---

Secretary drew attention to other factors which undermined the legal value of the treaties in question when he stated: 'There has of course been a great alteration in the circumstances of Nigeria since these Treaties were entered into seventy years ago. I think we all know, the British Crown has for a great many years exercised without question full jurisdiction over all the areas comprised in the Protectorate of Nigeria, including the particular areas to which the various Treaties relate, and has made provisions by various Orders in Council for the government of the whole country.' Pointing out the diminished authority of the Chiefs who signed the Treaties in the past, the Colonial Secretary said: '. . . but they have long since ceased to exercise the functions of government, and it is no longer possible to say that there now exist authorities who can be regarded as effective successors to the Nigerian parties to the Treaties.' (See ibid., p. 42.)

[1] See *Report by the Resumed Nigeria Constitutional Conference*, op. cit. The general principle is that treaties concluded by the Crown are considered as acts of state which cannot be interpreted by British courts unless they affect the rights of a British subject. See Hood Phillips, op. cit., p. 220.

[2] Schwarzenberger, p. 94.

[3] Fawcett, Treaty Relations . . . , op. cit., p. 91.

and the Shaikhdoms, object to any unilateral reference of these treaties to an international tribunal on the ground that the customary rules of international law regarding the interpretation of treaties do not apply to treaties which, in her view, have no international standing.

However, there are a number of factors which operate to exclude the treaties of the Shaikhdoms from the same category as those of tribal chiefs of colonial protectorates. In contradistinction to the treaties of the tribal chiefs, which are described as no more than 'public contracts' concluded 'under the municipal law of the colonial power concerned', the treaties with the Shaikhdoms acknowledge, both expressly and by implication, the sovereignty and the international personality of the Rulers.[1] Therefore, the result is that while tribal chiefs are treated as no more than subjects of the Crown, the Rulers of the Shaikhdoms are regarded as sovereigns of independent States under British protection or as 'States in special treaty relations with the British Government'.[2] Liebesny appears to entertain the view that since these Shaikhdoms still possess most of the attributes of sovereignty, their treaties may, therefore, be placed 'in a special category somewhat similar to that of the French Protectorate Treaties with Tunisia and Morocco.[3] Consequently, it is suggested that these treaties should not be dismissed as having no binding force under international law whatsoever.[4]

Having considered the legal value of the treaties of the Shaikhdoms on the international plane, the question arises what legal consequences might follow from the unilateral abrogation or the disregard of these treaties?

(a) *The unilateral abrogation of treaties*

According to Oppenheim, 'A treaty may terminate in four different ways: it may expire, or be dissolved, or become void, or be cancelled.'[5]

The question as to how and when a protected State can bring to an end its treaties of protection with another State is a difficult one. In the first place it is necessary to consider the question whether treaties between protected and protecting States are terminable by notice, and if so, in what circumstances, and what procedure is required for their termination?

The treaties of the Shaikhdoms appear to provide no solution to this question; they embody no provisions concerning their termination or their replacement, after a period of time, by new agreements. On the contrary, there seem to be grounds for suggesting that the language of

---

[1] See Part One.   [2] See above, pp. 78–9.   [3] Liebesny, op. cit., p. 167.
[4] Ibid. It is to be noted, however, that unlike the treaties with Morocco and Tunisia, the treaties with the Shaikhdoms have not been defined by an international tribunal.   [5] Oppenheim, pp. 936–7.

the treaties implies that they are of a perpetual nature, for almost all the Rulers of the Shaikhdoms pledge themselves, 'their heirs and successors', to observe fully the obligations contained in the treaties.[1] However, it seems only reasonable to say that too much stress must not be placed on the language of these treaties, since there is nothing in the nature of treaties of protection between two States to suggest that the arrangements under such treaties are to remain in a permanently static position without being affected by the course of events. According to Oppenheim, 'all treaties must be interpreted according to their reasonable, in contradistinction to their literal sense'.[2] It may be true, however, to say that when a treaty is made for the cession of territory it can be regarded as of a perpetual nature. This is on the ground that the object of such a treaty is, in the words of Hall, 'to set up a permanent state of things, and not barely to secure the performance of the act which forms the starting point of that state'.[3] But the treaties of the Shaikhdoms are not treaties of cession. They are treaties of protection which were concluded at the request of the Rulers themselves, as explained before.[4] If it is true, therefore, that there is nothing in the nature of these treaties that makes them perpetually binding, the question may be asked how, and in what manner, can they be terminated?

It can be argued that, since these treaties were concluded by the consent of both contracting parties—the Rulers and the British Government—it is only logical to assume that their modification or termination can be effective only by the consent of both contracting parties. In his statement of 29 July 1957, on the British treaty relations with the Shaikhdoms, the British Foreign Secretary appears to have confirmed this principle when he stated that

Any change in the nature of these relations could not be determined by Her Majesty's Government only, but would be a matter for agreement between Her Majesty's Government and the Rulers concerned.[5]

This statement is significant in that it establishes, beyond any doubt, that the question of terminating British treaty relations with the Shaikhdoms does not lie solely within the jurisdiction of the British Government. According to this statement the British Government appears to regard these treaties as terminable on the basis of direct negotiations with the Rulers concerned.

The principle of negotiation as a basis for the termination of treaties with protectorates seems to have been accepted by the United King-

---

[1] See Part One.   [2] Oppenheim, p. 952.
[3] Hall, p. 404.   [4] See Part One.
[5] See *House of Commons Debates*, vol. 574, *Written Answers*, col. 107, 29 July 1957.

dom as applicable to her treaty of 1952 with the Sultan of Lahej. In this case, the United Kingdom was reported as saying that

the provisions of the treaty, made in 1952, are not terminable except by negotiation between the Sultan and the Governor of Aden, representing the United Kingdom.[1]

The acceptance by the United Kingdom of the principle of negotiation as a basis for terminating her treaties with a State under her protection is significant in that it seems to place indirect emphasis on the international character of the relations between her and such a protected State. The principle of terminating treaties which are of 'perpetual duration' by negotiation is the basis of British normal practice in the field of international law.[2]

Accordingly, if it is correct to assume that the Shaikhdoms' treaties can be terminated by direct negotiations between the Rulers and the British Government, the question arises whether a failure on the part of the British Government to accede to the Rulers' request for the total abolition of these treaties would give the Rulers the right to abrogate them unilaterally? This is a difficult question to answer. The customary rules of international law on the manner in which treaties between independent States may be terminated by negotiations or, if negotiations fail, by unilateral denunciation are explained by text writers as follows:

Lord McNair states:

It is probably true to say that in the case of political treaties, bipartite or multipartite, there is a greater disposition to go into conference at the request of a party with a view to revision of the mutual obligation so as to bring them more into accord with modern conditions, and that a refusal to confer upon these lines would in some degree mitigate the censure which would still be due to a state which, with or without some moral justification to support it, announced its intention to regard a burdensome obligation as no longer binding upon it.[3]

On the same point, Oppenheim says that:

when a State is of the view that the obligations of a treaty have, through a vital change of circumstances become unbearable, the proper course for it is first to approach the other party (or parties), and request it to agree to the abrogation of the treaty. If the party or parties thus approached refuse to accede to the request—which ought to be coupled with an offer to submit

---

[1] See *The Times*, 17 April 1958. The principle that treaties of protection are terminable by negotiation has been applied in the case of the Kuwaiti Agreement of 1899 with Britain which was terminated in 1961 by the concurrence of both parties. This is a lucid example of how treaties of protection in the Arabian Gulf can be brought to an end by the agreement of both the British Government and the Rulers of the Shaikhdoms concerned.

[2] McNair, *Treaties*, p. 351.   [3] Ibid., pp. 369–70.

any disputed issue to judicial determination—then the requesting State may be justified in declaring that it can no longer consider itself bound by the treaty.[1]

Basic change in circumstances, or the rule *rebus sic stantibus*, have also been accepted by many writers as a ground for unilateral denunciation of treaties.[2] But it appears that the normal practice of the United Kingdom weighs greatly against unilateral abrogation, under any circumstances, of a treaty of which she is a party. To this effect, Lord McNair states:

The normal basis of approach adopted by the United Kingdom towards a treaty is that it is intended to be of a perpetual duration and incapable of unilateral termination, unless, expressly or by implication, the treaty contains a right of a unilateral termination or some other provision for its coming to an end. There is nothing judicially impossible in the existence of a treaty creating obligations which are incapable of termination except by the agreement of all parties.[3]

When on 8 July 1947 Egypt presented a complaint to the Security Council against the United Kingdom in which she appears to have relied, though not specifically, on the doctrine *rebus sic stantibus* as a basis for the termination of her treaty of 1936, the United Kingdom's reply to the complaint was no exception to the British normal practice, explained above. Accordingly, replying to the Egyptian representative's argument that the Anglo-Egyptian Treaty of 26 August 1936 'cannot bind Egypt any longer, having outlived its purposes besides being inconsistent with the Charter', Sir Alexander Cadogan, for the United Kingdom, stated:

... There is no decision of an international tribunal where this doctrine has been applied in any remotely similar case, and the constant practice of States has been to insist on the doctrine that a treaty can only be revised or modified by the consent of the parties. The argument against the Treaty of 1936 on *rebus sic stantibus* lines would seem to have no legal foundation whatsoever.[4]

It is noteworthy that the above principles of law regarding the termination of treaties are applicable to relations among equally

[1] Oppenheim, pp. 941–2.
[2] Ibid., pp. 938–9. 'Almost all the theorists agree', says Westlake, 'that to many treaties the tacit condition *rebus sic stantibus* is attached: they are concluded in and by reason of special circumstances, and when those circumstances disappear there arises a right to have them rescinded.' See Westlake, p. 295. For the views of other writers on the doctrine of *rebus sic stantibus*, see Brierly, pp. 260, 263–4; Schwarzenberger, *A Manual of International Law*, 4th ed., vol. 1 (1960), p. 157; Hyde, vol. 2, p. 1524.
[3] McNair, *Treaties*, p. 351.
[4] See Briggs, Herbert W., 'Rebus sic stantibus before the Security Council; The Anglo-Egyptian Question', *A.J.I.L.*, 43 (1949), pp. 764–5.

independent States. Therefore, they cannot, probably, be invoked as a
basis for determining the position of treaties between protecting and
protected States. Consequently, it may seem difficult to say whether
the doctrine *rebus sic stantibus*, doubtful as it is, can safely be invoked as a basis for terminating the treaties of the Shaikhdoms.
Moreover, occasions have not arisen where a protected State has
abrogated its treaties with the protecting Power without the concurrence of the latter. It appears, therefore, that a renunciation on the
part of the protecting Power of its protectorate rights over the protected State is a necessary step for the independence of the latter.[1]
But this is not always the case. While it seems that normally a recognition by the protecting Power of the independence of the protected
State is a basic step for paving the way for other States to recognise
the independence of the protected State, that recognition is, however,
not the sole basis for the independence of this State. The independence of the protected State lies basically in its existence as a State
and in the effective establishment of its independence and the extent
of its ability to defend that independence, if necessary against the
protecting State. The protected State exists as a State from the time it
separates itself from the 'community' upon which it is dependent.
'The existence of the State *de facto*', says Wheaton, 'is sufficient, in
this respect, to establish its sovereignty *de jure*. It is a State because it
exists.'[2] However, once this independence is established, it becomes a
question of recognition on the part of third States of the protected
State's independence. Accordingly, if third States are prepared to
recognise the latter's independence, the protecting State's objection
to this independence becomes of no legal value.[3]

(b) *Disregard of treaty obligation: remedies for breaches*

The question to be considered here is whether there are legal remedies
for breaches of these treaties by either the Rulers or the United
Kingdom. What happens, for example, if the Rulers correspond with
a foreign State, apply for membership in the Arab League, or decide
to join a federal Arab Union[4] without obtaining the sanctions of the

[1] For Britain's renunciation of her protectorate in Egypt, see above, p. 65, n. 3.
For France's declarations of the independence of Tunisia and Morocco, see *U.N.*,
Everyman's United Nations (1959) pp. 156–7. Reference should also be made to
the British-Kuwaiti Treaty of 1961 which implies Britain's renunciation of her
protectorate rights over Kuwait.

[2] Wheaton, E., *Elements of International Law*, 6th ed., vol. I (1929), pp. 42–3.

[3] Lauterpacht, pp. 9, 26–30.

[4] It was rumoured in 1959, nearly two years before Kuwait's independence,
that she was going to join the Arab League as a member. But this rumour was
later denied by a British Foreign Office spokesman. It was true, however, that the
Secretary of the Arab League visited Kuwait and discussed the possibility of
Kuwait joining the League. See *The Times*, 30 September, 2 October 1959. It is to
be noted, in this respect, that Article 1 of *The Pact of the Arab League* of 22 March

United Kingdom? Has the United Kingdom reserved for herself the right to interpret these treaties at her own discretion?

These are difficult questions to answer. However, it appears, in view of what has been stated above, that the United Kingdom would object to referring these treaties to an impartial tribunal for interpretation in cases of disagreement between her and the Rulers on the obligations arising from such treaties. Thus, interpretation of these treaties by the International Court of Justice is ruled out on the ground that they are not treaties between independent States.[1] Nor does their interpretation lie within the jurisdiction of British courts. The latter would regard them as acts of state which 'cannot be challenged, controlled, or interfered with by municipal courts'.[2]

In the controversy which arose in 1958 between the United Kingdom and the Sultan of Lahej, the former appears to have taken the view that she retains discretionary powers to interpret obligations arising from treaties of protection between her and a State under her protection. The facts, as revealed in this controversy, were that the Sultan was alleged to have made an approach to President Nasser with a view to joining the United Arab Republic. The United Kingdom took the view that any such approach would have been a breach of the treaty of 1952, by which the Sultan agreed to refrain

from entering into any political correspondence, agreement or treaty with any foreign state or government except with the knowledge and sanction of Her Majesty's Government.[3]

Consequently, in reply to a question in the House of Commons about the precise nature of the protest made by the Sultan of Lahej about

---

1945, provides that 'Any independent Arab State has the right to become a member of the League.' However, according to Article 2 of the Economic Council of the Arab League, 'Any Arab country which is not a member of the Arab League has the right to join the Council.' Accordingly, Kuwait which did not, at the time, qualify for membership in the Arab League, was able to join the League's Economic Council. See The Arab League, *Press Release* (Arabic), 4th Year, No. 38, Cairo, 25 June 1959; the *Financial Times*, 30 January 1961.

[1] See above, pp. 87–90.

[2] See Wade, E. C. S., 'Acts of State in English Law: Its Relations with International Law', *B.Y.I.L.*, 15 (1934), pp. 102 et seq. At p. 105, the writer states: 'If the municipal system treats certain acts of the sovereign power, be they in regard to internal or external policy, as conclusive, it is not competent for the municipal courts to control these acts, as they are outside their jurisdiction. Their legality or illegality in another jurisdiction, that of international law, is irrelevant.' See also *Salaman* v. *Secretary of State for India* [1906] 1 K.B. 613; *Doss* v. *Secretary of State for India* [1875] 5 L.R. 19 Eq. 509.

[3] See *The Times*, 17 April 1958; Ibid., 1 May 1958. It is reported here that the Sultan denied 'reports that he was thinking of abrogating the Protectorate treaty and joining the United Arab Republic'.

the entering of British troops into the Protectorate, the Colonial Secretary stated:

The Sultan has told the Governor (of Aden) that he considers that the movement of British troops into Lahej for the arrest of the Jifris and other purposes without his prior consent to be not in accordance with his Protectorate Treaty.

The Governor made it clear to the Sultan that in order to carry out Her Majesty's Government treaty obligations, British troops must be at liberty to go anywhere in the Protectorate at will, including Lahej as well as the other States.

This statement has my full approval and endorsement.[1]

It is noteworthy that this statement appears to interpret the United Kingdom's obligation under the treaty of 1952 as implying the right to station troops, if necessary, in Lahej for combating subversion within the Protectorate. This right was claimed by the United Kingdom despite the fact that the terms of her treaty with the Sultan did not give her the right to interfere in the internal affairs of Lahej. The Sultan himself considered the British action in his territory as 'illegal' and accused the British Government of 'violating' the treaty of 1952.[2] Later, the United Kingdom took far more serious action against the Sultan by formally withdrawing her recognition from him. This virtually meant that he was banned from returning to Lahej.[3]

The Lahej controversy seems to suggest that the United Kingdom may be seeking to retain quite wide powers of interpretation of her treaties with protectorates.

Whether the United Kingdom would be inclined, in cases of disputes between her and the Shaikhdoms, to interpret her treaty obligations with the latter in the same manner as she did in the case of Lahej is a question which is difficult to answer in strict legal terms. However, it can be argued that since the recognition by the United Kingdom of a sovereign ruler under her protection is closely connected with the right of protection exercised over the ruler concerned, the withdrawal of such recognition would only deprive him of British

---

[1] *House of Commons Debates*, vol. 587, *Written Answers*, col. 111, 8 May 1958.

[2] *The Times*, 11 July 1958.

[3] *The Times*, 11 July 1958. 'The removal of a native ruler', commented the Editor of *The Times*, 'for whatever cause, is apt to have serious consequences.' It is interesting to note that in June 1965, a similar incident happened in the Arabian Gulf when the Shaikh of Sharjah, Saqr ibn Sultan, 'was deposed, officially, by a unanimous decision of his own family and replaced by a cousin'. It was no secret then that the Ruler's deposition was the work of the British Government which objected to his determination to accept Arab League financial assistance. The other six Trucial States' Rulers refused to accept the Arab League's funds unless they were channelled through the British sponsored Development Fund (T.S.D.F.). See the Economist Intelligence Unit, *Quarterly Economic Review*, No. 22, July 1965, p. 21.

H

protection and no more. In other words, the withdrawal of British recognition from a ruler does not automatically deprive him of his inherent title as a ruler. In the case *Mighell* v. *Sultan of Johore* (1894), Kay, L. J. analysed the obligations arising from a treaty of protection concluded between the Sultan of Johore, a ruler of one of the former States of Malay, and the British Government as follows:

> The Agreement of the Sultan not to enter into treaties with other Powers does not seem to me to be an abnegation of his right to enter into such treaties, but only a condition upon which the protection stipulated for is given. If the Sultan disregards it, the consequence may be the loss of that protection . . .[1]

By way of conclusion, it may be stated that if there is any right for the United Kingdom to depose, by the use of force, a ruler who disregards his treaties of protection, this appears to be a matter of power, as it has been illustrated in the Lahej controversy. The legal problem in terms of strict law remains unresolved.

Treaties with third states

The question to be considered here is whether the Gulf States have the capacity to conclude treaties with foreign States. At the outset, it is necessary to distinguish between the position of the Sultanate of Muscat on the one hand, and the Shaikhdoms on the other.

(i) Treaty-making capacity of Muscat

Muscat, not being under the protection of the United Kingdom or any other State, has full capacity to conclude treaties or international agreements with foreign Powers. It has, in fact, concluded treaties not only with the United Kingdom, but also with France, the Netherlands, United States of America and India. British treaties with Muscat are published in both the British official treaty series and the United Nations treaty series.[2]

It has been argued, however, that, in some respects, the treaty-making power of the Sultan of Muscat is limited. Owing to the provisions of the Agreement of 1891,[3] he cannot conclude treaties with foreign Powers the object of which is 'to cede, sell . . . or otherwise give for occupation . . . the dominions of Muscat and Oman or any of their dependencies'. However, there is no basis for this argument now, because the Agreement of 1891 which had long been regarded by the parties as obsolete, was already formally terminated by exchange of letters in 1958.[4]

---

[1] [1894] 1 Q.B., 149, at pp. 161–2.   [2] See above, pp. 52–7.
[3] See above, p. 48.   [4] See above, p. 69.

(ii) *Treaty-making capacity of the Shaikhdoms*

It appears from the provisions of the treaties of the Shaikhdoms with the United Kingdom that the Rulers deprived themselves of the right to enter into treaties or international agreements with foreign States without first obtaining the consent and approval of the British Government.[1] This, however, does not mean that these Shaikhdoms have lost their treaty-making capacity *in toto*, but that their power to conclude treaties has been conditioned by the consent of the British Government.[2] This limitation on the treaty-making power of the Shaikhdoms presents the following question: What are the effects of treaties concluded by these Shaikhdoms with foreign States without the consent of the United Kingdom Government? Can such treaties be considered as internationally binding?

The general principles of international law on this question are as follows:

As regards treaties concluded by protected States in disregard of their treaties of protection, Oppenheim states:

Protected States may conclude treaties if so authorised by the protecting State or the treaty establishing the protectorate. An instrument is void as a treaty if concluded in disregard of the international limitations upon the capacity of the parties to conclude treaties.[3]

On the question whether treaties concluded by protected States in excess of their power are void or merely voidable, there are differences of views among writers. Thus, according to Hyde,

. . . such a limitation does not necessarily imply that treaties at variance

---

[1] See Chapters 2–5. As already mentioned, this discussion deals with the former status of Kuwait as a British protected State. Now, after her independence on 19 June 1961, Kuwait possesses full treaty-making capacity.

[2] Examples of cases where treaty-making capacity has been lost completely can be found in Hertslet, *Map of Africa by Treaty*, op. cit., pp. 290 et seq. By virtue of these treaties the African tribal chiefs placed themselves and their territories under the sovereignty of the Crown. See also for a description of these treaties, Snow, op. cit., p. 126, where he states: '. . . treaties with aboriginal tribes, instead of attempting to regulate the relations between the State exercising sovereignty and the tribe . . . are made for the purposes of arranging the terms of guardianship to be exercised on the tribe.' These tribes are described as possessing no treaty-making capacity whatsoever. See ibid., pp. 118–26.

[3] Oppenheim, pp. 882–3. On the treaty-making capacity of protected States Hersch Lauterpacht says: 'There is an occasional tendency to assume that such States, "not being members of the international community", possess no power to conclude treaties. This statement, which is probably inaccurate, seems to beg the question. The status of a political entity as a member of the international community depends on various factors, including the capacity to conclude treaties. This does not necessarily mean that the capacity to conclude treaties depends on the status as a member of the international community'. See *International Law Commission*, 1953, op. cit., p. 144.

with it which are concluded by the dependent entity are without any legal value.[1]

He explains his statement by saying:

In a word, the weakness of a treaty attributable to the dependent status of a contracting party is generally such as to render voidable rather than void commitments with States other than the protector. The practice of nations seemingly supports this conclusion.[2]

Hall, on the other hand, takes a different view. He says:

All contracts therefore are void which are entered into by such (protected) States in excess of the powers retained by, or conceded to, them under their existing relations with associated or superior States.[3]

As regards the United Kingdom Government's practice, Lord McNair states:

Whether treaties which a dependent State purports to conclude in defiance of this incapacity or in excess of this limited capacity, as the case may be, are *ipso facto* void or merely voidable at the instance of the dominant State, is a question upon which it is believed the United Kingdom Government has not found occasion to define its position.[4]

However, he maintains the view that this is a question

which does not admit of a general answer, since the precise terms and circumstances of the connection between the two States require analysis in each case.[5]

In one instance, Lord McNair refers to the Opinion of the British Law Officers of the Crown expressed on the validity of the Treaty of 27 April 1896, concluded by the South African Republic (known formerly as the Transvaal Republic) in violation of its Convention of

---

[1] Hyde, 2, p. 1377.

[2] Ibid., p. 1378. According to Hyde, 'In the course of the nineteenth century, some States paid no nice regard to the conditions or relationship of dependency upon Turkey of certain backward countries with which treaties were sought and concluded.' See ibid. See also for examples of such treaties, Hackworth. *Digest of International Law*, vol. V (1943), pp. 153–4. It is stated here that in the case of the United States of America Treaty of 1805 with Tripoli, the United States of America took the view that 'its treaty of 1805 with Tripoli was valid and binding although it was made with the Regency of Tripoli at a time when Tripoli was semi-independent. There was no indication that Turkey, the suzerain, was consulted.' Moreover, Hyde says, 'The relationship of Bulgaria to the Sultan of Turkey roughly and perhaps vaguely set forth in the Treaty of Berlin of 1878, did not serve greatly to deter the former from concluding various treaties with numerous States. Such few objections as were raised by the suzerain generally proved to be ineffectual.' See Hyde, p. 1378.   [3] Hall, p. 380.

[4] McNair, *Treaties*, p. 173. But see now the attitude of the United Kingdom as shown in 1958, in the case of the Treaty concluded between Bahrain and Saudi Arabia, below, pp. 104–6.   [5] McNair, *Treaties*, p. 138.

27 February 1884 with Great Britain. The Law Officers of the Crown were of the opinion that the Treaty of 1896 was invalid. They stated: 'Although the particular Treaty now in question may not be in itself of great importance the principle involved is obviously of the utmost gravity. . . .'[1]

On the other hand, Lord McNair suggests that where the

dependent State is allowed to conclude treaties subject to the communication of them to the dominant State and to the latter's veto within a certain period, it would seem probable that the former's treaties are only voidable, being made subject to a resolutive condition, and are valid until timously vetoed.[2]

He mentions as an example of such treaties which were regarded as voidable rather than void, the Treaty of the Transvaal Republic of 1896, referred to above.

On the question of the nature of the international responsibility of States contracting with protected States without the knowledge or consent of the protecting Power, the general principles of law are formulated as follows:

According to Hyde,

In the negotiation of treaties with dependent States the burden rests upon the other contracting parties to ascertain the scope of the agreement-making power retained by the former, as well as the mode by which it is to be exercised. Those parties assume the risk of obtaining provisions that a superior, if alive to its rights and interests, may both regard as voidable and encounter no difficulty in rendering valueless, at least if recourse be had to an arbitral forum.[3]

Similarly, Lord McNair states:

Moreover, it is believed that it is the duty of a State when contracting with a dependent State to satisfy itself as to the scope of the latter's treaty-making power and the procedure prescribed for its exercise, and that a State concluding in ignorance with a dependent State a treaty which is in excess of the latter's powers has no legal redress against the latter or its dominant State.[4]

The views of writers regarding the treaty-making capacity of protected States are inconclusive. In the opinion of Hersch Lauterpacht, the distinction between the view that such treaties are void and the

---

[1] Ibid., p. 140.

[2] Ibid., p., 138.

[3] Hyde, 2, pp. 1378–9. According to Hyde (who quotes from the *A.J.I.L.*, Suppl. No. XXXIX, p. 709), there exists no decision of an international tribunal 'which declares that a treaty is invalid for a lack of capacity of a party which had previously placed itself under obligation to another State agreeing not to enter such a treaty'. See ibid., p. 1379, n. (8).

[4] McNair, *Treaties*, p. 145.

view that they are merely voidable 'is probably without a practical difference'. But he sums up his view on this question thus:

> As the question is one of status imposed not as the result of any general operation of a rule of law but in consequence of a—usually bilateral—treaty, it is probably unnecessary in this case to follow what is apparently the correct logical conclusion and to hold that a treaty concluded in disregard of the contractual capacity of the dependent State is unalterably and irremediably void. It is preferable to regard the absence of protest on the part of the superior State as equivalent to acquiescence amounting to a renunciation of the limiting provisions of the original treaty.[1]

Bilateral treaties

Generally speaking, the only foreign State with which the Gulf Shaikhdoms have maintained treaty relations is Saudi Arabia. There exist in these Shaikhdoms no constitutional procedures for the conclusion or ratification of treaties. The Rulers of these Shaikhdoms are, in fact, the sole authority from which the right to conclude treaties can be derived.[2] However, owing to their treaties with the United Kingdom, to which reference has been made, the Rulers are required to obtain the approval of the United Kingdom's Government before they can commit themselves to any sort of treaties with foreign States. As pointed out above, these treaties do not deprive them of the capacity to conclude treaties, but they only limit their capacity to do so.[3] The result is that if the Rulers conclude treaties with foreign States, without obtaining the consent of the British Government, these treaties do not, in the light of the preceding principles of international law, possess international validity.

In connection with the consent of the British Government required for the conclusion of treaties by the Rulers, there appears to be in practice no special procedure by which this consent can be obtained. This question, however, does not seem to present an important problem, since in concluding their treaties with Saudi Arabia, the Shaikhdoms were, with only one exception which will be noted below, always represented by the British Government. This may, perhaps, be more clearly explained by referring to the following examples of the particular procedure adopted in each treaty or agreement concluded by an individual Shaikhdom:

1. *Agreement between Bahrain and Saudi Arabia, 16 November 1935*[4]

This agreement is entitled, 'Exchange of Notes Between His Majesty's Government in the United Kingdom and the Government of Saudi Arabia Regarding Transit Dues at Bahrain, 16 November 1935.'

---

[1] See *International Law Commission*, 1953, op. cit., p. 144.
[2] See Chapter 1.   [3] See Chapters 2–5.
[4] *Treaty Series*, No. 7 (1936), *Cmd.* 5168.

The British Note to the Saudi Minister for Foreign Affairs, signed by the British Minister at Jiddah, states:

I have the honour to inform your Royal Highness, in accordance with instructions addressed to me by His Majesty's Principal Secretary of State for Foreign Affairs, that His Majesty's Government in the United Kingdom have taken cognisance of the proceedings at the conference held in March and April of this year between delegates of the Governments of Saudi Arabia and Bahrain, and that they are prepared to enter into an agreement, *on behalf of and with the consent of the Government of Bahrain* regarding the treatment of goods destined for or exported from ports in Saudi Arabia. . . .

The last paragraph of the Note (Paragraph 7) states:

I am instructed to suggest that, if the arrangements set forth above are agreeable to the Government of Saudi Arabia, your Royal Highness will inform me accordingly, and that this note and your reply thereto shall be held to constitute a binding agreement between the parties.

(Signed) Mr A. S. Calvert.

It can be seen from the above provisions that the negotiations for the agreement in question took place directly between the Governments of Bahrain and Saudi Arabia without the participation of the British Government, but that the agreement did not assume its binding force in view of the British Government until the Notes were exchanged between the United Kingdom Government and Saudi Arabia. Nevertheless the italicised sentence in the first paragraph of the Note suggests that the British Government did not consider itself entitled to conclude such an agreement without first obtaining the explicit consent of the Bahrain Government.

2. *Treaties between Kuwait and Saudi Arabia, 1942*

(a) *Agreement for Friendship and Neighbourly Relations between The Government of the United Kingdom (acting on behalf of His Highness the Shaikh of Kuwait) and the Government of Saudi Arabia, Jiddah, 20 April 1942*[1]

(b) *Trade Agreement between Kuwait and Saudi Arabia (The United Kingdom Government acting on behalf of Kuwait), Jiddah, 20 April 1942*[2]

(c) *Agreement for the Extradition of Offenders (The United Kingdom Government acting on behalf of Kuwait), Jiddah, 20 April 1942.*[3]

---

[1] *Treaty Series*, No. 1 (1942), *Cmd.* 6380; U.N. *Treaty Series*, No. 57, vol. 10, p. 117.
[2] *Treaty Series*, No. 2 (1942), *Cmd.* 6381; U.N. *Treaty Series*, No. 58, vol. 10, p. 151.
[3] *Treaty Series*, No. 3 (1942), *Cmd.* 6386; U.N. *Treaty Series*, No. 56, vol. 10, p. 99.

As the terms of the above-mentioned agreements are of a technical nature, they, therefore, do not require any comment at this point. Suffice it to say, however, that they were concluded with Saudi Arabia by the British Minister Plenipotentiary in the Kingdom of Saudi Arabia. Their titles show clearly that the British Government in signing them was acting on behalf, and with the consent, of the Ruler of Kuwait.

It is worthy of note that an article is inserted in the agreements under discussion respecting their ratifications which reads:

Instruments of ratification shall be exchanged by the two contracting parties as soon as possible. It shall come into force as from the date of the exchange of instruments of ratification and shall be valid for a period of five years from that date.[1]

It is not clear whether this provision refers to ratification by the British Government in the United Kingdom, or by the Ruler of Kuwait himself. If the provision refers to ratification by the United Kingdom Government, the question arises whether a Ruler can decline to recognise an agreement so ratified if he is not satisfied with its terms. It is submitted that if the interests of the Rulers are considered to be paramount in every single agreement concluded for them, it may, therefore, be reasonable to assume that a Ruler cannot be forced to accept an agreement the terms of which do not meet with his approval. It is probably equally true to say that the United Kingdom would be unwilling to ratify an agreement concluded on behalf of a Ruler without first consulting him and satisfying herself that the agreement as a whole was accepted by him.[2]

3. *Sea-Boundary Agreement between Bahrain and Saudi Arabia, 22 February 1958*[3]

This agreement defines the respective rights of Bahrain and Saudi Arabia in the off-shore areas lying between their territories. A summary of the contents of this agreement is to be found in chapter 17 below. The significance of the reference to this agreement in this context lies in the fact that it represents what appears to be a major

[1] See Articles 12 and 10 of the above Agreements.

[2] But see above, pp. 88–9 regarding the controversy over the Anglo-Ethiopian treaty of 1897, concluded by the British Government in the name of the Somaliland Protectorate without the consent of the people of the Protectorate. This case is, however, not analogous to the position of the Shaikhdoms. Thus, where in the case of the Somaliland Protectorate (a colonial Protectorate) sovereignty lies in the British Crown, in the case of the Shaikhdoms (sovereign protected States) sovereignty is inherent in the Rulers themselves.

[3] For text, see Appendix X, and Map 4 at p. 262 below. For Arabic text, see Bahrain Government's Gazette: *Al-Jaridah al-Rasmiyah*, 15 Sha'ban 1377 (corresponding to 6 March 1958).

departure from the established practice regarding the procedure of concluding agreements between the Shaikhdoms and third States. The significant features of the agreement are that it was negotiated, concluded and ratified personally by the Ruler of Bahrain, representing his Government, and King Sa'ud during a friendly visit by the Ruler of Bahrain to Saudi Arabia. Thus, contrary to former practice, the United Kingdom took no actual part in its conclusion or ratification. However, it appears from two private letters which were exchanged between the Ruler of Bahrain and the British Political Agent in Bahrain, after the Ruler's return from his visit to Saudi Arabia, that the 'consent' of the British Government required for the validation of the Agreement was given after its conclusion.

Because of the new light which these two letters shed on the conclusion and ratification of the agreement by the Ruler and the procedure by which the United Kingdom communicated her approval, it seems desirable to quote some relevant extracts from these letters.

On 16 *Ramadhan* 1377, corresponding 5 April 1958, the Ruler of Bahrain wrote a letter to the British Political Agent in Bahrain in the following terms:

With reference to the letter of His Excellency the Political Resident of 21st December, 1957, concerning the frontiers between Bahrain and Saudi Arabia, and what was mentioned in it about the possibility of settling the matter directly by us and Saudi Arabia, and concerning the agreement of Her Majesty's Government to that step. . . .

During our visit to Riyyad an offer for a frontier settlement was presented to us. We studied, amended and gave it initial signature because we saw that it was in the interest of our country. That term of settlement was presented to His Excellency the Resident and yourself immediately on our return, and when it received your acceptance we arranged for ratification of the agreement in a final form, copies of which were sent to your Excellency together with a frontier map.

We are aware of the fact that the agreement does not include all the required points to implement it. As it was ratified in a friendly attitude and good will, we thought it best not to try to include them in the text of the agreement itself, leaving it to the suitable time to deal with it, at which it could be cleared by an agreement acceptable to both parties.

Finally, we consider that agreement which we have made is in the interest of our country and Government, and we therefore ratified it after it having met our and your acceptance.

(Signed) Salman bin Hamad Al-Khalifa.[1]

---

[1] This is a translation by the Bahrain Government Secretariat of an Arabic letter from the Ruler of Bahrain to the British Political Agent in Bahrain, obtained from the Archives of the Bahrain Government, Secretariat, *File of Confidential Correspondence Regarding Bahrain-Saudi Arab Boundaries*, 1959.

The Political Agent in Bahrain replied on 21 April 1958 saying (*inter alia*) that:

Her Majesty's Government in the United Kingdom were prepared formally to waive the provisions of the Agreements of 1880 and 1892 in so far as the Agreement between the Ruler and King Saud was concerned, and that, so far as Her Majesty's Government were concerned, the Agreement was thereupon given international validity.[1]

Multilateral treaties: accession to international agreements and participation in international organisations

(a) *The general practice of the United Kingdom in respect of the application of international agreements to territories for whose international relations she is responsible*

In so far as British treaty practice is concerned, it is recognised that

a treaty concluded by the United Kingdom might not be applicable *ipso facto* in its overseas territories, and it was thought necessary to make express provisions for the application of the treaty to all the Dominions and possessions of the contracting parties. . . .[2]

According to J. E. S. Fawcett, there are three possible ways by which a treaty concluded by the United Kingdom can apply to her overseas territories:

provisions for application *ipso facto* upon acceptance of the treaty by the United Kingdom, provisions for some or all of the overseas territories to become separate parties to the treaty and inclusion of the colonial application clause.

But, in cases, he says, where

there is no express provision in the treaty itself, it becomes a question of interpretation whether it is to be read as applicable to the overseas territories as well as to the United Kingdom.[3]

The present practice of the United Kingdom with regard to the conclusion of treaties for her overseas territories is in concurrence with the adoption of the so-called 'colonial' clause.[4]

According to Fawcett, the function of the 'colonial article' has been

to bridge the gap between the dependent status of the overseas territories in international law and their independence of the Government of the

---

[1] Extract from a letter from Deputy Legal Adviser of the Foreign Office, 2 June 1958, published by E. Lauterpacht, *I.C.L.Q.*, 7 (1958), p. 519.

[2] McNair, *Treaties*, p. 77.

[3] Fawcett, J. E. S., 'Treaty Relations of British Overseas Territories', *B.Y.I.L.*, 26 (1949), p. 101.

[4] For illustrations on this practice, see *U.N.L.S.*, Treaties (1953), 123; McNair, *Treaties*, p. 77.

United Kingdom in certain administrative and technical fields under constitutional law and practice.[1]

There appears to be no one rigid form for expressing the 'colonial clause' in treaties.[2]

The United Kingdom has encouraged the practice of allowing some of her overseas territories which are self-governing to become separate parties to agreements 'creating international organisations'.[3] The formalities of concluding such agreements are, of course, being executed by the United Kingdom.[4] On this principle, self-governing territories and other foreign overseas territories (i.e., protectorates and protected States) are, in some respects, allowed to acquire separate memberships in International Organisations.[5] The practice of allowing such territories to join, as separate members, International Organisations is, in principle, based on the recognition that they possess 'a measure of treaty-making power' and a degree of international personality.[6] It may be desirable to mention some instances where an originally non-self-governing territory is granted by the Crown a self-government and certain aspects of international personality, including the right to enter into treaties, or certain categories of treaties, with foreign States. More recent examples of this practice are (i) The Federation of Rhodesia and Nyasaland; (ii) The State of Singapore. In the case of (i), a joint announcement in London in April 1957 between the Government of the Federation of Rhodesia and Nyasaland and the Government of the United Kingdom stated that

the Federal Constitution provides that matters of External affairs may, from time to time, be entrusted to the Federation.[7]

As regards (ii), the Constitution of the State of Singapore (formerly Singapore colony) entrusts to the State the conduct of certain classes of foreign relations, including entering into some treaties, as follows: Section 73 (1) & (2) states that:

(1) The Government of Singapore, acting with the assent of the United Kingdom, shall be responsible for the conduct of matters concerning the trade and cultural relations of Singapore with other Countries.[8]

---

[1] Fawcett, op. cit., p. 106.

[2] For illustrations, see *U.N.L.S.*, op. cit., p. 124.

[3] Fawcett, op. cit., p. 101.

[4] See Oppenheim, p. 882; Fawcett, op. cit., p. 102.

[5] Ibid.   [6] Oppenheim, p. 884.

[7] *House of Commons Debates*, vol. 569, col. 537, 2 May 1957; See also Lauterpacht, E., 'Contemporary Practice of the United Kingdom in the Field of International Law, Part IV', *I.C.L.Q.*, 6 (1957), p. 506.

[8] See *The State of Singapore Act*, 1958, 6 & 7 Eliz., 2.c.59; *The Singapore (Constitution) Order in Council*, 1958, *S.I.* 1958, No. 1956. See also Lauterpacht, E., 'Contemporary Practice of the United Kingdom in the Field of International Law, Part VII', *I.C.L.Q.*, 8 (1959), p. 146.

(b) *Past and present practice regarding accession by the Gulf States to international agreements*

The United Kingdom had in the past applied certain international conventions to the Arabian Gulf region, without specifically mentioning that she was doing so on behalf of the States concerned in that region.[1] For example, in the International Sanitary Convention, signed by the United Kingdom in Paris on 17 January 1917, a provision was incorporated regarding the Arabian Gulf States generally. This provision was made in Article 83 (Section VI, Part 2) which stated:

La règlementation sanitaire telle qu'elle est instituée par les articles de la présente Convention, en ce qui concerne le Golfe Persique . . . et ses ports.[2]

Similarly, Article VI, No. 3 (Ch. II) of the International Convention Relative to the Control of the Trade in Arms and Ammunitions signed by the United Kingdom on 10 September 1919 provided:

La Zone maritime comprenant le Golfe Persique . . . et ses ports seront subordonnés a l'observation des prescriptions analogues mises en vigueur par le Gouvernement qui exerce l'autorité.[3]

It may be observed that in this Convention the Shaikhdoms were not mentioned separately. Subsequently, Muscat acceded to the Convention as a separate party.[4]

Later, in 1949, the Shaikhdoms became separate parties to the International Wheat Agreement which they signed on 29 March

---

[1] It should be remarked again that this discussion does not include Muscat, since as an independent State she has full capacity to enter into international agreements without the requirement of the consent of the United Kingdom. As regards Kuwait, the discussion is applicable to her only during the time when she was still a British protected State.

[2] See Hertslet, *Commercial Treaties*, vol. 27 (1917), p. 337.

[3] Ibid., vol. 29 (1919), p. 124.

[4] Hertslet, op. cit., p. 124. Note that there is nothing in practice to prevent protectorates becoming separate parties to international organisations. However, such practice appears to have been restricted to certain types of protectorates—the International Protectorates—which are regarded as possessing certain attributes of international personality. For example, the former Protectorates of Tunisia and Morocco were separate parties to a number of International Conventions, such as: (1) Sanitary Convention of 21 June 1926; (2) International Convention for the Protection of Industrial Property of 2 June 1934; (3) Convention of the Unification of the Methods of Analysis of Wines in Industrial Commerce, 5 June 1935.
   For a fuller account about the procedure of accession to these Conventions, see Hudson, *International Legislations*, vol. III (1925–27), pp. 1903–4; Ibid., vol. VI (1932–4), pp. 307–71; Ibid., vol. VII (1935–7), pp. 88–9. For the separate memberships of the Protectorates of Tunisia and Morocco in the Convention on Anti-Diphtheritic Serum, signed at Paris, 1 August 1930, see The League of Nations, *Treaty Series*, No. 2932, vol. CXXVIII, 1932, p. 9.

1949. But they withdrew from it in June 1950.[1] The Shaikhdom's application for both accession to and withdrawal from this Agreement was made for them by the British Government.[2]

The Shaikhdoms are now parties to a number of multilateral conventions which were applied to them by the United Kingdom under the so-called 'territorial application clause', entitled 'other non-metropolitan territories for the international relations of which the United Kingdom is responsible'.[3] Although it is not practicable to make an exhaustive list of all the international conventions to which the Shaikhdoms have automatically become parties through this procedure, it may be useful to examine the procedures under which some of these conventions and agreements were applied to the Shaikhdoms:

1. International Bank for Reconstruction and Development Agreement (IBRD) and International Monetary Fund Agreement (IMF) of 27 December 1945[4]

The United Kingdom's signature and acceptance of the Articles of Agreements of the IBRD and the IMF took place on 27 December 1945. By Article XI(2) (g) of the IBRD Agreement and Article XX(2) (g) of the IMF Agreement, it is provided that by their signature of these Articles of Agreements all States accept them 'both on their own behalf and in respect of their colonies, overseas territories, all territories under their protection, suzerainty or authority. . . .' Consequently, the United Kingdom's acceptance of the Agreements extended automatically to the Shaikhdoms in their capacity as States under her

---

[1] See *British and Foreign State Papers*, vol. 153 (1950), p. 154.

[2] Ibid. For the International Wheat Agreement, 1959, see *Treaty Series*, No. 28 (1960), *Cmnd.* 1074. United Kingdom's acceptance of the Agreement was deposited on 14 July 1959. This Agreement was extended to British Colonies on 25 November 1959. Among these, some British protectorates, such as Zanzibar, were included. The Federation of Rhodesia and Nyasaland acceded to it separately, on 9 July 1959. No mention of the Gulf States was made either under the list of accession or under the list of extension.

[3] In addition, the United Kingdom has, through the procedure of the 'territorial application clause', applied to the Shaikhdoms a number of bilateral treaties which she has concluded with foreign governments. Examples of such bilateral treaties are: Consular Convention with Norway (*U.K.T.S.*, No. 55 (1958), *Cmd.* 509); Consular Convention with the United States (*U.K.T.S.* No. 37 (1958), *Cmd.* 524); Consular Convention with Sweden (*U.K.T.S.* No. 70 (1954), *Cmd.* 9340); Consular Convention with France (*U.K.T.S.* No. 4 (1959), *Cmd.* 617); Consular Convention with West Germany (*U.K.T.S.* No. 2 (1959), *Cmd.* 607); Exchange of Notes with Switzerland on the Abolition of Visas for British Protected Persons (*U.K.T.S.* Suppl. List, No. 61 (1958), *Cmd.* 642); Agreement with UNESCO on Aid to United Kingdom's Dependent Territories (*U.K.T.S.* No. 46 (1956), *Cmd.* 9873); Agreement with UNICEF on Assistance in any Territory for which the United Kingdom is Responsible (*U.K.T.S.* No. 75 (1953), *Cmd.* 8981); Agreement with Special Fund on Assistance to Territories for which the United Kingdom is Responsible (*U.K.T.S.* No. 15 (1960), *Cmd.* 995).

[4] *U.K.T.S.*, No. 21 (1946), *Cmd.* 6885; *U.N.T.S.* vol. 2, pp. 40, 134.

protection, as provided in the above-mentioned Articles. As regards Kuwait, she ceased to be bound by the Agreements after 1961, since the 'territorial application clause' in the Agreements could no longer apply to her after that date. However, on 13 September 1962 Kuwait formally accepted the Articles of the two Agreements in her own right as an independent sovereign State.[1]

2. The General Agreement of Tariff and Trade (GATT), dated 30 October 1947.[2]

The United Kingdom which became a signatory to GATT from 28 July 1948, notified the Secretary-General of the United Nations on that date that she proposed under Article XXVI, 5(a) of the Agreement, to apply it provisionally to all territories for the international relations of which she was responsible, with the exception of Jamaica. In this respect, the Arabian Gulf Shaikhdoms have become bound by the provisions of the Agreement.[3] Regarding Kuwait, in particular, the United Kingdom specifically applied the Agreement to her in 1951.[4] And in November 1961, a few months after Kuwait's full independence, the United Kingdom, in line with procedures adopted by the Contracting Parties in 1957, informed the Executive Secretary of GATT that Kuwait had acquired full autonomy in her external commercial relations, and that it was then for her to decide on the question of her future position *vis-à-vis* the Agreement. Consequently, as Kuwait wished to become a contracting party to the GATT in her own right, she was advised to adopt one of three methods: (*a*) To become a contracting party under Article XXVI 5(c), 'immediately and automatically', by virtue of sponsorship by the United Kingdom which was formerly responsible for Kuwait's international relations. (*b*) To request that the Contracting Parties should, for a period of two years, apply the GATT to Kuwait on a *de facto* basis provided that she continues to apply the GATT *de facto* to other Contracting Parties. (*c*) To apply for accession in her own right as a new member, under Article XXXIII, and negotiate her way with Contracting Parties 'with a view to exchanging tariff concessions on a reciprocal and mutually advantageous basis'.[5] Having considered these three alternatives with regard to her membership of the GATT, Kuwait decided in November

[1] Archives of the Ministry of Foreign Affairs, Kuwait.

[2] *U.K.T.S.* (1961), *Cmnd.* 7258 and *Cmnd.* 9413; *U.N.T.S.*, vol. 55, p. 194.

[3] Ibid. The provisions of Article XXVI 5(a) of the GATT states that 'each Government accepting this Agreement does so in respect of its metropolitan territory and of the other territories for which it has international responsibility, except such separate customs territories as it shall notify to the Secretary-General of the United Nations at the time of its own acceptance'.   [4] Ibid.

[5] Private Correspondence and Notes on the Procedures for Accession to GATT and the Advantages for Less-Developed Countries, Issued by the Executive Secretary of GATT in October 1961 and January 1962, MGT (61)30.

1962, to apply the Agreement on a *de facto* basis for a period of two years, as provided in (*b*) above. The two-year period was to run from 19 June 1961, the date on which Kuwait formally assumed full responsibility for her international relations. After the expiry of this period, Kuwait opted to join the GATT under Article XXVI 5(c), through the United Kingdom's sponsorship.[1]

3. The Geneva Conventions relating to (a) the amelioration of the condition of the wounded and sick in armed forces in the field, (b) the amelioration of the condition of the wounded, sick and shipwrecked members of armed forces at sea, (c) the treatment of prisoners of war, and (d) the protection of civilian persons in time of war, signed at Geneva on 12 August 1949.[2]

At the time of the deposit of the instrument of ratification of the above four conventions on 23 September 1957 the United Kingdom made the following declaration to the Swiss Federal Political Department:

The United Kingdom . . . will apply each of the above-mentioned Conventions in the British Protected States of Bahrain, Kuwait, Qatar and the Trucial States to the extent of Her Majesty's power in relation to these territories.[3]

4. Supplementary Convention on the abolition of slavery, the slave trade and institutions and practices similar to slavery, done at Geneva on 7 September 1956.[4]

The United Kingdom ratified this convention on 30 April 1957, the same date on which it entered into force. And on 6 September 1957 the United Kingdom had, in compliance with the convention's territorial application Article 12(2), notified the Secretary-General of the United Nations of its extension to 'Bahrain, Qatar, The Trucial States (Abu Dhabi, Ajman, Dubai, Fujairah, Ras al-Khaimah, Sharjah and Umm al-Qaiwain)', as being part of those 'other non-metropolitan territories for the international relations of which the United Kingdom is responsible'.[5] Similarly, under this Article the United Kingdom extended the convention to Kuwait on 21 October 1957.[6] After her independence, Kuwait ceased to be bound by this convention under the procedure mentioned above. It was therefore

---

[1] Archives of the Ministry of Foreign Affairs, Kuwait.
[2] *U.N.T.S.* vol. 75, p. 85, vol. 78, p. 366, and vol. 84, p. 414.
[3] Ibid., vol. 278, pp. 259–66.
[4] *U.N.T.S.* vol. 266, p. 40; *U.K.T.S.* No. 59 (1957), *Cmnd.* 257.
[5] *U.N.T.S.* vol. 276, p. 370. It is to be noted that Article 12(2) under which the convention was applied to the Gulf States provides for obtaining the consent of the non-metropolitan territory concerned before applying the convention to it.
[6] *U.N.T.S.* vol. 278, p. 313; *U.K.T.S.*, No. 59 (1957), *Cmnd.*, 257.

necessary for her to accede to the convention as a new fully fledged member under Article 11(2). This procedure was finally adopted when Kuwait acceded to the convention in her own right on 18 January 1963.[1]

(c) *Membership of international organisations*

The Shaikhdom of Kuwait may be cited as an example of how an Arabian Gulf Shaikhdom can, while still being under the protection of the United Kingdom, become, as a separate entity, a member of certain Specialised Agencies of the United Nations. It may be useful, therefore, for the purpose of ascertaining the extent of the treaty-making power of the Gulf Shaikhdoms, to mention here some of the International Organisations of the United Nations joined by Kuwait when she was technically still a British protected State. In chronological order, these are: (1) International Telecommunication Union of 22 December 1952.[2] (2) World Health Organisation of 7 April 1948.[3] (3) International Civil Aviation Organisation of 7 December 1944.[4] (4) Universal Postal Union of 5 July 1947 (as revised at Brussels on 11 July 1952).[5] (5) Inter-Governmental Maritime Consultative Organisation of 6 March 1948.[6] (6) United Nations Education, Scientific and Cultural Organisation of 16 November 1945.[7]

---

[1] *U.K.T.S.* (1st. Suppl. List of Ratification, etc., for 1963), No. 51 (1963), *Cmnd.* 2070. Also for Kuwait's accession to the Slavery Convention, as amended by the Protocol signed on 7 December 1963, see *U.K.T.S.* (3rd. Suppl. List of Ratification, etc., for 1963), No. 91 (1963), *Cmnd.* 2225.

[2] For text, see Peaslee, A. J., *International Organisations*, vol. II, 1956, p. 394. And see *U.K.T.S.*, No. 76 (1950), *Cmd.*, 8124. Kuwait's accession to the Convention of the Union on August 14, 1959. See *U.K.T.S.* (3rd. Suppl. List of Ratification, etc., for 1959), No. 76 (1959), *Cmnd.* 866, p. 6.

[3] For Constitution, see *U.N.T.S.* vol. 14, p. 185. And see *B.Y.I.L.*, 24 (1947), p. 451. Kuwait's accession to the Constitution of WHO was on 9 May 1960. See *U.K.T.S.* (3rd. Suppl. List of Ratification, etc., for 1960), No. 74 (1960), *Cmnd.*, 1186, p. 5.

[4] *U.N.T.S.* vol. 15, p. 295. And see *U.K.T.S.*, No. 8 (1953), *Cmd.*, 8742. Kuwait acceded to the Convention of the Organisation on 18 May 1960. See *U.K.T.S.* (3rd. Suppl. List of Ratification, etc., for 1960), No. 74 (1960), *Cmnd.*, 1186, p. 2. It is to be noted also that Kuwait concluded with the United Kingdom on 24 May, 1960, an Agreement for Air services between and beyond Respective Territories. See *U.K.T.S.*, No. 6 (1960), *Cmnd.* 1168.

[5] For text, see Peaslee, op. cit., p. 736. And see *U.K.T.S.*, No. 57 (1949), *Cmd.*, 7794. For Kuwait's accession in June 1960, see U.N. *Press Release*, New York, I.C.A.O./426, 15 June 1960.

[6] *U.N.T.S.* vol. 11, p. 107. Kuwait joined the Organisation on 5 July 1960. See *U.K.T.S.* (3rd. Suppl. List of Ratification, etc., of 1960), No. 74 (1960), *Cmnd.*, 1186, p. 6. It is to be noted also that, through the United Kingdom's sponsorship, Kuwait acceded to the International Load Lines Convention of 5 July 1930, and the International Convention of Safety of Life at Sea of 10 June 1948, on 12 January 1959. See *U.K.T.S.*, No. 39 (1959), *Cmnd.*, 727, pp. 4–5.

[7] For Constitution, see *U.N.T.S.*, vol. 4, p. 275. And see *U.K.T.S.*, No. 50 (1946), *Cmd.* 6963. Kuwait acceded to UNESCO as full member on 25 July 1960, having

It is noteworthy that the Constitutions of a number of International Organisations contain provisions for membership of States which are not members of the United Nations. Moreover, some of these Constitutions provide for full membership of States which are not fully independent, and these Constitutions also provide for associate membership of non-independent territories whose international relations are controlled by a State member of the United Nations.[1] It appears that Kuwait joined the above International Organisations under those provisions for membership of sovereign States which are not members of the United Nations.[2]

The procedure by which Kuwait acceded to the Constitution of UNESCO will now be described.

On 2 June 1960 the Director-General of UNESCO wrote to the Secretary-General of the United Nations saying:

I have the honour to inform you that on 28th April, I received application dated 25th April, 1960, from His Highness the Ruler of Kuwait, for Kuwait's admission to membership of the UNESCO.

I enclose a copy of the application, together with a copy of a letter from the United Kingdom Foreign Office stating that Her Majesty's Government regards Kuwait as responsible for the conduct of her international relations, and I should be grateful if you cause it to be laid before the Economic and Social Council in its 30th Session.[3]

The application of the Ruler of Kuwait, dated 25 April 1960, for membership of UNESCO was couched in the following terms:

In accordance with the provisions of Chapter XVI of the Rules of Procedure of the General Conference of (UNESCO), I hereby submit an application on the part of Kuwait for admission to full membership of the Organisation. I request that this application be transferred to the Economic

---

first joined on 30 April 1958, as an Associate Member. See 10th Session of General Conference of UNESCO, 1958, Document 10C./30.

It is to be noted that Bahrain has become an Associate Member of UNESCO, and Qatar had joined the organisation earlier.

[1] Examples of the above provisions can be found in Article 93 of the I.C.A.O. Convention, in Article 3 of the U.P.U. Convention, and in Article 6 of the WHO Constitution. Kuwait was thus admitted to WHO under Article 6 of the WHO Constitution which provides for membership of States which are not members of the United Nations. The admission of Kuwait to WHO was by Resolution WHA 13.11 of 9 May 1960 which stated: 'That the 13th WHA admits Kuwait as a Member of the WHO, subject to the deposit of a formal instrument. . . .' See WHO Bulletin, vol. 23, Nos 2–3, 1960.

[2] For illustrations, see above examples in n. 1.

[3] U.N. *Economic and Social Council*, 30th Session, 1960, Agenda Item 23. Kuwait was admitted to membership of UNESCO on 25 July 1960 (E/Resolution 774(XXX)). For the Note of the Secretary-General of the U.N., dated 17 June, and for the letter of the Director-General of UNESCO, see ibid., E/3363/Add. 2, pp. 1–2.

I

and Social Council of the United Nations in accordance with Article II of the Agreement between the United Nations and (UNESCO) and that it be placed before the Executive Board and, as appropriate, the General Conference of the Organisation, in accordance with the provisions of Article II, paragraph 2, of the Constitution, at the earliest opportunity.

I hereby state, in accordance with the provisions of Rule 92, paragraph 1, of the Rules of Procedure of the General Conference of (UNESCO), that Kuwait is willing to abide by the Constitution of the Organisation, to accept the obligations contained therein, and to contribute to the expenses of the Organisation.[1]

In support of this application, a letter, dated 23 May 1960, from the United Kingdom's Foreign Office to the Director-General of the UNESCO stated:

I am directed by the Secretary of State for Foreign Affairs to state that Her Majesty's Government have been informed that a communication has been addressed by the Ruler of Kuwait to the UNESCO making application on behalf of Kuwait for admission to UNESCO as a full Member State in accordance with paragraph 2 of Article II of the Constitution of the Organisation. Her Majesty's Government hope that arrangements will be made for the application of Kuwait to be considered at the 11th Session of General Conference of UNESCO to be held next November.

I am to state in this connection that Her Majesty's Government regard Kuwait as responsible for the conduct of her international relations.[2]

It may be submitted that the significance of the above-mentioned procedure of admitting Kuwait to full membership of the UNESCO lies in the fact that this Shaikhdom was admitted to the Organisation under the provisions of Article 2, paragraph (2) of its Constitution. This Article specifically provides for membership of 'States not members of the United Nations'. The procedure for membership under this Article requires, as a qualification for such membership, 'two-thirds majority vote of the General Conference' of the Organisation. By securing membership under this procedure, Kuwait was thus regarded by the members of the Organisation as a sovereign State having capacity to enter into international agreements. And the British Government's statement—that 'Her Majesty's Government regard Kuwait as responsible for the conduct of her international relations'—was a confirmation of this fact.

WAR

It has been generally assumed that one of the essential characteristics of States of full international status is their power to declare war, or

---

[1] For the text of the Ruler of Kuwait's Application, signed by Deputy Ruler, Shaikh Sir Abdulla as-Sabah, see U.N. *Economic and Social Council*, E/3363/Add. 2, p. 3.

[2] For the British Foreign Office letter, signed by J. G. Tahourdin, see U.N. Economic and Social Council, E/3363/Add. 2, p. 4.

maintain a position of neutrality on their own authority.[1] Do the Gulf States possess such power and if so to what extent can they go to war independently of the United Kingdom or declare their neutrality in a war in which the United Kingdom Government is a party?

1. *Does a declaration of war on the part of the United Kingdom involve the Gulf States?*

(i) *Muscat*

As already stated, Muscat is not bound to Great Britain by treaties of protection. She is an independent State with full international status and she conducts her own foreign affairs. The British Government is not responsible, on the basis of any treaty arrangements, to defend Muscat against external aggression.[2] The right to declare war or to remain neutral in a universal war or in a war in which the United Kingdom is a party is part of the prerogatives exercised by the Sultan in his capacity as the Head of the State of Muscat. Consequently, the Sultan of Muscat is free to exercise such right independently of the wishes of the Government of the United Kingdom. In his earlier treaties with the United Kingdom, the Treaty of Commerce of 1839, the Sultan specifically expressed his right to go to war independently of the Government of the United Kingdom and to be neutral in a war declared by this Government. Thus Article 13 of this treaty referred to the respective obligations of the two parties during a war in which only one of the parties was involved as follows:

If it shall happen that either the Queen of England or His Highness the Sultan of Muscat should be at war with another country, the subjects of Her Britannic Majesty and the subjects of His Highness the Sultan of Muscat shall nevertheless be allowed to pass such country through the dominions of either power with merchandize of every description except warlike stores, but they shall not be allowed to enter any port or place actually blockaded or besieged.[3]

The present Treaty of 20 September 1951 between the Sultan and the United Kingdom contains no provisions similar to the provisions of the above Article. However, it certainly does not follow from the absence of such provisions in the Treaty of 1951 that the Sultan has lost his right to declare himself neutral in a war in which the United Kingdom is a party.[4] There is nothing in his treaties with the United Kingdom to show that the Sultan has actually surrendered his right

---

[1] Keith, A. B., *The Dominions as Sovereign States*, (1938) p. 46; Brierly, J., 'International Law and Resort to Armed Force', *Cambridge Law Journal*, 4 (1932), pp. 308, 31–112.
[2] See Chapter 6.   [3] Aitchison, p. 296.
[4] For the Treaty of 1951, see above, p. 52. The Sultan can deprive himself of the right of making war only by surrendering this right by treaty.

to declare war independently of the United Kingdom or to become neutral in a war declared by this Kingdom.[1]

It is clear, therefore, that a declaration of war on the part of the United Kingdom does not involve Muscat. Practice confirms this view. Muscat was not affected by the declaration of war on 3 September 1939, against Germany, and to all appearances remained outside this war. But it was reported in *The Times* that on 11 September 1939

> The Sultan of Oman . . . has expressed his hope that the British Forces may be successful and his desire to render such assistance as he can.[2]

This clearly shows that the Sultan supported the British cause in the war of 1939 against Germany. But there was no formal declaration of war by Muscat against Germany.

(ii) *The Shaikhdoms*

A more difficult question arises regarding the position of the Shaikhdoms in respect of a war declared by the United Kingdom. It may be presumed that the Shaikhdoms, having placed themselves under British protection, have, impliedly, deprived themselves of the right to observe strict neutrality in a war declared by the United Kingdom. However, it does not seem to follow that, as a consequence of their protectorate relations, the Shaikhdoms are necessarily automatically bound by a declaration of war on the part of the Queen of England. While there is a consensus of opinion that a declaration of war by the British Crown operates automatically in all British territories and, most probably, in British colonial protectorates, there appears to be some doubt whether such a declaration similarly operates in British protected States or in protectorates (such as the former Ionian Protectorate) which are not internally governed by the Crown.[3] There

---

[1] See Chapter 6.

[2] *The Times*, 11 September 1939.

[3] On the question of automatic belligerency of the British Dominions, see Keith, *Dominions*, op. cit., pp. 46–8, 605–6; Stewart, op. cit., pp. 380–8; Oppenheim, II, p. 238. According to Oppenheim, 'Since colonies are a part of the territory of the empire or mother-country they fall within the region of a war between the latter and another State, whatever their position may be within it.' For the development of the status of the British Commonwealth in this respect, see Noel-Baker, P. J., *The Present Juridical Status of the British Dominions in International Law* (1939), pp. 229–30; Stewart, op. cit., pp. 380–8. And see Oppenheim, p. 207. Here the author states: 'However with the passing of the doctrines of the indivisibility of the Crown and of common allegiance, it is doubtful whether there is any longer room for the view that a declaration of war by any of the members of the Commonwealth would involve in war all other members of the Commonwealth, including Great Britain.'

Accordingly, it seems that at present a British declaration of war does not automatically involve in war the Commonwealth of Nations. See for separate declarations of war by the Commonwealth Members during the 1939 war against Germany, Oppenheim, p. 207, n. (3); *The Times*, 11 September 1939.

seems to be some authority in saying that, generally, such protected States and protectorates remain neutral in a war in which the Crown is a party, unless and until a declaration of war is separately made by their own respective governments, or by the Crown, on their own behalf.[1] However, it is undeniable that the fact that the Crown is responsible for the defence of such protected States against external aggression makes it quite difficult, in practice, for the latter to observe a strict neutrality in a war declared by the former on the same footing as independent States which are recognised to possess this right of neutrality by international law. For example, it may be of practical difficulty for protected States or protectorates of this kind to deny the Crown, as a protecting Power, facilities for stationing troops or war-like materials in their territories, since these facilities, it may be contended, are part of the defence of such territories. In these circumstances, it may be suggested that such protected States, as long as they do not declare themselves by unequivocal statements issued on their behalf at war on the side of the Crown, may probably be able to observe some limited measures of neutrality in the war declared by the Crown. For example, they may not be required by the Crown to raise an army or to participate militarily in its operations against the enemy. Also, they may not be prohibited from trading with the Crown's enemy in merchandise goods of non war-like nature.[2]

The view that a protected State or a protectorate in the real sense is not necessarily a party in a war declared by the protecting Power seems to find favour with a number of distinguished authorities, such as Oppenheim,[3] Wheaton,[4] Keith[5] and Westlake.[6]

However, it is remarkable that all the above authorities appear to base their views regarding the position of a protectorate or a protected State in a war declared by the protecting Power upon a single decision, namely, the judgment of Dr Lushington in the *Ionian Ships* case (1855). This case gave rise to the question whether the Ionian Islands, a British protectorate between 1815 and 1863,[7] became a party to the Crimean War declared by Great Britain (and other States) against Russia. The decision in that case was that the Ionian Islands remained neutral in the War in question in spite of the fact that under the terms of the Protectorate Great Britain had the right of making war and

---

[1] The assumption that a British declaration of war does not automatically operate in a sovereign Protected State is based on the judgment in the *Ionian Ships* and on the views of text-book writers which will be explained below.

[2] This is based on the judgment of the *Ionian Ships*, explained below.

[3] Oppenheim, p. 139; Ibid., II, pp. 138–9, n. (2).

[4] Wheaton, op. cit., pp. 87–8.

[5] Keith, *Dominions*, op. cit., pp. 51–2.

[6] Westlake, Collected Papers on International Law (1914), pp. 181–2. See also Hall, p. 29.

[7] For the Ionian Islands legal position, see above, p. 62.

peace for the Ionian Islands. Dr Lushington held that the Ionian Islands were not *'ex necessitate* at war' as a result of the declaration of war made by Great Britain against Russia.[1] However, it is remarkable that in his judgment, Dr Lushington made it quite clear that had Great Britain intended to place the Ionian Islands at war with Russia, she had the power to do so. Accordingly, he said:

I know of no act of the protecting Power to place the Ionians in that predicament. Great Britain may have power to do so, as the protecting Power is possessed of all the rights of treating with foreign nations, and of the right to place them in the category of enemies; but she has not thought proper to do so.[2]

It is worthy of note that Dr Lushington's judgment was held to be 'in direct conflict' with the view taken by the Law Officers of the Crown regarding the position of the Ionian Islands during the war in question.[3] These Law Officers, however, although according to Lord McNair, 'adhering to their former opinion' that the Ionian Islands were not free to remain neutral, submitted on 10 May 1855 a Report in which they clarified the status of the subjects of the Islands during the war declared by the Crown as follows:

... yet, we think that the 'status' of a native of the Ionian Republic under the protection of the British Crown is very different from the 'status' of a natural born English subject, and that Ionians, being under the protection of the British Crown, are not in any degree liable, under the Proclamation, to be proceeded against for the committal of any of the treasonable acts therein referred to, but that it will be proper to declare that the protection of the British Crown will be withdrawn from all Ionians in any manner aiding or abetting Her Majesty's enemies.[4]

It may be submitted, in the light of the views expressed above, that the *Ionian Ships* case may, perhaps, be regarded as establishing the principle that a declaration of war on the part of the Crown does not automatically involve British protected States or protectorates (not of the colonial type) unless a separate declaration placing them at war is expressly made on their behalf. This principle was further approved by the Supreme Court of the Federated Malay States in its decision in *H. C. van Hoogstraten* v. *Low Lum Seng* of 16 October 1939. In that case it was held that the Federated Malay States were at war with Germany as a result of the declarations of the British High Commissioner (representing the Federations' Executive), which clearly and unequivocally placed them at war with Germany.[5]

---

[1] [1855] 2 Spinks 212; And see Green, L. C., *International Law Through the Cases*, 2nd ed. (1959), pp. 67–70.   [2] Green, op. cit., pp. 67–70.

[3] For an explanation of British diplomatic practice in this connection, see Smith, I, pp. 68–76.   [4] McNair, *Opinions*, I, p. 40.

[5] *Annual Digest*, 1938–40, case No. 16.

Having clarified the position of British protected States in a war in which the United Kingdom is a party, it can now be stated, in answer to the question asked at the beginning of this discussion regarding the position of the Shaikhdoms in a British war, that these Shaikhdoms are, most probably, not involved in a war as a direct result of a declaration of war on the part of the United Kingdom. The practice in the last war had shown that these Shaikhdoms were, for all practical purposes, not placed at war with Germany as a result of the British declaration of war of 3 September 1939 against Germany.[1] During the period of the war no specific mention of the Shaikhdoms being placed at war with Germany was ever made. However, according to *The Times*, the Rulers of the Shaikhdoms sent messages of support and sympathy to Her Majesty's Government in the United Kingdom.[2] It may be argued that the Rulers of the Shaikhdoms had, by sending messages of sympathy to the British Government, declared themselves, though informally, as enemies of Germany.[3]

2. *Do the Gulf States have the right to declare war against the British Government or against Third States?*

(i) *Muscat*

Having stated above that Muscat is an independent State with full international personality, it would seem to follow, therefore, that her sovereign right of making war or peace with any other State, including the United Kingdom, has remained in full force. Muscat has not, in law, curtailed or surrendered this right, and she is therefore responsible for her own international delinquencies. Consequently, it follows that a conflict between Muscat and any other independent State, including the United Kingdom, would most probably be regarded as 'an international conflict' to which the provisions of the Geneva Convention Relative to the Treatment of Prisoners of War of 12 August 1949 apply without condition.[4] Although Muscat is not a party to

---

[1] For the Announcement from the Privy Council Office regarding British declaration of war against Germany on 3 September 1939, see *The Times*, 4 September 1939.

[2] *The Times*, 11 September 1939.

[3] For a general statement regarding the Shaikh of Bahrain's support to the British cause during the war, see Bahrain Government, *Annual Report* (1358), February 1939–February 1940, p. 1.

It may be remarked in this connection, that by the Persian Gulf States (Emergency) Order in Council, 1939, the Trading with the Enemy Act, 1939, was applied, 'with certain modifications', to the Gulf States, within the limits of Her Majesty's jurisdiction therein. The Order of 1939 was later revoked by the Persian Gulf States (Emergency) (Revocation) Order, 1953. For these enactments, see 2 & 3 Geo. 6. C. 89; *S.R. & O.* 1939/1293; *S.I.* 1953 No. 1670; *Persian Gulf Gazette*, Suppl. No. 2, 1 *January* 1945.

[4] *Treaty Series*, Misc., No. 4 (1950), *Cmd.* 8033, p. 44.

this Convention, it should be possible for her to accede to it under the provisions of Articles 139 and 140.[1]

(ii) *The Shaikhdoms*

By their treaties with the United Kingdom the Shaikhdoms have clearly bound themselves to 'abstain from all maritime aggressions of every description, from the prosecution of war, piracy and slavery by sea. . . .'[2] They have also agreed to appoint the British Resident in the Gulf to supervise all matters connected with the observance of the peace and tranquillity of the Gulf waters at all times. Likewise, by these treaties the British Government has assumed the responsibility of defending the Shaikhdoms against external aggression, as pointed out above. In these circumstances, it is clear that the Shaikhdoms are not free to go to war against the wishes of the British Government.

Consideration may, however, be given to the question of what laws would apply in the event that hostilities were to break out between the United Kingdom and one of the Shaikhdoms. It seems doubtful whether the laws of war govern a conflict arising between two States in protectorate relations. The question whether a conflict between a protected and a protecting State can be regarded as an international conflict depends on various factors, one of which is the extent to which the protected State is accorded recognition as a belligerent power by either the protecting State or by third States.[3] This is on the ground that only States are, generally, recognised as possessing the right of belligerency. 'To be at war, the contention must be between two States,' says Oppenheim.[4]

Regarding the Shaikhdoms, it may be suggested, in the light of the above principles, that the question whether an armed conflict between them and the United Kingdom can be regarded as war depends on a number of factors. These are *inter alia*: (a) the extent to which this conflict presents a threat to the international peace within the meaning of Articles 35 and 39 of the United Nations Charter, and (b) the extent to which the Shaikhdoms' belligerent status is recognised by third States or by the British Government. So long, however, as an

[1] *Treaty Series*, Misc., No. 4 (1950), *Cmd.* 8033, p. 85.

[2] See Chapters 2–5.

[3] For recognition of belligerency generally, see Chen, Ti-Chiang, *The International Law of Recognition* (1951), p. 350; Briggs, op. cit., pp. 991–2.

[4] See Oppenheim, II, p. 203; Westlake, II, p. 1. But see Oppenheim, II, pp. 248–50, where examples are given of wars which broke out in 1877 between vassal states under Turkish suzerainty, such as Serbia and Roumania, and Westlake, p. 24, where the writer does not seem to exclude the possibility of existence of war between protected and protecting States. He thus cites the war between Madagascar and France, in 1895, as an example. But he further adds that 'if by the arrangement between them the protecting power has a larger share in the executive authority of the protected state, the subjects of the latter may not be able to organise such a war without being insurgents in their own country'.

armed conflict between the Shaikhdoms and the United Kingdom is
not regarded as an international conflict, or a war between sovereign
independent States, this conflict would appear to come within the
provisions of Article 3 of the Geneva Convention relating to the
Treatment of Prisoners of War of 12 August 1949. This Article
provides:

> In the case of armed conflict not of an international character occurring
> in the territory of one of the High contracting Parties, each Party to the
> conflict shall be bound to apply, as a minimum, certain humanitarian
> obligations regarding the treatment of prisoners captured during this armed
> conflict.[1]

This Article, says a commentator,

> is like a 'convention in miniature'. It applies to non-international conflicts
> only, and will be the only Article applicable to them until such time as a
> special agreement between the Parties has brought into force between them
> all or part of the other provisions of the Convention.[2]

And, according to Gutteridge:

> The present article is of a much more limited character. It was inten-
> tionally so drafted that the application of the Convention in the case of
> non international conflicts should in no wise depend upon the recognition
> of insurgents as belligerents, either by outside states or by the legitimate
> Government.

Quoting H. Lauterpacht, Gutteridge then continues:

> There is, at present, 'no question of international law conferring a right of
> recognition upon the belligerents or imposing a corresponding duty upon
> the lawful government.'[3]

It is worthy of note, however, that the 'armed conflicts' to which
Article 3 of the Geneva Convention under discussion is intended to
apply are defined as those

> armed conflicts, with armed forces on either side engaged in hostilities—
> conflicts, in short, which are in many respects similar to an international
> war, but take place within the confines of a single country. In many cases,
> each of the Parties is in possession of a portion of the national territory,
> and there is often some sort of front.[4]

Consequently, it may be observed, in the light of the above interpretation of Article 3, that the specific reference in this Article to an

[1] *Treaty Series*, Misc., No. 4 (1950), *Cmd.* 8033, p. 44; See also Gutteridge,
J. A. C., 'The Geneva Convention of 1949', *B.Y.I.L.*, 26 (1949), pp. 300–1.
[2] Uhler, O. M., Coursier, H., and others, *The Geneva Conventions of 12 August,
1949, Commentary IV.* (1949), English translation by Major Ronald Griffin and
C. W. Dumbleton, pp. 34–6.
[3] Gutteridge, op. cit., p. 301.   [4] Uhler and others, op. cit., p. 36.

armed conflict occurring 'in the territory of one of the High contracting Parties' seems, clearly, to exclude the application of this Article
to such conflicts as those occurring in the territories of the protected
States of one of the 'High Contracting Parties'. This is because the
territories of protected States cannot be, properly, described, within
the meaning of Article 3, as a mere portion of the territory of the 'High
Contracting Parties', in the same sense as colonies are.[1] *Prima facie*,
therefore, if an armed conflict occurs in the territory of a protected
State of one of the 'High Contracting Parties', this conflict, not being
covered by this Article, which refers only to an armed conflict 'in the
territory of one of the High Contracting Parties', would, probably,
be susceptible of being described as 'an international conflict' to which
the other provisions of the Geneva Convention under consideration
apply.

NATIONALITY

The inhabitants of the Gulf States, though not British subjects, normally enjoy British protection. This is the result of two fundamental
instruments, namely (*a*) British Nationality Act, 1948, and (*b*) the
British Protectorates, Protected States and Protected Persons Order
in Council, 1949.

(*a*) The British Nationality Act, 1948,[2] gives, for the first time,
statutory recognition to nationals of British protectorates and protected States as 'British protected Persons'. It should be observed,
however, that the term 'British protected Persons' was in use before
the passing of this Act, but this class of persons was not clearly
defined.[3] Consequently, the Act of 1948 defines British protected
persons as a separate category of British nationals to whom, by virtue
of their connection with protectorates or protected states, British
protection is extended.[4] This is provided under Article 32, section (1)
of the Act as follows:

'British protected person' means a person who is a member of a class of
persons declared by Order in Council made in relation to any protectorate,

---

[1] Commentators do not seem to associate the application of this Article with
conflicts taking place on the territories of protected States. Article 3 itself specifically refers to conflicts which 'take place within the confines of a single territory'.
  The fact that a conflict in a protected State is a conflict on one single territory
directed against the government of another single territory (in this case the protecting Power), seems to exclude the application of this Article to such a conflict.
For an interpretation of this Article, see Uhler and others, op. cit., pp. 34–43;
Gutteridge, op. cit., pp. 300–1.

[2] 11 & 12 Geo. 6. CH. 56.

[3] For the status of British protected persons before 1948, see Jones, J. Mervyn,
'Who Are British Protected Persons?', *B.Y.I.L.*, 22 (1945), p. 127.

[4] Jones, J. Mervyn 'British Nationality Act, 1948', *B.Y.I.L.*, 25 (1948), pp.
158–79.

protected state, mandated territory or trust territory to be for the purposes of this Act British protected persons by virtue of their connection with that protectorate, state or territory.[1]

(b) The British Protectorates, Protected States, and Protected Persons Order in Council, 1949,[2] issued in accordance with Sections 30 and 32 of the British Nationality Act, 1948, enumerates which territories are British Protectorates (the First Schedule), which territories are protected states (the Second Schedule) and which territories are trust territories (the Third Schedule). This Order defines under Sections 9 and 12, two main categories of British protected persons as follows:

Section 9 (1) . . . a person shall be a British protected person by virtue of his connection with a protectorate or a trust territory—
(a) if he was born (whether before or after the date of this Order) in a protectorate or trust territory; or
(b) in the case of a person born elsewhere than in a protectorate or trust territory before the date of this Order, if his father was born in a protectorate or trust territory; or
(c) in the case of a person born elsewhere than in a protectorate or trust territory after the date of this Order, if his father was born in a protectorate or trust territory and was a British protected person at the time of that person's birth.

Section 12 (1) A person who, under any law providing for citizenship or nationality in force in any protected state, is a citizen or national of that state shall be a British protected person by virtue of his connection with that state.
(2) If in any protected state no such law as is mentioned in the preceding sub-section is in force, the provisions of section 3, section 4, section 9, section 11 and section 13 of this Order shall have effect in relation to that state as if it were a protectorate.

British protected persons are, therefore, either (a) those who are such by virtue of their connection with protectorates specified by the Order (Section 9), or (b) those who are such by virtue of being nationals of protected states specified by the Order, in accordance with the terms of nationality laws issued by these states (Section 12). If any such protected State has no local nationality law of its own, Sections 9, 11 and 13 would then apply to it as if it were a protectorate.[3]

[1] Regarding the definition of protectorates and protected States, Article 30 of the Nationality Act, 1948, provides: 'His Majesty, may in relation to states and territories under His protection through His government in the United Kingdom, by Order in Council declare which of those states and territories are protectorates and which of them are protected states for the purpose of this Act.'
[2] S.I. 1949, No. 140. See also Parry, C., Nationality and Citizenship Laws of the Commonwealth and of the Republic of Ireland (1957), pp. 358–60.
[3] By Section 12 (2) is meant that a national of a protected State which has no nationality law would be regarded as a British protected person in accordance with Section 9 (1) as if he were a national of a protectorate. See text above.

In connection with the Gulf States, it should be observed that since Muscat is not a British protected State, she is not, therefore, covered by the provisions of this Order. With regard to the Shaikhdoms, they are, for the purposes of the Order, enumerated under the Second Schedule of the Order as protected States.[1] At present the only Shaikhdoms which have separate nationality laws of their own are Bahrain, Kuwait and Qatar. They thus fall under Article 12 (1) of the Order. The Trucial Shaikhdoms do not seem to have issued separate nationality laws, and to these Section 12 (2), therefore, applies.[2]

In the light of the above-mentioned Sections of the Order, an attempt will be made (1) to explain the relevant provisions of the nationality laws of those Shaikhdoms which have such laws, and (2) to elucidate the nature of the rights and privileges enjoyed by the nationals of these States in the eyes of English law.

1. *Nationality laws of Bahrain, Kuwait and Qatar*

The nationality laws of these States define who can be properly described as a citizen or national of Bahrain, Kuwait or Qatar respectively. The Ruler or the government of each State has the power to grant to, and withhold from, any person resident in these States the right to become a national of any of the Shaikhdoms in question, provided that an application is made and certain conditions are satisfied by the applicant. The provisions of these laws are, briefly, as follows:

(*a*) The Bahrain Nationality Law of 8 May 1937,[3] comprises 5 Articles. Article 1 regards nationals:

(a) All persons born in Bahrain before or after the promulgation of this law except as provided in Article 2.

---

[1] Muscat is not mentioned in any of the Schedules of the Order. For the Shaikhdoms, see Second Schedule of the Order, 1949, cited above.

[2] This means that the nationals of the Trucial Shaikhdoms are defined as protected persons as if they are connected with protectorates. See text above.

It should be noted, in this connection, that the above discussion applies to Kuwait in so far as she was still a British protected State, within the meaning of the above-mentioned Order in Council of 1949.

[3] Law No. 20/1356, dated 27 Safar 1356, Government of Bahrain, *Collection of Laws and Notices* (Arabic text), 1958, pp. 67-8. It should be pointed out that the Law of 1937 has now been replaced by the Bahraini Nationality Law of 1963 (Bahrain Government, *Official Gazette* (Arabic text), No. 534, 19 September 1963). The new Law does not substantially differ from the old one. It is however, more extensive and it contains 12 Articles. It classifies Bahrainis into three categories by adding a new category, namely, Bahrainis by descent. The new changes are: (*a*) It requires fifteen years (instead of ten) for obtaining nationality by naturalisation. (*b*) It omits Article 2 of the old law regarding the non-application of Bahraini nationality to persons born in Bahrain who are registered with the British Political Agency as foreigners. (*c*) It attributes Bahraini nationality to foundlings found in Bahrain. (*d*) It entrusts the Ruler with the right to return to a person his Bahraini nationality which was withdrawn from him previously.

(b) Persons born abroad before or after the promulgation of this law whose fathers or paternal grandfathers were born in Bahrain, except persons whose fathers during the minority of such persons registered at the Political Agency in Bahrain in accordance with Article 2 or might have so registered if resident in Bahrain.

By a Supplementary law dated 20 February 1955 the conditions for naturalisation under the Bahraini nationality law were stated to be as follows:

(1) The possession of immovable property in Bahrain.
(2) The continuance of residence in Bahrain for a period of ten years.
(3) The applicant should be of a good character.
(4) The applicant should have a fair knowledge of Arabic.
(5) The payment of a fee of 25 rupees by the applicant.

Article 5 of the Bahraini nationality law gives the Ruler the right to 'grant Bahraini nationality to any person resident in Bahrain who applies for it and' to 'cancel the grant if such person ceases to reside in Bahrain'.[1]

(b) The Qatari Nationality Law No. 2 of 1961,[2] as amended by Law No. 19 of 1963 and Law No. 17 of 1966, comprises 17 Articles. According to the provisions of this Law and its amendments, there are three categories of Qatari nationals, namely, Qataris by descent, by birth and by naturalisation. Qataris by descent, or original Qataris, are those who resided in Qatar prior to 1930. As regards Qataris by birth, they are those born to a Qatari father, whether inside or outside Qatar. In order to acquire nationality by naturalisation, the applicant must fulfil certain conditions which include the following:

(a) He must have lawfully continued residence in Qatar for a period not less than 20 years, or 15 years in case of an Arab belonging to an Arab country, from the date of his application for naturalisation, (b) he must have a lawful means of living and must be of good conduct, (c) he must have a fair command of Arabic.

Qatari nationality acquired in accordance with the above conditions can be withdrawn by decree from a *bona fide* Qatari national if he (a) acquires a foreign nationality; or (b) joins the military service of a foreign country against the wishes of the Qatari Government; or (c) works for the interests of a foreign country which is in a state of war with Qatar.

---

[1] *Collection of Laws*, op. cit. And for granting nationality by naturalisation, see ibid., Law No. 33/1374, dated 28 Jumada I 1374, p. 58.

[2] For this Law and its various amendments, see *Al-Jaridah al-Rasmiyah* (Government of Qatar's Official Gazette), No. 2, 3 April 1961. And see the same, 3rd Year, No. 5, 22 July 1963, and 6th Year, No. 5, 19 September 1966. It appears that Qatari nationality in the past was governed by the Qatari Nationality Regulation of 12 April 1951 (See Government of Qatar, *Laws and Regulations*). And see Parry, op. cit., pp. 370–2. But the nationality law of 1961 completely ignores the previous Regulation as if it never existed.

(c) The Kuwaiti Nationality Law, 5 December 1959,[1] comprises 24 Articles. Article 1 states that 'Kuwaitis in origin are those who are deemed to have permanently resided in Kuwait before 1920 and who have continued to reside in Kuwait up to the date of the publication of this Law.' Article 2 states that 'a person is deemed to be a Kuwaiti if he is born in Kuwait or outside Kuwait from a Kuwaiti father'. Article 3 states that the following are deemed to be Kuwaiti subjects:

(1) Any person born in Kuwait or outside Kuwait from a Kuwaiti mother so long as his relationship to his father has not been legally established.

(2) Any person born in Kuwait of unknown parents. A foundling in Kuwait is considered to be born in Kuwait unless the contrary is proved.

Articles 4 and 5 provide for nationality by naturalisation. By Article 4, nationality by naturalisation is conferred on any adult who satisfies the following conditions:

(1) That he has been permanently resident in Kuwait for at least 15 years, or for 10 years if he is an Arab belonging to an Arab country, before his application for naturalisation.

(2) That he has a lawful means of livelihood and is of good character, with no criminal records.

(3) That he has knowledge of Arabic.

By Article 5, Kuwaiti nationality may also be granted by the Kuwaiti authorities concerned to persons who do not satisfy the conditions of Article 4, but who may be granted Kuwaiti nationality on the following grounds:

(1) A person who has rendered useful services to Kuwait provided that he is an Arab belonging to an Arab country.

(2) A person who has been residing in Kuwait before 1945 and has continued this residence until the publication of this Law, provided that he is an Arab belonging to an Arab country.

(3) A non-Arab who has been residing in Kuwait before 1930 and has continued his residence until the publication of this Law.[2]

2. *The Rights enjoyed by nationals of the Shaikhdoms abroad: British diplomatic protection*

In the eyes of English law the nationals of the Shaikhdoms, although

---

[1] Law No. 15/1959, dated 5 Jamada II 1379 (corresponding to 5 December 1959), *Al-Kuwait Al-Yawm*, No. 253, Supplement, 14 December 1959. In an Explanatory Note attached to this Law, it is provided that a Kuwaiti Nationality Law was first issued in 1948 by the Law No. 2/1948, but that this Law based on the Egyptian Law of 1929, was rarely applied in practice. Accordingly, no definition of Kuwaiti nationals, in compliance with the provisions of this Law, was ever made.

[2] The provisions of Articles 4 and 5 are stated above as amended by Law No. 2/1960 of 12 Sha'ban 1379 (corresponding to 9 February 1960). See *Al-Kuwait Al-Yawm*, No. 262, Supp. 15 February 1960, p. 7.

Translation of the text of these nationality laws has been made by the author.

not British subjects, are declared, for the purposes of the Nationality Act, not to be aliens.[1] As British protected persons, they are not subject to the disabilities and restrictions imposed on aliens residing in the United Kingdom in regard to registration with the police and employment.[2] They may land and reside freely in the United Kingdom without being required to obtain special permission. They are also eligible to become British subjects by naturalisation on more favourable terms than those applicable to aliens.[3] Further, as British protected persons, the nationals of the Shaikhdoms

cannot be guilty of treason under the law of the United Kingdom in respect of any conduct [on their part] elsewhere than within the dominions of the Crown.[4]

But it is presumed, on the authority of *Joyce* v. *Director of Public Prosecutions* (1946), that

a British protected person who is the bearer of a British passport may be tried for a treasonable act committed abroad.[5]

From the point of view of international law, the nationals of the Shaikhdoms are classified as British nationals who, on the same footing as British subjects, normally enjoy Her Majesty's protection through her diplomatic representatives in the Commonwealth and in foreign States.[6] But, according to Mervyn Jones:

Neither British subjects nor British protected persons may claim as of right a passport or diplomatic protection.

However, 'a passport', he says, 'is *prima-facie* evidence of British nationality'.[7] The nationals of the Shaikhdoms are, therefore, accorded British protection abroad on the basis of the passports, or the travel documents, which they carry. The Shaikhdoms have their own separate passports which are issued subject to the authority of the Rulers.[8]

[1] Parry, op. cit., pp. 352–3; Jones, J. Mervyn, *British Nationality Law*, Rev. ed. (1956), pp. 194–5.

[2] Jones, *B.Y.I.L.* (1948), op. cit., p. 176; Parry, op. cit., p. 353; Jones, *British Nationality Law*, op. cit., pp. 78–81.

[3] Parry, op. cit., p. 353: A British protected person can become a British subject by naturalisation in accordance with Article 10 of the British Nationality Act, 1948. See ibid.

[4] Parry, op. cit., p. 353, Jones, *B.Y.I.L.* (1948), op. cit., p. 176.

[5] *Joyce* v. *Director of Public Prosecutions*, [1946], A.C. 347; See Parry, op. cit., p. 353, n. (11).

[6] Jones, *B.Y.I.L.* (1948), op. cit., p. 175.

[7] Jones, *British Nationality Law*, op. cit., p. 195.

[8] For example, the 'Passport of the Bahrain State and Dependencies' contains this Note:
'To all whom it may concern:—Greeting, Honourable friends, the Officials of the Great Powers and the Representatives of other Kingdoms abroad, are required and requested to allow the bearer to pass freely without let or hindrance and to

However, there is no mention in these passports of the fact that the bearers are British protected persons or that they are 'entitled to Her Majesty's protection'.[1]

Nationals of Muscat also have their own passports. The position of these nationals in the United Kingdom is, in all respects, similar to that of aliens. Like other aliens, they have to obtain visas for coming to England, and they have to abide by all the restrictions imposed on foreigners while residing in England. Muscati nationals in foreign States receive British diplomatic protection on the basis of courtesy, since, unlike the nationals of the Shaikhdoms, they do not possess the status of British protected persons.

---

afford him every assistance and protection of which he may stand in need.

'Issued by order of His Highness the Ruler of Bahrain.'

[1] In comparison, the passports issued for the former Indian States certified that 'the bearer is a subject of the state of . . . a state in India in subordinate alliance with Her Majesty, and as such is entitled to Her Majesty's protection.' See Lee-Warner, op. cit., p. 265. No such certificate is attached to the Shaikhdoms' passports. See p. 127, n. 8.

9

International responsibility[1]

RESPONSIBILITY FOR THE INTERNATIONAL DELINQUENCIES OF THE GULF STATES

Imputability of acts of Protected States to the Protecting Power

There seems to be general agreement among writers of authority and in the practice of States that a protecting State is responsible for the delinquencies of its protected State.

(*a*) *The views of writers:* The rule regarding the responsibility of the protecting State for the delinquencies of dependencies, protectorates and protected States under its protection has received virtually unanimous recognition by such writers as Hall, Eagleton, Oppenheim, Hyde, Wheaton, Dunn, Starke and Garcia Amador.[2] However, many writers relate the responsibility of the protecting State for the delinquencies of the protected State to the extent and degree of 'control' exercised by the former over the internal affairs of the latter, and to the extent to which the protected State controls its external affairs.[3] Thus, for instance, where the arrangement between the protecting and protected State leaves to the latter the freedom of administering justice internally, 'that State', says Eagleton, 'would appear to have sufficient control to accept responsibility for injuries suffered by aliens therein'.[4] But even in this particular case Eagleton admits that the protecting Power may be expected to prevent the claimant State from enforcing directly its claim against the delinquent protected State.[5] Garcia Amador makes an attempt to clarify the practical difficulties regarding the imputability of responsibility for the acts and omissions

---

[1] International responsibility has been defined as 'a duty to make reparation for the injury sustained, a duty incumbent upon the State which violated, or did not comply with, an international obligation'. See Garcia Amador, F. V., 'Report on State Responsibility', *Yearbook of International Law Commission*, vol. II (1956), p. 180 (Document A/CN.4/96, 20 January 1956). See also Eagleton, C., *The Responsibility of States in International Law*, 1928, p. 22.

[2] See Hall, pp. 150, 154; Eagleton, op. cit., pp. 36, 37–8, 43; Oppenheim, pp. 339–40; Hyde, 1, pp. 45–7; Wheaton, op. cit., p. 422; Dunn, F. S., *The Protection of Nationals: A Study in the Application of International Law* (1932) pp. 122–3; Starke, J. G., 'Imputability in International Delinquencies', *B.Y.I.L.*, 19 (1938), p. 117; Garcia Amador, op. cit., p. 187.

[3] Eagleton, op. cit., p. 43.

[4] Ibid., p. 36.

[5] Ibid.

of the protected State to the government of the protected State itself. He presents the issue thus:

Nevertheless, in a case involving a protectorate or like entity (these being the only cases presenting serious difficulties) one must determine whether, in addition to enjoying full internal autonomy, the entity in question has a measure of international personality and whether this personality carries with it the capacity to enter directly into international commitments with other States. This legal phenomenon, which is to be observed with increasing frequency in contemporary practice, is of great significance when the issue to be decided is: To whom should the responsibility be imputed for the acts or omissions of those semi-sovereign entities.[1]

It may be deduced from the above quotations that while it seems possible, from the point of view of municipal law, to allocate responsibility between the agencies of the protecting and the protected State, in international law there is only one State that can be held responsible, namely, the protecting State or the State in which, by virtue of its nternational status, the responsibility of the protected State merges.[2]

(b) *State practice:* The United Kingdom has consistently accepted international responsibility for the delinquencies of her protectorates and protected States. A dispatch, dated 27 February 1895, by the Foreign Office to the Law Officers of the Crown contains the following principles on the responsibility of the protecting Power:

That all Powers, other than the Protecting Power, are excluded from interference in the internal affairs of the protected country, and from asserting by force directly against the Government of the protected State any claims for redress they may have against it. . . . It is presumed that if any international wrong is committed against the protected Power redress would be sought only through the medium of the Protecting Power.[3]

---

[1] Garcia Amador, op. cit., p. 187.

[2] Eagleton, op. cit., pp. 32–4; Starke, op. cit., p. 117. It is agreed that in the case of States under suzerainty, their delinquencies are imputable to the suzerain State. As regards the position of the self-governing dominions of Great Britain, it is said that 'each Dominion will accept responsibility for internationally injurious acts within its jurisdiction'. See Eagleton, p. 35; Lewis, M. M., 'International Status of the British Self-Governing Dominions', *B.Y.I.L.*, 3 (1922–3), p. 21.

[3] McNair, *Opinions*, vol. 1, pp. 58–9. It seems clear that British practice is in accord with Hall's statement that where no internal jurisdiction or 'external sovereign power' is assumed by a superior State over a territory, 'no definite responsibility consequently is incurred' by it. See Hall, p. 154 (footnote). The case of *R. E. Brown Claim*, 1923, before the Anglo-American Pecuniary Claims Arbitration of 1923, may be cited as an example of this British practice. In this case, it was decided that since by the Convention of 1884, the British Government 'reserved only a qualified control over the relations of the South African Republic with foreign powers, there were, therefore, no grounds for invoking the international responsibility of Great Britain for tortious acts' of the South African Republic. For this Award, see *B.Y.I.L.*, 5 (1924), pp. 210–21.

The same view is reflected in French practice relating to the former protectorates of Tunisia and Morocco.[1]

(c) *Judicial decisions:* The principle that acts and omissions of a protected State are imputable to the protecting State has also been applied in a number of decisions of international tribunals. For example, in the *Casablanca case* between Germany and France, 1909,[2] claims were addressed to France in respect of occurrences in Morocco. And in the *Spanish Zone of Morocco Claims* (Great Britain v. Spain), of 23 October 1924, it was held that Spain, as the protecting Power of the Zone, was primarily responsible for the injuries suffered by British nationals residing in that Zone.[3] Furthermore, in the case *Adolph G. Studer,* before the American and British Claims Arbitration (1926), the British Government appeared in its capacity as the State responsible for the wrongs which were alleged to have been committed by the former British protected State of Johore, 'for whose acts the British Government admitted responsibility'.[4]

The Gulf States

It may be assumed, on the basis of the above principles, that acts and omissions of the Shaikhdoms are *ipso facto* imputable to the British Government in its capacity as the protecting Power. Muscat, as a State responsible for its own international relations, can be held directly responsible for its own delinquencies. However, it seems that the invocation of the international responsibility of Muscat by a foreign State presents some practical difficulties owing to the fact that it maintains diplomatic representation neither with the United Nations nor with foreign States other than the British Government.[5] It is true that by virtue of its long-standing treaties of friendship and of its capitulatory rights in Muscat, the British Government has been entrusted with certain duties in regard to the conduct of the foreign affairs of the Government of the Sultan.[6] In practice, the British Government is now looking after the interests of the Sultan *vis-à-vis* foreign Powers. However, there can be no ground to assume that the British Government by agreeing to act as a representative of the government of the Sultan internationally, would incur responsibility for delinquencies of that government. The British Government cannot accept responsibility for delinquencies of a State for whose foreign affairs it is not responsible. It follows, therefore, that delinquencies committed in Muscat are not *ipso facto* imputable to the British

---

[1] Eagleton, op. cit., pp. 37–8.

[2] For the *Casablanca* case of 22 May 1909, see Scott, *The Hague Court Reports* (1916), pp. 110–20.

[3] *Annual Digest*, 1923–4, case No. 85.

[4] For reference, see below, p. 33.

[5] See above, p. 67.   [6] See above, pp. 67–8.

Government. Indeed the position of the British Government in assuming certain duties in respect of the external affairs of the Sultan can be assimilated to that of an agent who acts according to the instructions of his principal without necessarily becoming a party to the contractual relations between the principal and the third party.

How can international claims be presented by a claimant State against Muscat? It can be assumed that since by special arrangement with the Sultan's government, the British Government has been representing the former in the international sphere, foreign States receiving injuries from the government of Muscat can therefore present their claims against that State through the diplomatic channels of the British Government, which in turn may make representation on their behalf to the government of the Sultan. Consequently, all negotiations for the peaceful settlement of the claims in question may be conducted with the government of the Sultan in this manner. It must be reiterated, however, that the mediation of the British Government in any such claims arising between the government of the Sultan and other claimant States does not, in any manner, entail the responsibility of the British Government for the former's delinquencies. Nor does the British Government, by acting as an intermediary in the disputes between Muscat and foreign States, confer on Muscat more rights or advantages than those actually possessed by the latter by virtue of her present status in international law. For example, the signature of the Optional Clause of the Statute of the International Court of Justice by the British Government does not confer any benefits on Muscat should she decide to appoint the British Government to act on her behalf in a dispute between Muscat and a third State before the International Court of Justice. In any such dispute Muscat has to sign the Optional Clause herself.[1]

Kinds of acts and omissions which give rise to the international responsibility of the Gulf States

1. *Acts and omissions of the rulers and their governments*

To what extent is responsibility borne by these States for injuries sustained by foreigners in consequence of acts and omissions of their Rulers or officials? For example, is responsibility arising from the expropriation of alien property by a Ruler in his territory *ipso facto* imputable to the British Government? If so, how can reparation be made by the British Government for the damage sustained by the alien concerned? It is difficult to show what attitude the British Government would adopt if such a case arises, since there has hardly been any precedent giving rise to the international responsibility of the Shaikhdoms in this respect. As regards British practice in other

[1] For an explanation, see below, pp. 143–4.

British protected States, there seems to be only one single case, namely, *Adolph G. Studer* (1925), which would, probably, shed some light upon the question under consideration. This case was in reality a claim for the destruction by the Ruler of the State of Johore—of the former protected States of Malay—of 'concessionary and other rights' owned by an American citizen, Adolph G. Studer, in the territory of that State.[1]

In dismissing this claim, before the American and British Claims Arbitration, the Tribunal, which gave its decision on 19 March 1925, relied upon a communication, dated 28 April 1906, from the British Foreign Office to the American Ambassador in which it was said:

> It is therein again pointed out that no valid reason has yet been adduced for the claimant's refusal to submit his claims in a regular manner before the proper court in Johore; and, as was stated . . . His Majesty's Government feel that until that step has been taken the Johore Government cannot be pressed to recognize the claim in any way.[2]

This communication further dealt with the argument of the claimant

> that the reason why he did not present his claim, in the first place, to the local courts of the Sultan of Johore was: 'That some difficulty was thought to exist in adopting this course, on the ground that 'the immunity of the Sovereign Power from suits at law within its territorial limits, unless by its own consent and in the manner in which it ordains', was a familiar principle at law.'[3]

It answered this argument thus:

> With a view of meeting this objection His Majesty's Government have thought it desirable to obtain a distinct assurance from the Sultan of Johore on the subject; and His Highness has now formally expressed willingness to waive all technical objections, and to agree to the case being tried by the Principal Judicial Officer in Johore in the presence of a British officer. It does not appear that any advantage was taken of this offer.[4]

The Tribunal, being satisfied with the assurances contained in the above British Communication, recommended that advantage should be taken of the British offer, and the claim should, thus, be referred to the courts of the State of Johore.[5]

It may be deduced from the above case that in an international claim of this nature against the Ruler of one of the Shaikhdoms, the British Government would accept international responsibility for the claim only after satisfying itself that all the legal remedies available

---

[1] Nielsen, F. K., *Report on American and British Claims Arbitration* (1926), p. 547.
[2] Ibid., p. 548.
[3] Ibid., p. 550.   [4] Ibid.   [5] Ibid., p. 553.

in the Shaikhdom against which the claim is primarily presented have been exhausted, unsatisfactorily, by the claimant.

2. *Denial of justice before the courts of the Gulf States*

This requires a discussion of the extent to which acts of the judiciary in the Gulf States give rise to their international responsibility. Responsibility of the protecting Power for denial of justice sustained by a foreigner in the courts of the protected State was established in the *Spanish Zone of Morocco* case, to which reference has been made above.[1]

The discussion of the problem of denial of justice in its relation to the Gulf States and the degree of imputability of responsibility arising from the wrongs of the judiciary in these States to the British Government requires a special distinction between two cases: (*a*) where denial of justice is sustained by an alien before the courts of the Rulers, and (*b*) where denial of justice is sustained by an alien before the British courts established under the system of foreign jurisdiction.[2]

Thus, in regard to the Shaikhdoms, it would appear that while in the case of (*a*) the British Government would, probably, bear 'vicarious' responsibility only, in the case of (*b*) British responsibility would be original. This is on the ground that responsibility arises in the latter case from the wrongs of a machinery of justice for whose administration the British Crown is directly responsible. Consequently, the Rulers of the Shaikhdoms would appear to bear direct responsibility for denial of justice sustained by aliens before their courts only. The practical importance of the above distinction arises in connection with the question: Who is directly answerable for reparation of injuries sustained by an alien in a claim for denial of justice in the territories of the Shaikhdoms? It may be presumed that since the wrongs of the British courts in the Shaikhdoms cannot, in law, be imputed to the Rulers, these Rulers are, therefore, not answerable for reparation of the wrongs of these courts. Responsibility in this respect rests with the British Government alone.

In regard to Muscat, it is, of course, clear that no responsibility for denial of justice in the courts of the Sultan is imputable to the British Government. This is so on account of the independent status of Muscat among the other Gulf States. However, owing to the fact that in this State there also exists a system of extra-territorial jurisdiction,[3]

---

[1] See above, p. 131.

[2] The British Government still maintains extra-territorial jurisdiction in the territories of the Shaikhdoms. (It was relinquished in Kuwait just before her independence.) This foreign jurisdiction, obtained with the consent of the Rulers concerned, is much limited today and it applies only to non-Muslim foreigners and Commonwealth citizens. See above, p. 10.

[3] But see above, p. 19. British extra-territorial jurisdiction in Muscat was relinquished as from January 1967.

the question arises if in these circumstances, responsibility for denial of justice sustained by an alien before the British courts in Muscat is imputable to the British Government? There are two relevant, though conflicting, considerations to be borne in mind. On the one hand, it would appear that *prima facie* the conferment by the Sultan of extra-territorial jurisdiction upon the British Government—as well as upon other governments—is a sovereign act which does not affect the independence of Muscat. Consequently, it would seem, from the point of view of international law, that Muscat cannot escape responsibility for derelictions of judicial institutions in her own territory by the mere fact that these institutions are directly administered by the British Government. On the other hand it may be argued, perhaps more cogently, that while it is true that the Government of the Sultan bears responsibility for denial of justice in its national courts, it seems difficult to impose on this Government a similar responsibility for derelictions of courts which are not under the authority of the Sultan. In other words, it may be presumed that the British Government, by obtaining the Sultan's agreement to the establishment of British courts of justice in Muscat, has, by implication, indicated its desire to bear alone responsibility for denial of justice in these courts. This is so because the conferment of jurisdiction by the Sultan upon the British Government carried with it not only rights but also duties and obligations. Responsibility for denial of justice in courts established under this jurisdiction is one aspect of these obligations.

3. *Violation of contractual obligations; disputes regarding oil agreements*

Failure on the part of the Gulf States to respect or perform their contractual obligations towards foreigners or foreign governments can give rise, in the last resort, to their international responsibility.

It is generally agreed that there can be no violation of international law for the mere breach of a contract by a government if such breach does not involve an arbitrary repudiation of this contract.[1] It is assumed that an alien who opted to enter into a contractual relation with a foreign government has already agreed, by implication, to settle all disputes regarding the interpretation or the application of his contract in accordance with the municipal law of the government in question. Accordingly, if an alien sustains injuries as a result of violation of the provisions of his contract by a foreign government which is a party to this contract, he has to institute a claim against this government in its local courts.[2] There is, therefore, no ground, at this stage, for an international claim to be presented by the government of the alien against the foreign government which is alleged to have

[1] Freeman, op. cit., p. 110; Eagleton, op. cit., pp. 157–8; Dunn, op. cit., p. 164.
[2] Freeman, op. cit., p. 112, n. (1).

violated or broken the provisions of this contract. According to Borchard, State practice has shown that

diplomatic interposition will not lie for the natural or anticipated consequences of the contractual relation, but only for arbitrary incidents or results, such as a denial of justice or flagrant violation of local or international law.[1]

Disputes regarding oil agreements: There appears to be general agreement, in the light of a number of arbitration awards relating to the Gulf States, that oil agreements entered into between the Rulers of these States and various oil companies are not subject—whether in their application or interpretation—to the local laws of the States within which they operate.[2] Usually, agreements of this nature contain some provisions indicating a legal system of law within which they are intended to operate and thus, impliedly, excluding the local system of either party to the transaction.[3] Moreover, references have very often been made in such agreements to the necessity of settling all disputes between the parties through arbitration which normally takes the form of appointing an arbitration tribunal or an umpire agreed upon by the parties concerned.[4]

In these circumstances, it can be stated that where a Ruler, who is a party to such an agreement, elects to violate, in any manner, the terms of the agreement, the other party—in this case the foreign Company—cannot invoke the diplomatic protection of its government unless it can prove that the matter of dispute was taken to arbitration according to the provisions of the agreement, or that the Ruler refused to arbitrate at all, or, if he accepted arbitration, intentionally and maliciously disregarded the award of the umpire or tribunal, or took some violent action against the employees or property of the Company. In other words, it is not enough in order to establish the responsibility of the Ruler or his government, to show that he infringed the terms of his agreement, but it must be clearly shown that he committed by his action an international wrong.[5]

The imputability of actions of the Rulers of the Shaikhdoms against oil companies to the British Government seems to present a difficult situation. This situation might arise as a result of wrongs committed by the Rulers against British oil companies in particular. Consequently, if, for example, a British oil company calls for the diplomatic interposition of the British Government against a Ruler who has

---

[1] Borchard, E. M., *Diplomatic Protection of Citizens Abroad* (1915), p. 284. And see Dunn, op. cit., p. 167.

[2] See Lord McNair, 'The General Principles of Law Recognised by Civilised Nations', *B.Y.I.L.*, 33 (1957), pp. 2–3.

[3] Ibid., pp. 3–4.

[4] See e.g. below, p. 284, Lord Asquith's Award in the Abu Dhabi Case, 1951.

[5] See Eagleton, op. cit., pp. 157–8; Dunn, op, cit., p. 164.

arbitrarily confiscated its property, this Government would then have, probably, to act in a double capacity (i.e., both as a claimant State and as a State which is 'vicariously' responsible for the wrong of the Ruler). In other words, it would have to redress claims by and against itself which seems to be, practically, absurd. This is actually a case of balancing the right of the British Government to intervene in favour of 'the protection of nationals who have their economic activities in foreign countries' with its duty to protect the interests of the Ruler in its capacity as a protector.[1]

The rule of the exhaustion of local remedies: the extent of the operation of this rule in the Gulf States

It seems necessary to supplement the above discussion by referring, briefly, to a problem which has been very closely associated by writers and States with international claims. This problem is referred to as 'the rule of the exhaustion of local remedies'. And it is often contended that the actual fulfilment of this 'rule' is a ground upon which an international claim can be based.[2]

Is the exhaustion of the local legal remedies in the Gulf States a pre-condition, or a necessary step, for a foreign claimant or his government to advance an international claim against these States or, vicariously, against the British Government? There are at least two cases which seem to shed light on this question, namely, *Adolph G. Studer*, 1925, and *Ziat Ben Kiran* (Great Britain *v.* Spain), 29 December 1924. These two cases are relevant in that (*a*) they both represent claims arising from wrongs committed in a protected State, and (*b*) they both establish the principle that local remedies available in the protected territory must first be exhausted before any international claim could be advanced against the protecting Power in respect of the delinquencies of the government of such territory.

In the *Adolph G. Studer* case, the Tribunal appeared to have accepted the British Government's argument (the British Government admitted responsibility in this case for the action of the Ruler of the protected State of Johore) that:

. . . the legal remedies which are open to the claimant in the Sultan's court must be exhausted before any question of treating the matter through the diplomatic channel or referring it to arbitration can be considered.[3]

---

[1] For a discussion of whether there are legal grounds for intervention by the State whose subjects have as shareholders in a British corporation 'suffered damage by the act of a foreign State inflicting damage on the property of the corporation', see Bagge, Algot, 'Intervention on the Ground of Damage Caused to Nations, with Particular Reference to Exhaustion of Local Remedies and the Rights of Shareholders', *B.Y.I.L.*, 34 (1958), pp. 162, 172–5.

[2] Freeman, op. cit., pp. 404, 423; Bagge, op. cit., p. 165; Briggs, op. cit., pp. 629–32.   [3] Nielsen, *Report*, op. cit., p. 550.

While in the *Ziat Ben Kiran* case,

a claim advanced by Great Britain on behalf of a British protected person, for damages caused in respect of riot in Melilla (in the Spanish Zone of Morocco) on 3 November, 1919,

it was held that the claim 'could not be entertained'. This was on the ground that

an international claim based on an alleged denial of justice cannot be entertained if the various instances of local jurisdiction have not been exhausted.

'This condition', it was stated, 'had not been fulfilled in the present case.'[1]

It may be assumed on the authority of the above two cases that an international claim advanced against a Gulf State cannot be accepted by the government of such State, or by the British Government on its behalf, if the rule of the exhaustion of the local remedies existing in this State has not been complied with. This would, probably, be the view most acceptable to the British Government.

There can be no question, of course, that the apportionment of the control of justice over foreigners in the Gulf States between the British Government—through the system of foreign jurisdiction—and the Rulers, who have their own courts of law, would in any manner hamper the requirements of the exhaustion of local remedies in these States on the part of the foreign claimant. Nor can it be presumed that the allocation of a certain class of foreigners to the jurisdiction of the Rulers' Courts has any bearing whatever on the consequent international responsibility of the British Government for injuries sustained by this class of foreigners. The only difference in regard to the position of this class of foreigners, from the standpoint of municipal law, is that they will be required in the first place, to exhaust their remedies by applying to the local Courts of the Rulers before they can invoke the international responsibility of these Rulers or their governments. It follows, therefore, that failure on the part of an alien injured in a Gulf State to comply with the local remedies rule, may, except in those conditions limiting the application of the rule,[2] give the British Government ground to refuse to accept responsibility for a claim arising from injuries sustained by this alien. According to Starke, in order to decide 'which authorities are to see to the fulfilment' of obligations arising from delinquencies of the protected State, a reference must be made 'to legal orders other than international

---

[1] *Annual Digest*, 1923–4, case No. 87.
[2] For cases where the local remedy rule may be waived, see Freeman, op. cit., pp. 420–3; Briggs, op. cit., pp. 629 et seq.

law'.[1] 'In effect,' Starke says, 'a double reference is required, first . . . to the law governing the relations between the protector and vassal state, and then to the law of the subordinate state. The agencies of . . . the vassal state are, *qua* performance of international obligations, really agencies of those entities, . . . which alone have an autonomous international position.'[2]

Conclusion

Having discussed the various aspects of the Shaikhdoms' delinquencies and the degree and nature of imputability of their responsibility to the Government of the United Kingdom, the question arises whether under some exceptional circumstance responsibility for these wrongs ceases to be imputable to the United Kingdom. In particular, this question brings to the fore the problem of Arab States' economic boycott of Israel. Are legislative and economic measures enforced by the Rulers in their territories against Israel *ipso facto* imputable to the United Kingdom?

Although it is not known whether the Government of Israel has delivered any such protest to the United Kingdom, it may be possible to say that such protests do not lie against the United Kingdom. The latter cannot, therefore, be held responsible for the Rulers' action in this respect. This is because the United Kingdom has no power to prevent the Rulers from prosecuting measures which are part of their own domestic jurisdiction and sovereignty so long as these measures do not cause injuries to foreign nationals in the Shaikhdoms, in the sense that they give rise to their international responsibility. It is clear that measures taken by the Rulers against Israel, trivial as they are, do not give rise to their international responsibility.[3] Moreover, the United Kingdom has no power, in law, to rescind the Rulers' decrees imposing the Israeli boycott in their territories, since the United Kingdom's legislation has no application in the Shaikhdoms which are independent governments.[4] The United Kingdom, for her part, does not seem to have raised objections to the functions of the Israeli Boycott Offices which are established in most of the Shaikhdoms and which are affiliated to the Israeli Boycott Committee of the Arab League.[5]

However, although it may be argued that the boycott measures taken by the Shaikhdoms against Israel do not give rise to their international responsibility, the question arises whether a third State

[1] Starke, op. cit., p. 116.   [2] Ibid.
[3] It is to be noted that the Jews who live in the Gulf possess the citizenships of the Shaikhdoms concerned.   [4] See above, p. 83.
[5] See *Arab Observer; The Middle East News Magazine*, 26 February 1961, p. 5, where Dr Ayedi, Commissioner General for the Economic Boycott of Israel, states: ' . . . the authorities in these emirates had assured him that regulations for the economic boycott of Israel were being strictly observed by them.'

friendly with the Shaikhdoms is entitled to protest diplomatically against measures taken in pursuance of this boycott, if such measures affect, directly or indirectly, the economic interests of its nationals who trade with Israel. In particular, this question relates to a protest which was made recently by the Government of the United States against some of the activities of the Kuwait Boycott Office. Thus, the United States was reported to have protested to the Government of Kuwait for alleged 'unwarranted interference in the commercial relationships of business firms'. This protest was made in consequence of letters sent to a large number of United States' commercial firms by the Israel Boycott Office in Kuwait in which they were asked to 'clarify the nature of their relations' with Israel and Israeli commercial concerns.[1] It is not known what reply was made by Kuwait to this protest. But it is noteworthy that the reports give the impression that the United States' protest was made directly to the Kuwait Government and not through the diplomatic channels of the United Kingdom.[2] This may well suggest that the United States had then recognised the international personality of Kuwait.[3]

RESPONSIBILITY FOR PROTECTION OF NATIONALS OF THE GULF STATES

It has been mentioned above that nationals of the Gulf States are treated, for the purposes of international law, as British nationals and that they, therefore, enjoy British diplomatic protection abroad.[4] According to Oppenheim,

A State may afford diplomatic protection to the subjects of a protected State or any other area under its protection or jurisdiction which does not form part of its territory.[5]

This principle was reaffirmed in the case *National Bank of Egypt* v. *Austro-Hungarian Bank* (Anglo-Austrian Mixed Arbitral Tribunal), 13 July 1923.[6] Is the British Government, by virtue of its diplomatic protection of nationals of the Gulf States abroad, entitled to espouse the claims of these nationals against foreign States?

Nationality of claims of British Protected Persons

The general principle regarding the nationality of claims is that a State is not entitled to espouse the claims of its nationals unless they possessed the nationality of the claimant State at the time of the occurrence of injuries to them and continued to do so until the claims

---

[1] See *The New York Times*, International Edition, Amsterdam, 28 August 1960; *Middle East Journal*, Autumn, 14 (1960), p. 449.   [2] Ibid.

[3] For a discussion about the international personality of Kuwait before independence, see above, pp. 76-7.   [4] See above, p. 127.   [5] Oppenheim, pp. 646-7, n. 3.

[6] *Annual Digest*, 1923-4, case No. 10.

were settled.[1] According to Cecil Hurst, the principle is defined as follows:

The person who suffered the injury out of which the claim arose must have possessed the nationality of the claimant state and not have possessed the nationality of the respondent state at the time of the occurrence . . . at the time when the claim is submitted to the Commission and continually up to the date of the award.[2]

It is clear from a number of arbitral awards that British practice supports the principle of espousal by the British Government of claims belonging to British protected persons.[3]

Presentation of claims on behalf of nationals of the Gulf States: appreciation of such claims in the light of generally accepted principles

It appears that in practice no case has arisen whereby a claim of a national of a Gulf State against a foreign government has been espoused by the British Government. Therefore, it is difficult to predict the attitude of the British Government towards such a claim should the occasion arise.

However, there seems no reason to assume that the British Government would not espouse claims presented by nationals of the Gulf States—the Shaikhdoms in particular—against foreign governments. The basis of British intervention in support of claims advanced by nationals of these States against foreign governments would be, provided all the other necessary conditions for the presentation of international claims were satisfied, that these nationals are, on the same footing as British nationals, entitled to British diplomatic protection abroad.[4]

---

[1] Garcia Amador, op. cit., p. 215; Sinclair, I. M., 'Nationality of Claims: British Practice', *B.Y.I.L.*, 27 (1950), pp. 129, 144; Briggs, H. W., *The Law of Nations, Cases, Documents and Notes*, 2nd ed. (1952), pp. 725–6.

[2] Hurst, Sir Cecil J. B., 'Nationality of Claims', *B.Y.I.L.*, 7 (1927), pp. 163, 180–2.

[3] For British practice in this matter, see the following awards: *Spanish Zone of Morocco Claims* (Great Britain v. Spain), 27 August 1924, *Annual Digest* (1923–4), Case No. 204; *National Bank of Egypt* v. *German Government and Bank für Handel und Industrie* (before the Anglo-German Mixed Arbitral Tribunal), 31 May 1924, and *National Bank of Egypt* v. *Austro-Hungarian Bank* (before the same tribunal), 13 July 1923, *Annual Digest* (1923–4), Cases No. 9 and 10. It should be pointed out, however, that, in the light of the principles enunciated in these cases, the British Government would not espouse a claim of a British protected person unless the claimant was a British protected person in the eyes of British municipal law at the time he suffered the injury giving rise to the claim and continued to be so until the claim was finally decided. And see, for example, *Spanish Zone of Morocco Claims* (Great Britain v. Spain), 29 December 1924, *Annual Digest* (1923–4), Cases No. 101 and No. 204. In this case the British espousal of the claim was rejected on the ground that the claimant, a British protected person, voluntarily renounced British protection before the date of arbitration.

[4] For the conditions for the presentation of such claims, see Meron, Theodor,

Settlement of claims of nationals of the Gulf States through the machinery of the International Court of Justice

It is relevant to discuss here whether the British Government can invoke the jurisdiction of the International Court for the settlement of such claims. Since the adjudication of disputes by the Court depends on the acceptance by the parties to the disputes (i.e., the two States) of the compulsory jurisdiction of the Court, through signature of the Optional Clause of Article 36 of the Statute of the Court, the question arises whether the signature of this Clause by the United Kingdom binds her in favour of the Gulf States.

(a) *Signature of the Optional Clause in favour of the Shaikhdoms*

There seems to be no difficulty in saying that the United Kingdom, by virtue of her international status and by virtue of her signature of the Optional Clause, is the only State which is capable of presenting international claims in favour of nationals—or governments—of the Shaikhdoms for settlement by the organs of the International Court. As mentioned before, the responsibility of the protecting State in espousing claims of nationals of a State under its protection 'proceeds from the fact that the protecting State alone represents the protected territory in its international relations'.[1] And so far as claims presented to the International Court by the protecting State on behalf of the protected State are concerned, Shabtai Rosenne states that

Article 35 (2) of the Statute does not, in as many words, limit the rights it gives only to *independent* States . . .[2]

Examples of State practice whereby claims were presented to the International Court by the protecting State partly on its behalf and partly on behalf of political units enjoying 'some recognisable international personality', though still lacking full independence, can be found without difficulty. Thus the decision of the Court in the *Rights of the United States Nationals in Morocco*, 1952, is a case in point. In this case, France made it clear that she was proceeding in the case both on her behalf and in her capacity as a protecting State. She also expressed her willingness to accept the decision of the Court 'as binding upon France and Morocco'.[3]

In conclusion, it may be submitted, in the light of the foregoing precedents, that the United Kingdom's signature of the Optional Clause binds her in favour of the Shaikhdoms.

'The Incidence of the Rule of Exhaustion of Local Remedies', *B.Y.I.L.*, 35 (1959), p. 100.

[1] *Annual Digest*, 1923–4, case No. 85.

[2] Rosenne, Shabtai, *The International Court of Justice* (1957), p. 235.

[3] *I.C.J. Reports*, 1952, pp. 178–80. And see Rosenne, op. cit., pp. 235–6.

(b) *Signature of the Optional Clause in favour of Muscat*

The question whether the signature of the Optional Clause by the United Kingdom binds her in favour of Muscat involves, no doubt, some complications. As explained elsewhere, Muscat is not a protected State, but the British Government has 'certain duties' in regard to the external affairs of Muscat. Muscat, in spite of her international status, is neither a member of the United Nations nor a party to the Statute of the International Court of Justice.[1]

However, the United Nations Charter makes provisions in Article 93 (2) for a State which is not a Member of the United Nations to become a party to the Statute, certain conditions being satisfied. In accordance with this provision Switzerland, for instance, became a party to the Statute in 1947, while Liechtenstein became a party to it in 1950.[2] According to Oppenheim,

the importance of becoming a party to the Statute lies, *inter alia*, in the fact that only a State which is a party to the Statute can effectively become signatory to the Optional Clause of Article 36 of the Statute and thus, by accepting the reciprocal obligations, secure for itself the benefits of the obligatory jurisdiction of the Court.[3]

It is clear that Muscat, as an independent State, can secure her admission as a party to the Statute under the above provisions and, therefore, become a signatory of the Optional Clause even though she is not a member of the United Nations.

But quite aside from the above procedure, Muscat is entitled in accordance with the resolution of the Security Council of 1946, to sign the Optional Clause at any time. It is, however, provided that 'such signature cannot be relied upon against States which are parties to the Statute unless they specifically agree'.[4] Moreover, the same resolution opens the door for States which are not parties to the Statute 'to become parties to disputes before the Court by accepting its jurisdiction with reference either to a particular dispute or to all disputes or particular classes of them'.[5] The State of Hyderabad made a declaration under the above provision in which it accepted compulsory jurisdiction of the Court in respect of its dispute with India 'concerning the interpretation of the principal Agreement, concluded in 1947, governing the relations between the two countries'.[6]

Consequently, Muscat, without even choosing to become a party to the Statute under Article 93 (2) of the United Nations Charter, can at any time that she becomes a party to a dispute with a foreign State—whether in connection with espousing claims of her nationals

---

[1] See p. 67. [2] Oppenheim, II, p. 53.
[3] Ibid., pp. 53–4. [4] For this resolution, see Oppenheim, II, p. 54.
[5] Ibid. [6] Ibid., p. 54, n. (2).

against a foreign government or other matters—accept the jurisdiction of the Court on any such matters. In so far as such claims are concerned, it seems clear that the British Government's signature of the Optional Clause will not apply to Muscat, being a non-protected State. The Government of Muscat is, therefore, originally entitled to espouse the claims of her nationals against foreign States. However, this does not mean that she cannot call on the British Government to act on her behalf in presenting such claims, or any other disputes, for international arbitrations.[1]

Nevertheless, it must be borne in mind that by espousing an international claim on behalf of Muscat, the British Government is merely acting as an agent and, therefore, it would be assumed that it cannot be in a better international position than the Government of Muscat while presenting such claims (i.e., Her Majesty's Government signature of the Clause will not cover Muscat).

---

[1] For an example of a dispute between Muscat and a foreign State in which the British Government acted on behalf of Muscat, see Chapter 13.

10

Immunity of the rulers of the Gulf States from the jurisdiction of foreign courts

THE PROBLEM OF JURISDICTIONAL IMMUNITIES OF PROTECTED STATES

The problem of the immunity of protected States and of their rulers from the jurisdiction of foreign courts arises from the generally accepted rule in international law that sovereigns and governments of independent States are entitled to jurisdictional immunities before foreign courts.[1] The question is whether semi-sovereign, or not fully independent, States are, on the same footing as independent States, entitled to immunity from the jurisdiction of foreign courts.

It seems that in practice the extent to which a State grants immunity from jurisdiction before its courts to rulers and governments of States under its protection is a matter of its own municipal law. Therefore, the question of granting immunity to such States is usually settled by a certificate issued by the executive; and the courts before which claims of immunity are put by such States generally regard the certificate as conclusive. But does this practice of granting immunity to not fully independent States indicate that there is a rule of international law to this effect?

(a) Position of British Protected States before British courts

It is clear from a number of decisions of English courts that these courts have constantly granted absolute immunity from their jurisdiction to rulers and governments of British protected States. However, it seems that English courts have acted in all, or the majority of, those cases on the advice of the authorities of the Crown, and thus treated the certificate received from those authorities as conclusive evidence regarding the immunity of the protected States concerned.[2] Lord McNair explains the principle upon which British protected States are granted jurisdictional immunities before British courts by saying

---

[1] Oppenheim, p. 272; Moore, *A Digest of International Law*, vol. II (1906), pp. 558–9; Hyde, 1, p. 813. And see *Le Parlement Belge* (1880), 5 P.D. 197.

[2] For examples of granting jurisdictional immunities to rulers and governments of British protected States before British courts, see the following cases: *Mighell* v. *Sultan of Johore* [1894] 1 Q.B. 149; *Duff Development* v. *Government of Kelantan and Others* [1924] A.C. 797; *Sayce* v. *Ameer Ruler Sadiq Mohammed Abbasi Bahawalpur State* [1952] 2 Q.B. 390; *Sultan of Johore* v. *Abubakar Tunku Aris Bendahara and Others* [1952] A.C. 318.

that it should not be implied that because 'many protected States within the British Empire and their Heads enjoy in British Courts, a degree of state immunity similar to that which is customarily accorded to foreign States and their Heads', such States possess 'international personality'. Immunity accorded to such States, he continues, is 'a matter of British constitutional law and not of international law'.[1] Similarly, Keith confirms this British judicial practice in his comment on *Duff Development* v. *Kelantan* [1924], when he states:

> From an imperial point of view, the case is interesting as reaffirming the fact that, although the foreign policy of Malay States is entirely in British hands, and although in varying measure their administration is conducted under British guidance, yet they remain genuine independent States for purposes of private international law.[2]

It should be pointed out, however, that from the point of view of British constitutional law, jurisdictional immunity before British courts is accorded only to sovereigns and governments of protected States as such; African chiefs of colonial protectorates, who unlike sovereigns of protected States are not regarded as possessing sovereign rights, are, therefore, denied immunity before British courts. A case in point is that of *Chief Tschekodi Khama* v. *S. Ratshosa and Others* [1931],[3] in which a letter was issued 'on behalf of the Secretary of State for the Dominions to the effect that the appellant was not recognised by His Majesty's Government as having sovereign rights'.[4]

In connection with the Gulf Shaikhdoms,[5] it may be assumed that owing to their sovereign status, they would be treated as immune from the jurisdiction of British courts, in accordance with the principle applied to the former Malay States. Therefore, they would clearly come within the scope of Dicey's rule which states:

> The Court has no jurisdiction to entertain an action or other proceedings against (1) any foreign State, or the head of government or any department of the government of any foreign State.[6]

Moreover, Dicey specifically includes within the scope of this rule 'any State under the protection of Her Majesty'. 'And the expression

---

[1] McNair, *Opinions*, 1, p. 23, n. 1.

[2] Keith, A. B., 'Notes on Imperial Constitutional Law: Jurisdiction in Respect of Sovereign States under British Protection', *Journal of Comparative Legislation and International Law*, 5 (1923), p. 127.

[3] [1931] A.C. 784.

[4] Ibid., p. 785.

[5] Muscat is excluded from this discussion because, on account of her full independence, her immunity before British courts is less doubtful. As regards Kuwait the discussion deals with her status as a British protected State (i.e., before her full independence in 1961).

[6] Dicey, A. V., *Conflict of Laws*, 7th ed. (1958), Rule No. 17, p. 129.

"foreign State" ', he says, 'as employed in the Rule is to be understood in this sense.'[1] On the other hand, regarding the position of a State under the protection of a foreign country before British courts, Dicey seems to be less certain. He thus states:

It is less certain whether a similar immunity is enjoyed by any State under the protection of a foreign sovereign State as such—for instance, Morocco, which was until very recently under the protection of France.[2]

The fact that the Gulf Shaikhdoms are accorded jurisdictional immunities before British courts within the meaning of the above-mentioned Dicey's rule has very recently been confirmed as a result of the judgment of the High Court of Justice (Queen's Bench Division) in *Antoun* v. *Harrison & Sons Ltd., and Others*, of 23 September 1965.[3] In this case, Mr Justice Waller gave judgment against granting Mr Antoun, stamp dealer, 'an interlocutory injunction to restrain' Harrison & Sons, Ltd, printers, and the Crown Agents 'from parting with possession of Ras al Khaiman stamps printed by Harrisons, or the proceeds of sale thereof alleged to be now in the defendant's possession'. In this judgment His Lordship

also set aside the writ in Mr Antoun's proposed action and stayed the proceedings, on the ground that the postage stamps and the proceeds of sale thereof, the subject matter of the action, were the property of a foreign sovereign, namely, the Ruler of Ras al Khaimah (Shaikh Saqr bin Muhammad bin Salem), and in his possession and control.

Summarising the facts of this case, His Lordship stated that it

arose out of an agreement—the nature of which was in issue—made between Mr Antoun and the Ruler of Ras al Khaimah, one of the Trucial States. It made arrangements, to the financial advantage of both parties, for the sale of stamps from that State, principally to philatelists. The Ruler had determined the agreement; and the plaintiff was seeking to obtain the stamps, and money received by the defendants for the sale of the stamps which was in their hands.

It is interesting to remark that this case establishes an unprecedented evidence in support of the principle of granting jurisdictional immunities to Rulers of the Arabian Gulf Shaikhdoms before English courts. The portions of the judgment in this case which deal with the sovereign immunity of the Ruler of Ras al Khaimah, on the basis of the principles of international law, are as follows:

The principle to be applied in considering the question of sovereign immunity had been stated by Viscount Simonds in *Rahimtoola* v. *Nizam of Hyderabad* (1958) . . . where he had cited from Lord Atkin's speech in . . . (the) *Cristina* (1938) . . . the two principles of international law which were

---

[1] Ibid., p. 134. [2] Ibid., pp. 134–5.
[3] *The Times*, 24 September 1965, p. 15.

... that the courts would not implead a foreign sovereign, and would not by their process, whether or not the sovereign was a party to the proceedings, seize or detain property which was his, or of which he was in possession or control. And Viscount Simonds had later (at p. 396) said that 'property' was not to be confined to valuables but included contract debts or other choses in action.

Furthermore, in upholding the Ruler's sovereign right to cancel by decree the agreement with the plaintiff, Mr Justice Waller stated:

It was agreed that the Ruler of Ras al Khaimah was an independent sovereign. Although the plaintiff made the first approaches, the stamps were ordered by a letter from the Ruler to Harrisons. Harrisons continued to deal with the plaintiff until the formal order by the Crown Agents was made on behalf of the Ruler on August 11.[1]

(b) *Position of British Protected States before foreign courts*

The problem of jurisdictional immunities of Rulers of the Gulf States becomes more difficult when one considers the position of these Rulers before foreign courts. The question arises whether such courts would extend to the Rulers of the Gulf States sovereign immunities similar to those which are usually extended in international law to sovereigns of independent States?

The general practice in America and in some continental countries has been in favour of extending jurisdictional immunities to semi-sovereign entities under their own protection. Some of these countries have even gone as far as to accord immunities to some of their colonial dependencies.[2] Concerning the position of semi-sovereign States under the protection of third States before the courts of these countries, the practice has also shown that some of these countries do, in fact, extend immunity to such semi-sovereign States. The general principle upon which immunity to such semi-sovereign entities has been accorded in continental countries is that 'the entity claiming the immunity need not be a "State" in the traditional sense, but it must be a person of international law'.[3] A reference to United States practice shows that the question of determining sovereign immunities of

[1] By a letter dated 12 August, the Ruler 'informed the plaintiff that the Agreement was cancelled, and that a decree to that effect had been made on August 11' *The Times*, 24 September 1965, p. 15.
[2] Sucharitkul, S., *State Immunities and Trading Activities* (1959), p. 109, n. 23 According to the author, States 'have granted immunities to colonial dependencies of foreign States on the ground that the actions in fact impleaded the foreign governments'. On United Kingdom's practice in this respect, Dicey states: 'But if an entity of this sort is not entitled to immunity *qua* a foreign State, it may well be so entitled *qua* a part of the State under whose protection it is.' See Dicey op. cit., p. 135.
[3] Allen, E. W., *The Position of Foreign States Before National Courts, Chiefly in Continental Europe* (1933), p. 239.

States of doubtful status, such as protected States, is usually decided not by the court entertaining the issue, but by the State Department.[1]

It may be deduced from the above statements that in a claim of immunity by a Ruler of one of the Shaikhdoms before an American court, the State Department would, probably, inquire about his legal status from the British Foreign Office before issuing a certificate to the court in question. This should not, however, be understood as implying that the State Department would be inclined to accept a statement made by the British Foreign Office in favour of the sovereign status of the Ruler concerned as conclusive. But in a claim of immunity by the Sultan of Muscat, it seems doubtful that the State Department would have recourse to the British Government for the ascertainment of his sovereign status since the United States has already recognised the full independence of the Sultan. Similarly, it may be presumed that in claims of immunity introduced by the Rulers of the Shaikhdoms before the courts of European and Commonwealth countries, these courts would give weight to declarations made by the British Foreign Office as to the sovereign status of such Rulers. It cannot, however, be suggested that in such cases European and Commonwealth courts would consider themselves bound by the declarations made by the British Government in favour of the sovereign immunities of the Rulers concerned.

LEGAL BASIS FOR IMMUNITY OF PROTECTED STATES

Does the above practice indicate that there is a general rule of international law regarding jurisdictional immunity in those cases? It has been shown from reference to a number of decisions of British and foreign courts on claims of jurisdictional immunity by not fully independent States, that such States have very often been granted jurisdictional immunities on the basis of certificates issued to the courts by the executive. In most of those cases immunities have been granted by a State to rulers and governments of territories under its protection, not on the basis of a rule of customary international law, but on a rule derived from its own constitutional system. However, the crucial issue in this discussion seems to be whether there is any general rule of international law recognising immunity before foreign courts of governments and rulers under the protection of third States. In view of lack of practice in this matter it is difficult to confirm the evolution

---

[1] Lyons, A. B., 'Conclusiveness of the Statements of the Executive: Continental and Latin American Practice', *B.Y.I.L.*, 25 (1948), p. 194; 'The Conclusiveness of the "Suggestion" and Certificate of the American State Department', *B.Y.I.L.*, 24 (1947), p. 116. According to the writer, 'when an application of this kind is made to the Department of State, the reply is often conveyed to the court by the medium of a procedural device known as a "Suggestion"'. And see for more details, Feller, A. H., 'Procedure in Cases Involving Immunity of Foreign States in United States Courts', *A.J.I.L.*, 25 (1931), pp. 83–96.

of such a rule. It is true, however, that in one French case, that of *Seyyid Ali Ben Hamod,* 1916,[1] the French court approved, in principle, the sovereign immunity of an ex-Sultan of Zanzibar, a ruler of a former British protectorate, from its jurisdiction. But apart from the fact that it is not clear from this decision whether the French court relied on a certificate from the executive, this seems to be an isolated decision which cannot be taken as a basis of a general rule of law.

It is therefore very difficult to establish, in the light of the above discussion, that breach of the sovereign immunity of any of the Rulers of the Gulf Shaikhdoms before non-British courts is breach of international law. With regard to the position of the Sultan of Muscat before foreign courts, it may be possible to say that breach of his sovereign immunity before the court of a State that has already recognised him as a sovereign could lead to breach of international law. But it is, perhaps, doubtful whether there exists a legal duty on the courts of those States which have not recognised the Sultan as an independent sovereign to extend to him sovereign immunities, in accordance with the rules of customary international law.

---

[1] *Wiercinski* v. *Seyyid Ali Ben Hamod,* 1916, *Journal du Droit International,* XLIV (1917), p. 1465, quoted by Allen, op. cit., p. 157. In this case, the ex-Sultan of Zanzibar was sued for the payment of a bill for medical treatment. However, although the court decided that the Sultan was entitled, in his capacity as a foreign sovereign, to jurisdictional immunity, it nevertheless treated the case as an exception to the rule on the ground that, in accordance with the provisions of the *Code civil,* the Sultan 'acted in his own personal interests'. As is known, European courts generally differentiate between *jure imperii* acts and *jure gestionis* acts. They grant immunity to foreign sovereigns only in respect of claims involving *jure imperii* acts of such sovereigns. Therefore, all the personal activities of the foreign sovereigns which come within the provisions of the *Code civil,* and to which the expression *jure gestionis* applies, are excluded from the application to them of sovereign immunity. For details on the practices of European courts in this matter, see Hamson, C. J., 'Immunity of Foreign States, the Practice of the French Courts', *B.Y.I.L.,* 27 (1950), pp. 293 et seq.; Walton, F. P., 'States Immunity in the Laws of England, France, Italy and Belgium', *Journal of Comparative Legislation and International Law,* 2 (1920), pp. 252 et seq.

11

Position within the framework of the United Nations

In practice, the United Kingdom has not treated the Gulf States at
non-self-governing territories, within the meaning of Chapter XI of
the Charter. Other States have concurred in this practice. However, it
may be desirable to explain, by reference to both theory and practice,
why there has been no problem in this respect.

The obligation under Chapter XI of the Charter

Chapter XI, entitled 'Declaration Regarding Non-Self-Governing
Territories', recites that Members of the Organisation who are
responsible for the administration of Territories that

have not yet attained a full measure of self-government recognize the
principle that the interests of the inhabitants of these territories are paramount, and accept as a sacred trust the obligation to promote to the
utmost, within the system of international peace and security . . . the well
being of the inhabitants of these territories . . .

To this effect, they undertake to observe a number of responsibilities regarding the political, economic and social advancement of
these territories, and, in particular, 'to develop self-government' in
them. Furthermore, they undertake, under Article 73(e),

to transmit regularly to the Secretary-General for information purposes,
subject to such limitation as security and constitutional considerations may
require, statistical and other information of a technical nature relating to
economic, social, and educational conditions in the territories for which
they are respectively responsible other than those territories to which
Chapters XII and XIII apply.[1]

The territories in respect of which information is required to be
submitted, under paragraph (e) of Article 73, are those territories
'whose peoples have not yet attained a full measure of self-government'. The significance of this phrase was clearly noted during the
early debates marking the preliminary work on the draft of Chapter

[1] The United Nations, *Charter of the United Nations and Statute of the International Court of Justice*, published by the United Nations, Department of Public
Information, New York, 1956.

XI, presented at the San Francisco Conference in 1945. The original draft of Chapter XI described the territories to be covered by this Chapter as those

territories inhabited by peoples not yet able to stand by themselves under the strenuous conditions of the modern world.[1]

This phrase was taken from Article 22 of the Covenant of the League of Nations. However, during the discussion on the draft it was thought desirable by the majority of delegates that this phrase should be deleted in favour of the phrase

territories whose peoples have not yet attained a full measure of self-government.

which was thus adopted.[2] The suggestion by the Chinese delegation that the words 'or independence' should be added after 'self-government' in the above phrase was defeated. But, as a compromise, the phrase 'self-government or independence' was adopted as a goal for 'Trust Territories' with which Chapters XII and XIII now deal.

The practice

In 1946, Members of the United Nations took the first initiative towards putting the declaration concerning non-self-governing territories, contained in Chapter XI, into effect. After a general review of the various aspects of the problems of these territories, the General Assembly adopted its first resolution 9(1) of 9 February 1946 on this question. In this resolution the General Assembly affirmed

the fact that the obligations accepted under chapter XI of the charter by all Members of the United Nations are in no way contingent upon the conclusion of Trusteeship agreement and that they are already in full force.[3]

During the 1947 session of the General Assembly a number of resolutions were adopted which approved the principle of the 'voluntary' nature of information transmitted under Article 73(e).[4]

Competence of the General Assembly to examine information transmitted: question of accountability to the Organisation

During the 1948 and the 1949 sessions of the General Assembly the controversy arose as to the extent to which Members administering non-self-governing territories were directly responsible to the General

---

[1] *UNCIO*, vol. 3, Document 2-G/26(e), pp. 615–18; ibid., vol. 10, Document 323 II/4/12, pp. 677; ibid., Document 892/II/4/36, pp. 525, 575.

[2] Ibid., vol. 10, p. 575.

[3] *U.N.G.A.*, 1st sess. 1st mtg, 27th plen. mtg (1946), pp. 366–76. For the report of the 4th Committee, see ibid., Annex 13, pp. 588–91.

[4] *U.N.G.A.*, 2nd sess., 108th plen. mtg. 3 Nov. (1947), p. 704 (Resolutions 144(II) and 146(II)); ibid., 4th Committee, 36th mtg (1947), p. 29.

Assembly in respect of their administration of such territories. This controversy was precipitated by the fact that the number of territories in respect of which information was transmitted in 1948 dropped from seventy-four (the figure for 1946) to sixty-three.[1] The ultimate result of the General Assembly's debate in 1949 was the adoption of a number of resolutions which vested the General Assembly with some obligations in respect of transmission of information under Article 73(e) and allowed for the establishment of a 'Special Committee' for this purpose. One of the most important resolutions adopted in 1949 was Resolution 334 (IV) of 2 December 1949. This resolution can be regarded as a victory for those Members who wanted the United Nations to take an active role in examining information transmitted under Article 73(e). It stated, *inter alia*, that the General Assembly

2. Invites any special committee which the General Assembly may appoint on information transmitted under Article 73(e) of the Charter to examine the factors which should be taken into account in deciding whether any territory is or is not a territory whose people have not yet attained a full measure of self-government.[2]

The determination of territories to which Chapter XI of the Charter applies

During the General Assembly's 1951 to 1953 sessions the controversy over the right of the General Assembly to determine whether a territory is or is not a territory whose people have not yet attained a full measure of self-government continued in full force. In these sessions also differences arose between Members of the administering Powers and some other Members on the interpretation of the term 'self-government'.[3] However, in 1953 the stalemate ended when the General Assembly, on the recommendation of the Fourth Committee, adopted Resolution 742 (VIII) of 4 August 1953 on the list of factors which should be taken into consideration in deciding whether a territory has or has not attained a full measure of self-government, in

---

[1] *U.N.G.A.*, 3rd sess., 1st part, 155th plen. mtg, 3 Nov. (1948), pp. 380–94. For details, see ibid., 4th sess., 4th Committee, 115th–118th and 120th–127th mtgs, 3–18 Nov. (1949), pp. 128–98.
[2] *U.N.G.A.*, 4th sess., 263rd plen. mtg, 2 December (1949), pp. 457–61.
[3] For the discussions of the 4th Committee and the *Ad Hoc* Committees regarding these questions, see *U.N.G.A.*, 7th sess., 4th Committee, 271st–279th mtgs, 12–19 Nov. (1952), pp. 151–208. See also ibid., 6th sess., Suppl. No. 14 (Report of the Special Committee of Information), 1951. For writers' definitions of the phrase 'self-government', see Kelsen, H., *The Law of the United Nations* (1950), pp. 555–6; Goodrich and Hambro, *The Charter of the United Nations* (1949), pp. 406–7; Baron von Asbeck, 'International Law and Colonial Administration', *Transactions of the Grotius Society*, 39 (1953), pp. 23–4, 28. von Asbeck maintains that '. . . once the obligations of colonial administration are essentially described in the Charter, an international treaty, they are lifted from the domestic into the international sphere. . . .'

accordance with Article 73 of the Charter. This resolution adopted a flexible definition of 'self-government' which does not exclude independence as an alternative. The list of some of the factors adopted in this resolution included the following: (a) The attainment of independence. (b) The complete freedom of the people of the territory to choose the form of government which they desire. (c) Political advancement of the population sufficient to enable them to decide upon the future destiny of the territory with due knowledge.[1]

United Kingdom's action

British criteria for the application of Chapter XI to non-self-governing territories for whose international relations the United Kingdom is responsible

In practice, the United Kingdom has, as stated above, declined to transmit information under Article 73(e) of the Charter in respect of the Gulf Shaikhdoms.[2] It should be recalled that when the United Kingdom enumerated, in 1946, in accordance with resolution 9 (I) and resolution 66 (I) of 1946, the non-self-governing territories under her administration, no mention was made in the United Kingdom's list of the Shaikhdoms.[3] Consequently, up to this date these Shaikhdoms have never appeared on the lists of non-self-governing territories introduced by the British Government, whether for the purpose of Article 73 of the Charter or for any other purpose of the United Nations' activities in relation to the problems of colonial or dependent peoples. Moreover, when the United Kingdom submitted in 1946 her list to the United Nations on the non-self-governing territories under her administration, no objections were made by Members to the non-inclusion within that list of the Gulf Shaikhdoms.[4]

The United Kingdom's action in not transmitting information to the United Nations on the Shaikhdoms, in accordance with Article

---

[1] *U.N.G.A.*, Suppl. No. 17, p. 21.

[2] The specific reference to the Shaikhdoms is intended to exclude the Sultanate of Muscat which, being an independent State, does not come within the scope of this discussion. The expression 'the Shaikhdoms', however, covers Kuwait prior to 1961, the date of her full independence.

[3] See above, pp. 152-3. The territories under British administration which were enumerated in 1946, included all British colonies, African Protectorates (including Zanzibar). In later years the British protected States of Malay were added. See *NSGT*, year 1946 (1947), Appendix IV; *Y.U.N.* (1946-7), p. 571.

[4] It is to be recalled that when administering Powers presented their lists of territories under their administration to the United Nations, these lists were accepted as a basis for future specification by administering Powers of territories under their control. See *NSGT*, year 1946, op. cit., Appendix IV. See also *UNCIO*, vol. 10, pp. 434, 446. There, the Chairman ruled that the obligation on the part of administering Powers was to refer specifically to 'individual territories' under their administration.

73(e), appears to be consistent with her own construction of Chapter XI of the Charter. As explained elsewhere in this discussion, the United Kingdom, together with other States responsible for the administration of colonial peoples, has always maintained that the basic element in judging whether a particular territory should come within the scope of Chapter XI or not is not independence, as argued by some other Members, but the extent to which this territory has its own indigenous self-government. In other words, in interpreting Chapter XI, the United Kingdom took the view that the phrase 'self-government' in the preamble of Article 73 is not an alternative to independence.[1] Accordingly she held that a British overseas territory could attain 'a full measure of self-government', which thus excludes it from the application of Chapter XI, while the United Kingdom still remains responsible for its external affairs.[2] During the second session of the General Assembly Mr Creech-Jones, for the United Kingdom, explained what he considered to be 'a flexible' meaning of 'self-government' in these words:

. . . self-government was a living process which differed from territory to territory. . . . There were United Kingdom territories which, while not in full control of their external affairs, were nevertheless fully responsible for the conduct of their internal affairs. These territories included Burma, Ceylon and Malta, and they fell completely outside chapters XI and XII.[3]

It can be assumed, in the light of the above statement, that the British Government, not being in fact responsible for the internal government of the Shaikhdoms, has, therefore, treated them as self-governing territories to which Chapter XI does not apply. Moreover, it can be argued that these Shaikhdoms are not non-self-governing territories in the sense envisaged in Chapter XI. And the fact that they are sovereign States which have, by treaties, entrusted the control of their external affairs to the United Kingdom does not reduce their status to that of dependent territories within the meaning of Article 73. The responsibility of the British Government towards these States is, therefore, not based on the obligations embodied in Chapter XI, as is the case with other British colonies and protectorates which are directly administered by the British Government, but on obligations embodied in the treaties between the British Government and these States. Further, it may be argued that even as self-governing territories, these States, unlike British self-governing territories, have not attained this status through an evolution from a colonial system within the British Dominion.

On the other hand, a construction of Chapter XI on the lines suggested by some other Members of the United Nations—the so-called

---

[1] See above, pp. 152–3. And see *NSGT*, year 1946 (1947), pp. 132–6.
[2] Ibid.   [3] *U.N.G.A.*, 2nd sess., 4th Committee, 43rd mtg (1947), p. 80.

anti-colonial group[1]—would suggest that so long as the Shaikhdoms, or any other territories which are not fully independent of foreign control, are internationally represented by the United Kingdom, they should remain subject to the obligations of Article 73 (e). Therefore, it can be contended, if this latter construction of Chapter XI is maintained, that by removing these Shaikhdoms from the scope of Chapter XI, the United Kingdom has not only escaped responsibility in respect of the affairs of these Shaikhdoms, which she still controls, but also deprived the peoples of the Shaikhdoms from the right to make their voice heard, on their own account, before an international forum such as the United Nations.

COMPETENCE OF THE UNITED NATIONS TO SETTLE DISPUTES ARISING BETWEEN THE GULF STATES AND THE UNITED KINGDOM

The problem

Is the United Nations entitled to intervene in disputes between a State Member of the United Nations and States or territories over which it exercises rights of protection? Since the relations between a protecting and a protected State are not equal to relations between two independent States, the question of settlement of disputes between them by the United Nations is, therefore, one of whether these disputes are within the 'domestic jurisdiction' of the protecting State, and of whether there is a threat to the peace. Article 2, paragraph 7, of the Charter provides:

Nothing contained in the present Charter shall authorize the United Nations to intervene in matters which are essentially within the domestic jurisdiction of any state or shall require the Members to submit such matters to settlement under the present Charter; but this principle shall not prejudice the application of enforcement measures under Chapter VII.

Chapter VII of the Charter, to which the above Article refers, deals with 'actions with respect to threats to the peace, breaches of the peace, and acts of aggression'. Article 39 of this chapter explains the jurisdiction of the United Nations in this matter as follows:

The Security Council shall determine the existence of any threat to the peace, breach of the peace, or act of aggression and shall make recommendations, or decide what measures shall be taken in accordance with Articles 41 and 42, to maintain or restore international peace and security.

It can be deduced from the above provisions that if a dispute between a protected and a protecting State can properly be described

[1] For the views of this group, see *NSGT*, year 1946 (1947), pp. 130–3. In the same meeting the Indian representative expressed his surprise whether 'a territory not yet in full control of its external affairs could be said to enjoy full self-government under the terms of Article 73'. See ibid.

as 'domestic', within the meaning of Article 2, paragraph 7 of the Charter, then the United Nations is not authorised to intervene in the settlement of this dispute, unless it constitutes a threat to the peace, as envisaged in Chapter VII of the Charter. The practice of the United Nations shows that States have regarded disputes between them and their protectorates or dependencies as domestic matters which do not come within the jurisdiction of the United Nations. Examples of such disputes which were referred to, and decided by, the United Nations are those relating to the complaints of Indonesia, Hyderabad, and Morocco and Tunisia against their former protecting Powers, the Netherlands, India and France, respectively.[1] All those disputes involving protected and protecting States were continuously discussed by the United Nations during the first decade of its life, despite the protecting States' objections to their discussion on the ground of the 'domestic jurisdiction' principle. On the other hand, the questions of Indonesia, Hyderabad and Tunisia and Morocco show that the intervention by the United Nations in disputes between States members of the Organisation and their not fully independent territories was actuated by the fact that those disputes gave rise to situations which were likely to threaten the peace, as envisaged in Article 39 of the Charter. Moreover, all those disputes were brought before the United Nations not as colonial issues, where the domestic jurisdiction clause has a stronger application, but as political issues involving the resort to military actions by States against territories which constitute neither part of their metropolitan territories nor part of their colonies.[2] Consequently, the recommendations of the United Nations regarding those disputes were based on the principle of seeking a reconciliation between the two disputing parties and thus calling upon them to negotiate a peaceful settlement of their dispute in the light of the principle of self-determination.

The question of Oman before the United Nations

The question of Oman may be discussed here as an example of a dispute involving both the Sultanate of Muscat and the United Kingdom: the first for denying 'the Imamate of Oman the right to self-determination', and the second for sending British troops to Oman for the suppression of the Omani revolt against the Sultan's

---

[1] On the question of Indonesia, see *U.N.S.C.*, 2nd Year, No. 67, 171st mtg, 31 July 1947, p. 1616; ibid., No. 74, 173rd mtg, Resolution S/459, 1 August 1947. On the question of Hyderabad, see *U.N.S.C.*, 3rd Year, 357th mtg, 16 September 1948, pp. 7–15, 19 et seq. And on the questions of Tunisia and Morocco, see *U.N.G.A.*, 7th sess., 379th, 392nd, and 397th plen. mtgs, 16 October, 10–13 November 1952; ibid., 7th sess., 407th plen. mtg, 19 December 1952; ibid., 7th sess., Annexes, Item 69, Resolution 612 (VII), 19 December (1952).

[2] For a fuller explanation of this point, see Toussaint, C. E., 'The Colonial Controversy in the U.N.', *The Yearbook of World Affairs* 10 (1956), pp. 193–4.

authority. Accordingly, the Omani question is fundamentally a dispute between the Imam of the 'hinterland of Oman', who claims independence or 'internal autonomy' from the Sultan of Muscat, on the one hand, and both the Sultan and the British Government, on the other. In this dispute which has been on the agenda of the General Assembly for the last eight years or so, the British Government has always espoused the position of the Sultan of Muscat and Oman which is to the effect that the Omani complaint is a domestic matter over which the United Nations has no jurisdiction.[1] The United Nations, however, has, despite British objection, continued its consideration of this dispute. The history and developments of the dispute in the United Nations will now be discussed.

The question of Oman was first introduced in the United Nations in August 1957, when representatives of eleven Arab States requested, under Article 35 of the Charter, the convening of the Security Council to consider

the armed aggression by the United Kingdom . . . against the independence, sovereignty and the territorial integrity of the Imamate of Oman . . .[2]

This motion failed to be placed on the agenda. However, in September 1960 ten Arab States requested that the 'question of Oman' be placed on the agenda of the General Assembly's fifteenth Session. In their request, the Arab countries submitted that the 'Imamate of Oman', described as the hinterland of what is erroneously called the Sultanate of Muscat and Oman, had been invaded by British-led forces, and its capital occupied in December 1955. The question was allocated to the Special Political Committee and was considered by that Committee.[3] At the sixteenth session of the General Assembly, the Omani Representative, who was granted hearing by the Special Political Committee, stated that Oman 'had enjoyed freedom and independence for centuries and that the treaty of Sib of 1920 had confirmed that independence'.[4] The British representative, who spoke in favour of the Sultan of Muscat, maintained that the Sultan's sovereignty and independence over Muscat and Oman has been recognised in international treaties. As regards British military assistance to the Sultan, the British representative said that it was rendered at the request of the Sultan to help him suppress 'the rebellion of certain Shaikhs in 1954–55'. This object, he continued, was achieved in 1959, when the rebellion was put down and thus 'the area had since been at peace'. Further-

---

[1] For similar objections to United Nations discussion of disputes between protected and protecting States, see above, p. 157.

[2] See *Report of the Ad Hoc Committee on Oman* (*U.N.G.A.*, A/5846), 22 January 1965, p. 31.

[3] *Report of the Ad Hoc Committee on Oman*, op. cit., p. 32.

[4] Ibid., p. 33; *Y.U.N.*, 1961, pp. 149–50.

more, he apprised the Political Committee of the fact that the current discussion of the question 'constituted interference in the Sultanate's internal affairs in violation of Article 2(7) of the Charter' which precludes United Nations intervention in matters falling within the domestic jurisdiction of States.[1]

At the seventeenth session of the General Assembly, the question of Oman was again considered by the Special Political Committee. Consequently, a draft resolution, sponsored by eighteen States was approved. It stated:

The General Assembly, deeply concerned with the situation in Oman and recalling its resolution 1514(XV) of 14 December 1960, containing a declaration on the granting of independence to colonial countries and peoples, would (1) recognise the right of the people of Oman to self-determination and independence; (2) call for the withdrawal of foreign forces from Oman; and (3) invite the parties concerned to settle peacefully their differences with a view to restoring normal conditions in Oman.[2]

The above resolution, however, failed to receive the necessary two-thirds majority in the plenary meeting of the General Assembly, and was thus not adopted.[3]

In August 1963, Mr de Ribbing, Swedish Ambassador to Spain, who was earlier authorised by the Secretary-General to conduct a fact-finding mission on Oman, submitted his report to the Secretary-General.[4] On 18 September 1963 the Assembly's General Committee recommended the allocation of the question of Oman to the Fourth Committee. The discussion of the question in the Fourth Committee revealed that some representatives had regarded the question as a colonial issue arising from 'a series of treaties imposing heavy and unreasonable obligations on the Territory'.[5] On the other hand, the United Kingdom's representative took the other extreme line of defending the independence of 'Muscat and Oman', under the sovereignty of the Sultan. He rejected totally the argument that Muscat and Oman was a colonial territory or that the 'British colonial system' did in fact apply to it. In his view, which reflected that of the Sultan,[6] the 'so-called question of Oman' was an internal matter which fell outside

---

[1] Ibid., p. 34; *Y.U.N.*, 1961, pp. 150–1. For a fuller account of the British Government's position on Oman, see *U.N.* No. 1 Oman (1963) *Cmnd.* 2087 (Report on the Proceedings of the 17th Session of the General Assembly of the United Nations on Oman, September–December, 1962).

[2] *Y.U.N.*, 1961, p. 149; *Report of the Ad Hoc Committee*, op. cit., pp. 35–7.

[3] *Y.U.N.*, 1962, p. 147; ibid, 1963, p. 70.

[4] Ibid., 1963, p. 70. And see A/5562. Note by Secretary-General transmitting report of Special Representative of Secretary-General on his visit to Oman.

[5] *Report of the Ad Hoc Committee on Oman*, op. cit., p. 43; *Y.U.N.*, 1963, p. 71.

[6] See A/C.4/619. Cable of 26 October 1963, from Sultan of Muscat and Oman, objecting to the discussion of the question by the United Nations.

the jurisdiction of the United Nations.[1] The third group of representatives which emerged in the course of this debate maintained that 'whereas previously the question of Oman had been posed as a question of aggression by one State, namely Muscat, against another, Oman, now what was being sought was the end of colonialism not only in Oman but also in Muscat'.[2] Recalling these developments of the question to mind, this group of representatives had, therefore, urged the Committee to provide them with further 'impartial information' on Oman. With regard to the report of the Secretary-General's Special Representative, Mr de Ribbing, on Oman, it was held that due to the limited scope of Mr de Ribbing's mission (being a mere fact-finding mission), the latter's report was, therefore, not complete.[3] Finally, at the conclusion of the debate thirteen Latin-American States submitted a new draft resolution which proposed the establishing of an *Ad Hoc* Committee to examine the question of Oman and to report to the General Assembly at its nineteenth session in 1964. The General Assembly, at its plenary meeting on 11 December 1963, adopted the Latin-American draft as Resolution 1948 (XVIII) by a roll-call vote of 96 to 1, with 4 abstentions.[4]

In accordance with its mandate, the *Ad Hoc* Committee on Oman, consisting of five Member States, made contact with the Sultan and British officials in London, as well as the Imam of Oman and his representatives in the Middle East. Having collected the information it needed on the position in the Omani dispute, the *Ad Hoc* Committee submitted its report to the nineteenth session of the General Assembly which, in turn, unanimously adopted it on 8 January 1965.[5] In its report, the Committee, after reviewing the history of the question of Oman in the United Nations, sets out and examines the information it gathered and states its conclusions. In these conclusions the Committee considers, *inter alia*, the question of Oman as 'a serious international problem' requiring the special attention of the General Assembly. Furthermore, it upholds 'the legitimate aspirations of the people of Muscat and Oman' and requests the Assembly to call upon all parties concerned to facilitate and 'encourage a negotiated settle-

[1] *U.N.* No. 1 (1963), *Comnd.* 2087, op. cit.; *Y.U.N.*, 1963, p. 71.

[2] Ibid.

[3] *Y.U.N.*, 1963, 71. And see Report of the Special Representative of the Secretary-General, *U.N.G.A.*, Official Records, 18th sess., Annexes, Agenda item 78, doc. A/5562. In his report, Mr Ribbing stated that 'his mission did not have the time, nor did it consider itself competent, to evaluate the territorial, historical and political issues involved'.

[4] *Y.U.N.*, 1963, p. 72.

[5] *Report of the Ad Hoc Committee on Oman*, op. cit., pp. 4–5. It is to be noted that although the Sultan accepted to meet the Chairman of the Committee in London, where he was then staying, he, however, refused to allow the Committee to visit Muscat and Oman. He also told the Committee that he objected to the discussion of the dispute by the United Nations.

ment' which does not prejudice the position taken by either party.[1] In December 1965 the General Assembly approved this report of the Committee and passed a resolution calling on Britain to withdraw her military forces from Oman and to remove all forms of British domination in the area. The resolution also called for 'self-determination' in Oman. Acting on behalf of the Sultan, the British Government disapproved the report in question and voted against the General Assembly's resolution.[2]

The Shaikhdoms

In connection with the Gulf Shaikhdoms, it may be submitted, in the light of the general principles referred to above, that their disputes with the United Kingdom can, probably, be brought before the United Nations if they give rise to situations analogous to those cases referred to above (i.e., if such disputes constitute a threat to the peace, as envisaged in Article 39 of the Charter). However, it should be stated that the United Kingdom would have no right to resort to force in the event of disputes with the Gulf Shaikhdoms. This is doubly so, because of her obligations under the United Nations Charter and of the nature of her treaties with the Gulf States which do not allow her to interfere in their internal affairs or act contrary to their political progress towards full independence.

QUALIFICATION FOR MEMBERSHIP OF THE UNITED NATIONS

Are the Gulf States eligible for membership of the United Nations? According to Article 4 of the Charter,

Membership . . . is open to all other peace-loving states which accept the obligations contained in the present Charter and, in the judgment of the Organization, are able and willing to carry out these obligations.

These are the only conditions of membership of new States in the United Nations.[3]

It is clear from the above Article that (a) the word 'states' refers to sovereign independent States,[4] and (b) the phrase 'in the judgment of

---

[1] *Report of the Ad Hoc Committee on Oman*, op. cit., p. 222.
[2] United Nations *Monthly Chronicle*, II, No. 8, 1965, p. 87.
[3] Oppenheim, p. 408.
[4] It is quite clear from the phrase '. . . able and willing to carry out these obligations' contained in Article 4, paragraph 1 of the Charter that the applicant State must be fully independent so that it can be able to meet the obligations contained in the Charter. For an account about the requirement of full independence as a basis for membership in the United Nations, see *UNCIO*, vol. 1 (Verbatim Minutes of the 5th plen. sess., 30 April 1945), pp. 345-9. And see Russell, R. B., *The History of the United Nations* (1958), p. 358.

M

the Organization' acts as a qualification for membership.[1] In its decision of 1948, the International Court of Justice affirmed the principle that a State applying for membership cannot demand to be admitted to the United Nations by right, even if it has all the qualifications mentioned in paragraph 1, Article 4, since this is a matter which exclusively rests within the discretion of the Organisation itself.[2] Accordingly, it was held that even if such qualifications, as required by the Article in question do exist,

... the candidate cannot himself judge whether the conditions are fulfilled in conformity with Article 4. This is the task of the Organisation, which may, or may not, accept the proposal by a judgment which it alone can render. . . .[The question is] therefore . . . not . . . of right but simply of interest . . .[3]

The conclusion of the Court on the question of the interpretation of Article 4 was that

... these conditions constitute an exhaustive enumeration and are not merely stated by way of guidance or example. The provision would lose its significance and weight, if other conditions, unconnected with those laid down, could be demanded. The conditions stated in paragraph 1, Article 4 must therefore be regarded not merely as the necessary conditions, but also as the conditions which suffice.[4]

The General Assembly adopted, in 1951, resolution (A 506) in which the above decision of the Court was affirmed. This resolution was to the effect that the conditions embodied in Article 4 of the Charter constituted the only basis upon which the decision of the Organisation should be based.[5]

The Gulf States

With regard to Muscat, there seems little difficulty in saying that owing to her independence and sovereignty, in law, she will be entitled to membership of the Organisation.[6] The independence of Muscat is now

---

[1] Humber, P. O., 'Admission to the United Nations', *B.Y.I.L.* 24 (1947), pp. 10 et seq. For a comparison between Article 4 of the Charter and Article 1 of the League of Nations Covenant which declares that 'any fully self-governing State Dominion or colony . . . may become member of the League', see Green, L. C 'Membership of the United Nations', *Current Legal Problems*, 2 (1949), pp. 262–

[2] *I.C.J. Reports*, 1948, pp. 57–63.

[3] Ibid., p. 77, per Judge Azevedo.

[4] Ibid., p. 62. For a fuller examination of the Court's opinion in this case and in the case on the *Competence of the General Assembly for the Admission of State to the United Nations* (1950), see Fitzmaurice, Sir G. Gerald, 'The Law and Procedure of the International Court of Justice: International Organs and Tribunals', *B.Y.I.L.*, 29 (1952), pp. 22–8.   [5] Oppenheim, p. 410, n. 1.

[6] In his cable of 20 June 1964 to the *Ad Hoc Committee on Oman*, op. cit., pp. 1– the Sultan stated that 'we . . . have not yet thought it desirable to join the United Nations'.

recognised *de facto* by five States Members of the United Nations, namely Britain, the United States, France, Holland and India. However, the fact that Muscat does not maintain diplomatic relations with foreign States, that she is still represented internationally by the United Kingdom, and that she still maintains treaties of alliance and friendship with the United Kingdom which derogate from her political independence,[1] could be regarded by States Members of the United Nations as grounds for opposing Muscat's application for membership in the United Nations. The practice of the United Nations, in this respect, shows that on a number of occasions applications for membership in the Organisation were opposed both in the Security Council and in the General Assembly on the grounds that the applicants either had no diplomatic representations with some States or group of States, or that they were bound by treaties of alliance which deprived them of their 'territorial integrity and political independence'.[2]

With regard to the Shaikhdoms, it can be stated that because (*a*) the requirements of the Charter for membership are largely subjective, and (*b*) these are not States in customary international law (they lack the capacity to enter into relations with other States), they are, therefore, not entitled to membership in the United Nations.

It is true, however, that there were among the original Members of the United Nations which took part in the United Nations Conference on the International Organisation at San Francisco, in April and June 1945, countries, such as India, the Philippines,[3] Ukraine and White Russia,[4] which lacked full 'statehood' or 'independence all round'.[5]

---

[1] See above, pp. 47–9, 159.

[2] For example, in 1946 and 1947, objections were made by the Soviet Union to membership of Ireland, Portugal, Transjordan (Jordan) and Siam on the ground that these countries had no diplomatic representations with the Soviet Union. For a fuller account of the debates on this question, see U.N.*S.C.*, 1st year, 2nd eries, 56th mtg, 29 Aug. (1946), pp. 81–97. On admission of new members generally, see U.N.*S.C.*, Suppl. No. 4, 28 Aug. (1946), pp. 17–148; Humber, op. cit., p. 102; *Y.U.N.* (1946–7), pp. 417, 569–73.

In the United Nations' questionnaire sent to the Government of Transjordan following its application for membership of 26 June 1946 Transjordan was asked to show the effect of its Treaty of Alliance of 22 March 1946 with the United Kingdom on the maintenance of its 'territorial integrity and political independence'. See U.N.*S.C.*, 1st year, 2nd Series, Suppl. No. 4, 28 Aug (1946), p. 5. For Transjordan's reply, see ibid., Annex 19, p. 145.

[3] According to Russell, during the Malta and Yalta Conferences the discussion of the draft Constitution of the present Charter did not take into account the anomalous position of India and the Philippines as signers of the Declaration by the United Nations despite their non-self-governing status . . .' See Russell, op. cit., pp. 351 (footnote), 354.

[4] With regard to the initial membership of the two Soviet Republics, the Ukraine and Byelo-Russia, the issue, says Russell, was clearly a political one; it was based on the commitments given by President Roosevelt to the Soviet Government during the Yalta Conference. See Russell, op. cit., pp. 631–2.

[5] Oppenheim, p. 119.

But it is doubtful that the procedure under which those countries were admitted, as original Members, in the United Nations is relevant to the discussion of the membership of the Shaikhdoms.[1] It is quite clear from that procedure that the original membership of the above countries in the United Nations was decided on political rather than legal grounds.[2] Therefore, the membership of these countries constituted a special case.

[1] Indeed, the former Shaikhdom of Kuwait was admitted to the United Nations only after, and not before, her full independence from the United Kingdom on 19 June 1961. For the developments on this issue, see below, p. 251.

[2] For the unanimous acceptance of the original membership of the Ukraine and White Russia by the Conference of the International Organisation, see *UNCIO*, vol. 1 (Verbatim Minutes of 2nd plen. sess., 27 April 1945, document 20 (English), p. 16), pp. 166–8.

PART THREE

TERRITORIAL CLAIMS

12

Iran's claim to sovereignty over Bahrain[1]

Diplomatic history of the Anglo-Iranian controversy

Bahrain's early history is obscure. According to classical historians, in about 1900 B.C. Arabs from the Yemen settled there.[2] Before the rise of Islam in the seventh century Persians as well as other nations seem to have dominated the island on account of its pearl-fisheries. Between the seventh and eleventh centuries it formed part of the Islamic Empire, under Arab governors who were subject to the authority of the Caliph. After the downfall of the Abbasid Caliphate in the eleventh century, Bahrain, on account of its nearness to the eastern Arabian coast, came to be governed by various independent Arab dynasties until the beginning of the sixteenth century, when it was occupied by the Portuguese. The Portuguese governed the island from 1522 to 1602, being finally expelled from the Arabian Gulf in 1622. In 1602, the Persians conquered the island and it remained under their domination until 1783. But even during these years the Persian occupation was not uninterrupted, for on many occasions the islands were wrested from the Persians by Arab Shaikhs, who occupied Bahrain for short periods. In 1718 and 1720, Bahrain was held by the Sultan of Muscat. Persia's final loss of Bahrain was in 1783 when it was conquered by the strong 'Utubi rulers of Zubarah, from the Qatar coast.[3] The sovereignty of the present dynasty of Al-Khalifah (descendants of the 'Utubi tribe) over Bahrain remains undisturbed until the present day.

The controversy between Persia and Britain over the sovereignty of Bahrain can be traced back to 1820, when Britain concluded the Treaty of Peace with the Ruler of Bahrain and with other Rulers of the Gulf States.

Although Persia had lost Bahrain to Al-Khalifah in 1783, she renewed her efforts to regain control of the islands. Owing to her military weakness she adopted the policy of encouraging the Sultan of

[1] 'Iran' and 'Persia' are synonyms referring to the same country. The former has in modern time been the official name of the country. In this chapter the name 'Persia' will be used because it is the name which is more frequently used in documents relating to this dispute.

[2] *Bombay Selections*, pp. 1–40; Oestrup J., Al-'Bahrain', *Encyclopaedia of Islam*, vol. 1 (1913) pp. 584–5.

[3] Ibid,; Al-Nabhani *Tarikh al-Bahrain* (Cairo, 1924) pp. 11–50, 78–140; F.O. 60/118 (1845), Chronological table of events connected with Bahrain, etc., op. cit. These records show that the occupation of Bahrain by the Portuguese took place between 1522 and 1602, and not between 1507 and 1622, as stated by Oestrup, op. cit.

Muscat to conquer Bahrain.[1] At this stage the British Government had no definite policy towards Bahrain but took a neutral stand, neither defending Bahrain nor assisting Persia.[2]

However, in 1822, the British Government in Bombay was taken by surprise at finding that an unauthorised agreement had been concluded between the Persian authorities in Shiraz and the British Political Resident in the Gulf, Captain William Bruce, in which the latter recognised the Persian title to Bahrain. The agreement, dated 30 August 1822, comprised five articles. In article 2, Bahrain was regarded as 'being always subordinate to the province of Fars'. And in articles 4 and 5, the British Government was committed to supply Persia with war vessels for the purpose of conquering Bahrain.[3]

This unauthorised agreement was disapproved of by the British Government in Bombay. Thus the Governor of Bombay, Mountstuart Elphinstone, immediately wrote to Captain Bruce expressing his surprise at the agreement which he said, 'is not only not authorised, but entirely inconsistent with the views of Government and with the obligation of the public faith'. He also denounced the admission of the King of Persia's title to Bahrain of which, he said, 'there is not the least proof', and which will be injurious to the 'independence of Uttubis, to whom we are bound by a treaty of friendship'. Finally, he concluded that he

has therefore been obliged to disavow the treaty in the most explicit terms . . . and . . . to remove you from your appointment of Resident at Bushire . . .[4]

Following his disavowal of Bruce's agreement, Mountstuart Elphinstone wrote to the Shaikh of Bahrain expressing his regret about the agreement and informing him of Britain's good intention towards Bahrain. In his letter to the Shaikh he said:

I beg leave to assure your Excellency that the British Government consider the relations with your State as existing in the same force as from the first and that it is my wish to preserve them undiminished.[5]

Bruce's agreement was also denounced by the Shah of Persia who expressed his displeasure to the Prince of Shiraz for entering into an

[1] F.O. 60/17, 1820. Correspondence between W. Grant Keir and Henry Willock, January–February 1920.
[2] Ibid., Bombay Government to Henry Willock, H.M.G. Chargé d'Affaires at Tehran, 15 December 1819.
[3] F.O. 60/21, 1822. Treaty of Shiraz, 30 August 1822.
[4] F.O. 60/112, 1845. Copy of a letter from the Secretary to the Government of Bombay to Captain Bruce, Resident at Bushire, Bombay Castle, 1 November 1822.
[5] F.O. 248/48. Draft of a letter from the Governor in Council to the Sheikh of Bahrain (no date), about November 1822.

engagement with the British authorities 'without his knowledge or injunction'.[1]

After this incident the Persian pretensions towards Bahrain were shelved for over twenty years, until 1845, when the Prime Minister of Persia, Meerza Aghassi, introduced his government's claim in an elaborate note to the British Government. Before discussing the reasons entertained by the Persian Premier in support of his Government's case it seems useful, for the purpose of this study, to refer to the occurrences between 1830–45 which seem to have overshadowed the formulation of the Persian claim.

Bahrain during this period was internally and externally unstable. Externally, the Ruler of Bahrain, who had previously paid tribute to the Wahhabi rulers of Najd, now stopped that payment and the relations between Bahrain and the Wahhabis underwent a great strain which, in 1833, developed into war between the two countries. The instability of Bahrain encouraged Persia to resume, with the co-operation of the Imam of Muscat, her threats to conquer it. But the Shaikh of Bahrain frustrated that threat by coming to terms, in 1836, with the Wahhabi Ruler who agreed to supply him with 'contingent of troops to repel any Persian invasion of Bahrain', while the Shaikh promised to pay a small tribute to the Wahhabi Ruler.[2]

The internal situation in Bahrain was disturbed from 1830 until 1843 by dynastic quarrels between the Shaikhs, which finally resulted in Shaikh Muhammad ibn Khalifah expelling his uncle Shaikh ʿAbd Allah, the Ruler, and seizing power himself. Shaikh ʿAbd Allah spent the rest of his life endeavouring to regain Bahrain by asking the help of the British, the Persians and the Sultan of Muscat. The Persians promised help, but the British refrained from taking part in a family quarrel.[3]

Thus, in an interview between Captain Hennell, British Resident at Bushire, and the Governor of Bushire, Captain Hennell informed the Persian Governor that he considered the dispute as a family affair and that, therefore,

so long as it was confined to themselves and the peace of the sea remained undisturbed by it, we did not favour one party more than the other.[4]

However, when it was known to the British Government that Persia was preparing a military expedition to Bahrain in support of the ex-Shaikh, who apparently had promised to accept Persian suzerainty once he succeeded in regaining the island, fresh instructions were

[1] I.O. Persia and Persian Gulf Series, vol. 35, 25 January 1823, p. 381.
[2] F.O. 60/118, 1845. Chronological table of events connected with Bahrain, etc., op. cit. May–June 1836–9.
[3] F.O. 60/98, 1843, Kemball to Sheil, 3 October 1843; F.O. 60/103, 1844, Sheil to Aberdeen, 25 January 1844.
[4] Ibid., Hennell to Sheil, 23 December 1843.

sent by the Government of India to the British authorities in the Gulf to meet the new circumstances arising from the Persian interference in the affairs of Bahrain.[1] The line of policy advocated in these instructions met with the approval of the British Foreign Secretary in London, Lord Aberdeen, who sent a Note to the British Minister at Tehran, Lt-Col Sheil, in which he supported the instructions of the Indian Government and added:

Unless Persia can show that she has a clear and undisputed right to the sovereignty of Bahrain, that she has exercised it without interruption under the dynasty of the Kajar family and consequently her present policy is directed to the maintenance of her lawful claims and not to the assertion of a pretension not founded in law, Persia must be prepared to encounter in any scheme of this kind the active opposition of the British Government in India.[2]

Lord Aberdeen further instructed Sheil to inform the Persian Minister

that Her Majesty's Government have heard with regret that it is reported to be in the contemplation of the Government of the Shah to take part in the disputes respecting the Government of Bahrain; that such proceeding will be viewed with much jealousy by the British Government . . .[3]

A prompt answer to Lord Aberdeen's Note was made by the Persian Prime Minister Haji Meerza Aghassi in a statement, dated 15 March 1844. In this, the Persian Premier attempted to introduce his Government's evidence for proving the right of Persia to the ownership of Bahrain. His arguments can be summed up as follows:

First, 'the Persian Gulf from the commencement of the Shatt ul-Arab to Muscat belongs to Persia, and that all the islands of that sea, without exception, and without participation of any other Government, belong entirely to Persia, as indeed in your Excellency's language, you call that sea the Persian Gulf.'
Secondly, 'Bahrain has always been under the authority of the Governor of Fars, from 1300 A.D.' But, he added, 'in the commencement of the reign of His Majesty the late Shah, the Arabs of the Beni Attubeh came . . . and conquered' it. 'From the tribe itself . . . presents have generally been sent to the Governor of Fars.'
Thirdly, 'all European and Turkish books of geography as well as the books of travellers considered Bahrain as Persian.'
Fourthly, Bruce's agreement of 1822 recognised Persia's ownership of Bahrain.[4]

---

[1] F.O. 60/102, 1844, Lt-Col Sheil, No. 23, F.O. 1 May 1844 (Extracts of Instructions from the India Board); F.O. 248/116, Bombay Castle, 29 February 1844, to the Secret Committee, East India Company.
[2] F.O. 248/116, 1844. Aberdeen to Sheil, 1 May 1844.   [3] Ibid.
[4] F.O. 60/113. Sheil to Aberdeen, 18 March 1845; F.O. 60/118, East India House, 31 July 1845, in reply to India Board; F.O. 31 May 1845. Enclosed Letter dated 15 March 1844, from Persian Prime Minister, Haji Meerza Aghassi.

In reply to the inquiries made by the India Board as regards the points raised by Haji Aghassi in his statement about Bahrain, the Secret Committee of the East India Company made the following observations in which it refuted the Persian claim:

First, 'with regard to the first point, the British Government has treated the Shaikhs of Bahrein as independent authorities' after their occupation of that island in 1783. The Egyptian Government, that of Mohammed Ali aimed at its possession and was deterred by the British representation in which no reference was made to Persia. The Imam of Muscat had repeatedly laid claim to it, and during some years it paid him tribute. The attempt to found an argument on the name of the Persian Gulf is open to the obvious remark, that the Red Sea is the Arabian Gulf, and that no one would venture to allege that all the islands in it belong to Arabia.'

Secondly, 'Bahrein may have been a dependency of Fars while the Persians were in actual possession of the island. But the allegation that they had possessed it from A.D. 1300 is contrary to the best evidence that can be produced on the subject.'

Thirdly, 'during the period when the Persians are admitted to have held possession of Bahrein travellers would of course speak of the island as a Persian possession. Chardin, however, speaks of the surrender of Bahrein by the Portuguese to the Persians in 1625 . . .'

Fourthly, 'with regard to the treaty made by Captain Bruce, the Committee noticed that it had no legal significance whatsoever, since it was expressly disavowed and Captain Bruce himself was removed of his office for having made it without authority.'[1]

From the preceding premises, the Committee concluded that Persia had no legitimate claim to the sovereignty of Bahrain. The British Government after hearing the comment of the Indian Government on the Persian Prime Minister's Note preferred not to deliver a formal reply of their views on this Note. Persia also did not press the matter any further and the affair was therefore forgotten for some years to come.

In the meantime, the agitation in the area continued and the Persian Prime Minister again found an occasion of presenting a fresh protest in 1848 to the British Minister at Tehran against what he alleged to be the interference by the British Resident at Bushire in the affairs of Bahrain. The truth about this allegation was that the ruler of the island, Shaikh Muhammad, made in the year preceding the Persian protest an overture to the British Resident seeking British assistance against an aggression which he apprehended on his country from his uncle, the ex-Shaikh, and his followers who were backed by Persia. Being aware of the genuineness of the Shaikh's apprehensions the Resident promised to afford to Bahrain military support in the case of any aggression directed against her by Persia. When the Persian

---

[1] F.O. 60/118, op. cit., Observations of the Secret Committee of the East India Company, 31 July 1845.

Government protested against these discussions which took place between the Shaikh and the British Resident, the British Minister at Tehran, acting on the instructions previously received by him from the home Government, delivered a Note dated 7 February 1848 to the Persian Government in which he stated that he

urges the Persian Government to take the necessary measures to prevent any aggression being made on Bahrain [and that his Government] do not recognise as valid the claim advanced by Persia to the sovereignty of that Island.[1]

The situation in Bahrain continued to be unstable owing to internal feuds and the Shaikh's position was precarious. To strengthen his hold and to ward off the intrigues of his ambitious neighbours he requested the British Resident to place his country under British protection.[2] But the British Government declined this request.[3] Subsequently, the Shaikh turned his face to the Turkish Government offering to become 'under the sovereignty or protection of the Porte'.[4] But after his overtures to Turkey, the Shaikh became involved in a maritime struggle with the Wahhabi Ruler, Amir Faisal, who in consequence of the Shaikh's refusal to pay tribute made preparation to attack Bahrain. Knowing that he had forfeited by his maritime activities the sympathy of the British Government, and in order to repel the Wahhabi attack, the Shaikh started playing off Persia against Turkey by asking them both for aid and protection against Wahhabi designs.[5]

The Shaikh's appeal for military aid was favourably considered by the diplomatic circles both in Turkey and Persia. Persia lost no time in dispatching an agent to Bahrain to represent her interests there. The Shaikh, on his part, flattered the Persians by hoisting their flag on the main port in Manama, and sending in April 1860 two letters—one addressed to the Shah and the other to the Governor-General of Fars—in which he expressed his loyalty to the Persian Crown.[6]

But it is interesting to know that following the arrival of the Persian agent in Bahrain the Shaikh was preparing to receive Turkish emis-

---

[1] F.O. 60/136. Farrant to Viscount Palmerston, 17 February 1848; ibid., Extract of a letter from Haji Meerza Aghassi to Lt-Col Farrant, 2 February 1848; ibid., Viscount Palmerston to Farrant, 2 May 1848. (In this communication Palmerston conveys to Farrant his approval of the latter's reply to Haji M. Aghassee.)

[2] F.O. 60/145. Farrant to Palmerston, 23 May 1849, enclosing letter, dated (15th Rabee Awwal) 19 February 1849, from Shaikh Muhammad ibn Khalifah, Ruler of Bahrain, to British Resident, Major Hennell, and the latter's reply to the Shaikh of 28 February 1849.

[3] F.O. 60/143. Foreign Office, to Farrant, 1 August 1849.

[4] F.O. 60/157. Palmerston to Canning, Foreign Office, 12 February 1851.

[5] F.O. 60/170. Sheil to Earl of Malmesbury, 11 May 1852.

[6] F.O. 248/251. Letters from Shaikh Muhammad ibn Khalifah, dated 9 and 12 April 1860, to the Persian Governor of Fars and to the Shah respectively.

saries. In order to give them their share of flattery and to demonstrate allegiance, he pulled down the Persian flag from the main port and hoisted the Turkish flag in its place.

It can be adduced from the Shaikh's behaviour that he was by no means sincere in his allegiance either to Persia or Turkey. He was, according to the British Resident of that time, Captain Felix Jones, 'playing fast and loose with all parties' for his own ends.[1] In support of the above assessment of the Shaikh's behaviour the following evidence may be given.

First, in a dispatch to the Foreign Secretary, the British Chargé d'Affaires at Tehran spoke of the Shaikh's attitude towards the Persian mission thus:

It is apparent . . . that the chief of Bahrein is not sincere . . . in his profession of loyalty to the Persian Government. He speaks of their flag with contempt; declares himself to be on the side of the strongest; and is prepared under certain contingencies to admit the sovereignty of Turkey.[2]

Secondly, the British agent at Bahrain reported to the British Resident at Bushire that the Shaikh said to the Turkish envoys:

I have given them (the Persians) no binding promises. If they can do what I desire I shall be on their side, otherwise, they have nothing to do with me, and, as to their flag, a slave can have it down.[3]

The British views about the Persian and the Turkish missions to Bahrain were explained at the time by Sir Henry Rawlinson, then British Minister at Tehran, who analysed the position in Bahrain as follows:

It seems to have been the normal conditions of Bahrein for some years past that three rival authorities, the Pasha of Baghdad, the Wahhabi Amir and the Prince Governor of Fars, should lay claim to the allegiance of the island and endeavour either by intimidation or intrigue to supersede the independence of the Sheikh.

He then proceeded to point out the line of policy which should be applied to the situation. He said:

Hostilities against Bahrain from any quarter are to be repelled by us by force of arms, whilst the voluntary tender of the Sheikh's allegiance to any Power, as long as it is not followed by military occupation, is to be ignored as of no practical importance.[4]

---

[1] F.O. 60/249. Felix Jones to Sir Henry Rawlinson, 17 April 1860.
[2] F.O. 60/249. Captain Lewis Pelly to Lord Russell, 23 May 1860.
[3] Ibid., translated purports of two letters from Hajee Jasem, British Agent at Bahrain to Felix Jones dated 23 and 25 April 1860.
[4] F.O. 60/249. Sir Henry Rawlinson to Captain Felix Jones, 4 May 1860.

In accordance with this line of policy, Sir Henry Rawlinson, in an interview with the Shah, informed the latter that

under no circumstances can the British Government be expected to concur in the proposed transfer of the sovereignty of Bahrain to the Persian Crown since we have contracted engagements with the Arab Shaikhs of the Island as independent chiefs, and since the maintenance of their independence is indispensable to the successful working of those plans of maritime police in the Persian Gulf which we have been at so much pains and expense to establish.[1]

The British Government was not satisfied with the behaviour of the Shaikh of Bahrain, Shaikh Muhammad, who by soliciting military aid from Persia and Turkey and by his aggression against Qatar, contrary to his Agreement of 1861, provoked the British authorities in the Gulf to take a military action against Bahrain.[2] This military operation against Bahrain, which was carried out by the British Resident in the Gulf, Lt-Col Pelly, elicited a furious protest on 19 November 1868 by the representative of the Persian Foreign Ministry at Fars. He condemned the British action against the ruler of Bahrain as an 'absolute and independent proceeding which violated the manifest and proved rights of the Persian Government in regard to the ownership of Bahrein'.[3] The Persian protest was ignored by the British authorities, but correspondence about the Persian complaints continued between the Persian and British Governments without results.

The Anglo-Persian controversy over Bahrain reached a new phase when it became the subject of prolonged negotiations in London. The starting point for those negotiations was a Note of Protest delivered by the Persian Chargé d'Affaires on 13 April 1869 to the British Foreign Secretary, Lord Clarendon. The Persian Chargé d'Affaires reiterated his Government's vigorous complaints of Col Pelly's actions in Bahrain and as a proof of Persia's sovereignty over Bahrain he furnished the British Foreign Secretary with the texts of two letters from Shaikh Muhammad, the deposed ruler, acknowledging his loyalty to the Persian Crown.[4]

On receiving the Persian protest Lord Clarendon approached the Duke of Argyll, Secretary of State of India, asking his views on the subject of the political status of Bahrain and her relations with the

[1] F.O. 60/249. Sir Henry Rawlinson to Captain Felix Jones, 4 May 1860, Sir Henry Rawlinson to Lord Russell, 10 May 1860.

[2] F.O. 248/247. Lt-Col Lewis Pelly to Charles Alison, British Minister at Tehran, 28 December 1868.

[3] F.O. 248/247. Translated purport of a letter, dated 19 November 1868, from Mirza Mohammed Ali Khan, Persian Agent for Foreign Affairs, Shiraz, to Lt-Col Lewis Pelly. Also see ibid., for resolution of the Secretary to the Government of India, dated 28 October 1868, approving Pelly's action against the Shaikh of Bahrain.   [4] See above, p. 172.

Shah of Persia. Because of the importance of the Duke of Argyll's reply, in so far as it formed the main basis for Lord Clarendon's Note to Persia on the question, a discussion of the main points raised in this reply is, therefore, necessary. In his reply the Duke stated:

The British Government have hitherto carefully abstained from recognizing either directly or indirectly the validity of the claims, on several occasions advanced by Persia, to the right of sovereignty over Bahrein. Moreover, the Sheikh of Bahrein, in his capacity of an independent sovereign, has contracted obligations towards the British Government for the suppression of piracy, war and slave trade, which are indispensable to the success of our measures of maritime police, of which the local Governor of Bahrein who is possessed of considerable naval resources, is alone competent to secure the fulfilment.

The last passage of Argyll's reply contained the suggestion that it may be expedient to notify the Government of the Shah, 'as a matter of courtesy' only, about any measures which the British Government may take in the future against the conduct of the Shaikh of Bahrain.[1] It appears that this suggestion met with the concurrence of Lord Clarendon who, in view of the friendly relations between his Government and Persia, sent a rather moderate and courteous Note dated 29 April 1869 to the Persian Chargé d'Affaires. In this Note Clarendon stated:

The British Government readily admit that the Government of the Shah has protested against the Persian right of sovereignty on Bahrein being ignored by the British authorities; and they have given due consideration to that protest.

But, after referring to the nature of the engagements which the Shaikh of Bahrain entered into with the British Government, Clarendon added:

If the Persian Government are prepared to keep a sufficient force in the Gulf for these purposes, (i.e., for policing the Gulf), this country would be relieved of a troublesome and costly duty, but if the Shah is not prepared to undertake these duties, Her Majesty's Government cannot suppose His Majesty would wish that in those waters disorders and crimes should be encouraged by impunity.

Then, after assuring the Persian Chargé d'Affaires of the friendly feelings entertained by his Government towards Persia, Clarendon made the following concessions:

Whenever it is practicable to do so, [he said] Her Majesty's Government will cause the Persian Government to be informed beforehand of any

---

[1] F.O. 248/251. India Office to Rt Hon. E. Hammond, Foreign Office, 21 April 1869.

measures of coercion against himself which the conduct of the Sheikh of Bahrein may have rendered necessary.[1]

On receiving Clarendon's Note, the Persian Chargé d'Affaires reported to his Government expressing his complete satisfaction with its contents. Persia construed Clarendon's Note, as it will be seen later, as forming a British recognition of the Persian claim to Bahrain.

Apart from minor protests by Persia on a few occasions during the beginning of this century, the Anglo-Persian controversy over Bahrain remained static after Clarendon's Note in 1869, for a period of over fifty years until it was revived again by Persia, in 1927. This time the Persian claim assumed a considerable measure of seriousness when Persia protested against Article 6 of the Treaty of Jiddah, dated 20 May 1927, concluded between Britain and the King of Saudi Arabia. Article 6 of this Treaty which provoked Persia's protest reads:

His Majesty the King of Hijaz and Nejd and its dependencies undertakes to maintain friendly and peaceful relations with the territories of Kuwait and Bahrain . . . who are in special treaty relations with His Britannic Majesty's Government.[2]

The Persian Note of protest, dated 22 November 1927, was sent to the British Government and stated:

As Bahrein is incontestably in Persian possession . . . the above mentioned article, so far as it concerns Bahrein, constitutes an infringement of the territorial integrity of Persia.

The Note further stated:

The Persian Government, therefore, protests emphatically against the part of the treaty referred to, and looks to the British Government to take steps to nullify its effects.[3]

On Persia's request this Note of protest was also communicated to all States Members of the League of Nations on 23 November. The attention of those States was particularly drawn by Persia to Article 10 of the Covenant of the League which 'guarantees the territorial integrity of the States Members of the League'.[4]

Sir Austen Chamberlain, then British Foreign Secretary, replied to the Persian protest on 18 January 1928, denying emphatically that there were 'any valid grounds upon which the claim of the Persian Government to the sovereignty over [Bahrain] is or can be based'.[5] Not satisfied with the British answer, Persia delivered again, on 2 August 1928, another Note in which her previous contentions were

[1] F.O. 248/251. Lord Clarendon to Haji Mohsin Khan, Persian Chargé d'Affaires, 29 April 1869.

[2] *Treaty Series*, No. 25 (1927), *Cmd.* 2951.

[3] L.N.*O.J.*, May 1928, pp. 605-6.

[4] Ibid.   [5] L.N.*O.J.*, May 1928, pp. 606-7.

reiterated.[1] To this, an elaborate reply, dated 18 February 1929, was made by the British Foreign Secretary who contested the Persian arguments juridically and historically.[2]

These two Persian Notes of 22 November 1927 and 2 August 1928, together with the British replies of 18 January 1928 and 18 February 1929, are important for the purposes of this study of the Persian claim to sovereignty over Bahrain because they embrace the main British and Persian points of view on the question.

Legal analysis of the Iranian claim

From the above statement of facts, it will be seen that the essential issues of law are the following:

(1) Did Persia acquire title to Bahrain prior to 1783?
(2) If the answer is in the affirmative, did Persia at any time thereafter lose title to Bahrain?

As to (1), the grounds on which it may be said that Persia acquired title to Bahrain are: (*a*) occupation, and (*b*) conquest.[3]

(*a*) *Occupation*: Occupation as a mode of acquiring territory operates on a territory which is *terra nullius* (i.e., not forming part of the dominion of another State).[4] There are two authoritative cases on the acquisition of title by occupation, namely, the *Clipperton Island* case (1932), between Mexico and France, and the *Eastern Greenland* case (1933), between Denmark and Norway.

The general principle accepted in these cases is that 'besides the *animus occupandi*, the actual, and not the nominal, taking of possession is a necessary condition of occupation'.[5] Therefore, there are two necessary elements for the establishment of a valid title to sovereignty by occupation, namely 'the intention and will to exercise such sovereignty and the manifestation of State activity'.[6] This amounts to effective occupation or 'effective control'.[7] Thus, it has been maintained that the fact that a territory has been under the authority of another State is irrelevant if that State has abandoned the territory, in the sense that it no more assumed jurisdiction over it.[8] And it is not necessary that the abandonment of an acquired territory should be voluntary. It suffices if the other element, namely, the manifestation of

---

[1] L.N.O.J., September 1928, pp. 1360–3.   [2] Ibid., May 1929, pp. 790–3.
[3] International law recognises five modes of acquiring legal title to a territory, namely, occupation, conquest, cession, prescription or accretion. See Oppenheim, pp. 543–6; Hall, p. 125. Only occupation and conquest, as means of acquiring title to territory, are relevant to this discussion.
[4] Brierly, p. 151; Schwarzenberger, pp. 296–7.
[5] Arbitral Award on the Sovereignty of the *Clipperton Island A.J.I.L.*, 26 (1932), p. 390.
[6] *Legal Status of Eastern Greenland* (1933), *P.C.I.J.*, Series A/B, No. 53, pp. 62–3.
[7] Schwarzenberger, pp. 298–9; Waldock, C. H. M., 'Disputed Sovereignty in the Falkland Dependencies', *B.Y.I.L.*, 25 (1948), pp. 334–5.
[8] Schwarzenberger, p. 297.

N

State activity, ceases to be exercised.[1] However, it may be stated, as an exception to this principle, that in the case of an uninhabited territory (i.e., islets, rocky islands, etc.), the other element of exercising in a positive manner State authority is not required. Thus, in the *Clipperton Island* case, it was decided for France that she did not lose her right on the uninhabited Clipperton Island

by *derelictio* since she never had the animus of abandoning the island, and the fact that she has not exercised her authority there in a positive manner does not imply the forfeiture of an acquisition already definitely perfected.[2]

In the case of Bahrain, an inhabited territory, the two elements of the intention to retain the territory, or the *animus*, and the positive exercise of State authority are both required for the establishment of Persia's title to the island. It has been argued by two Iranian writers, in support of their country's claim, that Persia never abandoned Bahrain, after the events of 1783, and still retains the animus.[3] But this *animus*, or the mere assertion of title by Persia, is not sufficient, if it was not followed by the exercise of State authority in Bahrain after 1783. Accordingly, Majid Khadduri rightly points out that the Bahrain case 'would be analogous to the *Palmas* case, rather than the *Clipperton* case',[4] since in this case, which will be explained more fully later, the principle of the peaceful and continuous display of authority is required as a basis for title to an inhabited territory.

(*b*) *Conquest*: If Persia has not acquired title to Bahrain on the ground of occupation, the question arises whether she acquired such title by conquest? For the legal evaluation of this question, it is necessary to refer to the conditions required for the acquisition of territory by conquest.

Conquest is defined as

the acquisition of the territory of an enemy by its complete and final subjugation and a declaration of the conquering state's intention to annex it.[5]

According to Norman Hill, title by conquest involves three elements:

Actual possession based upon force, an announcement of intention to retain the territory and an ability to hold it.[6]

---

[1] Schwarzenberger, p. 298; Brierly, p. 152.
[2] *A.J.I.L.* (1932), op. cit., pp. 390–4. See also Schwarzenberger, p. 298, where he quotes the following from the Award: 'In that of a relinquished and uninhabited island, as the Clipperton Island, an initial display of sovereignty may suffice even to maintain the title . . .'
[3] Esmaili, Malek, *Le golfe persique et les îles de Bahrein* (1938) pp. 200–4; Adamiyat, Fereydoun, *Bahrein Islands, A Legal and Diplomatic Study of the British-Iranian Controversy* (1955), p. 229.
[4] Khadduri, M., 'Iran's Claim to Sovereignty of Bahrayn', *A.J.I.L.*, 45 (1951) p. 638.   [5] Brierly, p. 155.
[6] Hill, N., *Claims to Territory in International Law and Relations* (1945) p. 161

This clearly indicates that title by conquest may well be lost as a result of another conquest by another State which is able to retain the territory as against the former conqueror.

Conquest alone [says Oppenheim] does not *ipso facto* make the conquering State the sovereign of the conquered territory, although such territory comes through conquest for the time under the sway of the conqueror. Conquest is only a mode of acquisition if the conqueror, after having firmly established the conquest, formally annexes the territory.[1]

It flows from the above principles that whoever succeeds in subjugating the territory originally acquired by conquest can, if he annexes the territory and establishes an effective State authority, assume a better title to the territory than his defeated adversary. It may be argued that even if Persia acquired a legal title to Bahrain on the ground of conquest she, nevertheless, was not able to maintain that title and hold it to the exclusion of others. Thus, by her expulsion from Bahrain in 1783, she lost her title for ever. In his reply of 18 February 1929 the British Foreign Secretary, Sir Austen Chamberlain, challenged the Persian right over Bahrain on the ground of conquest by stating:

. . . it would still be necessary for Persia to prove that she is, or ever has been, the lawful owner of Bahrain, and that such rights as she may have acquired in former ages by conquest and the exercise of force outweigh those not only of the Portuguese but of the Arab inhabitants themselves.[2]

As to (2), the grounds on which Persia may have lost her title to Bahrain are: (*a*) conquest by a foreign State, (*b*) assertion of independence by Bahrain, (*c*) prescription.[3]

(*a*) *Conquest by a foreign State:* There is no dispute among writers that conquest by a foreign State also operates as a mode of losing territory. Thus if the conquering State takes possession of the territory

---

[1] Oppenheim, pp. 566–7.

[2] L.N.O.J., May 1929, op. cit., p. 791. Toynbee confirms the fact that the Persians acquired Bahrain by the right of conquest, but that they lost this right to the present rulers of the island, who conquered it from them in 1783. See Toynbee, A., 'The Dispute between Persia and Great Britain over Bahrayn (1927–1934)', *Survey of International Affairs* (1934), p. 222. However, he, like other authorities, refers to the date of the Persian occupation of Bahrain, as from 1622 to 1783. The right date of the Persian conquest of Bahrain from the Portuguese is 1602, as explained above, p. 167.

[3] There are five modes of loss of title to territory, corresponding to the above five modes of acquiring title to territory. These five modes of losing territory are: cession, dereliction, operation of nature, subjugation (conquest) and prescription. To these is also added a sixth mode, namely, revolt or independence. See Oppenheim, pp. 578–81; Hyde, 1, pp. 117–19.

Since not all of these modes are applicable to this discussion, an examination will be made of the above-mentioned modes only.

of the defeated State 'through military force', and annexes it, it becomes the new sovereign of the conquered territory. The

subjugated territory [says Oppenheim], has not for one moment been no State's land, but passes from the enemy to the conqueror not through cession but through annexation.[1]

In support of her contention that she has not lost her sovereignty over Bahrain either as a result of the ʿUtubi conquest in 1783, or by the assertion of the independence of Bahrain in the following years, Persia introduced in a Note, dated 2 August 1928, an alleged principle of international law which reads:

A territory belonging to a sovereign State cannot be lawfully detached so long as the right of ownership has not been transferred by this State to another State in virtue of an official act, in this case a treaty, or so long as its annexation by another State or its independence have not been officially recognised by the lawful owner of the territory.[2]

In his reply, dated 18 February 1929, to the above Note, Sir Austen Chamberlain denied

that any such principle, if alleged to be of universal application, forms part of international law. The assertion [he said] that the consent of the dispossessed State is invariably required to validate a change of sovereignty is contradicted both by international practice and the facts of history. Moreover, it would, if it existed, seriously prejudice the maintenance of peace and international order.[3]

What are the merits of the Persian argument?[4] The assertion that conquest does not operate as a means of loss of territory without the conclusion of a treaty of cession (which formally transfers the subjugated territory from the possession of the conquered State to that of the conqueror), as implied in the Persian argument, seems repugnant

[1] Oppenheim, pp. 566–7, 568; See also Hill, op. cit., p. 161.
[2] L.N.O.J., September 1928, p. 1360.
[3] L.N.O.J., May 1929, p. 791.
[4] It appears that the Persian argument is based on a report submitted in 1925 to the League of Nations, by a Commission of three persons (the Wirsen Commission) which was appointed by the Assembly of the League of Nations in September 1924 for the purpose of collecting facts and data regarding the dispute between Turkey and Iraq over the 'Mosul District'. This district, which was at the time occupied by British and Iraqi troops, was claimed by Turkey as part of her territories. On the legal side of the Iraqi-Turkish dispute, the Commissioners stated that Turkey 'retains her legal sovereignty over the disputed territory so long as she does not renounce her rights'. Iraq has no legal rights or right of conquest over that territory. 'The territory', the Commissioners continued, '. . . still belongs in law to Turkey until she renounces her rights.' See League of Nations, C. 400, n. 147, 1925, VII, pp. 84–5. For a general discussion of the League's Assembly on the merits of this report, see L.N.O.J., vol. 11 (1925), pp. 1307 et seq.

to international law principles.[1] Cecil Hurst discusses various cases of conquest based on unilateral annexation.[2] And according to John Fischer Williams, the consent or the recognition of the dispossessed State, although

in most cases settles the problem whether in the view of international law there has been a valid transfer of dominion, this assent is not the only condition of which it is necessary to take account.[3]

Conquest has been recognised by international law as a mode of losing territory without 'regard to the justice or injustice of a particular acquisition'.[4] There are cases, says Westlake, where States ceased to exist, without their own consent, by conquest. He cites the annexation of the former South African Republic by Great Britain as an example of such cases. He further quotes the American Vice Chancellor James as saying, as late as the past century, that

any government which de facto succeeds to any other government whether by . . . or conquest . . . succeeds . . . to all rights . . . of the displaced power . . .[5]

Finally, according to Max Huber,

Possession, in international law, is the exercise of power in and from a territory. The territory of a state is that of which it can take physical possession. Whoever succeeds in obtaining this possession has sovereignty (*Herrschaft*) over everything that is in the territory. When one state follows after another on the same territory there is a change in the exercise of power. The change may be the result of the concurrent wills of both the states concerned, but nevertheless, the consent of the predecessor is unnecessary.[6]

The implication of this view is that conquest can operate as a ground for loss of territory even without the conclusion of a treaty of cession with, or obtaining the consent of, the conquered, or dispossessed, State.[7]

---

[1] Williams, Sir John Fischer, 'Sovereignty, Seisin, and the League', *B.Y.I.L.*, 7 (1926), pp. 24–42. In an analysis of the legal conclusions of the 'Wirsen's Commission' on the Turkish-Iraqi dispute over the 'Mosul District', the writer concludes that there exists, in international law, no such principle as that stated by the Commission.

[2] Hurst, Sir Cecil, J. B., 'State Succession in Matters of Tort', *B.Y.I.L.*, 5 (1924), p. 172.

[3] Williams, op. cit., p. 30.   [4] Lindley, p. 161.

[5] Westlake, J., 'The Nature and Extent of the Title by Conquest', *Law Quarterly Review*, 17 (1901), pp. 392–401.

[6] Huber, M., *Die Staatensuccession* (1898), quoted by Williams, op. cit., p. 30.

[7] Conquest, although 'a moral wrong', is not illegal and it produces legal results. See Williams, op. cit., p. 41. It is to be noted, however, that, at present, the legality of conquest has been modified by the presence of the United Nations (formerly the League of Nations). Therefore, conquest is not, today, a basis of acquiring or losing territory. See Oppenheim, pp. 570–1.

However, it may be argued that the legality of the acquisition of title to Bahrain by the ʿUtubi Arabs on the ground of their conquest of it in 1783 can be doubted, since the war between them and Persia was not 'a war between two States'. And thus, the requirement of conquest as a mode of loss of sovereignty (i.e. as being a war between two States whereby 'by reason of the defeat of one of them sovereignty over territory passes from the loser to the victorious State')[1] was not satisfied. Although it cannot be doubted that the conquest of Bahrain by the ʿUtubi Arabs was not a conquest by a State in the international sense, there seems to be, nevertheless, no lack of evidence to the effect that the ʿUtubis were not, at the time, mere 'invaders' who belonged to no land, but the actual rulers and overlords of the settlement of Zubarah in the peninsula of Qatar.[2] At any rate, the fact that the ʿUtubis (the predecessors of the present reigning family of Al-Khalifah) did not conquer Bahrain in the name of an established State in international law, does not seem to affect the present legal status of the island, the independence of which has been continuously maintained from Persia since the date of its conquest in 1783.[3]

(b) *Assertion of independence by Bahrain:* It can, safely, be contended that Persia has lost her title to Bahrain as a result of the assertion by the latter of her independence during past years. The argument introduced by Persia that the recognition of the original owner is required for rendering lawful a change of sovereignty over a territory belonging to that owner seems to be untenable.[4] What seems to be essential in this case is, actually, the *de facto* establishment of the independence of the territory itself, irrespective of the recognition or the assent of its original sovereign. If, for instance, a dominion revolts against its colonial regime and succeeds in overthrowing that regime and establishing a sufficiently stable national government, it can be presumed that a change of sovereignty in favour of the new government has been effected. It follows, therefore, that

if the recognition of such change of sovereignty was given by the Powers, even if the owner was not among them, the territory would be regarded as an independent sovereign state.[5]

---

[1] *Legal Status of Greenland* (1933), op. cit., p. 47.

[2] See *Bombay Selections*, 'Historical Sketch of the Uttoobee Tribe Arabs, 1716–1817', by F. Warden, pp. 362–5. It can be seen from this document that the ʿUtubis were originally the rulers of Zubarah, and that the conquest of Bahrain by them from the Persian garrison in Bahrain was in retaliation of a former attack which was dispatched against their country, Zubarah, by the Persian governor of Bahrain, Shaikh Nasir.

[3] See below, pp. 184–6 for other factors on which Persia may be regarded as having lost her title to the island.

[4] See above, p. 180.

[5] Khadduri, op. cit., p. 637. See also Oppenheim, p. 579.

International practice furnishes many examples in support of this argument. The most clear example, perhaps, is that of the former Spanish colonies in South America which, after a successful revolution against Spain, declared their independence in 1810. The United States recognised the independence of the new States in 1822, and Great Britain in 1824. The Spanish Government, which was making efforts to suppress the revolution, protested against the American and the British recognition of the new States. In its reply of 6 April 1822 to the Spanish protest, the United States Government argued that it

yielded to an obligation of duty of the highest order, by recognising as Independent States, Nations which, after deliberately asserting their right to that character, have maintained and established it . . .

The recognition, it continued, was 'the mere acknowledgement of existing facts'.[1] The British reply, dated 25 March 1825, to the Spanish protest was based on the principle of State responsibility. Thus, in support of her recognition of the South American States, Great Britain held that the 'Mother Country' (Spain) could not, in her view, have 'continued responsible' internationally 'for acts over which it could no longer exercise the shadow of a control'.[2] Further examples may be cited with regard to Greece, in 1827, and Belgium, in 1831, whose independence was recognised in this manner (i.e., without the consent of their Mother Countries). The independence of the United States of America, and the recognition by France of that independence in 1778, without the consent of Great Britain, furnishes another demonstrative example.[3]

It can hardly be suggested that in all the cases cited above the recognition by the Powers of the independence of those new States was unlawful, and that, until the Mother Countries of those States recognised their independence, they continued to be regarded, in international law, under the sovereignty of their Mother Countries.

'International law,' says Lauterpacht, 'does not condemn rebellion or secession aiming at acquisition of independence.'[4] However, it requires for recognition by Powers of a new government, revolutionary in origin, certain conditions which should be fulfilled by the new government seeking recognition. These are the *de facto* existence of an independent government exercising effective authority within a defined area.[5] In other words, there must be established a permanently stable government. For it is held that any premature recognition as a new State may be considered a violation of the rights of the mother State. But it is equally held that a recognition too long delayed is not legally

[1] Lauterpacht, pp. 12–25.   [2] Ibid., p. 16.
[3] Ibid., pp. 8–9; See also for more examples, Oppenheim, pp. 128–9.
[4] Lauterpacht, p. 8.
[5] Ibid., pp. 26–30; Brierly, pp. 129 et seq.

justified.[1] There is, however, no definite test whether a recognition of a revolutionary government is premature. On the other hand, it is considered to be an indication of the existence of the new State when it

has utterly defeated the mother-State, or that the mother-State . . . is apparently incapable of bringing the revolutionary State back under its sway.[2]

It may be seen from the above principles of international law on recognition that there is no condition which requires for the validity of the recognition of a new State the prior 'consent' of the parent State. On the contrary, it has been maintained by Lauterpacht that

the formal renunciation of sovereignty by the parent State has never been regarded as a condition of the lawfulness of recognition. For parent States are naturally slow in acknowledging the independence of revolted provinces.[3]

The writer further elucidates this principle as follows:

On the other hand, the refusal of the mother Country to recognise such independence is not conclusive. The legal title of the parent State is relevant to the extent that conclusive evidence is required showing that it has been definitely displaced and that the effectiveness of its authority does not exceed a mere assertion of right. But once such evidence is available, the illegality of the new State's origin from the point of view of the constitutional law of the parent State is of no consequence.[4]

(c) *Prescription:* Finally, it can be maintained that Persia lost her title to Bahrain on the ground of prescription.[5] According to Brierly,

prescription as a title to territory in international law is so vague that some writers deny its recognition altogether. But in fact most existing frontiers are accepted by international law simply because they existed *de facto* for a long time. . . . It is therefore no paradox to say that prescription is the commonest of all titles to territory.[6]

It is defined as

the acquisition of sovereignty over a territory through continuous and undisturbed exercise of sovereignty over it during such a period as is necessary to create under the influence of historical development the general conviction that the present condition of things is in conformity with international order.[7]

Writers on the subject have based prescription on the theory that the State which maintains law and order in a territory and develops it

---

[1] Williams, Sir John Fischer, 'Recognition', *Transactions of the Grotius Society*, XV (1930), pp. 63–4.

[2] Oppenheim, p. 129; Brierly, pp. 132–5; Williams, 'Recognition', op. cit.

[3] Lauterpacht, p. 9.   [4] Ibid., p. 26.

[5] See Schwarzenberger, pp. 565–6, 307–8, for distinction between 'acquisitive' and 'extinctive' prescription.

[6] Brierly, p. 157.   [7] Oppenheim, p. 576.

is entitled to sovereignty over it as against another 'State which, though originally possessing the same territory, had neglected it'.[1] The majority of writers, as explained above, accept prescription as part of international law. Leading cases on prescription, such as the *British Guiana Arbitration* (1899),[2] between Great Britain and Venezuela, and the *Chamizal Arbitration* (1910–11),[3] between the United States of America and Mexico, show that States have recognised prescription as a valid principle of international law. Still more important authorities on the law of prescription are the decisions of the Permanent Court of Arbitration in the *Island of Palmas* case (1928),[4] between the United States and the Netherlands, and of the Permanent Court of International Justice in the *Eastern Greenland* case (1933),[5] between Denmark and Norway. In these two cases it was accepted that the effective peaceful and continuous display of authority in a territory establishes a valid sovereignty over that territory. In the *Island of Palmas*, Judge Huber confirmed the principle of acquisitive prescription when he stated in his judgment that the Netherlands Government had proved 'continuous and peaceful display of State authority during a long period of time' on the Palmas Island.[6] In another part of his judgment, Judge Huber held that the principle of 'continuous and peaceful display of authority would prevail even over a prior definitive title'.[7] This can be taken to mean that title by prescription overrides any other title based on occupation or conquest.

It should be mentioned that some writers object to the principle of prescription mainly on the ground that there is 'no fixed time laid by international law within which a title by prescription could be established'.[8] But against this, Lauterpacht, as quoted by Johnson, argues

that the lack of a fixed period of time for the operation of the doctrine of acquisitive prescription in international law is no more fatal to that doctrine than is the absence of a settled rule regulating the rate of interest fatal to the principle that interest may be awarded in international law.[9]

Thus, it may be argued that the disagreement of jurists on a fixed period for the operation of prescription is no reason why this doctrine should be treated lightly. However, international practice shows that in the *British Guiana Arbitration*, it was stated in the Treaty of 1897,

---

[1] Johnson, D. H. N., 'Acquisitive Prescription in International Law', *B.Y.I.L.*, 27 (1950), p. 333.

[2] *Venezuela-British Guiana Boundary Arbitration*, *A.J.I.L.*, 11 (1917), pp. 700–1.

[3] *Chamizal Arbitration* (1911) Mexico-United States, *A.J.I.L.*, 5 (1911), pp. 782–833.

[4] *Island of Palmas Arbitration*, *A.J.I.L.*, 22 (1928), pp. 867–912.

[5] *Legal Status of Eastern Greenland* (1933), *P.C.I.J.*, Series A/B, No. 53.

[6] *A.J.I.L.*, 1928, op. cit., p. 910.

[7] Ibid., pp. 867, 884.   [8] Johnson, op. cit., p. 334.

[9] Ibid., quoting Lauterpacht, *Private Law Sources and Analogies of International Law* (1927), p. 117, n. 4.

that 'adverse holding or prescription during a period of fifty years shall make a good title'.[1] Jurists, such as Grotius, favoured more than one hundred years, while others required more. Nevertheless, the majority of writers seem to concur in the view that the time for the operation of prescription varies with the facts of each case which has to be decided upon its own merits.[2]

In applying the doctrine of acquisitive prescription, explained above, to the case of Bahrain, it can be argued that 'the peaceful and continuous display of State authority'[3] by Al-Khalifah Shaikhs—the successors of the former 'Utubi Arabs—in Bahrain during the past years (from 1783 up to this date), has operated as a ground for the loss of Persia's title to the island. The refusal, on the part of Persia, to recognise this fact can hardly affect the established rights of the present Government of Bahrain.

Finally, it is desirable to consider two issues which may be regarded, from the point of view of Persia, as a ground for interrupting the operation of prescription against Persia's right in Bahrain. These are: (1) Alleged British recognition of Persian sovereignty over Bahrain. (2) Submission of a former Shaikh of Bahrain to Persia. To these, a third issue will be added, namely, continued protests by Persia against the authority of the present Government in Bahrain.

Alleged British recognition of Persian sovereignty over Bahrain

As a ground for her sovereignty over Bahrain, Persia relies upon alleged British recognition of this sovereignty. It is asserted that two nineteenth-century documents establish British recognition. One of these documents is the disavowed draft Agreement of 1822, between a former British Resident in the Gulf, Captain Bruce, and the then Persian Governor of Shiraz. The other is Lord Clarendon's Note to Persia, dated 29 April 1869. These two documents will be discussed as follows:

(i) *The Bruce 'Agreement'*: It will be convenient first to examine Captain Bruce's Agreement which stated that Bahrain was 'being always subordinate to the province of Fars'.

It has been explained that Bruce's 'Agreement' was negotiated without any authorisation on the part of the Governments of the two negotiators, that, on the strength of these facts, the Agreement was disavowed by the British and the Persian Governments, and that the British Government removed Captain Bruce from his post for acting without authority.[4]

Yet, Persia still insists that this Agreement, 'though disavowed,

---

[1] Johnson, op. cit., p. 340.   [2] Ibid., p. 347.
[3] See *Island of Palmas*, op. cit., pp. 910, 867, 884; *Legal Status of Eastern Greenland*, op. cit., pp. 45–6.   [4] See above, pp. 168–9.

continued to be an historical document of inestimable value'. The historical truth about this Agreement, she maintains, is that it confirmed the fact that 'Bahrain then formed part of the Persian province of Fars'. And accordingly, she says that

no disavowal will ever invalidate this historical truth which was definitely established so far back as 1822 by a British official, who was in an excellent position to know the facts.[1]

The British reply of 18 February 1929 to this Persian assertion stated that

The main reason for the recall, and the prompt disavowal of this tentative agreement is that it acknowledged the King of Persia's title to Bahrain, of which there is not the least proof.[2]

The weakness of the Persian argument seems to lie in the fact that it forces upon Britain the admission of a document whose validity she has never recognised. Moreover, Persia argues that Bruce recognised her title to Bahrain because he 'was in an excellent position to know the facts'.[3] But the evidence of history shows that Bruce was actually 'given to the practice of making unauthorised agreements',[4] and that in July 1816 he himself recognised the independent status of Bahrain, and concluded with her ruling Shaikh an unauthorised agreement designed to defend Bahrain against external aggression.[5] If Bruce was, to quote the Persian statement, 'in an excellent position to know the facts' he would not have contradicted himself by recognising Bahrain in 1822, as part of Persia after he had admitted her independence in 1816.[6]

(ii) *The Clarendon Note:* The second document on which Persia relies is Lord Clarendon's statement, discussed above. The interpretations placed on this statement by both the Persian and the British Governments are at variance. In her Note of 2 August 1928 Persia construed Lord Clarendon's statement as a recognition on the part of Britain of Persian sovereignty over Bahrain.

The British point of view about Lord Clarendon's statement of 29 April 1869 was explained by the British Foreign Secretary, Sir Austen Chamberlain, in two replies dated 18 January 1928 and 18 February 1929. In these, he emphatically disputed the Persian contention that by the terms of Lord Clarendon's statement 'any recognition of the

---

[1] L.N.*O.J.*, September 1928, p. 1362.

[2] Ibid., May 1929, p. 792.

[3] Ibid., September 1928, p. 1362.

[4] Kelly, J. B., 'The Persian Claim to Bahrain', *International Affairs*, 33 (1957), p. 58.

[5] *I.O.*, *Bombay Secret Proceedings*, vol. 41, *Secret Consultation*, 29, 31 July 1819, p. 1413. (Communication from Captain Bruce to Chief Secretary, Bombay, 31 July 1916.)   [6] See ibid., and Kelly, op. cit.

validity of the Persian claim to sovereignty in Bahrain was at that time intended'.[1]

Let us now examine the Persian and the British interpretations of Lord Clarendon's statement.

It is clear from the Persian interpretation of that statement that Lord Clarendon's recognition of Persia's claim was not expressly mentioned but was implied. Thus, a reference was made in the Persian Note of protest of 22 November 1927 to the recognition by Lord Clarendon of 'the justice of the Persian protest',[2] and not of the Persian claim outright. But it can be argued that if Lord Clarendon admitted that Persia had protested in the past against the British refusal to take notice of her 'rights of sovereignty over Bahrain' and that the 'British authorities' considered that protest, this does not seem to imply recognition of Persia's sovereignty over Bahrain, or even the 'justice of the Persian protest'.[3] It merely means that the British Government considered the Persian protest. If a reference be made to the Duke of Argyll's reply of 27 February 1869 to Lord Clarendon about the Persian Protests, it will be observed that it was never in the intention of Lord Clarendon, or the Duke of Argyll, who advised the former on the question, to recognise the Persian claim. Argyll's reply, which formed the basis of Clarendon's statement, clearly stated that the British Government abstained from recognising the Persian claim. But the Duke advised Lord Clarendon, if he believed it to be more expedient to do so, to notify the Government of the Shah, 'as a matter of courtesy', about other measures concerning the conduct of the Shaikh and the peace of the Gulf.[4]

Thus, it can be maintained on the basis of this correspondence that while any recognition of the Persian claim was out of the question, it was the intention of Lord Clarendon to offer Persia a share of responsibility, with the British Government, in policing the Gulf.[5] He also offered to inform Persia, as a result of her accepting responsibility in policing the Gulf with the British Government, of

any measures of coercion against himself which the conduct of the Sheikh of Bahrein may have rendered necessary.

With regard to British engagements with the Shaikh, Clarendon confirmed that they were designed for that purpose (i.e., the maintenance of peace in the Gulf). Those concessions made by Lord Clarendon to

[1] For reference, see above, p. 177. See also *The Times*, 9 April 1957, where the Persian Foreign Minister, Mr Ardalan, reiterates the same arguments based on Lord Clarendon's Note of 29 April 1869.

[2] L.N.*O.J.*, May 1928, p. 605.

[3] Ibid.   [4] See above, p. 175.

[5] It is maintained, with justification, that 'the right to police the Gulf (which was conceded by Britain) would not necessarily constitute recognition of its [Persia's] sovereignty over Bahrayn'. See Khadduri, op. cit., p. 635.

Persia, whether they were connected with the punishment of the Shaikh against committing piratical acts in the future, or with other matters, were only natural if Persia were to accept responsibility and to act in concert with the British Government in policing the Gulf. It would be irrelevant, therefore, for Persia to consider those concessions as 'an acknowledgement of the necessity of rendering account to the legitimate sovereign', or, in other words, a recognition of Persian sovereignty over Bahrain. On the contrary, it may be assumed that Lord Clarendon had actually referred, though indirectly, to the independence of Bahrain from the authority of the Shah when he stated that

. . . the Sheikhs of Bahrein have at different periods entered directly into engagements with the British Government . . .[1]

It is true, however, that he did not expressly refer to the independence of Bahrain, nor did he refute the validity of the Persian claim. But the position of the British Government on this point, at the time, was explained by Chamberlain in his reply of 18 February 1929 when he stated that 'although they did not consider Persia's claims to ownership to Bahrain as valid, they were not at that time directly concerned in refuting them. The special treaties by which they eventually agreed to accept the control of the Shaikh's foreign relations were concluded in a later period.'[2]

Finally, it can be contended that even if it is assumed that the United Kingdom has recognised the Persian claim, this recognition does not in the least affect the right of sovereignty enjoyed by the Shaikh of Bahrain and his people for the past hundred and eighty-three years during which Persia exercised no symbol of authority in Bahrain. Moreover, Bahrain is not under the sovereignty of the United Kingdom, and the latter cannot, therefore, transfer to Persia the sovereignty of the island which she herself does not possess.[3]

But the fact that the United Kingdom has never recognised Persian sovereignty over Bahrain was reiterated in a statement to the House of Commons on 27 November 1957 by the then Secretary of State for Foreign Affairs, Mr Ormsby Gore, who stated that the Iranian claim was 'unfounded' and added:

The Iranian Government have been so informed on numerous occasions and can be in no doubt of Her Majesty's Government views on this matter. Her Majesty's Government will continue to fulfil their obligation to

---

[1] See above, p. 175, and see L.N.*O.J.*, May 1929, pp. 790–3.

[2] L.N.*O.J.*, May 1929, p. 793.

[3] On this ground the suggestion that 'it would only be if Britain had to transfer general predominance (over Bahrain) to any other Power that Persia might be preferred to others' should be regarded as absurd. See *The Times*, 'An Untenable Claim', 9 April 1957.

safeguard the independence of Bahrain, and the Ruler of Bahrain has received an assurance to this effect.[1]

Submission of the Shaikh of Bahrain to Persia

A further argument presented by Persia in support of her claim is the alleged declaration of loyalty and the payment of tribute by the rulers of Bahrain to the Government of the Shah. The Persian Note of protest of 2 August 1928, makes a reference to this point by saying:

> The Sheikhs of Bahrein have always accepted Persian sovereignty. Later authentic documents exist in which they declare their entire submission and loyalty to the central Government . . . and they paid taxes.[2]

The 'authentic documents' to which the Persian Government refers in the above passage are two letters dated 9 and 12 April 1860, from Shaikh Muhammad ibn Khalifah to Persia, in which he declared his loyalty to the Shah. It seems doubtful whether such an isolated act of loyalty in a certain period of Bahrain's history can give credit to the Persian claim to Bahrain's sovereignty. To see what motivated Shaikh Muhammad to send those letters of allegiance to Persia, it should be recalled that during the period 1850–60, Shaikh Muhammad, in an effort to retain his shaky position in the island, made overtures to the British Government, to the Ottoman Empire and to the Wahhabis respectively, requesting each of them to place Bahrain under their suzerainty. He even paid tribute of 4000 dollars to the Wahhabi ruler. When in 1859, Shaikh Muhammad became involved in hostile activities with the Wahhabi ruler, there was no alternative for him, especially after alienating the sympathy of the British Government by his maritime activities, but to write to Persia asking for military aid against the Wahhabis. It is in the prosecution of this policy that Shaikh Muhammad sent the two letters of loyalty to the Shah in 1860.[3] To suggest, therefore, that these two letters were a sincere declaration, on the part of the Shaikh, of Persian sovereignty over Bahrain is nothing but distortion of the facts.

Sir Austen Chamberlain in his reply of 18 February 1929 to this point challenged the Persian argument by stating that the British Government

have always been well aware that the unfortunate rulers of the islands, surrounded by warlike and more powerful States which menaced their

---

[1] *House of Commons Debates*, vol. 578, *Written Answer*, cols 115–16, 27 November 1957. In fact, Britain has continuously refuted similar claims.

[2] L.N.O.J., September 1928, p. 1361.

[3] See above, p. 172. It is observed from the diplomatic history of the island, explained above, that the Shaikh's letters of loyalty to the Persian Government were sent after the Shaikh's request to the British Government to extend protection to his country was refused.

independence, professed on various occasions, during the first sixty or seventy years of the nineteenth century, an unwilling allegiance to Muscat, to Persia, to Turkey, to the rulers of the mainland of Arabia, even to Egypt —to any Power, in short, who would agree to offer them protection and seemed at the time in a strong enough position to do so; and that at different times for short periods they paid tribute to Muscat, Egypt, or the Wahhabi Arabs of the mainland.

Any argument based on payment of tribute would therefore be available in support of a claim to sovereignty over Bahrain by any of the States to which tribute was in fact paid.

Chamberlain then referred to an important point when he stated that

. . . in any case it is evident that this timid and vacillating policy pursued on occasion by his predecessors cannot be held to affect the position of the present Shaikh, who is firm in his determination to resist the Persian Government's claims . . .[1]

Persian diplomatic protests

It has been argued, on behalf of Persia, that the Persian sovereignty over Bahrain 'cannot be challenged' on the ground of 'a change of international title to the Island' by prescription, because Persia, by her renewed protests to Britain, has interrupted the operation of prescription, and thus kept 'alive' her rights on Bahrain.[2]

On the face of it, this argument is not devoid of some truth, especially when one has to consider that for the operation of prescription, or adverse holding, the exercise of State authority must be peaceful and continuous.[3] In the view of many writers, protest estops the operation and continuity of the adverse holding.[4] It was held in the *Chamizal Arbitration* that 'possession maintained in teeth of constant opposition did not amount to prescription'.[5] But the question at issue is whether a mere diplomatic protest can, by itself, be regarded as an adequate action for the purpose of interrupting prescription?

According to Verykios, as quoted by Johnson, 'a protest not followed by other action becomes in time "academic" and "useless" '.[6] 'The other action that was formerly required', says Johnson, 'was forceful opposition of some sort. Since 1919 it was reference of the matter to the League of Nations or the Permanent Court of International Justice. Since 1945 it has been, where possible, reference of the matter to the United Nations or the International Court of Justice.'[7] In his view, 'The advent of this new machinery for settling international disputes has altered the role of protest in the matter of acquisitive prescription.' Therefore, diplomatic protest, he continues, 'is of

---

[1] L.N.*O.J.*, May 1929, p. 792.   [2] Adamiyat, op. cit., p. 249.
[3] Johnson, op. cit., pp. 347–8; MacGibbon, I. C., 'Some Observations on the Part of Protest in International Law', *B.Y.I.L.*, 30 (1953), p. 306.
[4] Hyde, 1, p. 387; Oppenheim, pp. 577–8.
[5] See Johnson, op. cit., p. 345.   [6] Ibid., p. 346.   [7] Ibid.

reduced significance and is certainly not now the principal method of interrupting prescription'.[1] Further, the ineffectiveness of diplomatic protests as a means of asserting sovereignty is confirmed in the following statement of Lauterpacht:

Thus mere protests and assertions of sovereignty unaccompanied by attempts to restore the challenged authority of the mother country can safely be and have been disregarded.[2]

Finally, MacGibbon, relying on the evidence of a number of international arbitration awards, sums up the principle about the inadequacy of diplomatic protests not accompanied by other affirmative actions, in interrupting an adverse holding or title by prescription by stating:

. . . Courts will require evidence of the assumption by the protesting State of some positive initiative towards settlement of the dispute in the form of an attempt to utilize all available and appropriate international machinery for that purpose.[3]

In connection with Persia, it is quite true to say that she has been since the beginning of this century, 'relentlessly' asserting her claim to sovereignty over Bahrain by means of diplomatic protests to the United Kingdom.[4] On one occasion in 1927 a protest was lodged with the Secretariat of the League of Nations which was also asked to communicate it to Members of the League.[5] However, it is quite clear that, apart from these verbal and written protests, Persia has never made an attempt to take a positive action on the lines explained above. For example, she has never called upon the United Kingdom to settle her claim through conciliations or international arbitrations. Nor has she been able to take any forceable measures to retain the island, or to challenge the effective authority of its present Government.[6] All that

---

[1] See Johnson, op. cit., p. 346.   [2] Lauterpacht, p. 9.
[3] MacGibbon, op. cit., pp. 310–13.
[4] See Adamiyat, op. cit., p. 249.
[5] See above, p. 176. Persia also protested to the British Government on 23 July 1930, against the Shaikh of Bahrain's grant of an oil concession to a British Company. A similar protest was made on 22 May 1934 to the United States against the purchase of the Bahrain oil concession by the Standard Oil Company of California. In her protest to the United States, Persia stated that a concession given by 'legally incompetent authorities cannot create any rights in favour of the Company'. She further stated that she reserved her rights 'to claim and demand the restitution of any profit that may accrue from such concession . . .' Such protests did not meet with favourable response. See L.N.O.J., July 1930, p. 1083; ibid., August 1934, p. 968.
[6] It is noteworthy that Kelly makes mention of the fact that in 1839, long before Bahrain came under British protection, Bahrain 'received no protection whatever from Persia' against the Egyptian attack. It was due to the interference of the British Royal Navy that the Egyptians were stopped from their premeditated attack. See Kelly, 'The Persian Claim', op. cit., pp. 59–60.

she has been able to do was to protest, on paper, to Britain and to pass legislation in Persia, the object of which is to renew the assertion of her claim to the island.[1]

Finally, in the light of the foregoing principles of law, it seems evident that the Persian Government's intermittent protests during the past and present centuries can afford no defence in face of the unequivocal rights of the present Government of Bahrain, as established by prescription or adverse holding.

Conclusion

It can be seen from the above legal analysis that the Persian claim to sovereignty over Bahrain lacks any valid legal grounds. But it appears from repeated Persian statements that Persia, essentially, bases her claim on her historical connection with the island in the past. Thus, it has often been alleged by Persia that

Bahrein has always and uninterruptedly formed part of Persia in past centuries, except during the Portuguese occupation from 1507–1622 [? 1522–1602], in which year the Persian Government resumed possession of this territory.[2]

It has been shown above that this statement does not correspond with historical facts.[3] As early as 1844, the British Indian authorities denied the allegations made by the Persian Prime Minister, Haji Meerza Aghassi, to the effect that Bahrain was 'a Persian possession'. Those authorities stated:

Bahrein may have been a dependency of Fars while the Persians were in actual possession of the Island. But the allegation that they had possessed it from A.D. 1300, is contrary to the best evidence that can be produced on the subject.[4]

Therefore, as a purely historical claim—based on an occupation lasting between 1602 and 1782—the Persian claim does not seem to stand today any chance of success. In the words of Hill:

Historic claims are difficult to assess, and cannot be taken at face value. Standing by itself, the historic claim is weak.[5]

---

[1] In 1957 a bill was passed by the Persian Parliament by virtue of which Bahrain was officially included as forming one of the administrative divisions of Iran. See *House of Commons Debates*, vol. 578, op. cit.
When the Persian Foreign Minister, Mr Ardalan, gave a press conference in Tehran on 8 April 1957 about his Government's claim to Bahrain, he stated that his Government, in spite of its differences with Britain, did not intend to place its dispute with Britain 'on the agenda of the Baghdad Pact council meeting' which was then due to be held in Tehran. He preferred 'to maintain discussions on this problem with Britain in a direct and friendly manner'. See *The Times*, 9 April 1957.
[2] L.N.O.J., September 1928, p. 1361.   [3] See above, pp. 167–8.
[4] See above, p. 171.   [5] Hill, op. cit., p. 171.

o

And stating State practice as regards the justiciability of territorial disputes, other than legal disputes, Hill then says:

The Root treaties made by the United States of America in 1908–9, for instance, provide for the arbitration of legal disputes only, thereby excluding territorial disputes in which the claims are of non-legal character.[1]

If a reference be made to the decisions of international arbitral awards, there also cannot be found much support for historic claims. In the case of *Eastern Greenland*, for instance, the Permanent Court of International Justice held that 'historic claims to dominion over the whole regions . . . lost weight and were gradually abandoned ever by the States which had relied upon them'.[2] Instead, the Court held:

International law established an ever closer connection between the existence of sovereignty and the effective exercise thereof, and States successfully disputed any claim not accompanied by such exercise.[3]

It can clearly be seen from the foregoing principles that a historical claim to territory which is unaccompanied by a proof of an effective exercise of authority in the territory cannot, successfully, be relied upon as a ground for the establishment of title to that territory.

Finally, it may be submitted that the independence of Bahrain from Persia has been established since her secession from the Persian dominion in 1783, and that by her secession, Bahrain satisfied the requirements of statehood in international law, namely, the existence of an independent Government exercising an effective authority on a defined territory.[4] The fact that Persia has not yet, from the point of view of her constitutional law, recognised this independence is, as pointed out above, irrelevant.[5] Nor can it be argued that, as a result of her becoming under British protection, Bahrain failed, for the purpose of the validity of her secession from Persia, to fulfil the requirements of statehood in international law.[6] This is because the sequence of events shows that the rulers of Bahrain established, effectively, their independence from Persia long before they entered into treaties of protection with Britain. Thus, the Treaty of Peace of 1820 by virtue of which Britain assumed political responsibility in the Gulf was signed by the rulers thirty-seven years after their conquest of Bahrain in 1783, while the first Agreement of protection of 1880, was concluded by them ninety-seven years after that conquest.[7] During

---

[1] Hill, op. cit., p. 202.
[2] *Legal Status of Eastern Greenland*, 1933, op. cit., p. 84.   [3] Ibid.
[4] See Lauterpacht, p. 31. These conditions, says the writer, 'are definitive and exhaustive. They have nothing to do with the degree of civilization of the new State, with the legitimacy of its origin, with its religion, or with its political system. For irrelevant tests of recognition of statehood, see ibid., pp. 31–2.
[5] See above, pp. 182–3.
[6] See Adamiyat's argument, op. cit., pp. 238–9.   [7] See Chapter 3.

this period, the Persian Government made no attempt whatever to regain control of Bahrain.[1]

Moreover, on the basis of the principle of nationality the Iranian case in Bahrain ceases to have any valid grounds. Bahrain was and has always been inhabited by Arabs who originally came to the island, according to some authorities, in 1900 B.C. The fourth census held in Bahrain in 1965 gives the Bahraini population as 143,814 and the number of Iranian subjects as 7,223, or about 4 per cent of the total population of 182,203.[2]

In his book in support of his country's claim, Dr Adamiyat makes a misleading statement about the population of Bahrain. He gives the number of the population of the island as 100,000. He then adds that 'approximately 50,000 of the total population belong to the Shia sect of Persia with the remainder belonging to the Sunni sect of Islam',[3] thus intending to give his reader the impression that those who belong to the Shia sect are Persians, and, therefore, sympathise with the union with Persia. But the writer seems to have failed to notice that those 50,000, according to his estimation, which is wrong, are, none the less, Arabs in the sense of race, language and national aspirations. The differences in Islam between the Shiis and the Sunnis are not so grave as to warrant a break in the unity of the Arabs of Bahrain who are determined to preserve their independence and to resist the Iranian claim to their country.

Arguments based on the religious beliefs of the population of a disputed territory can hardly be accepted as a decisive factor for settling that dispute. In the Mosul dispute, when the Turkish representative to the League of Nations referred to the religion of the Mosul's population (who belong to the Sunni sect of Islam) as one of the reasons for exercising Turkish sovereignty over Mosul, Mr Amery, the British representative, made a good point by replying:

There is no difference between Shias [Shiis] and Sunnis as would give any foundation whatever for the idea that this should be a factor in drawing the boundaries between Iraq and Turkey.[4]

---

[1] It has been explained above, at p. 168, that before the conclusion of the unauthorised Bruce Agreement, 1822, the British authorities adopted a strictly neutral attitude to the Persian claim, and therefore, had the Persian Government been able to re-establish its authority in Bahrain during any time before 1822, the British authorities would not have interfered to stop them from doing so.

[2] In 1959 there were 118,734 Bahraini nationals and 4,203 Iranian subjects (about 2·9 per cent of the total population of 143,135. Neither the 1959 nor 1965 censuses gives the total number of naturalised Persians in Bahrain. These may be estimated as not exceeding 10,000, or nearly 7 per cent of the total Arab population of the island. This shows that Iran has no ethnical or national case in Bahrain. See Govt. of Bahrain, *The 3rd Population Census*, 1959, and *The 4th Population Census*, 1965.   [3] Adamiyat, op. cit., p. 208.

[4] L.N.O.J., vol. 11 (1925), p. 1333. (See debate on the question of frontier between Turkey and Iraq.)

13

British-Saudi controversy over the sovereignty of Buraimi

INTRODUCTION

Historical and diplomatic background

The establishment after the First World War of the present independent Kingdom of Saudi Arabia, which succeeded to the former Ottoman provinces of Najd, Hasa and the Hijaz,[1] gave rise to a number of boundary problems. Although in 1922 agreements were concluded by Saudi Arabia with Iraq and Kuwait delimiting her northern boundaries with these countries,[2] no agreements were concluded by Saudi Arabia concerning the definition of her eastern and south-eastern boundaries with Qatar, the Trucial States or the Aden Protectorate. The present dispute over Buraimi is essentially a dispute over the definition of the Saudi Arabian eastern boundaries.

The problem of the Saudi Arabian eastern boundaries first arose in 1933, as a result of the grant of an oil concession by Saudi Arabia to the Standard Oil Company of California on 29 May 1933.[3] This problem assumed further importance when in 1935, 1937 and 1939, the Rulers of Qatar, Muscat and the Trucial States, respectively, granted to affiliates of the Iraq Petroleum Company oil concessions in respect of their territories.[4] It appears that the first step towards

---

[1] Amir'Abd al-'Aziz ibn Sa'ud, later proclaimed as King 'Abd al-'Aziz, conquered the district of Najd in 1902 and the district of Hasa—from the Turks—in 1913, and thus established what came to be known as the Kingdom of Saudi Arabia. The ancestors of King 'Abd al-'Aziz, formerly known as the Wahhabi House of Sa'ud or the Wahhabis (meaning the Arabian Reformation), governed Arabia proper between the middle of the eighteenth and the middle of the nineteenth centuries. In 1871, the House of Sa'ud was driven by the Turks from the province of Hasa. They retreated to Riyadh and central Najd until its occupation by the House of Rashid in 1891. Between 1891 and 1902, Amir'Abd al-Rahman, the father of King 'Abd al-'Aziz, and his family took refuge in Kuwait. In 1902, 'Abd al-'Aziz attacked and conquered Najd in his first attempt to regain the lands of his forefathers, the Wahhabis or the Arabian Reformation.

For a detailed analysis of the rise of Saudi Arabia, see Aitchison, pp. 187–8; Toynbee, A. J., *Survey of International Affairs*, vol. 1 (1925), pp. 271–88; Philby, H. St J. B., *Saudi Arabia* (1955), chapters 9–10; *Saudi Memorial*, I, chapter IV.

[2] See Appendix VIII.

[3] For text of the concession agreement, see *Umm al-Qura* (Saudi semi-official gazette) no. 448, dated 21 Rabi' 1 1352 (14 July 1933).

[4] Lenczowski, G., *Oil and State in the Middle East* (1960), pp. 141–2.

196

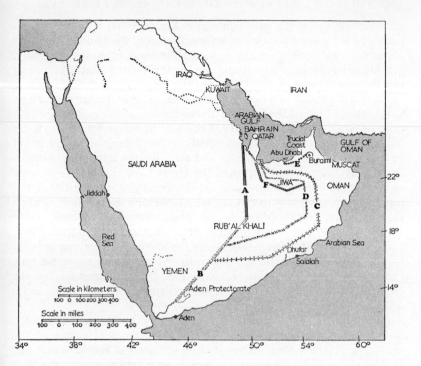

A Unratified Anglo-Turkish Treaty, 1913.
B Anglo-Turkish Treaty, 1914.
C Suggested by Saudi Arabia, 1935, rejected by British.
D Proposed by British, 1935–7. U.K. declared it approximate boundary of disputed territory seized Oct. 1955.
E Claimed by Saudi Arabia, 1949 north-eastern limit of Buraimi arbitration area.
F Claimed by British, 1952 west-south limit of Buraimi arbitration area.

MAP 2: Buraimi boundary lines

Extracted from the Map published by the Permanent Delegation of the Kingdom of Saudi Arabia to the U.N., New York, January 1956.

the clarification of the problem was taken in 1934, by the Government of the United States when it formally asked the United Kingdom about the legal position of the eastern boundaries of Arabia. In reply, the United Kingdom communicated to the United States copies of two documents, commonly known as the Anglo-Turkish Conventions of 29 July 1913 and 9 March 1914,[1] and stated that, in her view, these Conventions formed the basis of the definition of the eastern boundaries of Arabia.[2] On 28 April 1934 the United Kingdom, through her Minister at Jiddah, officially informed the Saudi Arabian Government of her reply to the United States and sent, for the information of the Saudi Government, two copies of the above Conventions.[3]

This communication marked the beginning of the British-Saudi diplomatic controversy over the eastern boundaries of Saudi Arabia. Consequently, on 13 May, Acting Saudi Foreign Minister, Fuad Hamzah, wrote to the British Minister at Jiddah, Sir Andrew Ryan, that his Government did not consider the above Conventions as binding upon it. However, Fuad Hamzah expressed his Government's desire to conduct negotiations with the United Kingdom for the purpose of reaching an equitable settlement of the boundaries question.[4]

Negotiations on the Saudi Arabian eastern boundaries continued intermittently between 1934-8. This formed the first phase of the negotiations which were interrupted by the Second World War.[5] The second phase of the negotiations which were resumed after the War took place between 1949-52. During this latter period two conferences were held, the London Conference of 1951, and the Dammam Conference of 1952, but no agreement was reached by the parties.[6]

The first Saudi Arabian proposal for defining her boundaries with Qatar, Muscat, the Trucial States and the Aden Protectorate was contained in a Memorandum of 3 April 1935. This proposal, commonly known as the 'Fuad Line', defined the Saudi Arabian boundaries as follows.

1. With Qatar, the line

begins at a point on the coast of the sea known as Dauhat Salwa and runs along the extension of the point of junction of Jabal Dukhan with the territory adjacent to the west, leaving to the Kingdom of Saudi Arabia the area to the west thereof, which lies between Jabal Dukhan and Jabal al-Nukhsh, and leaving to Qatar Jabal Dukhan and whatever lies beyond it to the east.

---

[1] For reference, see below, pp. 218-19.
[2] *British Memorial*, II, Annex D, No. 3, See Map 2.
[3] *Saudi Memorial*, II, Annex 4, p. 18; *British Memorial*, II, Annex D, No. 4.
[4] *Saudi Memorial*, II, Annexes 5, 6 and 7.
[5] *Saudi Memorial*, I, pp. 400-18.
[6] Ibid., pp. 419-42.

The line then extends to various places on

to the seacoast, leaving Niqyan Qatar to Qatar and Khaur al 'Udaid to the Kingdom of Saudi Arabia.

2. With Abu Dhabi and the other Arab Shaikhdoms on the Arabian Gulf,

the line begins at a point on the seacoast 25 kilometers from Khaur al-'Udaid. It then runs to the south and southeast through the territories known as al-Majann, Sabkhat Matti, and Kaffat al-Liwa (Qafa al-Jiwa) leaving the land of Kaffat al-Liwa to the Arab Amirates and the land west thereof to the Kingdom of Saudi Arabia. The line extends from the limits of the land of Kaffat al-Liwa to the point of intersection of Longitude 56°E. and Latitude 22°N. It then runs along the 56th meridian to the point of its intersection with Latitude 19°N. It then runs in a straight line to the point of intersection of Latitude 17°N. and Longitude 52°E. Thence it runs west a straight line along the 17th parallel to its intersection with Longitude 46°E. From this point it runs in the same direction until it intersects the line known as the Violet Line.[1]

The British Government made a counter-proposal in a Memorandum dated 25 November 1935 which drew a new line, often referred to as 'Ryan's Line' or the 'Riyadh Line', as a basis for the definition of the boundaries. The frontier line laid in this proposal starts from the

head of Dauhat as-Salwah at a point little to the east of Qasr as-Salwah, runs in a southeasterly direction, skirting the southern edge of the Sabkhat Matti, and then turning eastwards along the northern edge of the Rub'al-Khali as far as latitude 55°E. This line left . . . Kaur al-'Udaid and the coast eastwards, Liwa, and Buraimi to Abu Dhabi. But it conceded the well of Banaiyan . . . to King Ibn Saud, together with a large section of Rub'al-Khali.[2]

The significance of this proposal is that it constituted a departure from the 'Blue Line' of the 1913 Convention which was drawn up arbitrarily along the 50th meridian.[3] This Ryan's line was unacceptable to the Saudi Government on the ground that it did not recognise its 'claim either to Jabal al-Nukhsh, on the western side of the peninsula, or to a stretch of seacoast east of Qatar, commencing in the vicinity of Khaur al-'Udaid'.[4]

[1] Ibid., pp. 405–7. See Map 2.
[2] *British Memorial*, I, p. 89. And see for the modification of this line in favour of Saudi Arabia, ibid., II, Annex D, No. 17. See Map 2.
[3] Lenczowski, op. cit., p. 143. For the 'Blue Line' provided for by Article 11 of the unratified Convention of 1913, and later incorporated in Article 3 of the Convention of 1914, see below, pp. 219–20. See Map 2.
[4] *Saudi Memorial*, I, p. 412; ibid., II, Annex 21, H.R.H. Prince Faisal to the British Minister at Jiddah, 19 December 1937.

After the Second World War, the controversy arose again in 1949, when the British Political Officer for the Trucial States objected to oil exploration activities made by a party of Aramco's geologists within an area which was regarded by the British Government as part of the Shaikhdom of Abu Dhabi. In a letter of protest of 22 April 1949 delivered by the British Officer to Mr Holm, the principal geologist with the party, it was said

His Majesty's Government in the United Kingdom have always recognised the Shaikhdom of Abu Dhabi as extending up to Khor al Odaid and it is, therefore, natural that the Ruler should regard Your Company's presence at points North of Sufk as an incursion, particularly as the Company have Saudi soldiers with them.[1]

This letter led to an exchange of notes of protests between the Saudi and the British Governments. As a result, negotiations on the boundaries were again resumed.[2]

On 14 October 1949 the Saudi Government presented a new definition of the boundaries which, it stated, was based on an 'exhaustive study of the camping places of the tribes and an investigation of the actual situation'. This new definition proposed two lines: (1) a boundary line between Saudi Arabia and Qatar which

begins at a point on the coast of Dauhat Salwah at Latitude 24°56′ (Point A). From Point A the line runs due east to the point of intersection of Latitude 24°56′ and Longitude 51° (Point B). From Point B the line runs straight to the seacoast at Latitude 24°48′ (Point C), leaving 'Amirah to Saudi Arabia. Here ends the boundary line.

(2) A boundary line between Saudi Arabia and Abu Dhabi which

begins at a point on the coast of the Gulf between Bandar al-Marfa and Bandar al-Mughaira, lying 2 kilometers east of Bandar al-Marfa (Point A). The line runs due southeast from this point until it meets Latitude 23°56′ (Point B). From this point the line runs straight until it meets Longitude 54° (Point C). From point C the line runs straight until it meets the point of intersection of Latitude 24°25′ and Longitude 55°36′ (Point D).

In addition, the above definition alluded to the Buraimi Oasis as follows:

As to the territory south and east of the last-named point . . ., it is under the authority of Shaikhdoms which have no treaty relationships with the British Government. For this reason, the boundary between the Kingdom

---

[1] *British Memorial*, I, pp. 92–3, Mr P. D. Stobart to J. Holm of Aramco, 22 April 1949.

[2] *Saudi Memorial*, II, Annex 25, Aramco to Mr Stobart, 25 April 1949; ibid., I, pp. 421–2; *British Memorial*, I, pp. 93–4.

of Saudi Arabia and these Shaikhdoms shall be agreed upon between the Saudi Arabian Government and the Shaikhdoms referred to.[1]

The British Government's reaction to the above Saudi proposal was conveyed in a Note dated 30 November 1949, in which it rejected the new Saudi frontier claim and stated, *inter alia*:

His Majesty's Government feel that they have no option but to take up their position on the basis of the legal claim, namely, the 'Blue Line' and the 'Violet Line' as defined by the Anglo-Turkish Conventions of the 29th July, 1913 and the 9th March, 1914.[2]

Further, the Note disputed the Saudi claim to 'the Oasis of Liwa and other areas previously admitted to belong to Abu Dhabi'. With reference to Buraimi, it stated that

here the claims of the Shaikh of Abu Dhabi give His Majesty's Government an undoubted right to negotiate on his behalf. His Highness the Sultan of Muscat claims that the areas south of Buraimi are under his authority and he has asked His Majesty's Government . . . to represent him in these negotiations.[3]

In an attempt to reconcile their differences, the British and the Saudi Governments agreed in 1951 to hold a conference at London. The only useful outcome of the London Conference, which took place between 8–24 August 1951, was that the parties agreed to call for a round table conference in Saudi Arabia, comprising, in addition to British and Saudi representatives, the Rulers of the Shaikhdoms involved in the boundary dispute.[4]

The Dammam Conference, 1952

In this conference much of the discussion was based on historical allegiance of the tribes in the disputed areas, particularly al-Manasir, Al-Murrah and Bani Yas. The collection of *zakah*, a religious tax, by Saudi Arabia or Abu Dhabi in the areas was often relied upon as a basis of the disputing parties' claims. The British delegation expressed their willingness to consider the Saudi 1935 proposal, Fuad's Line, as representing the Saudi Government's official view. But the Saudi delegation denied the validity of that proposal, which, they said, was only offered as a compromise which, having been rejected by the

[1] *Saudi Memorial*, II, Annex 26, The Government of Saudi Arabia to the Government of the United Kingdom, 14 October 1949. See Map 2.

[2] *British Memorial*, Annex D, No. 27, H.M. Embassy at Jiddah to the Saudi Arabian Ministry of Foreign Affairs, 30 November 1949.

[3] Ibid. The Saudi Government replied to the above communication saying that it was impossible for it to adhere to 'the so-called Blue and Violet Lines'. See *Saudi Memorial*, II, Annex 28, The Government of Saudi Arabia to the Government of the United Kingdom, 10 December 1949.

[4] *Saudi Memorial*, II, Annexes 43–5, Records of London Conference, August 20–3, 1951.

British Government, 'became defunct'.[1] A new development in this conference was a statement presented by the British representative, Sir Rupert Hay, on behalf of the Rulers of Abu Dhabi and Qatar in which two boundary lines were claimed. With regard to Qatar, the line claimed runs from 'Ghar al-Buraid on the Dauhat al-Salwah through three named points to Saʿuda Nathil, and thence through ʿAqlat Manasir to a named point on Khaur al-ʿUdaid'. As regards Abu Dhabi, the frontier claimed begins at 'a line drawn from Saʿuda Nathil to the southernmost tip of Sabkhat Matti, including within Abu Dhabi ʿAqlat al-Rimth and Batr al-Tarfa; then a line from the southernmost tip of the Sabkhat Matti to al-Qaraini and thence to Umm al-Zamul'.[2] This represented a claim by Abu Dhabi to lands beyond those defined by the Ryan's Line of 1935.

The Standstill Agreement, 1952

As a means of asserting its claim, the Saudi Government dispatched in August, 1952, a party headed by Amir Turki ibn ʿUtaishan to take up his position as the Governor of Buraimi. According to Saudi sources, Ibn ʿUtaishan, who established himself in the village of Hamasa, 'was accompanied by a civilian staff of between thirty to forty persons—clerks, attendants, technicians, and policemen'.[3] The British Government termed this Saudi action as an armed 'invasion of Buraimi'.[4] After further negotiations on the new situation which arose from the presence of the Saudi party in Buraimi, the two parties agreed to conclude a 'Standstill Agreement' dated 26 October 1952. The purpose of this agreement was to neutralise the activities of the disputing parties in Buraimi, pending a final settlement of the dispute. Thus, it was agreed:

(a) The British shall remove the restrictions and obstacles imposed by them . . ., it being understood that the Saudis are also to desist from provocative actions . . .

(b) The two sides shall remain at present at Buraimi and maintain their present positions.

(c) After that discussions will be resumed between the British and the Saudis.[5]

---

[1] *Saudi Memorial*, I, pp. 423–4, 436–8; ibid., II, Annex 47, Records of Conversations between H.R.H. Prince Faisal and the British Ambassador at Jiddah (Excerpt), 28 February 1952; *British Memorial*, I, pp. 98–100.

[2] *British Memorial*, I, 98–9; ibid., II, Annex D, No. 36. The spot 'Umm al-Zamul' is shown on the map submitted as lying at about latitude 22° 35′ N., longitude 55° 10′ E. See *Saudi Memorial*, I, p. 438. See Map 2.

[3] *Saudi Memorial*, I, p. 444. Buraimi was visited a few months before the arrival of the Saudi party by the British Political Officer of the Trucial Coast. This drew a protest from Saudi Arabia. For this protest and for the British reply to it, see ibid., II, Annex 55, 30 March 1952, and see *British Memorial*, II, Annex D, No. 39.

[4] *The Times*, 27 May 1954; Lenczoweski, op cit., pp. 146–8.

[5] *Saudi Memorial*, II, Annex 76, Buraimi Standstill Agreement, 26 October 1952.

The final stages of negotiations ended in 1954, when the parties agreed to refer their dispute to arbitration by a special tribunal to be agreed upon.[1] The proceedings of this tribunal and the developments ensuing from it will be discussed below.

The Arbitration Agreement of 30 July 1954, and the Geneva Arbitration, 1955

By the Arbitration Agreement of 30 July 1954[2] it was agreed to refer the dispute between the United Kingdom, acting on behalf of the British protected Shaikhdom of Abu Dhabi and on behalf of the Sultan of Muscat, at his own request, and Saudi Arabia

as to the location of the common frontier between Saudi Arabia and Abu Dhabi and as to the sovereignty in the Buraimi Oasis,

to a tribunal consisting of five members chosen by both parties.

By Article II of this agreement, the tribunal was asked to decide:

(a) The location of the common frontier between Saudi Arabia and Abu Dhabi, within the line claimed by the Saudi Arabian Government in 1949 and that claimed on behalf of Abu Dhabi at the Dammam Conference in 1952;

(b) Sovereignty in the area comprised within a circle whose centre is in Buraimi village and whose circumference passes through the point of junction of latitude 24 degrees, 25 minutes North and longitude 55 degrees, 36 minutes East.

By Article IV the tribunal was asked to

have due regard to all relevant considerations of law, fact and equity brought to its attention by the Parties under Article V and VI or disclosed through the exercise of the powers conferred upon it by Article VII.

And, in particular, it was asked to

take into account various historical facts relating to the rights of His Majesty the King of Saudi Arabia and his forefathers and the rights of the other Rulers concerned and their forefathers.[3]

The Geneva Arbitration

After a preliminary meeting in Nice the tribunal, composed of Dr Charles De Visscher (Belgium), President, Sir Reader Bullard (Britain), Shaikh Yusuf Yasin (Saudi Arabia), Dr Mahmoud Hasan (Pakistan)

---

[1] Ibid., II, Annex 90, February (no date), 1954.

[2] *Treaty Series*, No. 65 (1954), *Cmd.* 9272; *Saudi Memorial*, II, Annex I.

[3] *Saudi Memorial*, II, Annex 1. To this agreement was attached Exchange of Notes, bearing the date of the agreement, by which the parties agreed to withdraw their forces from the Buraimi Zone to undisputed areas, and to maintain a small police force of fifteen men by each party in the Zone.

and Dr Ernesto Dihgo (Cuba), began its proceedings in September 1955 at Geneva.[1] These proceedings, which took place between 11–16 September were held at the request of the British Agent who informed the President of the tribunal that he had some complaints to submit against Saudi Arabia for what he alleged to be a violation of the terms of the Arbitration Agreement. At the beginning of its session on 11 September, the British Agent presented the following charges against Saudi Arabia:

(a) That the Saudi police contingent in the area exceeded the maximum number of 15, agreed upon by the Arbitration Agreement;
(b) That attempts were made to send arms to disputed areas;
(c) That passengers and supplies were flown to the area;
(d) That a Saudi bribery on a wide scale was offered to Buraimi Shaikhs to win them over to the Saudi side.[2]

The Saudi Agent presented evidence to refute the above charges. As a result, the tribunal devoted its sessions to considering evidence in support or against these charges.[3] The final verdict of the tribunal was expected on 16 September. But instead of giving its verdict on the British charges at this session, the tribunal suspended its proceedings *sine die*. This followed the sudden resignation of the British nominee of the tribunal, Sir Reader Bullard, who, despite the advice of the

---

[1] *The Times*, 29 July, 12 September 1955.

[2] *Buraimi Arbitration Tribunal, Minutes of Sittings*, 11–15 September 1955, *Complaints by the United Kingdom Against Saudi Arabia to the Tribunal*. These complaints were made to the Tribunal by the British Counsel on 11 September, before the beginning of the actual arbitration proceedings on the substance of the Buraimi dispute. In his submission, the British Leading Counsel, Sir (now Lord) Hartley Shawcross, complained that the Saudi Government 'has been engaged in a deliberate, a systematic and persistent policy of large-scale bribery, and other improper practices which are calculated . . . to destroy the *status quo* as it existed at the time of the Arbitration Agreement. . . .' He introduced witnesses, who included Buraimi shaikhs, to testify before the tribunal in support of the British complaints.

[3] Ibid. And see *The Times*, 13–16 September 1955. The Saudi Leading Counsel, Dr Richard Young, introduced to the tribunal one leading witness, 'Abd Allah al-Quraishi, who consistently denied the charges of 'improper practices' which were brought against him by the British Counsel. In his submission, Dr Young held that 'the evidence before the tribunal does not substantiate the charges' brought by the United Kingdom against Saudi Arabia in respect of 'alleged violation by (the latter) of the interim regime in the disputed areas'. The Counsel also cast doubts on the evidence of the United Kingdom's witnesses who, he said, included 'two brothers of the Ruler of Abu Dhabi, two shaikhs of the Dhawaher tribe, and a British officer'. On the bribery charge Dr Young stated that sums of money received by shaikhs and notables were 'notoriously exaggerated by rumour of what perhaps sometimes be called common knowledge'. Such sums of money, he said, 'cannot be construed as bribery'. Finally, he gave an assurance, on behalf of Saudi Arabia, to withdraw from the Buraimi Zone the Saudi officials whose withdrawal was demanded by the United Kingdom.

President, left the session of the tribunal.[1] Later, it was announced that the President had also handed his resignation. The proceedings were thus abruptly brought to an end.[2]

It appears from the terms of Sir Reader Bullard's letter of resignation that his main complaint was against what he considered to be 'the complete partiality' of the Saudi member of the Tribunal, Shaikh Yusuf Yasin, who was also the Deputy Foreign Minister of his country.

It has become abundantly clear [he said], that Shaikh Yusuf Yasin is, in fact, in effective control of the conduct of the proceedings on behalf of the Saudi Arabian Government, and is representing that Government on this tribunal rather than acting as an impartial arbitrator.[3]

After the breakdown of the Geneva proceedings the British Prime Minister announced on 26 October 1955, that the British-officered forces of Trucial Oman had taken the Buraimi Oasis and ejected the Saudi police contingent from it. At the same time he informed the Saudi Government of his Government's decision to reconsider a settlement of the boundary dispute on the basis of the Riyadh Line, as modified in 1937, in favour of Saudi Arabia.[4] The Saudi Government protested at what it termed to be an 'arbitrary action taken by the Government of the United Kingdom in resorting to military force against the Saudi Arabian Oasis of Buraimi'.[5]

The Saudi Government regarded the charges made by the British Government against it as unfounded and called upon the British Government to agree to the resumption of arbitration which did not, in its view, lose its legal force as a result of the withdrawal of the British member of the tribunal.[6] The British Government rejected

---

[1] *The Times*, 17 September 1955; *Minutes of Sittings of the Buraimi Arbitration Tribunal*, op. cit.

[2] *The Times*, 24 September 1955.

[3] *The Times*, 17 September 1955. In reply to the allegations made by Sir Reader Bullard, Shaikh Yusuf Yasin said that 'the tribunal had thus been frustrated in expressing its views on the charges', as a result of the resignation of the British member. About himself, he said that 'the whole tribunal has always been aware that, in addition to my duties as a member, I have continued to discharge my duties as Deputy Foreign Minister' of Saudi Arabia. See ibid., 19 September 1955.

[4] *The Times*, 27 October 1955. In a statement to the House of Commons on 20 February 1956, the then British Prime Minister, Sir (now Lord) Anthony Eden, reported to the House the military measures taken by the British Government in Buraimi in the previous year, and reiterated his Government's wish to uphold the Riyadh Line, as amended in 1937. But he added that his Government was ready to discuss 'any minor rectifications of the line which may seem convenient in the light of local circumstances'. See *The Times*, 21 February 1956.

[5] *The Times*, 27 October 1955.

[6] It is noteworthy that Britain's abrupt withdrawal from the Arbitration Tribunal at the time and her unexpected seizure, five weeks later, of the Buraimi Oasis was criticised by neutral observers as arbitrary and high handed. It is noted,

this Saudi request for the resumption of arbitration and declared its intention to maintain the position which arose from the occupation of Buraimi by the Trucial Oman Levies (now Scouts).[1]

Latest developments of the dispute

In August 1960 it was announced that the British and the Saudi Governments had agreed on the appointment of a neutral observer by the Secretary-General of the United Nations with the object of sending 'a fact-finding mission' to Buraimi.[2] The Secretary-General at the time chose Mr Herbert de Ribbing, Swedish Ambassador to Spain, to head this mission. The purpose of the mission was to ascertain the number of 'Buraimi inhabitants, shaikhs and notables who fled to Saudi Arabia' after the occupation of Buraimi in 1955 by the British-led Trucial Oman Levies. Saudi Arabia has maintained that the return of these Buraimi inhabitants to the Oasis is a necessary condition before any progress could be made on the settlement of the dispute by negotiations.[3] In September 1960, Mr de Ribbing visited Buraimi, and in October of that year he submitted to the Secretary-General his report in which he recommended that a number of genuine Buraimi inhabitants (who are now living in Saudi Arabia) should be allowed to return to their settlements in the Oasis.[4] Following the

---

in particular, that the British member on the tribunal had seen fit to resign from the tribunal on the same day it was reconvened for the purpose of delivering its findings on the British charges against the Saudis.

See *The Times*, 25 November 1955; ibid., 28 April 1958. And for a critical review of the Buraimi arbitration, see Mann, C., *Abu Dhabi* (1964), p. 97, where the writer makes this comment on Sir Reader's resignation: 'As a member of the tribunal, Sir Reader (Bullard) was fully aware of the outcome of the deliberations regarding the British allegations; therefore, it is doubtful that he would have resigned if the decision were going to substantiate British claims and allegations.'

[1] Legally speaking, the British Government could be held at fault for not giving effect to Article I(c) of the Arbitration Agreement of 1954, which provides for the method of replacing a member of the tribunal in the case of his resignation or death.

For a legal analysis of the Buraimi proceedings at Geneva in 1955, see Goy, Raymond, 'L'Affaire de l'Oasis de Buraimi', *Annuaire français de droit international* (1957), pp. 188–205. The writer seems to question the legality of the action of the British member of the tribunal, Sir Reader Bullard, in withdrawing, without notice, in the following remarks: 'A vrai dire, le droit de démissionner ne pouvait être en soi contesté à l'agent britannique: il se trouvait prévu par le compromis (art. 1 34. lib c.) Mais son usage dans les circonstances de l'affaire est critique, parce qu'il serait intervenu pour certains motifs partiaux et à seule fin de bloquer l'arbitrage.' See ibid., p. 201.

[2] *The Times*, 11 August 1960. For earlier reports about Buraimi, see ibid., 1 December 1959.　　　　[3] *The Times*, 14 November 1960.

[4] *The Times*, 11 August, 20 September and 14 November 1960. It seems that the recommendations of Mr de Ribbing on the status of the Buraimi refugees living in Saudi Arabia were quite unacceptable to the British Government. See *The Times*, 19 October 1960.

resumption of diplomatic relations[1] between Britain and Saudi Arabia on 16 January 1963, it was announced that the two countries had decided to continue their efforts in the discussion of the Buraimi dispute under the personal supervision of the Secretary-General of the United Nations.[2] Although discussions on the question have continued ever since, with some intermissions, there is yet no hopeful sign in sight of a solution to the problem.

Conclusion

The Buraimi dispute is, in principle, a dispute between Saudi Arabia, on the one hand, and the Shaikh of Abu Dhabi and the Sultan of Muscat, on the other, over two main issues, namely, (*a*) the definition of the common eastern frontiers between Saudi Arabia and Abu Dhabi, and (*b*) the determination of sovereignty over the Buraimi Oasis. The United Kingdom has been acting in this dispute on behalf of the Shaikh of Abu Dhabi, for whose foreign relations she is responsible, and the Sultan of Muscat, who appointed her to represent him in so far as the dispute relates to part of the 'territory in the Buraimi Oasis claimed by him to belong to Muscat'.[3] The Oasis comprises nine villages, six of which are claimed by Abu Dhabi and three by Muscat, while Saudi Arabia is claiming them all.[4] The claims of both sides to the Oasis appear to rest upon their historical connections with the area, and upon allegiance and payment of the *zakah*, or political tributes, by the tribes belonging to the area. As regards the issue relating to the determination of the eastern frontiers of Saudi Arabia, the British Government claims that the Anglo-Turkish Conventions of 1913–14, defining the Turkish possessions in Arabia, formed the basis of the Saudi eastern frontiers, and that no developments have taken place in Arabia since 1914, which could establish a Saudi Arabian claim to areas lying to the west of the 'Blue Line'. The Saudi Government does not recognise the validity of the Blue Line, as defined in the above Conventions, in delimiting its eastern frontiers with Qatar and Abu Dhabi. Nor does it agree to the definition of its frontiers on the basis of the 1935 boundary line—so-called Ryan's line. Instead, it contends that its frontiers should be delimited on the basis of its 1949 boundary claim.[5]

---

[1] Diplomatic relations between Britain and Saudi Arabia were severed following the Suez conflict in 1956.

[2] *The Times*, 17 January 1963.

[3] The preamble of the Arbitration Agreement of 30 July 1954, op. cit.

[4] *The Economist* (London), 28 March 1955; *The Times*, 'A Guide to Buraimi', 1 December 1959.

[5] For these developments, see above, pp. 200–01.

FACTS RELATING TO THE TERRITORY IN DISPUTE

Situation of the oasis

The Buraimi Oasis is an agglomeration of nine settlements. These are: *Hili, Al-Qattarah, Al-Qimi, Al-Muʿtaradh, Al-ʿAin, Al-Muwaiqiʿi, Saʿra, Hamasa* and *Buraimi*. The first six are settled by the Bani Yas and the Dhawahir tribes; Saʿra and the Buraimi are settled by the Nuʿaim and Hamasa by the tribe of Al Bu Shamis.[1] The name Buraimi is taken from that of the biggest villages. The population of the whole settlement is estimated at 10,000.[2] It lies on the extreme boundary of south-east Arabia proper in a tract referred to geographically as 'Independent Oman'. Lorimer, in his great work on Arabia and the Arabian Gulf, classifies the promontory of Oman, an area extending from the mountains of 'Ras Musandam at the extreme north of the Gulf of Oman to the Dhafar district at the extreme south-west', into three different political districts or units. The Buraimi Oasis, he says, lies 'in the heart of the promontory, at or near its base'. He calls it 'Independent Oman' so as to emphasise its independence from any link with either of the two other units, namely Trucial Oman and the Oman Sultanate. He thus says: 'Independent Oman is not subject to either the Sultan or any of the Trucial Shaikhs of Oman.'[3]

The exact situation of the Oasis is shown by Lorimer to be 'a little south of a straight line drawn between the coastal towns of Sohar and Abu Dhabi about 65 miles west by south of the former, and 85 miles east by south of the latter.'[4] The Oasis, says Lorimer, 'is nearly circular and its diameter is about six miles'.[5] It lies north of the famous *Jabal Hafit*. According to Article II of the Arbitration Agreement of 30 July 1954 the Oasis is located within 'a circle whose centre is in the Buraimi village and whose circumference passes through the point of junction of latitude 24 degrees, 25 minutes North and longitude 55 degrees, 36 minutes East'.

History of control over the oasis

(a) *1800–69*

The following chronology of events will show that for the most part of their reign in Arabia during the nineteenth century the Wahhabis[6] exercised authority over Buraimi.

1. In 1800 Buraimi was occupied by a Wahhabi expedition

---

[1] *Saudi Memorial*, I, pp. 31–7; *The Times*, 1 December 1959. See Map 3.
[2] Lenczowski, op. cit., p. 144.   [3] Lorimer, II, pp. 1368–9.
[4] Ibid., p. 260.   [5] Ibid.
[6] For the relationship of the Wahhabis to the present ruling family of Saudi Arabia, see above, p. 196, n. 1.

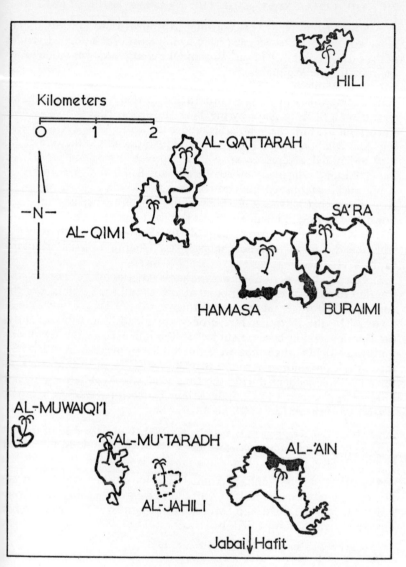

MAP 3: The villages of Buraimi

dispatched from Najd.[1] According to Ibn Ruzaiq, the Wahhabi Amir ʿAbd al-ʿAziz 'succeeded in reducing most of the northern tribes of the eastern coast of Arabia'. Buraimi, he continues, 'was made head-quarters for the Wahhabis'.[2]

2. The Wahhabis continued their control over Buraimi and the surrounding areas of Oman until 1818.[3] In that year the Wahhabis were dislodged from Najd by the Turkish forces of Ibrahim Pasha of Egypt. But in 1824, the Wahhabis, under the leadership of Amir Turki ibn ʿAbd Allah, regained their position in Arabia and in the year 1828, they appointed a representative in Buraimi by the name of ʿUmar ibn ʿUfaisan.[4] During 1824–30, Lieutenant S. Hennal reported that Amir Turki established his control over the whole eastern region of Arabia and that he was governing 'with great prudence and modera-tion'. And in 1831, Lieutenant A. B. Kemball reported that 'the whole of the Arabian coast from Ras-ool-Hud [Ras-al-Hadd] to Koweit, with the exception of Aboothabee [Abu Dhabi], became tributary to the Wahabees'.[5]

3. During this period, the Wahhabis continued to govern the Buraimi region through an appointed agent until the beginning of the year 1838.[6] However, at the end of this year the Wahhabis were again attacked by the Egyptian forces of Muhammad ʿAli. Consequently, the Buraimi region became subject to the influence of the Egyptians until May 1840,[7] when they were finally driven away from Najd and the eastern province of Arabia. British records confirm that Buraimi remained independent during the time when the Wahhabis were not holding it. According to Captain Atkins Hamerton, who wrote to the British Government in 1840, about Buraimi:

... Brymee has been generally held by the Wahabis to the date of the fall of their power and influence, when the Naeem tribes assumed possession in independence ...[8]

4. In 1843, a new Wahhabi Amir, Faisal ibn Turki, came to power. He immediately communicated with the Buraimi tribes. In 1844, Amir Faisal dispatched Saʿd ibn Mutlaq al-Mutairi to Buraimi as his representative, accompanied by Nasir al-ʿUraini as Qadhi. British

---

[1] *Bombay Selections*, pp. 152–3; Lorimer, p. 1053.

[2] Badger, G. P., *History of Imams and Seyyids* (English translation) by Humaid ibn Ruzaiq (1871), p. 230, Introduction, p. lviii.

[3] Ibid., pp. 230, 298. And see *Bombay Selections*, p. 153, where A. B. Kemball states in a report in 1808 'the preponderance of the Wahhabis [was] com-pletely established in Oman'.

[4] *Bombay Selections*, pp. 435–7; and see *Saudi Memorial*, I, p. 158.

[5] *Bombay Selections*, pp. 153–4, 437–9.

[6] Ibid., pp. 154–5, 440–4. According to A. B. Kemball, 'the *zakah* or tribute of 5 per cent began to be exacted and his influence, [Turki] was completely estab-lished over the inhabitants of the coast'.

[7] *Bombay Selections*, p. 449.   [8] Ibid., pp. 116–18.

records describe how he was greeted by the tribes of Nu'aim, Dhawahir and al-Bu Shamis who all 'hastened to tender their submission when they heard of his approach'.[1] And in 1853, Amir Faisal sent his son, Amir ʿAbd Allah, to Buraimi with a mission to reconcile differences between some tribes in the interior of Oman. According to British records, Amir ʿAbd Allah 'took up his position at Brymee, and summoned the chiefs to attend him'.[2]

5. The predominant position which the Wahhabis occupied during this period among the Shaikhs and tribes of the whole eastern region of Arabia is clearly shown in a report submitted in July 1854 by Lieutenant A. B. Kemball to the Government of India. In this report, Kemball stated:

These states are independent, but acknowledge the feudal supremacy of the Wahabi ruler whenever his own power, or their dissensions, may place him in a position to exercise it. Their chiefs are expected to afford military aid in his expeditions, and to furnish supplies to his troops when present, as in the case of the garrison at Brymee in Oman . . .[3]

6. In 1865, Amir Faisal died and he was succeeded by his son, ʿAbd Allah, who was proclaimed in the same year as the new Amir of the House of Al-Saʿud.[4] Very shortly after Amir ʿAbd Allah's reign the British Government accused the Wahhabi Agent at Buraimi of sending troops to Sur, a territory under the authority of the Sultan of Muscat, and attacking Indian subjects resident in that territory. The British Government, therefore, sent an ultimatum in July 1866 to Amir ʿAbd Allah requiring reparations for the damages sustained. At the same time the British Government gave military aid to the Sultan and encouraged him to oust the Wahhabis from the territories of Oman.[5]

Later, however, the differences between the British Government and the Wahhabi Amir were reconciled when they both arrived at an understanding based on a declaration, made on behalf of Amir ʿAbd Allah, dated 21 April 1866. According to Lorimer, in that declaration, Muhammad ibn Maniʿ assured the British Resident at Bushire, on behalf of his Master, Amir ʿAbd Allah that:

(1) British subjects would be protected in the Wahhabi dominions.
(2) Beyond collecting the tribute established by ancient custom, the Wahhabis would not in future interfere with Arab principalities in alliance with the British Government, in particular, the Sultanate of Oman.[6]

7. In April 1869 the Wahhabi Agent at Buraimi, Turki al-Sudairi, was shot dead while he was on a visit to the town of al-Sharjah, on the

---

[1] Ibid., p. 456.   [2] Ibid., pp. 232, 456, 460.   [3] Ibid., p. 292.
[4] *Saudi Memorial*, I, p. 237.   [5] Lorimer, pp. 474, 1121–2.
[6] Lorimer, p. 1124. For an accurate translation of Amir ʿAbd Allah's letter, see Aitchison, p. 206.

Trucial Coast. At or about this time, a certain Omani chief, called Sayyid ʿAzzan ibn Qais, usurped the Sultanate of Oman from the legitimate Sultan, Turki, who was on a visit abroad, and declared himself, in his place, as a Sultan. ʿAzzan was also encouraged by the death of the Wahhabi Agent at Buraimi and his followers to send troops to that place and occupy it, which he did 'after a trifling resistance' on the part of the small Wahhabi garrison. The surrender of Buraimi to ʿAzzan's forces took place on or about 18 June 1869. According to Lorimer, the occupation of Buraimi by Sayyid ʿAzzan resulted in the 'disappearance of the Wahhabis from Buraimi which they occupied, almost continuously, for nearly seventy years'[1] (i.e., from 1800 to 1869). And according to Ibn Ruzaiq:

> In July (1869) he [ʿAzzan] captured the fortress of el-Bereimy—long the frontier stronghold of the Wahhabis . . . and established friendly relations with Beni Yas [of Abu Dhabi] and the El-Kawasim.[2]

8. Amir ʿAbd Allah ibn Faisal made some attempts to recover Buraimi from ʿAzzan in the following year, but he failed to do so.[3] The British Government also 'reminded' him, says Lorimer, 'of his promise, given in 1866, not to commit aggressions upon Arab states having friendly relations with the British Government.'[4]

9. The expulsion of the Wahhabis from Buraimi in 1869 concluded the period of their control over it, lasting from 1800 to 1869. During this period they were twice dispossessed of Buraimi: from 1818 to 1824 and from 1838 to 1842. In May 1871, the Turkish Government sent another expedition to Arabia and occupied the province of Hasa.[5]

(b) *1869–1952*[6]

During their occupation of Hasa (including the ports of Qatif and Uqair), a period lasting from 1871 to 1913, the Turks had not exer-

---

[1] Lorimer, p. 1127.

[2] Badger, op. cit., Introduction, p. cxv. And see Lorimer, p. 1127. According to Lorimer, 'Azzan was regarded as a mere usurper and the British Government therefore declined to recognise him as a legitimate ruler of Muscat. 'The arrogant and fanatical character of his ('Azzan) Counsellors, the unfavourable influence of his administration on trade, and the fact that he was not of the line of Said, whom British Officers had come to recognise as the natural rulers of the country, were the principal objections against him.' See Lorimer, p. 487. 'Azzan met his death early in 1871 in a battle with the legitimate Sultan, Turki Al-Bu-Saʻid. See ibid. p. 490.   [3] Lorimer, p. 1127.   [4] Ibid.   [5] Lorimer, p. 1128

[6] The year 1952 is chosen as the 'critical date' in this dispute, the date after which the actions of the parties cannot affect their legal positions or rights as they then stood. This is because in August of this year Saudi officials established control over the Oasis after they left it in 1869. After this year the parties proceeded to make arrangements for the settlement of the dispute. On the other hand, the year 1934 may be suggested as a critical date since it marked the beginning of negotiations on the Saudi Arabian eastern boundaries, as stated above in the introduction.

cised any jurisdiction over the Buraimi region. The British Government itself was not in favour of any Turkish expansion in Arabia beyond those parts which were actually under their hands. The British Government thus took the view, in 1878, that Turkish sovereignty should not be admitted to exist

as far southeast as Ojair [Uqair'], and that on this understanding the Turks may be held responsible for maritime disorders within the confines of the coast of al-Hasa ending at Ojair.[1]

Lorimer makes only brief references to the political status of Buraimi after 1869. He states:

After the expulsion of the Wahhabis in 1869, Buraimi ceased to play an important part in the general history of Trucial Oman and became an annex to the principality of Abu Dhabi.[2]

and

Buraimi is independent, but the influence of the Shaikh of Abu Dhabi in the district is strong and increasing.[3]

But in a third statement Lorimer seems to lay emphasis on the political independence of Buraimi:

The district . . . is not subject to any recognised ruler.[4]

As regards Ibn Ruzaiq, he also makes a brief reference to the independent position of Buraimi after 1869 when he states:

Azzan, however, left Bereimy after its capture . . . and it remained under the authority of the Benu-Naim who paid tribute for a while.[5]

An attempt will now be made to show the extent of control over Buraimi during this period, by (a) Muscat, (b) Abu Dhabi and (c) Saudi Arabia.[6]

[1] Saldanha, J. A., *Précis of Turkish Expansion on the Arab Littoral of the Persian Gulf, the Hasa and Katif Affairs, Political and Secret Department* (1904), pp. 100–2. It appears that the British Government could not, at the time, enter into discussions with Turkey for the limitation of her influence on the Arabian coast on the basis of the above view taken by the British Government. This was because Turkey did not recognise such limitations on her sovereignty and jurisdiction. (See Saldanha, ibid., pp. 100–7.)
[2] Lorimer, p. 770.
[3] Lorimer, II, p. 264.
[4] Lorimer, p. 1368.
[5] Badger, op. cit. Introduction, p. cxvi.
[6] The following illustration is based on Lorimer and on the views of British officials and travellers who paid occasional visits to Buraimi during this period. This appears to be the only data available.

(a) *Extent of control by Muscat*

1. In November 1875, almost five years after 'Azzan's conquest of Buraimi, Lieutenant Colonel Miles, British Political Agent in Muscat, visited the region. He expressed the following view:

The most powerful and predominant Ghafiri tribe at present is the Naim . . . They occupy el-Bereymi proper and Suareh, and their possession of the fort enables them to overawe the whole of the settlement. Since the time of Seyyid Azan, *they have been practically uninterfered with by the Muscat Government*, but of course own allegiance to the present Sultan.[1]

In his report of 1878-9 on Muscat, Miles made a list of the towns and districts which were governed by officials appointed by the Sultan. The district of al-Dhahirah or Buraimi was not mentioned in that list.[2]

2. According to Lorimer, '. . . the Buraimi Oasis and the Mahadhah tract, though they belong to Oman, *are not included in the Sultan's possessions*'.[3] The Sultan, Lorimer says, 'had no authority at a distance from his capital'.[4]

3. Buraimi was visited in May 1901 by Samuel Zwemer, an American missionary. He stated that:

The principal tribes east of Bereimi . . . *do not acknowledge the authority of the Sultan of Maskat*, but have their own chiefs, and are, alas, nearly always at a feud with each other.[5]

4. Lovat Fraser, a British journalist, recorded this about his visit to Muscat:

Even within the state of Oman the authority of the Sultan can rarely be safely exercised outside the two contiguous towns of Muscat and Matra [Matrah].[6]

5. The British Admiralty Handbook on Arabia refers to Buraimi as an 'independent tract' as follows:

There are two small independent tracts between Oman Sultanate and Trucial Oman, *to which the Sultan of Oman has never laid claim* . . . (These two independent tracts are referred to as 'Jau and the Buraimi Oasis'.)[7]

6. Captain Eccles, an officer of the Indian Army who was in command of the Muscat levies in 1920, gave a talk on 27 October 1920 to the Central Asian Society, London, on Muscat. In that talk,

---

[1] Lt-Col Miles, 'On the Route between Sohar and el-Bereymi, in Oman', *Journal of the Asiatic Society of Bengal*, 46 (1877), p. 52.

[2] Government of India, *Annual Report of the Persian Gulf Residency and Muscat Political Agency* (1878–1879), p. 116.

[3] Lorimer, pp. 1369, 1382.   [4] Ibid., p. 517; ibid., II, pp. 1419.

[5] Zwemer, S. M., 'Three Journeys in Northern Oman', *Geographical Journal*, 19 (1902), p. 63.   [6] Fraser, L., *India under Curzon and After* (1911), pp. 90–1.

[7] Great Britain; British Admiralty, *A Handbook on Arabia*, vol. 1 (1916), pp. 281–2.

Captain Eccles referred to what he called ' . . . the independent oasis of Biraimi'. He then remarked that 'in fact the greater part' of the territory over which the Sultan claims suzerainty 'is entirely independent'. In the discussion which followed, Sir Percy Cox agreed with Captain Eccles that ' . . . the Sultan's writ practically does not carry beyond the walls of Muscat'.[1]

7. Brigadier Longrigg, formerly an executive of the Iraq Petroleum Company, described the position of the Sultan in 1932 by stating that he 'was far from enjoying undisputed authority' beyond his capital, Muscat.[2]

8. Thesiger, a British traveller, visited Buraimi in November 1948. Two years after this visit he stated that the shaikhs of Buraimi 'clamorously rejected' the claim of the Sultan to their territory.[3]

9. Ronald A. Codrai, once a representative of the Iraq Petroleum Company in the Trucial Coast, described, in an article on Oman, 1950, the Buraimi Oasis as an independent 'small neutral zone', not subject to the government of the Sultan who, he said, 'is left with control over only Muscat and the adjoining coastal region'.[4]

(b) *Extent of control by Abu Dhabi*

1. Reference has been made above to Lorimer's statement that

Buraimi is independent, but the influence of the Shaikh of Abu Dhabi in the district is strong and increasing.[5]

Explaining how the Shaikh of Abu Dhabi came to establish his influence in Buraimi, Lorimer continues:

He [the Shaikh] has had recently acquired (and is now engaged in developing) an estate at Jahali, while Masudi is being formed into a village by his eldest son. Moreover, a regular tribute . . . is paid to him by the Dhawahir, who are numerically a majority in the oasis . . .[6]

2. On the relationship between Abu Dhabi and the tribes of Buraimi, Lorimer records that throughout the period 1875–1904,

. . . a state of war existed between the Beni Yas [the name of the ruling house of Abu Dhabi] and the Naim [owners of Buraimi].

Further, Lorimer states that the Shaikh of Abu Dhabi, after establishing his influence through the use of force against the tribes of

---

[1] Eccles, G. J., 'The Sultanate of Muscat and Oman', *Journal of the Central Asian Society*, 14 (1927), pp. 19, 38.

[2] Longrigg, S. H., *Oil in the Middle East* (1954), p. 99.

[3] Thesiger, W. P., 'Desert Borderlands of Oman', *Geographical Journal*, 116 (1950), p. 140.

[4] Codrai, R. A., *Canadian Geographical Journal*, (1950), p. 184, as quoted in *Saudi Memorial*, I, p. 369.

[5] See above, p. 213.   [6] Lorimer, II, p. 264.

Buraimi, proceeded to adopt 'measures for the virtual annexation of Buraimi'. And, in 1904, he continues,

> About the same time he proved the strength of his influence in the Baraimi neighbourhood generally by obliging the Beni Qitab to pay blood-money for two citizens of Ibri town in Dhahirah, whom they had slain.[1]

3. On the boundaries of Abu Dhabi, Lorimer says:

> Inland, the frontiers of Abu Dhabi are not defined: it is asserted that on the east they reach to the Buraimi oasis, but without taking it in . . .[2]

4. Describing his journey from Abu Dhabi to Buraimi in May 1902, Sir Percy Cox, then the British Political Agent in Muscat, makes the following remarks: About Buraimi, he says that he found the Nuʿaim tribe enjoying 'a special position by virtue of their past history'. In regard to the influence of Abu Dhabi in Buraimi, he confirms Lorimer's statement, previously mentioned, that the Shaikh and his son acquired 'material possessions', 'date gardens' and settlements, in some of the villages of the oasis, such as *al-Jahali* and *al-ʿAin*. He then refers to what he noticed to be commercial ties existing between Buraimi and Sharjah and Dubai.[3]

5. According to the *Peace Handbook* on Arabia, issued by the historical section at the Foreign Office in 1920, the Trucial Shaikhs have never 'wielded effective rule over any considerable territory'.

> Their power [the *Handbook* continues], relative to one another and to that of Oman proper, which lies in the rear of all and in undefined territorial relation to them, depends on the ruling personalities even more than on the shifting politics of Oman; it is therefore of little service to discuss the actual distribution of their authority or *the validity of their respective territorial* claims.[4]

On Abu Dhabi's particular claim to territories in the Oman region, the *Handbook* remarks:

> Abu Dhabi claims a considerable territory on its northwest, reaching to Khor Odaid, and including all that lies between the intervening Gulf shore and the Great Desert; but this is a lean region of no social and political importance.[5]

---

[1] Lorimer, pp. 770–2. Lorimer explains the 'measures' taken by Shaikh Zaid for the annexation of Buraimi by saying: 'About 1897, or possibly earlier, he appropriated or reclaimed the estate of Jahali on the south-western border of the cultivated area; and since then divers pieces of land . . . in Baraimi . . . have been purchased by Shaikh Zaid and his sons . . .' See ibid.

[2] Lorimer, II, p. 405.

[3] Cox, Sir Percy, 'Some Excursions in Oman', *Geographical Journal*, 66 (1925), pp. 200, 207, 208. The writer gives the exact distance between Abu Dhabi and Buraimi as 100 miles. (See ibid., p. 203.)

[4] Great Britain, *Peace Handbook*, No. 61 (1920), pp. 22, 34.

[5] Ibid., pp. 4–5, 33.

6. Wilfred Thesiger gives his account of the Buraimi villages which he visited in 1948, as follows:

Buraimi village belongs to Saqr bin Sultan Shaikh of the Naim, and Hamasa to the Shuamis. The other villages are ruled from Muwaiqih by Zaid bin Sultan of Al Bu Falah, Shakbut's representative.[1]

(c) *Extent of control by Saudi Arabia*

1. The Wahhabis who lost Hasa to the Turks in 1871 continued to rule Najd until about the year 1890. From 1890 to 1902, Najd became subject to the rule of the House of al-Rashid, who, with the indirect backing of the Turks, forced the Saudi Amir, ʿAbd al-Rahman ibn Faisal, to retire at Kuwait. This brought an end to the rule of the Wahhabi House of Saʿud in the nineteenth century.[2]

2. In 1902, the Wahhabi Amir, who since 1890 had taken refuge in Kuwait, fought and overthrew the rule of the al-Rashid House in Najd, thereby re-establishing his authority over it. In the spring of 1913, his son Amir ʿAbd al-Aziz, who later became the first King of the present Saudi Arabian Kingdom, conquered the province of Hasa from the Turks.[3] At the end of 1913, Amir ʿAbd-al-Aziz had his first official contact with Britain by meeting in the port of ʿUqair both the British Political Agents for Bahrain and Kuwait.[4]

3. The establishment of Saudi authority in Hasa had not affected Buraimi itself which seemed to have remained outside Saudi control. However, British travellers and explorers who visited the district between 1920 and 1946 appear to refer in their accounts of these visits to some evidence of Saudi influence among the tribes of the district. Thus, for example, Captain Eccles says that in or about 1924 'the Wahhabi governor of al-Hasa sent messengers to all the northern tribes of Oman', who, he says, 'are Wahhabi in sentiment', demanding 'in the name of his master, Ibn Saud, the payment of zakat or tithes'. These tribes, he continues, 'would probably prefer Wahhabi domination to that of Oman confederacy'.[5] Bertram Thomas, a former British Finance Minister and Wazir of Muscat, says that when he wanted to visit Buraimi in May 1927 in his official capacity, he was told by the 'Naim shaikh of Baraimi' that 'these places belong to Al-Hamuda, and after them they belong to Ibn Saud'. Further, the writer describes the presence in the district, during that year, of a Saudi tax-collector by saying:

The Dhahirah rang with news of the visit of a tax-collector from Ibn

[1] Thesiger, op cit., p. 163.
[2] Lorimer, pp. 1132–8. And see Amin al-Rihani, *Tarikh Najd Al-Hadith*, 2nd ed. (1954), pp. 104–5.
[3] Aitchison, p. 188.   [4] Ibid.   [5] Eccles, op cit., pp. 23-4, 36.

Jaluwi, Bin Saud's Viceroy in the Hasa, and many of the Dhahirah tribes were paying tribute . . .[1]

St J. B. Philby refers, in his account about his exploration of the Empty Quarter, to an interview which he had with one of the Saudi tax-collectors in the district of Buraimi. He describes this district as 'a Wahhabi centre of long standing'.[2] In December 1946, Wilfred Thesiger visited the district. He gives the following account about a conversation which he had with one of the Shaikhs of the tribes:

> Here we met a Rashidi Shaikh. . . . We heard from him that many of the Murra, Manasir, and Awamir were assembled in Dhafra and Rabadh for the yearly assessment of taxes. This was unwelcome news. If we encountered any tax collectors we should probably be taken to Hufuf to explain ourselves, since we were here without the permission of Ibn Saud . . .[3]

4. In August 1952 Saudi Arabia sent an official, with a contingent of 40 men, to the Buraimi district to take up his position as a governor of Buraimi under the authority of the Saudi Amir of Hasa.[4] The Saudi governor remained in the district until October 1955, when the Saudi contingent was forced to leave Buraimi by the British-officered Trucial Oman Levies (Scouts).[5]

Treaties relevant to the dispute

In this section reference will be made to some of the important provisions of the treaties which have relevance to this dispute because they either (*a*) define a boundary line which leaves the disputed areas on one side of the line or the other, or (*b*) relate to some of the legal questions raised in this dispute.

(i) *Anglo-Ottoman Draft Convention on the Arabian Gulf Area, 29 July 1913.*[6]

This Convention constituted a settlement of outstanding issues between the Ottoman and the British Governments in relation to their respective spheres of influence in the Arabian Gulf area. After long negotiations, the two parties, Ibrahim Hakki Pasha on behalf of Turkey and Sir Edward Grey on behalf of Britain, agreed on signing a first draft convention, referred to as 'the Persian Gulf Convention, July 29, 1913'. Provisions were made for the ratification of the convention within a period of three months; but for some reason the date for ratification was extended to 31 October 1914. As a result of the

---

[1] Thomas, B., *Alarms and Excursions in Arabia* (1931), pp. 173-4.

[2] Philby, H. St J. B., *The Empty Quarter* (1933), p. 28.

[3] Thesiger, W. P., *Geographical Journal*, 111 (1948), pp. 6-7, as quoted in *Saudi Memorial*, I, p. 358.

[4] See above, p. 202.   [5] See above, p. 205.

[6] French text in Gooch, G. P., and Temperley, H., *British Documents on the Origins of the War*, 1898–1914, vol. 10 (ii) (1938), pp. 190-4. English text in Hurewitz, I, op. cit., pp. 269–72.

outbreak of war between the two Governments on that date, the convention was never ratified. It is divided into five parts as follows: (1) The status of Kuwait and its boundaries; (2) Qatar boundaries; (3) Bahrain; (4) Turkish recognition of certain British rights relating to navigation and policing in the waters of the Gulf; (5) Technical measures connected with the demarcation of the eastern boundaries of Arabia on the basis of the provisions of the Convention.

The part of the Convention relevant to the present dispute is Part II, Article 11 of which deals with the demarcation of the boundaries of 'El-Katr' [Qatar]. Article 11 reads as follows:

The Ottoman *Sanjak* of Najd, the northern limit of which is indicated by the demarcation line defined in Article 7 of this Convention, ends in the south at the gulf facing the island of *al-Zakhnuniyah*, which belongs to the said *Sanjak*. A line beginning at the extreme end of that gulf will go directly south up to the *Rub'al-Khali* and will separate the Najd from the peninsula of *al-Qatar*. The limits of the Najd are indicated by a blue line on the map annexed to the present Convention. The Ottoman Imperial Government having renounced all its claims to the peninsula of al-Qatar, it is understood by the two Governments that the peninsula will be governed as in the past by shaykh Jasmin bin Thani and his successors. The Government of Her Britannic Majesty declares that it will not allow the interference of the shaykh of Bahrein in the internal affairs of al-Qatar, his endangering the autonomy of that area or his annexing it.[1]

Article 7 of the Convention deals with the boundaries of Kuwait.

(ii) *Anglo-Turkish Convention, 9 March 1914*[2]

This Convention constituted a settlement between the British and the Turkish Governments of the boundaries of Aden Protectorate. It confirmed a demarcation line drawn up in 1903–5 by experts of both Governments between Aden Protectorate and the so-called, at the time, 'Turkish Wilayat of Yemen'. Ratification of this Convention was accomplished on 3 June 1914. Article 3 of this Convention embodied Article 11 of the unratified Convention of 1913. This Article recites:

. . .The boundary of Ottoman territory shall follow a direct line which runs from Lakmat al-Shu'ub north-eastwards to the desert of Rub'al-Khali at an angle of 45 degrees. This line shall join in the Rub'al-Khali on parallel 20 degrees, the straight and direct line southwards which leaves the Gulf of al-Uqair at a point on the south coast, and which separates the Ottoman territory of the Sanjak of Najd from the territory of Qatar, in accordance

---

[1] Gooch and Temperley, op. cit., p. 193; Hurewitz, I, op. cit., p. 271.

[2] See *Saudi Memorial*, I, p. 390. For French text, see Gooch and Temperley, op. cit., pp. 340–1; Aitchison, pp. 42–3. It is to be noted that this Convention was not published in the Official List of British Treaty Series or in any other publication, such as British and Foreign State Papers.

with Article 11 of the Anglo-Ottoman Convention of the 29th July, 1913, relative to the Persian Gulf and the surrounding territories. The first of the two lines is shown in violet and the second in blue on the special map annexed hereto . . .

THE FACTS IN THE LIGHT OF RELEVANT LEGAL PRINCIPLES

The question of continuous occupation of Buraimi by either party

This discussion will be devoted to an examination of the parties' historical title to the Buraimi Oasis. Therefore, the question to be considered here is whether either party to this dispute has established an effective authority over the territory. It will be convenient to deal with the extent of rights acquired by the parties in the territory in dispute by adhering to the preceding division of the history of control over it as follows:

(i) *1800–69*

In the light of the historical facts set out above, it appears that for the most part of this period the Buraimi Oasis had, undisputably, remained under Saudi sovereignty. The argument in favour of Saudi Arabia's title to the area during this period runs as follows: The Saudi original title was based on conquest. This was perfected by establishing a prescriptive right in the area for a period of nearly seventy years.[1] As regards the kind of activity that is required from a State to display in a territory, as a prerequisite for proving its sovereignty over that territory, the World Court, in its decision in the *Minquiers and Ecrehos case*, 1953, felt content with what it called 'the acts which relate to the exercise of jurisdiction and local administration and to legislation'.[2] The Saudi administration of Buraimi was tribal in nature, but there was also an appointed Saudi Official in that place who was responsible to the Saudi Amir who had his seat of government at Najd. On the other hand, it is undisputable that during this period neither the Sultan of Muscat nor the Shaikh of Abu Dhabi had any connection with Buraimi. It is clear that while the Wahhabis during the most part of this period were in full control over the Oasis, all the tribal Shaikhs of the Omani coast, including those of Muscat and Abu Dhabi, were tributary to them.[3]

In view of those facts, and according to the doctrine of the 'inter-temporal law', as interpreted by Max Huber,[4] it can be submitted

[1] See *Arbitral Award Concerning the Island of Palmas* (1928), *A.J.I.L.*, 22 (1928), pp. 873, 876, 907–8.

[2] *I.C.J. Reports*, 1953, p. 65.   [3] See above, pp. 208–12.

[4] Waldock, C. H. M., 'Disputed Sovereignty in the Falkland Dependencies', *B.Y.I.L.*, 25 (1948), p. 320. According to the writer, the doctrine of 'inter-temporal law', as interpreted by Max Huber in the Palmas case, means that a 'juridical fact must be appreciated in the light of the law contemporary with and not of the law in force at a time when a dispute in regard to it arises or falls to be settled'.

that the Saudi sovereignty over the Oasis, during this period, was sufficiently established.[1]

(ii) *1869–1952*

It is agreed that the main criteria for establishing a title to territory is the proof of 'peaceful and continuous display of State authority'.[2] The question now arises whether any of the parties in this dispute has possessed such a title (a title based on peaceful and continuous display of authority) in respect of Buraimi.

(a) *The rights of the Sultan of Muscat*[3]

It appears, in the light of the above-mentioned facts, that the Sultan of Muscat has been far from establishing any right of sovereignty over the Oasis; British authorities confirm that during this period, or the greater part of it, the Sultanate's rule was limited to the coastal towns only. The Sultan of Muscat had, thus, wielded no power in the interior of Oman and the Buraimi region which remained, for all practical purposes, to be governed by independent tribal Imams and Shaikhs. The fall of Buraimi into the hands of ʿAzzan ibn Qais, the self-imposed Imam, in the summer of 1869 did not establish a legal title for the Sultanate, since ʿAzzan himself was not the legitimate Sultan; he was then a mere usurper of the Sultanate rule, and the British Government for that reason declined to recognise him as the legitimate Sultan of Muscat. Moreover, the facts show that ʿAzzan was merely called upon by the Buraimi tribe of Nuʿaim to assist them in their action to drive out the Wahhabi governor, ʿAbd al-Rahman al-Sudairi, and to take possession of Buraimi. Having accepted this offer, ʿAzzan, with the assistance of Nuʿaim, succeeded, after a fierce battle, in occupying Buraimi which he left after a few months to be administered independently by its own tribes. Traditionally, Buraimi had been regarded as being under the control of the Nuʿaim tribe throughout this period.[4] There is also no evidence that in 1952—the date of the arrival in Buraimi of the Saudi party under the command of Turki ibn ʿUtaishan—or during any period before that date, Buraimi was, in fact, administered jointly by the Sultan of Muscat and the Shaikh of Abu Dhabi.[5]

---

[1] See *The Legal Status of Eastern Greenland*, 1933, *P.C.I.J.* Series A/B. No. 53 (1933) pp. 45–6: A title to territory must consist of two essential elements, namely, 'the intention and will to act as sovereign, and some actual exercise or display of such authority'.

[2] *The Island of Palmas*, op. cit., pp. 907–8.

[3] See above, pp. 214–15.

[4] See above, pp. 214–15. And see Arabian American Oil Company, *Oman and the Southern Shore of the Persian Gulf* (1952), p. 145.

[5] See above, pp. 214–16. And see *The Times*, 27 May 1954, where no mention is made of local resistance in Buraimi against the arrival of the Saudis. In fact,

(b) *The rights of the Shaikh of Abu Dhabi*

A reference has been made above to Lorimer's statement that after the Wahhabis defeat from Buraimi in 1869, it lost its significance as a Wahhabi outpost and became almost 'an annex to the principality of Abu Dhabi'. Although making such a vague statement, Lorimer does not appear to say whether Buraimi was later administered by the Shaikh of Abu Dhabi as part of his territories.[1] On the other hand, although Lorimer refers to Buraimi as 'independent', he, nevertheless, confirms that the 'influence of the Shaikh of Abu Dhabi in the district is strong and increasing'. This influence of Abu Dhabi in Buraimi is attributed by Lorimer to the fact that the Shaikh owned lands, date-gardens and, perhaps, one or two small settlements in the Oasis. Other British writers and travellers, who paid occasional visits to Buraimi during the first half of this century, also took notice of the Shaikh's property rights in the district.[2] These facts clearly confirm the great influence enjoyed by the Shaikh of Abu Dhabi in the Oasis. But it may be argued that this influence is not relevant. The essential issue is whether the Shaikh has, beyond any doubt, established his sovereignty over the Buraimi Oasis. The distinction between ownership and sovereignty is drawn by Professor Waldock in these words:

The emphasis has shifted from the taking of physical possession of the land and the exclusion of others to the manifestation and exercise of the functions of government over the territory. This change is a natural consequence of the recognition that in modern international law occupation is the acquisition of sovereignty rather than of property.[3]

In order to establish Abu Dhabi's title to Buraimi it must therefore be clearly shown that she was, and has been, continuously and undisputably exercising State functions in the territory. In other words,

---

British records admit that the Saudi officials were invited to assume control of Hamasa village by loyal Shaikhs of that village. See *British Memorial*, I, p. 45.

However, it should be mentioned that, contrary to the above conclusions, the British Government maintains that 'since 1869, the Sultan has maintained his sovereignty over the three settlements of the Naʿim tribe appointing their paramount Shaikh as his representative. . . . At the same time, he has had special arrangements with the Ruler of Abu Dhabi, whereby . . . (the latter) undertook to supervise the Sultan's interests in the Oasis. . . .' See *British Memorial*, I, pp. 8, 35. In view of the opinions expressed by a number of writers and British officials, who paid visits to Muscat and Oman, on the complete lack of the Sultan's authority in the interior of Oman for the last 100 years, it would seem difficult to accept the above British argument without question.

[1] See above, p. 213. Lorimer points out at pp. 770–72 that during 1875–1904, fighting never ceased between the Shaikhs of Abu Dhabi and the tribes of Buraimi. This statement testifies to the fact that the Buraimi tribes were far from being submissive to the influence of the Abu Dhabi Shaikhs.

[2] See above, pp. 215–16.   [3] Waldock, op. cit., p. 317.

it must be established that the territory in question, which was formerly under the sovereignty of another country, has effectively passed into the sovereignty of the Shaikh of Abu Dhabi through the process of prescription or adverse holding. The prescription, in order to be of legal value, must be manifested in the peaceful and continuous display of government's functions over the territory acquired. The manifestation of State functions over a territory, moreover, 'entails', according to Professor Waldock,

a duty to protect within the territory the rights of other States both in regard to their security and in regard to the treatment of their nationals in the territory.[1]

In support of Abu Dhabi's claim to sovereignty over Buraimi, the British Government maintains that 'the Ruler of Abu Dhabi and the Sultan of Muscat and Oman possessed valid and subsisting titles to the sovereignty of their respective parts of the Zone, by continuous and peaceful display of authority ever since the final eviction of' the Saudis in 1869. 'Throughout the period', the British argument continues, 'the Ruler of Abu Dhabi, by agreement with the Sultan of Muscat and Oman, exercised a general supervision of the Sultan's interests in his parts of the Oasis, co-operating with the *Tamimah* of Nu'aim and the Wali of Sohar in this regard.'[2]

In addition, the British Government contends that the Ruler of Abu Dhabi 'exercised complete authority over the Dhawahir settlements', and he, through his representative in Buraimi, 'regularly collected *zakat* on dates in the Dhawahir settlements, controlled through his officials the management of water-channels, and collected the water taxes'.[3]

It seems questionable that the above British contentions provide solid proof of continuous and peaceful display of state activities in the Buraimi Zone by either the Sultan of Muscat or the Shaikh of Abu Dhabi.[4] It is noteworthy, however, that evidence of the exercise of jurisdiction by the Ruler of Abu Dhabi over Buraimi and the disputed areas, which are subject to Article II(a) of the Arbitration Agreement, is provided in Part VI of the British Memorial.[5] This

---

[1] Ibid.   [2] *British Memorial*, I, pp. 121–2, 129.
[3] Ibid., pp. 69–70.
[4] In his comment on the *Minquiers and Ecrehos case*, 1953, Sir Gerald Fitzmaurice, 'The Law and Procedure of the International Court of Justice: Points of Substantive Law, Part II', *B.Y.I.L.*, 32 (1955–6), at p. 56 states: 'The question of private activities such as fishing, visits to the group, quarrying there, building houses, etc., was a good deal discussed in this case. But it was contended on the French side, and tacitly admitted on the United Kingdom's side, that such activities certainly could not *per se* be a basis of title, in the sense of conferring it, and could only within limits afford evidence of it.' And see ibid., p. 45, note (6).
[5] *British Memorial*, I, pp. 65–73.

evidence in support of the Ruler's jurisdiction in the area is worth considering by an impartial reader, despite its inconsistency with the above-mentioned quotations from British authorities on the lack of the Ruler's authority there.

In connection with Abu Dhabi's claim to the disputed areas which are the subject of Article II(a) of the Arbitration Agreement, the British Government contends that it has since 1878, recognised Abu Dhabi's sovereignty over a piece of uninhabited coastal land, called Khaur al-'Udaid,[1] lying at the base of the Qatar promontory. This British view was officially stated to the Saudi Government in the discussion on the Abu Dhabi–Saudi Arabia frontiers which was held at Jiddah on 19 March 1937 between representatives of both Governments. The attribution of Khaur al-'Udaid to Abu Dhabi, which in effect extends that country's territory farther 200 miles westward, amounts to barring Saudi Arabia from access to al-Jiwa (Liwa), Buraimi, and, generally, the rest of territories to the east of Qatar.[2] It is noteworthy that both British proposed boundary lines (i.e., the so-called Ryan or Riyadh Line of 1935 and the 1952 Line presented on behalf of Abu Dhabi) were generally drawn from a point starting from Khaur al-'Udaid. This is in line with the British recognition of that place as belonging to Abu Dhabi.[3] The Saudi Government which claims sovereignty over al-'Udaid maintains that British 'traditional support of Abu Dhabi's claim to the Khaur al-'Udaid could not operate to transfer sovereignty over the area to the Ruler (of Abu Dhabi)'.[4]

---

[1] Khaur al-'Udaid was maintained between 1869 and 1880 as a settlement by a certain section of Bani Yas tribe of Abu Dhabi, called the Qubaisat. When the Turks occupied that place in 1871, the Qubaisat fell largely under the Turkish influence, and accepted the Turkish flag. The British Government, therefore, found it difficult to take military measures under the Treaty of Peace of 1853, against the Qubaisat to prevent them from committing piratical acts, unless they were brought under the authority of the Shaikh of Abu Dhabi who was a party to the treaty. During 1871, Colonel Pelly, then British Political Resident in the Gulf, found a solution to this problem by suggesting to the Government of India to recognise Khaur al-'Udaid as forming part of Abu Dhabi. This suggestion met with the concurrence of the Government. Accordingly, the Shaikh of Abu Dhabi was officially informed, later in that year, of this decision which now forms the basis of Abu Dhabi's claim to this strip of land lying 200 miles westward of the coast of Abu Dhabi. For a detailed account about Colonel Pelly's decision, see I.O., *Proceedings of the Government of India, Foreign and Political Department*, March 1872, No. 368, dated 11 March 1872. And see ibid., No. 370, dated 4 March 1871.

[2] *Saudi Memorial*, II, Annex 19, p. 51. Conversation between Shaikh Yusuf Yasin and Mr Rendel (Excerpt), 19 March 1937.

[3] The Riyadh Line, proposed on 25 November 1935, is a modification of the 'Blue Line' which has its basis in the 1913 Convention. See *Saudi Memorial*, I, pp. 354, 411–12.

[4] *Saudi Memorial*, I, p. 439.

(c) *The rights of Saudi Arabia*

It is evident from what has been stated above that after the end of their rule in Buraimi in 1869, the Saudis did not occupy that area or any part of it, except comparatively recently in 1952. However, quite apart from the fact that Buraimi remained beyond Saudi control during this period, evidence of Saudi continued influence among the tribes of the district does not seem to be lacking.[1]

But it may be submitted that the fact that Saudi Arabia had sovereignty over the Oasis in the past (i.e., during the period 1800–69), does not necessarily mean that she has such sovereignty at present. In view of legal principles, sovereignty in order to be established must be 'peaceful' and 'continuous'. In other words, there is an essential requirement of continued display of State functions in the territory acquired. In the case of the *Island of Palmas*, this principle was put as follows:

> The admission of the existence of sovereignty (at two given periods) . . . would not lead . . . to the conclusion that, unless the contrary is proved, there is a presumption for the existence of sovereignty in the meantime. . . . No presumption of this kind is to be applied in international arbitration. . . .[2]

Similarly, in his comments on the *Clipperton Island* case, 1932,[3] Professor Waldock clarifies this principle in the following:

> It is therefore improbable that any formal state annexations that may be proved in the nineteenth century could have greater legal effect than to reinforce a more recent display of state activity in the present century by the same state.[4]

On the other hand, it is recognised in this same case that

> . . . state activity may be slight when the territory is uninhabited and when there is no competing state activity.[5]

Consequently, in so far as the Saudi Government's claim to the Buraimi Oasis is concerned, the question arises whether that Government, even in the absence of its actual physical possession of the Oasis during the last eighty-three years (from 1869 to 1952), has, nevertheless, continued to display State activities in the area concerned? In view of the independent character of the tribal regime in the Oasis, and in view of the fact that the 1913 conquest of Hasa by the Saudis did not affect this territory which remained beyond Saudi control,[6]

---

[1] See above, pp. 217–18.   [2] *The Island of Palmas*, op. cit., p. 904.
[3] *Arbitral Award on the Sovereignty over the Clipperton Island* (Mexico v. France) 1932, *A.J.I.L.*, 26 (1932), p. 390.
[4] Waldock, op. cit., p. 325.
[5] *Clipperton Island*, op. cit., pp. 390–94.   [6] See above, p. 217.

Q

it is therefore difficult to answer this question in the affirmative. The Saudi Government for its part contends that its sovereignty over Buraimi and the disputed areas which are subject to Article II(a) of the Arbitration Agreement has never been extinguished. In support of this claim it gives certain facts as evidence of its continuous and peaceful exercise of authority in the disputed territories. These facts which are expounded in full detail in the Saudi Memorial relate to the following:

(a) The presence in the disputed areas, including al-Jiwa (Liwa), of Saudi tribes such as Al-Murrah and the Manasir whose *dirahs* are claimed to be within 'the region westward of Sabkhat Matti'. As regards Buraimi, there the allegiance of the Nuʿaim to Saudi Arabia is claimed.[1] (b) The systematic collection of *zakah*, the religious tithe, from the inhabitants of the disputed areas: *Zakah* payments from members of such tribes as Al-Murrah, the Manasir, the Awamir and Nuʿaim are claimed.[2] (c) The preservation of public security.[3]

Consequently, the Saudi Government argues that its sovereignty over the disputed areas, 'as based essentially on effective possession *longi temporis*', has not been lost as a result of the temporary interruption of Saudi authority in 1873 (actually 1869).[4]

The validity of the Anglo-Turkish Conventions of 1913 and 1914 vis-à-vis *Saudi Arabia*

Since Saudi Arabia was not originally a party to any of these conventions, she cannot, therefore, be bound by them unless it is established that (a) they were perfectly valid instruments, and (b) they devolved upon her as a successor State of the Ottoman Government.

(a) The formal validity of the Conventions

As regards the Convention of 29 July 1913, it has been explained above that this instrument was not ratified within the prescribed period

---

[1] *Saudi Memorial*, I, pp. 488–504.
[2] Ibid. In the third volume of the Saudi Memorial eighteen tax registers have been reproduced. The volumes given cover 'the years from 1354 (1935–6) to 1370 (1950–1) inclusive'.
[3] *Saudi Memorial*, I, pp. 470–1. Examples of the Saudi Government's preservation of public security in the disputed areas are given in full in Annex 109 of the *Saudi Memorial*, II. There 'an official statement' by Saʿud ibn Jiluwi (the Amir of the Eastern Province) sets forth 'the details of twenty-nine representative instances in which Saudi officials took action with respect to wrongdoing or wrongdoers in the disputed areas. The examples stretch in time from the year 1337 (1918–19) through 1366 (1947), the eve of the present controversy. They range in space from the vicinity of Buraimi . . . westward through ʿIrqan . . . into al-Dhafrah. . . .'
[4] *Saudi Memorial*, I, pp. 470–84.

of three months. Although the period for ratification of this conven-
tion was extended from time to time, it never, in fact, took place.[1]
On this basis, this convention can have no legal validity whatsoever.
According to Oppenheim,

The function of ratification is . . . to make the treaty binding; if it is
refused, the treaty falls to the ground in consequence.[2]

On the other hand, the Convention of 9 March 1914 was ratified on
3 June 1914,[3] and is, therefore, a perfectly valid treaty. Although this
convention is basically connected with the boundaries between Aden
and Yemen, which was at the time under the Turkish suzerainty, its
significance in the present dispute over the eastern boundaries of
Saudi Arabia lies in the fact that it provided in Article 3 for the adoption of Article 11 of the unratified Convention of 1913. It appears
from this arrangement that Article 11 of the unratified Convention of
1913, which specifically refers to the 'Blue Line', has been given legal
validity by its adoption in a completely different treaty which has, by
its subsequent ratification, assumed international validity. This seems
to be a peculiar way of giving validity to a single article of a draft
convention which never acquired legal force owing to its non-ratifica-
tion. It is clear from this procedure that the parties to the 1914
Convention took the definition of the 'Blue Line' provided by Article
11 of the 1913 Agreement as final in Article 3 of this convention, and
thus brought it into force.[4] But the question arises whether the 'Blue
Line' can be made valid in this manner when the instrument from
which it basically derived its validity was not ratified at all?

It is obvious that had the 1913 Agreement been ratified at any time
after the ratification of the 1914 Convention, Article 11 defining the
Blue Line' would then have been given full legal force by virtue of
the 1913 Agreement rather than by the 1914 Convention. Therefore,
had the parties been able to ratify the 1913 Agreement, this would
have changed the whole basis of the 1914 Convention. Moreover, it
may be argued that on 3 June 1914, the date of the ratification of the
1914 Convention, Article 11 itself was not actually devoid of any
legal validity[5] because on that date the 1913 Agreement was still open

[1] See above, p. 219.   [2] Oppenheim, pp. 903–4.
[3] Aitchison, p. 43, and see above, p. 219.
[4] The British Government's argument on this point runs as follow: '. . . While
the Anglo-Turkish Convention of 1913 was not ratified, the boundary laid down in
Article 11 of that Convention is mentioned, adequately defined and definitely
adopted in Article 3 of the ratified Convention of 1914, which in view of His
Majesty's Government remains operative . . .' See British Memorial, II, Annex D,
No. 4, Sir A. Ryan, British Minister at Jiddah to Fuad Bey Hamza, Deputy Saudi
Arabian Minister for Foreign Affairs, 28 April 1934.
[5] A treaty which provides for ratification is 'not devoid' of legal effects. See
Oppenheim, p. 904.

for ratification which was to take place on 31 October 1914.[1] But that Article lost its legal force later, on the expiration of the final date prescribed for the ratification of the 1913 Agreement (i.e., 31 October 1914).[2] It cannot be argued that Article 11 was alone ratified by the 1914 Convention, because this would have amounted to 'a partial ratification' of the 1913 Agreement which is illegal. According to Oppenheim, 'a treaty cannot be ratified in part'. Nor are 'alterations of the treaty . . . possible through the act of ratification'.[3]

(b) *The question of succession by Saudi Arabia to the above Convention.*

Quite apart from the lack of the formal validity of the Convention of 1913 and 1914, as explained above, the question to be considered is whether these conventions are perfectly valid *vis-à-vis* Saudi Arabia. In other words, the question arises whether Saudi Arabia, which was not originally a party to these conventions has, as a successor to the Turkish possessions in Arabia, become bound by the conventions?

The general principles of law regarding state succession to treatie are that treaties are not, in principle, subject to state succession; th successor State is not bound by treaties of its predecessor. However it is agreed that, as an exception to this rule, certain treaties that ar of strictly local character (in other words, treaties creating 'rea rights') can be made subject to state succession.[4] According to D

[1] It is to be noted that on the date of the ratification of the 1914 Conventio (i.e., 3 June) the date prescribed for the ratification of the 1913 Convention wa 26 June 1914. But this date was again extended to 31 October 1914. See Gooc and Temperley, op. cit., pp. 241, 282.

[2] The Saudi Government's argument on this point runs as follows: '. . . It wholly implausible that the parties intended to take the Blue Line out of its contex where it was intimately tied to the question of Kuwait and Bahrain, and bring alone into effect by means of a brief reference in the 1914 Convention. It is muc more consonant with reason to view its mention in 1914 merely as a convenie method of defining a terminus *ad quem* for the Violet Line—a terminus whic would match, without further revision, the anticipated boundary coming dow from the north.' See *Saudi Memorial*, I, p. 397.

[3] Oppenheim, p. 904. And see footnote (4) ibid., where the author questio the legality of Ecuador's action in 1934, when in order to become an origin member of the League of Nations, she ratified the Covenant of the League alo without ratifying the Treaty of Versailles itself. He treats this case as 'exce tional', since Ecuador's ratification of the Covenant did not, in law, amount to implied ratification of the Treaty of Versailles.

[4] For international practice regarding the discontinuance of treaties on annex tion or cession of territory, see Keith, A. B., *The Theory of State Succession, w Special Reference to English and Colonial Law* (1907), pp. 17, 19–20; O'Conne D. P., *The Law of State Succession* (1956), p. 15; Jones, J. M., 'State Succession the Matter of Treaties', *B.Y.I.L.*, 24 (1947), p. 362; McNair, *Treaties*, pp. 389– For the practice regarding treaties creating 'real rights' which thus pass to t State acquiring the territory, see McNair, *Treaties*, p. 470, and see Jenks, C. \ 'State Succession in Respect of Law-Making Treaties', *B.Y.I.L.*, 29 (1952), pp. 1 et seq.

Muralt, such treaties (i.e., treaties concerning boundaries, etc.) remain 'binding in respect of the territory over which the expanding State extends its powers'.[1] With respect to Saudi Arabia, the question arises whether, in the light of the above principles, she can be bound by the conventions under discussion?

There is no doubt that the Conventions of 1913 and 1914 define, or purport to define, former Turkish territories to which Saudi Arabia has succeeded. On this basis, it can be argued that since these conventions are classified as dispositive treaties, or treaties creating 'real rights', Saudi Arabia would, therefore, be bound by them. However, the fact that the Saudi Arabian succession to the Turkish territories in Arabia preceded the conclusion of these conventions seems to give rise to the question whether Saudi Arabia has properly succeeded to the conventions.[2] If she has not, the treaties in question cannot be binding upon her without her own consent and agreement. Therefore, in order to bind Saudi Arabia by the Conventions of 1913 and 1914, it must be shown that she has not only succeeded to a territory which was formerly under the Turkish sovereignty, but also succeeded to obligations under these conventions from the time the territory was acquired by Saudi Arabia. In other words, it must be shown that when Ibn Sa'ud conquered the province of Hasa from the Turks that territory was already 'burdened' by the Anglo-Turkish conventions.

It is believed that the Saudi conquest of Hasa from the Turks took place on 5 May 1913.[3] It is clear that on that date neither the Convention of 1913 nor the Convention of 1914 had any legal existence. Therefore, there were, in fact, no recognised boundaries of the territory before the conquest. A successor State can be bound by the boundaries of the territory of its predecessor only if that territory had recognised boundaries before the conquest or the act of transfer. This principle seems to be reflected in Keith's statement:

The boundaries of the territory acquired by the cession or conquest are regulated by the treaty of cession or by *the recognised boundaries before the conquest*.[4]

Similarly, Alf Ross says:

. . . A succession of B to A's legal status is recognised to a certain extent

---

[1] De Muralt, R. W. G., *The Problem of State Succession with Regard to Treaties* (1954), p. 20. On the practice of the World Court in relation to 'subrogation' or state succession of treaties of 'a strictly localised character', see Schwarzenberger, p. 178.

[2] Saudi Arabia succeeded to the Turkish territories nearly a year before the conclusion of the 1914 Convention. This is explained in the next paragraph.

[3] This is the date given by Philby, H. St J. B., in his book *Arabian Jubilee* (1952), p. 30. The *Saudi Memorial*, II, Annex 6, p. 21, gives the date of Saudi's conquest of Hasa as 5 Jumada I 1331 (corresponding to 13 April 1913).

[4] Keith, op. cit., p. 27 (emphasis supplied).

in the case of treaty obligations with a special local connection with the territory in question. That at any rate applies to treaties in which *the boundaries of the territory towards a third State are established*.[1]

According to the principles of international law, Saudi Arabia was, after 5 May 1913, the only recognised International Person responsible for the territory in question. 'With the extinction of an International Person', says Oppenheim, 'disappears its rights and duties as a Person.'[2] If the Ottoman Government subsequently concluded a treaty with the United Kingdom purporting to demarcate a territory over which it already lost all marks of sovereignty, its action can be regarded illegal *ab initio*. On this basis, it seems doubtful that the conventions under discussion have devolved upon Saudi Arabia.[3] However, it can be argued on behalf of the United Kingdom, that the conventions are only statements of facts accepted by the Ottoman Government as to what part of Arabia it had exercised authority over during its rule between 1871 and 1913, irrespective of the fact that the said territory was in the material date (i.e., 1913) under the control of Ibn Saʿud. Thus, it may be contended that since Ibn Saʿud had, in fact, been unable to extend his authority beyond Hasa, he is, therefore, not allowed to regard his succession from Ottoman Turkey extended to lands which were beyond Turkish authority. But the Saudi Arabian answer to this contention is that Ibn Saʿud's claim to the disputed boundaries is not based upon succession to former Turkish territories, but upon succession to territories of his forefathers, the Wahhabi rulers. Accordingly, the Saudi argument goes on, since Ibn Saʿud's forefathers had established their control over territories which extended beyond Hasa, he was, therefore, entitled to disavow a treaty

[1] Ross, A., *A Textbook on International Law* (1947), p. 125 (emphasis supplied).
[2] Oppenheim, p. 158.
[3] In a Note dated 15 June 1934, Sir Andrew Ryan, the British Minister at Jiddah, wrote to Fuad Bey Hamzah, Deputy Saudi Foreign Minister: '. . . So far as the boundaries now in question are concerned, they do not consider that any developments in Arabia since 1914 have been such as to render inappropriate to present circumstances the blue line laid down in the Anglo-Turkish Convention of 1913 and duly confirmed by the Convention of 1914.' See *British Memorial*, II, Annex D, No. 6. The above Note was replied to by Fuad Bey Hamzah on 20 June 1934. The Saudi Government's reply was as follows:
'His Majesty's Government cannot admit . . . that the boundary known as the Blue Line . . . was agreed upon by Governments actually having any real concern (in the matter) . . . It is (also) perfectly obvious that not only did the authority of the Ottoman Government over the region under discussion not extend beyond the limits of the inhabited towns and villages, . . . but in fact (even this authority) ceased as soon as His Majesty the King recovered the lands of his forefathers and established his legal authority in them by taking Hasa on (13 April 1913). Any agreement (made) by the Ottoman Government regarding these regions after that is not valid, since it was issued by a Government that had no concern with the matter.' See *Saudi Memorial*, II, Annex 6, pp. 20-1.

imposing upon him a boundary line drawn on the basis of former Turkish possessions in Arabia between 1871 and 1913.[1]

Consequently, if it is assumed that Saudi Arabia has not succeeded to these conventions from Turkey two questions arise: First, whether she can be bound by them on the ground of her recognition of, or adherence to, them on a date subsequent to their conclusion or ratification. Secondly, whether she has, at a time prior to the conclusion of the conventions, acknowledged some sort of Turkish suzerainty. These will be considered in turn.

The question of recognition or adherence by Saudi Arabia to the Conventions

It is agreed that 'treaties are binding only between the contracting parties'.[2] And in the words of Oppenheim,

According to the principle *pacta tertiis nec nocent nec prosunt*, a treaty concerns the contracting States only; neither rights nor duties, as a rule, arise under the treaty for third States which are not parties to the treaty.[3]

On the other hand, third States which 'may be interested in such treaties', are free, in certain cases, to subscribe to them either by voluntary adherence or recognition.[4] In the light of these principles, it can be stated that if Saudi Arabia has, directly or indirectly, recognised the above conventions, then she could be bound by them. The attitude of the Saudi Arabian Government towards these conventions will be examined below.

It is contended by Saudi Arabia that she had no knowledge whatsoever of these conventions before 1934, and that the first occasion on which the British Government officially informed her of the existence of the agreements was marked by the Note dispatched on 28 April 1934 by the British Minister at Jiddah, Sir Andrew Ryan, to the Saudi Arabian Under-Secretary for Foreign Affairs, Fuad Bey Hamzah. This Note prompted a reply from the Saudi Arabian Government rejecting the validity of these conventions.[5] There appears to be nothing in the diplomatic correspondence—from 1934 to 1954—between the British and the Saudi Governments, as revealed in the Saudi Memorial presented to the Geneva Arbitration Tribunal in

---

[1] See *Saudi Memorial*, I, pp. 397–8. And see ibid., p. 399, where it is maintained that the British Government was estopped from its claim on the basis of the Blue Line by the Treaty of Darin of 26 December 1915, in which it recognised Ibn Sa'ud's succession to territories which belonged to 'his fathers before him'. For the Anglo-Saudi Treaty of 1915, now superseded by the 1927 treaty, see Aitchison, pp. 206–8.

[2] Schwarzenberger, p. 176.   [3] Oppenheim, pp. 925–6.

[4] Oppenheim, p. 933. For differences between adherence to treaties and recognition of treaties, see Schwarzenberger, p. 131.

[5] See above, p. 198.

1955, to suggest that the Saudi Government has ever recognised, directly or indirectly, the Anglo-Turkish Conventions of 1913 and 1914, as a basis for settling the dispute in respect of its common frontiers with the Trucial Coast Shaikhdoms.[1] Moreover, it is contended that by Article I of the Treaty of 26 December 1915 between Britain and Saudi Arabia, the former recognised Ibn Sa'ud's sovereignty over the territories of 'Najd, Al-Hasa, Qatif and Jubail' which territories were, according to this article, not defined, but 'will be discussed and determined hereafter'.[2] Surely, it is asked, if in view of the British Government the above-mentioned territories of Ibn Sa'ud were previously defined by either the Convention of 1913 or by the subsequent Convention of 1914, a clear and an express reference to these conventions should have been made in the Anglo-Saudi Treaty of 1915. On the contrary, it is apparent that this treaty expressly confirmed that the territories to which Ibn Sa'ud succeeded had no previously defined boundaries.[3] It may also be assumed that Ibn Sa'ud had no foreknowledge of the 1913–14 Conventions since they were not published officially by the British Government.[4] However, mention should be made of the fact that a brief reference to the 'Blue Line' of the unratified Convention of 1913 was made in the 'Uqair Agreement between Kuwait and Saudi Arabia, dated 2 December 1922.[5] But the Saudi Government contends that a reference to the 1913 boundary line 'was included (in the 1922 agreement) in order to simplify the geographical description; but there was no suggestion that the 1913 Convention or any part of it was binding'.[6]

The question of acknowledgement by Saudi Arabia of Turkish suzerainty

It appears that the United Kingdom has taken the view that Saudi Arabia was bound by the Anglo-Turkish Conventions of 1913 and 1914 not only on the ground that she succeeded to former Turkish territories in Arabia, but also on the ground that she acknowledged Turkish suzerainty, or protection, by virtue of a treaty concluded

[1] See *Saudi Memorial*, I, Part V.
[2] Ibid., p. 399.
[3] Ibid. Note that British interpretation of the 1915 treaty varies from that of the Saudis. From the British viewpoint, the 1915 treaty 'constituted a formal recognition by Ibn Sa'ud of the fact that Saudi territory in eastern Arabia extended almost to the furthest limits of Nadj and Hasa'. Accordingly, Ibn Sa'ud 'recognised the territorial situation upon the basis of which the Blue Line had been delimited in the Anglo-Turkish Conventions of 1913 and 1914'. See *British Memorial*, I, p. 125.
[4] The Anglo-Turkish Conventions were published neither in the official British Treaty Series nor in the publications of the British and Foreign State Papers. According to Philby, 'the British Government put away these instruments, which were all open to inspection, until such time as it might suit their interests to produce them'. See Philby, H. St J. B., 'Arabia To-day', *International Affairs*, XIV (1935), p. 630.
[5] See Appendix VIII.   [6] *Saudi Memorial*, I, p. 401.

with Turkey on 15 May 1914.[1] The British Government claims that
this treaty was found in the Turkish archives captured at Basrah.
The provisions of this treaty are summarised as follows:

Under Article 2, Ibn Sa'ud, for himself and his descendants, accepted
the appointment from the Ottoman Government of the post of Wali of
Najd. Under Article 4, he recognised the right of the Ottoman Government
to station soldiers at Qatif and 'Ujair in Hasa. Under Article 7, . . . he
agreed to use the Turkish flag, while under Article 9, he agreed (not) to
enter into any correspondence about foreign affairs, or to grant concessions
to foreigners.

Consequently, the British Government argues that 'when the Anglo-
Turkish Convention (of 1914) was ratified and came into force on
June 3, 1914—a mere three weeks after the execution of the agreement between Ibn Sa'ud and the Turks—Ibn Sa'ud was a subject of
the Turkish Government, and the Turkish Government was competent
to enter into a Convention binding the territory of Ibn Sa'ud'.[2]

Saudi Arabia, for her part, denies, categorically, that Ibn Sa'ud
had signed a treaty with Turkey accepting her suzerainty over his
country. She contends that the 'Saudi archives have failed to yield
any text of a perfected Saudi-Turkish agreement' of this sort. However, she admits that there were negotiations between Ibn Sa'ud and
the Turks during 1914, the aim of which was to reach a reasonable
settlement on outstanding problems between Ibn Sa'ud and Turkey.
But those negotiations in which, she says, the question of Turkish
suzerainty over Arabia was mooted, had never been formulated into
an agreement.[3]

[1] The British Government's legal argument is fully expounded in an *aide-
mémoire*, dated 25 July 1950, which was delivered to the Saudi Government. It
runs as follows:
'According to International Law, His Majesty King Abdul Aziz Al Saud is the
successor authority of the Turkish Government, to which His Majesty acknowledged his dependence in the treaty of 15 May 1914, with that Government. The
Turkish Government, by signing the Anglo-Turkish Conventions of 1913 and 1914,
acknowledged that their authority in Arabia did not extend east of the lines laid
down in these Conventions. His Majesty cannot, therefore, base a claim to territory lying east of these lines on any event or circumstances existing prior to the
conclusion of the Conventions. If, then, His Majesty desires to establish a claim to
any such area, it is for him to prove that since 1914 he has acquired sovereignty
in that area in accordance with International Law and for this purpose to put
forward any facts and events subsequent to that date on which he relies to support
his claim.' See *British Memorial*, II, Annex D, No. 30.
[2] *British Memorial*, I, p. 80. For the full text of the 1914 treaty, see ibid., II,
Annex A, No. 8.
[3] In conversations held between Shaikh Yusuf Yasin and Mr Rendel on 19 March
1937, the former stated the Saudi Government's view on the treaty of 15 May 1914
as follows:
'There does not exist any treaty at all recognised by His Majesty (to this effect).
If there exist some copies of letters these papers are perhaps not authentic. I have

The above conflicting statements of the British and the Saudi Governments show that there is a difference of opinion as to the exact legal status of Ibn Saʿud following his succession to the formerly held Turkish territories in eastern Arabia, viz, whether he held the territories in question in his capacity as an independent ruler or as a mere Turkish vassal? The British Government appears to regard the Agreement of 15 May 1914, signed by Ibn Saʿud with the Turkish Government as a confirmation of the former's dependent status *vis-à-vis* the Porte. On the other hand, the Saudi Government denies the validity of the agreement against it. From the legal point of view, it seems questionable that the legal status of Ibn Saʿud at the time could be determined on the basis of this agreement alone which, in any case, is not in itself an internationally binding instrument.[1]

The historical evidence shows that subsequent to his conquest of Hasa from the Turks in 1913, Ibn Saʿud was able to establish his authority, beyond any doubt, over territories which were formerly under Turkish authority. According to Philby, 'in 1913, Ibn Saʿud thus became master of the last Turkish province in central and eastern Arabia'.[2] There is also no evidence that Ibn Saʿud had in fact extended, during any period of the year 1914, Turkish suzerainty over his country, or acted, in any manner, as though he was a Turkish vassal or dependent. For example, he never used the title of *Qaim Maqam* conferred upon him by the 1914 treaty, nor did he, for that matter, refrain from corresponding with foreign Powers. Also a clear evidence of Ibn Saʿud's independence from Turkey at the time can be seen in his decision to enter into war, on the side of Britain, against Turkey. According to Philby, Ibn Saʿud 'was quite firm in his refusal to co-operate with the Turks when they became involved in war'.[3] Furthermore, contrary to its present contention that Ibn Saʿud was in 1914 a Turkish dependent, the British Government had never, in fact, refrained at the time from dealing with him directly, in his capacity as an independent ruler. It is evident that subsequent to his conquest of Hasa in May 1913, the British Political Agents for Bahrain and Kuwait met him personally somewhere in Arabia and had friendly talks with him. Also in the winter of 1914, Captain W. H. I. Shakespeare, the then British Political Agent at Kuwait, paid him

---

made an extensive search but found nothing regarding this alleged treaty nor any of these letters.' See *Saudi Memorial*, II, Annex 19, p. 52.

[1] If any such treaty of suzerainty had, in fact, existed between Ibn Saʿud and Turkey, it should not be excepted from the category of treaties that have been discussed elsewhere in this work. As is shown above, such 'treaties' do not actually have the status of internationally binding treaties and foreign States have often tended to disregard the legal relationship arising from them. See pp. 74-5, 100 n. 2.

[2] Philby's article, op. cit., p. 629.

[3] Philby, H. St J. B., *Arabian Jubilee* (1952), p. 38.

friendly visits in Riyadh.[1] According to Philby, 'Captain Shakespeare
. . . had little difficulty in establishing friendly personal relations with
the ruler of Najd by a series of visits to his territories culminating in
his journey via Riyadh . . . across Arabia to Suez in the early months
of 1914.'[2]

It may be argued that if in the British view Ibn Saʿud was then a
Turkish vassal, the British officials should have been discouraged
from dealing with him directly, regardless of the authority of the
Porte.

The British Government's contention seems to be that it did not
accord Ibn Saʿud *de jure* recognition as the independent ruler of
'Najd, Al-Hasa, Qatif and Jubail, and their dependencies and territories . . .' before the end of 1915, when it concluded with him the
Treaty of 26 December 1915. During this time, the Saudi Government
was already bound by the Anglo-Turkish Conventions of 1913–14
which preceded the conclusion of the 1915 treaty.[3] However, the
question arises whether the British Government had not already
accorded Ibn Saʿud *de facto* recognition as the ruler of the above-
mentioned territories prior to the conclusion of the 1915 treaty, as a
result of the friendly relations which it consistently maintained with
him, through its officials on the spot, throughout the period 1913–14?
It seems clear from the content of a dispatch published by *The Times*
on 19 July 1914, that the British Government thought it expedient to
establish relations with Ibn Saʿud at the time no matter what were his
legal relations *vis-à-vis* the Porte. In that dispatch, British policy
towards Ibn Saʿud, who was referred to as being 'in the position of
beatus possidentis in El Hasa', was clarified as follows:

It is understood that an Article in the Anglo-Turkish convention debars
the British Government from entering into relations with Ibn Saud as Emir
of independent Nedjd. Now that he has occupied the Gulf Ports El Beida
and El Ajeir, *it will be impossible for Great Britain not to have relations with
him, either if he accepts the Ottoman offer as Turkish Vali or if he remains
in occupation of the ports as an independent Chieftain. The British Embassy
(in Constantinople) is taking, or has taken steps, to provide for the former
contingency.* The latter depends upon the Porte's ability to conduct military
operation in Arabia.[4]

---

[1] Aitchison, p. 188; Philby, H. St J. B., *Saudi Arabia* (1955), p. 270.

[2] Philby, H. St J. B., *Report on the Operations of the Najd Mission*, 29 October
1917 to 1 November 1918 (Government Press, Baghdad), pp. 1–2.

[3] *British Memorial*, I, p. 125.

[4] *The Times*, 20 July 1914. Italics supplied. According to British sources, the
British Foreign Office was formally informed of the 1914 treaty appointing Ibn
Saʿud as an Ottoman Wali of Najd by the Turkish Ambassador in London in a
Note dated 9 July 1914 (i.e., nearly seven weeks after the date of the treaty of
15 May 1914). For the text of the Note of the Turkish Ambassador, see *British
Memorial*, II, Annex D, No. 40.

It seems clear from the italicised words of the above quotations that the British Government was not prepared to debar itself from establishing relations with Ibn Saʿud even if he had apparently 'accepted the Ottoman offer' as Turkish Wali. The British Government did not, thus, seem to view with great concern the apparent pledge of Turkish loyalty by Ibn Saʿud, as long as Ottoman Turkey had not the military ability to dislodge Ibn Saʿud from his *de facto* independent position in Arabia.[1]

On the other hand, it may be argued that even if the British Government had, in practice, regarded Ibn Saʿud as a Turkish vassal, as a result of his conclusion of the treaty of 15 May 1914, this, however, does not make the 1914 Convention binding upon Saudi Arabia just because it happened to be ratified a few weeks after the date of the signature of the treaty of suzerainty.[2] This may be explained as follows: Firstly, the 1914 Convention, the ratification of which followed the date of the signature of the treaty of suzerainty, was in fact formally concluded on 9 March 1914, nearly two months before the signature of the treaty. During that period Ibn Saʿud, who had already, since 5 May 1913, established himself 'in the position of *beatus possidentis* in El-Hasa', was still, in the eyes of the law, the only *de facto* sovereign of the Turkish named 'sanjaq of Najd'.[3] Yet he was never consulted or informed about the conclusion of a convention which purported to define the boundaries of Arabian territories over which Ottoman Turkey had not even a shadow of control at the time. Consequently, the 1914 Convention was, basically, not binding upon Saudi Arabia since it was negotiated and finally concluded with a government which held no legal authority over the territories in question.[4] Secondly, even in her capacity as a vassal State, Saudi

---

[1] It seems clear from British state practice that the British Government had often in the past objected to Turkish pretensions of suzerainty over the petty Arab Shaikhs and Rulers of the Arabian peninsula. Consequently, it proceeded to establish direct relations with those Arab Rulers regardless of the Turkish claims of authority over them. For example, the British Government was not deterred in the past from concluding with the then Ruler of Kuwait, Shaikh Mubarak Al-Sabah, the Agreement of 1899, which placed Kuwait under British protection, although it ostensibly acknowledged Turkish suzerainty over Kuwait. For details, see Chapter 5.

[2] See *British Memorial*, I, pp. 9, 80.

[3] *The Times*, 20 July 1914. And see above, p. 235.

[4] The British contention, as explained above, appears to attach great importance to the date of the ratification of the 1914 Convention since it took place after the date of the treaty of suzerainty. But this contention loses sight of the fact that at the time of the conclusion of the Convention Turkey had no legal standing whatsoever, since Ibn Saʿud had not yet transferred to her authority over the subject-matter of the Convention. The significance of the date of the conclusion of a treaty which provides for ratification should not be ignored, since 'according to the most accepted opinion', such a treaty is not 'devoid altogether of certain (legal) effects'. Moreover, it is agreed that such a treaty 'is always dated from the day when it

Arabia could not have become bound by a treaty (i.e., the 1914 Convention) of which she had never heard. It is an accepted principle of international law that when an independent State accepts, through a freely negotiated treaty, the protection or suzerainty of a superior State, it does not, however, surrender its sovereignty as a State and as an International Person. It follows, therefore, that such a vassal State does not, *inter alia*, lose its capacity to enter into treaties with foreign powers. However, because the suzerain State conducts the foreign relations of its vassal, it also conducts the latter's treaties. But this does not mean that such treaties can be concluded without the knowledge or the consent of the vassal State. According to Oppenheim,

> Modern suzerainty involves only a few rights of the suzerain State over the vassal State which can be called constitutional rights. The rights of the suzerain State over the vassal are principally international rights. Suzerainty is by no means sovereignty.[1]

CONCLUSION

The Buraimi controversy involves two essential issues: (*a*) the location of the common frontiers between Saudi Arabia and Abu Dhabi, and (*b*) the determination of sovereignty over the Buraimi Oasis. These were the two issues which the abortive Geneva Arbitration Tribunal of 1955 was requested to decide, in accordance with Article II of the Arbitration Agreement of 30 July 1954.

As to (*a*), the British Government has invited the Saudi Government to agree to a mutual settlement based on the Blue and the Violet Lines of the Anglo-Turkish Conventions of 1913–14, as modified by the proposed Riyadh Line of 1935. Such a settlement has been rejected by the Saudi Government on a number of legally justifiable grounds which have been examined in some detail above. On this basis, it seems difficult to bind Saudi Arabia by these Conventions without first making a full examination as to their legal propriety by an impartial tribunal appointed by the parties concerned. It may be that a reference of these Conventions by the parties for interpretation by the International Court of Justice will be justified.

As to (*b*), the question which has to be determined, in the light of the historical facts referred to above, is whether Saudi Arabia has, through any lack of effective state activities in the Buraimi Zone, lost her original title based on the conquest of Buraimi in 1800. If so, has either Muscat or Abu Dhabi, or both, established in the Oasis a better title than that of Saudi Arabia during any time after 1869? If it is shown in this dispute that Saudi Arabia lost her title to the Oasis after 1869, because she was not able to establish full control over it,

---

was duly signed by the representatives, and not from the day of its ratification'.
See Oppenhem, pp. 903–4.   [1] Oppenheim, pp. 188–9.

or because her state activities in it after this period were very slight, it does not follow that Muscat and Abu Dhabi have acquired such a title if they cannot show sufficient proof of their 'effective possession' over the Oasis throughout this period. In other words, the sovereignty of Muscat and Abu Dhabi over Buraimi can be proved by showing that these countries have established a 'superior' title to that of the Saudis.

The British Government has claimed sovereignty over the Buraimi Oasis, on behalf of both Muscat and Abu Dhabi, on the ground that after 1869 it came under the joint jurisdiction of the rulers of the two countries who have continuously displayed and exercised unchallenged state activities in the Oasis. The Saudi Government has, of course, made a similar claim of jurisdiction over Buraimi. However, except for their temporary occupation of the village of Hamasa in 1952, the Saudis do not appear to have been able to establish their 'effective possession' over the Oasis since their eviction from it in 1869. Consequently, if it is proved that during this period both Abu Dhabi and Muscat have, in fact, established 'a prescriptive title' to the territory, this title, as manifested by a continuous and peaceful display of authority, would, undoubtedly, prevail upon the original Saudi title to that territory. However, it seems questionable that the *fait accompli* settlement which prevailed in Buraimi after 1955, as a result of what a distinguished British writer calls 'a continuous build-up' of the British-officered Levies of Trucial Oman,[1] could, legally and judicially, be relied upon as proof of the 'effective control' established by both the Sultan of Muscat and the Ruler of Abu Dhabi in the Oasis.

[1] Mann, C., *Abu Dhabi* (1964), p. 98.

14

Disputes over Inner Oman and Zubarah

THE CLAIM OF THE IMAM OF OMAN TO SOVEREIGNTY OVER INNER OMAN

The dispute between the Imam of Oman and the Sultan of Muscat over the sovereignty of Inner Oman was little known to the outside world before the events in Muscat of July 1957, which precipitated British intervention in Oman and which led, in consequence, to a debate in the United Nations Security Council.

In connection with the merits of this dispute between the Imam of Oman and the Sultan of Muscat as to sovereignty over Oman, it is convenient to examine separately the historical and the legal aspects of the claim to sovereignty over Oman, or more properly Inner Oman.

The historical aspect

The territory of Oman lies at the extreme strip of the Arabian peninsula. It is the hinterland of what is now called the Sultanate of Muscat and Oman. As early as the sixteenth century the name Oman was applied to the whole country which was governed, 'as it had been generally since 751 A.D., by an elective Imam or ruler possessing supreme religious, military and political authority'.[1]

In the year 1793, an ancestor of the present Sultan of Muscat, Imam Sa'id ibn Ahmad, was the last genuinely elected Imam of Oman. This Imam became unpopular with his subjects because he altered the Imamate rule and established a new 'hereditary sovereignty' in Muscat confined in his family, the Al-Bu-Sa'id, and transferred the capital from Rustaq in the interior to Muscat on the sea coast.[2] This arbitrary action of Imam Sa'id ibn Ahmad, whose successors came to be known as 'sultans', seriously prejudiced the effectiveness of the Sultanate rule. Thus, in the first place, the action divided the country into two rival systems of government; a secular government in Muscat under the Sultan and an elective religious government in Nazwa, the capital of the interior, known as the 'Imamate of all Oman' under the leadership of the Imam.[3]

Secondly, the Omani tribes, under the leadership of their religious Imam, continued to revolt against the rule of the sultans of Muscat

---

[1] Lorimer, p. 397.
[2] Ibid., pp. 414–19. And see the history of the Imamate in Wingate, Sir Ronald, *Not in the Limelight* (1959), p. 72.   [3] Lorimer, p. 455.

who were, and have always been, declared by the Omanis as 'irreligious' and non-representative of the people of Oman. And, according to Lorimer, in the years 1877 and 1895, Muscat and Mutrah were 'occupied unopposed' by the forces of the Imam, in spite of 'a written remonstrance from the British Political Agent'.[1] The British Agent, although abstaining from supporting the Sultan against the Imam's revolution, had not in fact favoured the demands of the Imam.[2] However, it appears that after the revolution of 1895 a reversal of British policy of strict 'neutrality' towards the affairs of Muscat and Oman was advocated by those concerned with British policy-making in the Gulf.[3] The initiative towards this aim came from the British Government of India which suggested one of three courses:

(a) The annexations of Muscat and Mutrah to the British Crown and sending the Sultan on pension;

(b) the establishment of British protectorate over Muscat and Oman, or,

(c) making it clear to the tribes of the interior

that, whatever differences they might have with their Sultan, the British Government would not, in view of the importance of British interests at those places, permit attacks upon Muscat and Mutrah.[4]

Subsequently the third course was adopted. This committed the British authorities in Muscat to supporting the authority of the Sultan in the towns of Muscat and Mutrah but not in Oman.[5] Oman, therefore, continued for many years past to be governed directly by an elective 'Imamate' which owed no allegiance to the government of the Sultan of Muscat. In fact, all authorities agree that the Sultan's writ had never, before 1955, reached Oman.[6] When the Sultan sent, in 1898, a garrison to Sur, in the interior of Oman, it was expelled by the Omanis by force of arms. Similarly, the work of the expedition sent by the Sultan in 1901, to examine the coal deposit in the hinterland of Sur was obstructed by the Imam.[7] But, whenever there was fighting between the Sultan and the Omanis, the British Government came to the assistance of the Sultan.[8]

[1] Lorimer, pp. 482–505.   [2] Ibid., pp. 536–9.   [3] Ibid.
[4] Ibid., pp. 550–1; Aitchison, pp. 277–8.   [5] Lorimer, pp. 578–9.
[6] See Thesiger, W., 'Desert Borderlands of Oman', Geographical Journal, vol. 116, October–December (1950), pp. 151–2. The writer states that the representatives of the Imam 'are to be found in every group or village where they administer justice and collect taxes . . . The "Badu" do . . . recognise the Imam as their overlord'; Eccles, G. J., 'The Sultanate of Muscat and Oman', Journal of the Central Asian Society, vol. 14 (1927), p. 27; The British Royal Institute of International Affairs, The Middle East, A Political and Economic Survey, 2nd ed. (1951), pp. 136–7; Johnson, P., Journey into Chaos (1958), p. 146; Philby, H. St J. B., 'Britain and the Sultan', The Manchester Guardian, 21 August 1957.
[7] Lorimer, pp. 580–1.
[8] Ibid., pp. 590–8; Aitchison, pp. 280, 284; Philby, op. cit.

In 1913, another major revolution occurred against the Sultan's interference in the internal affairs of Oman. This led to protracted negotiations between the Sultan and the Imam, through the mediation of the British authorities in Muscat, for reaching a *modus vivendi* for the situation.[1] But it was not until 1920 that an arrangement acceptable to both the Sultan and the Imam was reached. It is this arrangement which has given rise to the legal aspect of the Omani-Muscati dispute.

The legal aspect: the Secret Treaty of Sib, 25 September 1920

As mentioned above, the Omani-Muscati dispute entered a new phase when the British Government thought seriously of taking practical steps which would reduce, or frustrate, the tension between the Sultan and the Imam. Thus, after long preliminary meetings and negotiations between the representatives of the Imam and the British Consul in Muscat, acting on behalf of the Sultan, the parties finally agreed on the terms of an Agreement, known as the Treaty of Sib, 1920,[2] in which the respective authority of the Sultan in Muscat and the Imam in Oman has been defined. This agreement which was concluded in Arabic was not published at the time, and when the Omani-Muscati conflict arose in 1955, and in 1957, the Sultan and the British Government refused to release details about its provisions. But the representatives of the Imam of Oman disclosed their own text of the agreement.[3]

The provisions of the agreement were divided into two parts, with four Articles pertaining to the 'People of Oman', in one part, and four Articles pertaining to the Sultan in the other.

In part one, Article (1) fixed the maximum of 5 per cent as a charge to be imposed by the Government of Muscat on goods of Omanis coming to the coastal towns under the jurisdiction of the Sultan. Article (2) provided for the security and freedom of Omanis in 'all the coastal towns', Article (3) provided for the removal of 'all restrictions upon everyone entering and leaving Muscat and Mutrah and

---

[1] Aitchison, p. 284. And see *House of Commons Debates*, vol. 574, col. 33, 22 July 1957 (Mr Selwyn Lloyd's speech). It is to be noted that Mr Selwyn Lloyd had incorrectly stated that 'until 1793, the Sultan of Muscat was also Imam of Oman. Then a separate Imamate was elected.' The historical facts are that until 1793, there was no Sultanate, but there was an Imamate. It was after this date that a Sultanate, which broke away from the Imamate, was established. See above, p. 239.

[2] Reference to the Treaty of Sib, 1920, is found in Aitchison, p. 284; Thesiger, op. cit., p. 162; Eccles, op. cit., pp. 23–4; Thomas, B., *Arab Rule Under the Al Bu Said Dynasty of Oman, 1741–1937* (1938), p. 26; Morris, J., *Sultan of Oman: Venture into the Middle East* (1957), pp. 148–51.

[3] For an English translation of the Arabic text of the Agreement, see The Arab Information Center, New York, *The Status of Oman and the British Omanite Dispute* (1957), Annex I. See Appendix V.

R

all the' coastal towns. Article (4) provided for the extradition of criminals between the Government of Muscat and Oman. By the same Article the Sultan promised not to 'interfere in the internal affairs' of the people of Oman.

In part two, by Article (1) all the tribes and the Shaikhs of Oman promised to be 'at peace with the Sultan' and not to 'interfere in his Government'. By Article (2) the subjects of the Sultan entering Oman for lawful trade or business were promised security and free movement. Article (3) provided for the extradition of criminals fleeing into Oman. By Article (4) the Sultan acknowledged the right of the Omani chiefs to look into the claims of 'merchants and others' from Muscat against the people of Oman and provided that justice should be dispensed in accordance with 'the law of Islam'.

It is clear from the above provisions of the Treaty of Sib, 1920, that Oman retained an internal independent character of its own. Thus the Omanis reserved full authority in respect of administration, justice and other aspects of government. The provisions concerning the extradition of criminals are significant in that they attribute to Oman a distinct personality and a separate existence. However, there is nothing in the treaty which shows that the Sultan by signing it had in fact intended to relinquish his sovereignty over Oman, although he did not expressly assert it. There does not seem any reference in the treaty to the independence of Oman or to the government of the Imam. Instead, the reference is being made to the 'people of Oman'.

On the other hand, the evidence of history shows that for over a century Oman has developed a separate existence with little or no connection with the Government of Muscat.[1] The head of the government of Oman, the Imam, has continually been elected in accordance with the traditions of the Omanis irrespective of the authority of the Sultan who, it is interesting to note, himself stood for the Imamate in 1954, when a new Imam was elected, but did not succeed.[2] Not until the rebellion of 1955, which was crushed by the Sultan with the assistance of British forces, could the Sultan exercise any authority in Oman at all. For many years the British Political Agent and Consul acted as mediator between the Sultan and the tribes of Oman.[3]

Consequently, it can be argued that the agreement, which was concluded through the mediation of the British Consul in Muscat, has

[1] See above, p. 40.
[2] See The Arab Information Center, op. cit., pp. 2, 13.
[3] See The Arab Information Center, op. cit., pp. 3–4. And see ibid., p. 9, for a reference to a communication, dated 8 March 1922, between Major Rae, British Consul in Muscat, and the Deputy Imam, connected with the treaty. This communication may well be regarded as a virtual acknowledgement of the independence of the Imamate, not only on the part of the Sultan, but also on the part of the British Government.

actually affirmed and recognised the independent status assumed by Oman in the past. According to *The Times*,

There appears to have been no definite denial of Omani independence in the Treaty but a refusal to affirm it.[1]

The legal issue ensuing from this agreement seems to centre round Article (4) of part one which assures the Omanis of non-interference in 'their internal affairs'. The representatives of the Imam contend that the Sultan by granting in 1937 an oil concession in the territory of Oman to a subsidiary of the Iraq Petroleum Company, without consulting the Imam, has infringed the terms of the agreement.[2] The British Government and the Sultan reject this contention.[3] The treaty of Sib, the British Government argues,

was in no sense an international treaty but an agreement, of a kind familiar in that area, between the sovereign and certain of his tribes, which did no more than allow the Omani tribes a measure of autonomy.[4]

The question of which contention is correct cannot be discussed in legal terms exclusively. It is true that if the terms of the treaty are regarded as establishing objectively and absolutely binding commitments between the two parties, then there is room for the view that a violation of the agreement occurred when the Sultan interfered in the internal affairs of Oman by denying the Omanis the right to control their own oil resources. However, it is questionable whether the agreement can be interpreted as creating legal commitment of this nature. One reason is that it is not an international treaty, in the strict sense of the term, since it was not concluded between two independent international persons. It was, rather, as the British representative pointed out in the United Nations, merely

an agreement, of a kind familiar in that area, between the sovereign and certain of his tribes, which did no more than allow the Omani tribes a measure of autonomy.

If the agreement is not a proper treaty and is not governed by international law, then if it is to enjoy legal validity, it must be governed by some other system of law. If that system of law is the law of

---

[1] *The Times*, 14 August 1957. And see *Report of the Ad Hoc Committee on Oman*, op. cit., p. 210.

[2] *The Times*, 14 August 1957. And see Johnson, P., op. cit., p. 147.

[3] *The Times*, op. cit.

[4] See U.N.S.C., 12th Year, 783rd mtg, 20 August 1957, pp. 7–9. It is to be noted that although the document is described as the 'Treaty of Sib', it should not be confused with real international instruments. It may be that a parallel with this kind of 'Treaty' can be found in the 'arrangements made by the Ottoman Sultans and their Walis'. See A British Contributor, 'Commentary on the Treaty of Sib' *Middle East Journal*, 12 (1958), pp. 366–8.

Muscat, then, presumably, it is open to modification by the Sultan; and there can, in technical terms, be no question of a breach.

The only remaining possibility is that the agreement is governed by some third system of law which binds both the Sultan and the Omanis. If any such system exists, it must be a local system, presumably derived from the custom and practice of the area. That such a system may exist cannot be denied *a priori*. On the other hand, if it is to be established, there must be some evidence of it; and there appears to be none. This being so, it is difficult to speak, with any confidence, of a breach in a technical legal sense of the treaty of Sib. Questions of the Sultan's honour or moral obligations are *prima facie* outside the concern of the lawyer.

Nevertheless, if the assumption is made that the Sultan was acting in the breach of the treaty in 1937, two questions then arise. The first is whether that violation by itself terminated the treaty in 1937. The second is whether, assuming the treaty to have subsisted, the 1937 breach could have been used in 1955 or in 1957, to justify the Omani revolt.

To both these questions it is submitted that the answer is in the negative. Apparently no allegation was made in 1937 by the Omanis that the treaty had been violated, or, if violated, that they were entitled to regard it as at an end. Indeed all the evidence points in the direction of the continuation of the treaty after that date. And if the treaty subsisted it seems contrary to the general principles of the law of contract, even when most broadly interpreted, to suggest that one party may assert a breach of the agreement by the other party as a justification for reprisal action taken eighteen years after the alleged breach. On the other hand, if, as is claimed by the Omanis, the violation of the agreement occurred in December 1955 when the Sultan, provocatively, conducted his military expedition to the interior against the legal authority of the Imam, then there would, probably, be a point in justifying the Omani revolt as an unavoidable reprisal action.

Nature of British obligations to the Sultan: legality of British armed intervention in Oman

Having examined the merits of the Omani-Muscati dispute as to sovereignty over Oman, it may be desirable to consider a relevant issue which overshadowed this dispute when it arose on the international plane in 1957, namely, British military action in Oman in July 1957. Is there any legal basis for the British Government to take military action in Oman at the request of the Sultan?

This is one of the complex legal issues in the Omani-Muscati dispute, and public opinion in Britain was at the time divided on the legality of British intervention in a purely domestic dispute between the Sultan and the Imam. In the United Nations, eleven Arab States,

Members of the Arab League, called upon the Security Council in a letter, dated 13 August 1957, to debate 'urgently' what they termed as British 'armed aggression' against Oman.[1] The Arab States' request to convene the Security Council was made under Articles 34 and 35 of the United Nations Charter. But when the question was debated in the Security Council on 20 August 1957 it failed to receive the seven affirmative votes required for its inscription on the agenda of the Council.[2]

The British Government's argument before the Security Council was to the effect that

The military action taken by the British forces was taken at the request of the Sultan in order to assist him in restoring order in the face of a revolt against his authority which had been encouraged and supported from outside.[3]

But when the question of British military intervention in Oman was debated in the House of Commons and the Foreign Secretary, Mr Selwyn Lloyd, was asked 'whether outside intervention has yet been formally established, and if so, from where', he replied that 'certain arms have been smuggled into the country from outside', but he declined to accuse specific outside countries of supplying arms to the forces of the Imam.[4] There were two reasons for the British Government's intervention in Oman. These were, in the words of the British Foreign Secretary:

First, it was at the request of a friendly ruler who had always relied on us to help him resist aggression or subversion. Secondly, there is the direct British interest involved and I have no need to stress to the House the importance of the Persian Gulf.[5]

However, the problem was complicated, from the British view-point, by the fact that Her Majesty's Government had no treaty obligations to defend the Sultan against aggression.[6] Therefore, some Members of both the House of Commons and the House of Lords took the view that

intervention by a foreign State in a country where there are civil disturbances

---

[1] See U.N.*S.C.*, op. cit., S/3865 and Add. 1. Letter of 13 August 1957, from Permanent Representatives of Arab States.

[2] U.N.*S.C.*, op. cit., 783rd mtg, pp. 1–2, and 784th mtg, pp. 1–18.

[3] Ibid., 783rd mtg, p. 7.

[4] *House of Commons Debates*, op cit., col. 36, 22 July and cols 231–2, 23 July 1957. Recently, *the Report of the Ad Hoc Committee on Oman*, op. cit., p. 215, revealed that the military assistance received by the Omanis was not 'of such a nature as to affect the character of the Imam's struggle and convert it into a foreign-controlled action being carried out essentially in the interest of a foreign Power'.　　[5] *House of Commons Debates*, op. cit., col. 872, 29 July 1957.

[6] Ibid., col. 875, 29 July 1957.

is contrary to international law, and that it was on these grounds that the Foreign Secretary condemned Russian intervention in Hungary.[1]

The above uncertainties about the legality of British intervention in Oman give rise to a controversial issue, namely, whether 'intervention by invitation' (to use the words of E. Lauterpacht) is lawful?[2] P. Benenson, and indeed a few other people, took the view that British intervention in Oman was contrary to the principles of international law.[3] He quotes an article in *The Times* by Lord Shawcross, in which the latter condemns the Russian intervention in Hungary as illegal.[4] In his article, Lord Shawcross was quoting from Hyde where he says:

> Foreign interference, howsoever invoked, is necessarily directed against a portion of the population of a State and is thus a denial of its right to engage in or suppress a revolution or of employing its own resources to retain or acquire control over the government of its own territory.[5]

Benenson then deduces from the above principles that the Omani revolt against the Sultan was an exercise of the 'Droit de Revolte', and he, therefore, concludes by saying:

> Where no constitutional machinery for legal change exists, the people of a country may have no option but to revolt against tyranny.[6]

Similarly, Quincy Wright is of the opinion that intervention by invitation is inadmissible. He formulates the principle of law in the following:

> International law does not permit the use of force in the territory of another state on invitation either of the recognised or insurgent government in times of rebellion, insurrection or civil war. Since international law recognises the right of revolution, it cannot permit other states to intervene to prevent it.[7]

Although E. Lauterpacht is of the opinion that

the government of a state may give what amounts to a licence to another

---

[1] *House of Commons Debates*, op. cit., col. 36, 22 July 1957. And see *House of Lords Debates*, vol. 205, col. 16, 22 July 1957.

[2] Lauterpacht, E., 'Intervention by Invitation', *The Times*, 24 August 1960. For an analytical discussion of the legality of British intervention in Oman, 1957, see Lauterpacht, E., 'The Contemporary Practice of the United Kingdom in the Field of International Law', *I.C.L.Q.*, 7 (1958), pp. 102–8.

[3] *The Times*, 13 August 1957. And see Philby's Letter in *The Manchester Guardian*, op. cit. See also Editorial Note, 'British Intervention in Oman', *Revue egyptienne de droit international*, 13 (1957), pp. 114–21.

[4] *The Times*, 'Intervention in Hungary', 13 March 1957.

[5] Hyde, 1, pp. 253–4. [6] *The Times*, 13 August 1957.

[7] Wright, Q., 'Subversive Intervention', *A.J.I.L.*, 54 (1960), p. 529. See also by the same writer, in the same Journal, 'The Prevention of Aggression', 50 (1956), pp. 514 et seq.; and 'U.S. Intervention in the Lebanon', 53 (1959), pp. 112 et seq.

state to do things on its territory which, if done without such consent, would constitute an unlawful intervention,

he, nevertheless, concedes that

this view yielded . . . to an acknowledgement that the principle of self-determination entitled the people of a territory to replace their government —if necessary, by forcible and even technically unconstitutional means— free of interference from outside states.[1]

Owing to the lack of agreement among authorities and the prevailing uncertainties as to the true nature of the rebellion in Oman in 1957, it is very difficult to express a firm view as to the legal propriety of the military assistance rendered by the United Kingdom to the Sultan at that time. However, it appears that a new light has been shed on this question after the publication in 1965 of the United Nations' sponsored Report of the *Ad Hoc* Committee on Oman. In that part of the report dealing with the legal propriety of British intervention in the armed conflict between the Imam and the Sultan of Muscat, the Committee says that it is not convinced by the British argument that 'the putting down of a rebellion by a lawful authority is no violation of human rights'. In the Committee's view, the British statements have placed the emphasis 'on the necessity of maintaining a government in power rather than on ensuring that basic human rights are not infringed'. Then the Committee states its conclusions as follows:

The action taken by the United Kingdom was extreme and difficult to justify. It feels that some kind of negotiations along the lines of those in 1920 might have been more appropriate particularly in the early stages before . . . 1955.[2]

THE ZUBARAH DISPUTE

The Zubarah question is, in reality, a claim by the Shaikh of Bahrain to ownership of a piece of land on the northern coast of the peninsula of Qatar. At present, Zubarah forms an integral part of Qatar and is in fact under the administration of the Ruler of Qatar.

The nature of the Shaikh of Bahrain's claim to Zubarah is historical; he claims it because it was the ancestral home of his family, Al-Khalifah, before their conquest of Bahrain in 1783.[3] The Shaikh of Bahrain has never relinquished his claim to Zubarah which remains today the main source of dissension between the two ruling families of Bahrain and Qatar. It appears that during the nineteenth century,

[1] Lauterpacht, E., *The Times*, op. cit.
[2] *Report of the Ad Hoc Committee on Oman*, op. cit., pp. 215–16.
[3] See Bahrain Government, *Annual Report*, March 1937–February 1938, p. 25; Belgrave, Sir Charles, *Personal Column: Autobiography* (1960), p. 153. And see above, chapter 1.

and before the British Government concluded the Agreement of 1916 with Qatar,[1] the Shaikhs of Bahrain claimed sovereignty over the whole peninsula of Qatar which they held to be tributary to them.[2]

The British Government of India took the view as early as 1873 that the Shaikh of Bahrain

had no clear or important rights in Qatar and that he should be restrained, as far as possible, from raising complications on the mainland.

The British Government, therefore, advised the successive Shaikhs of Bahrain, on various occasions thereafter, to relinquish their claim to Qatar, or to Zubarah, but the Shaikhs did not accept this advice.[3] Moreover, the British Government, specifically, undertook by Article 11 of the unratified Anglo-Turkish Convention of 29 July 1913 not to

allow the interference of the Shaikh of Bahrain in the internal affairs of al Qatar, his endangering the autonomy of that area or his annexing it.[4]

At present, the Shaikh of Bahrain claims Zubarah, firstly, because it was his ancestors' home, and, secondly, because it is inhabited by the Nuʿaim tribe who owe him their allegiance. He regards the Nuʿaim tribe, who settled in Zubarah as early as 1874, as his subjects over whom he should exercise jurisdiction while they are staying in Zubarah.[5]

In 1937, the Nuʿaim complained to the Shaikh of Bahrain that the Shaikh of Qatar tried to establish a customs post in Zubarah. As a result, the Shaikh protested to the British Government against what he termed to be an interference by Qatar in the affairs of his people. Subsequently, the British Government arranged for negotiations to take place between the parties for the settlement of the dispute between them, but no satisfactory solution was reached.[6]

Again, in 1949, an attempt was made, through the mediation of C. J. Pelly, the British Political Agent at Bahrain, to reach a *modus vivendi* between Bahrain and Qatar on this question.[7] It is understood that in the negotiations which were held in Bahrain, the Shaikh of Bahrain agreed to disclaim the ownership of oil resources which might be discovered in Zubarah, provided that the Shaikh of Qatar agreed

---

[1] See above, Chapter 4.   [2] See above, Chapter 3.
[3] See Lorimer, pp. 815–16.   [4] See Hurewitz, I, p. 271.
[5] Belgrave, op. cit., pp. 152–4. And see Kelly, J. B., 'Sovereignty and Jurisdiction in Eastern Arabia', *International Affairs*, 34 (1958), p. 18. Dr Kelly presents the Shaikh of Bahrain's argument about his claim to Zubarah by saying that in answer to the assertion that he cannot exercise jurisdiction over people who are within the territory of another State, the Shaikh argues that 'the sea coast of Qatar cannot automatically be taken to constitute the maritime frontier of that State to the exclusion of his claim to Zubarah, especially as the coast has not explicitly been recognised as such a frontier in any written agreement'.
[6] Belgrave, op. cit., p. 154; Bahrain Government, *Annual Report*, op. cit.
[7] Belgrave, op. cit., pp. 157–8.

neither to interfere with his subjects, the Nuʿaim, nor to rebuild the old fort at Zubarah which belonged to his ancestors. However, no formal agreement was concluded by the parties on these matters, which now remain as complex as before.[1]

Although the Shaikh of Bahrain seems to be still willing to reach a conciliatory agreement with Qatar on the question of Zubarah, it is quite unlikely that he will ever be dissuaded by any means, short of an agreement which satisfies his own pride, from asserting his rights to Zubarah.[2] The great importance which the Shaikh of Bahrain attaches to Zubarah is described by Sir Charles Belgrave, formerly Adviser to the Shaikh, in the following words:

It [Zubarah] ranked higher in the eyes of the Shaikhs than any other political issue and it took up more time and presented more difficulties than any of the problems in which I had to deal. The individual attitudes towards the Zabara Question of the long string of Residents and Political Agents who came and went during my thirty-one years in Bahrain coloured the relations between the Shaikhs and the British authorities throughout the whole of my time there. To the outer world it was an affair of no importance, . . . but to the Shaikhs of Bahrain it was a matter affecting their dignity, prestige and honour, and it was this which made it so difficult to arrive at any sort of agreement.[3]

It can be seen from the above explanation that the question of Zubarah, as it stands today, cannot be fitted in any legal classification. It is not, in reality, a claim to territory; it is a claim to jurisdiction over the subjects of a State in another territory.

---

[1] This information is based on notes taken during an interview with Sir Charles Belgrave on 1 April 1961.

[2] Interview with Sir Charles Belgrave.

[3] Belgrave, op. cit., p. 152. It is doubtful if Belgrave's description of the Zubarah question still represents Bahrain's position on this issue, the importance of which has now greatly receded. Instead, Bahrain is now giving top priority to the settlement of her offshore boundaries with Qatar, while avoiding any reference to the Zubarah issue which will only mar such a settlement.

The latest discussions on the Bahrain-Qatar offshore boundaries were held in Qatar in March 1967, during an official visit by the Ruler of Bahrain to Qatar. It is understood that in these discussions, the Ruler of Qatar raised the question of Huwar islands which, in his view, stands against reaching an equitable boundary settlement. These small islands (better known as one island), $1\frac{1}{2}$ miles from Qatar are under Bahrain's sovereignity. But Qatar now demands their ownership as a condition for agreeing to an offshore boundary settlement satisfactory to Bahrain. Not surprisingly, Bahrain refused to accede to Qatar's demand, and the discussions were therefore suspended *sine die*.

See below, pp. 300, 302–3, for an account of offshore boundary disputes.

15

Iraqi claim to sovereignty over Kuwait

Background

On 19 June 1961 the late Amir of Kuwait, Shaikh ʿAbd Allah al-Salim Al-Sabah, and the then British Political Resident in the Arabian Gulf, Sir William Luce, signed in Kuwait an Exchange of Notes[1] by virtue of which the Agreement of 1899 was terminated and Kuwait was recognised by the British Government as a sovereign independent State. Following the signing of this new treaty, the Government of Kuwait formally applied on 22 June for the membership of the Arab League. But on 25 June, General ʿAbd al-Karim Qasim, then President of the Iraqi Republic, laid a claim to Kuwait as 'an integral part of Iraq'.[2] This claim was reiterated on 26 June in a formal statement, issued by the Iraqi Foreign Ministry, which formulated the legal grounds for the Iraqi claim as follows:

Foreign powers including the British Government itself recognised the sovereignty of the Ottoman State over Kuwait. The Ottoman Sultan used to appoint the Shaikh of Kuwait by a decree conferring on him the title of *Qaim Maqam* and making of him a representative of the Governor of Basrah in Kuwait. Thus, the Shaikhs of Kuwait continued to derive their administrative powers from the Ottoman authorities in Basrah and affirm their allegiance to the Ottoman Sultan until 1914.[3]

The statement went on to say that the 'secret Agreement of 1899', concluded with the then Ruler of Kuwait, Shaikh Mubarak, was invalid because it was made in defiance of the authority of the Ottoman Sultan. As regards the treaty of 1961, which terminated the 1899 Agreement, the statement continued, it was equally invalid, because it aimed 'under the new cloak of nominal independence . . . to maintain imperialist influence and to keep Kuwait separated from Iraq'.[4]

The Kuwaiti Government reacted swiftly to the Iraqi claim by issuing a statement on the following day in which it repudiated the Iraqi claim which it regarded as untenable. The Kuwaiti statement said that Kuwait was never subjected to Turkish sovereignty and that 'the title of *Qaim Maqam*, . . . was never used in Kuwait and never influenced the course of life or the independence of Kuwait from the

[1] *U.K.T.S.* No. 1 (1961), *Cmnd.* 1409, See Appendix XI.
[2] *The Times*, 23, 26 June 1961.
[3] The Republic of Iraq (Ministry of Foreign Affairs), *The Truth About Kuwait*, July (1961), p. 24.
[4] Ibid., pp. 24–5.

Turkish Empire'. Regarding the 1899 Agreement, the statement continued, it was terminated on 19 June 1961, and Kuwait consequently emerged as a fully sovereign and independent State.[1] Following reports of movements of Iraqi troops to the Kuwaiti borders, the Ruler requested the British Government for military assistance under the provisions of the treaty of 1961.[2] He also requested on 2 July the Security Council of the United Nations to consider the Iraqi 'threat of the invasion of Kuwait'. Simultaneously, he formally applied for the membership of his country to the United Nations Organisation. But on 7 July the Soviet Union's representative at the Security Council vetoed a resolution aiming at recognising the independence of Kuwait.[3] By the end of July, the independence of Kuwait was formally recognised by all the Arab League countries, with the exception of Iraq, and by a number of European nations, also by the United States of America. On 20 July Kuwait was admitted, against Iraq's opposition, to the full membership of the Arab League.[4] In October, the British troops completed their withdrawal from Kuwait, at the request of the Ruler. Another request for United Nations membership was again rejected by the Security Council in November, owing to the Soviet Union's veto.[5] The latter's objection was based on the argument that Kuwait was not yet qualified as an independent State, and that the 1961 treaty with Britain subjected her to foreign political influence.[6]

On 8 February 1963 a military revolution overthrew the Government of ʿAbd al-Karim Qasim and assumed power in Iraq. The Council of Ministers of the new Iraqi Government declared its intention to ease the state of tension which was then prevailing between Iraq and Kuwait. Consequently, the new Iraqi regime took steps aiming at the gradual relinquishment of Qasim's claim to Kuwait. Meanwhile, the Russian hostility towards Kuwait receded. And on 7 May 1963 Kuwait's application for membership of the United Nations was approved by the Security Council, upon the recommendation of which Kuwait was elected by the General Assembly as the 111th member of the United Nations.[7]

[1] The Government of Kuwait (Printing and Publishing Department), *The Kuwaiti-Iraqi Crisis* (1961), pp. 3–4; *The Times*, 27 June 1961.

[2] *The Times*, 27, 28, 29 June 1961. And see above, Chapter 5.

[3] For these developments, see *The Times*, 3, 6, 7 July; *Middle East Journal*, 15 (1961), pp. 433–5.

[4] *The Times*, 22 July 1961; *Middle East Journal*, op. cit.

[5] *Y.U.N.*, 1961, pp. 168–9; *Middle East Journal*, 16 (1962), pp. 70–1.

[6] *Y.U.N.*, 1961, pp. 168–9; Kuwait Government Centre, New York, *Press Release*, 1 December 1961.

[7] *Y.U.N.*, 1963, pp. 91–2; *MEES*, 24 May 1963. For earlier developments, see *Middle East Journal*, 17 (1963), pp. 120 et seq.; *MEES*, No. 24, 19 April 1963; *The Observer* (London Weekly), 2 June 1963.

Finally, on 4 October 1963, Iraq officially recognised the independence of Kuwait and confirmed Iraq's adherence to the status of the Iraqi-Kuwaiti boundaries, as described in the Exchange of Letters dated 21 July and 10 August 1932, between the then Prime Minister of Iraq and the Ruler of Kuwait, respectively. Later, on 12 October 1963, Kuwait and Iraq signed a financial agreement providing for the payment by the former to the latter the sum of KD £30 million as a loan to be re-paid, without interest, in nineteen instalments over twenty-five years.[1]

Legal validity of the Iraqi claim

When on 2 July 1961 Kuwait brought her complaint against Iraq before the Security Council, the Iraqi representative to the Council objected to the acceptance of the Kuwaiti complaint in accordance with Article 35(2) of the United Nations Charter.[2] He argued that since Kuwait was not a State, in the international sense of this meaning, she could not, therefore, invoke the procedure envisaged in paragraph 2 of this Article. Despite Iraqi objection, however, all the members of the Security Council, with the exception of the Soviet Union, voted in favour of the independent statehood of Kuwait.[3] As is shown in the above background, the Iraqi claim to Kuwait is based on two issues, namely, (a) the historical connection of Kuwait with the Ottoman Empire, and (b) the succession of the new State of Iraq to the territorial sovereignty of that Empire over Kuwait.[4] But in order to establish this claim, it seems necessary to prove: (1) That Kuwait was, legally, an integral part of the Ottoman Empire and was administered as a district of the *Wilayat* of Basrah. (2) That Iraq had succeeded to the Turkish territorial sovereignty, or suzerainty, over Kuwait. (3) That Iraq had continued to maintain, effectively and without disturbance, her sovereign claim to Kuwait. The merits or demerits of the above propositions will now be analysed.

The original Ottoman historical title to Kuwait

The Kuwaiti Government's argument against the alleged subjection of Kuwait to the authority of the Ottoman Empire is that 'Kuwait has been governed, without direct Turkish interference, by the same dynasty of Al-Sabah since 1756, and that the independent status of Kuwait was maintained even after Midhat Pasha, the Wali (Governor) of Baghdad, who led in 1871 an expedition into al-Hasa . . . to subdue the area . . .'[5] What are the historical facts? On the basis of historical

---

[1] *MEES*, No. 49, 11 October and No. 50, 18 October 1963.
[2] *Y.U.N.*, 1961, pp. 168–9. Article 35(2) of the United Nations Charter refers to a 'State which is not a member of the United Nations'.
[3] Ibid.   [4] See above, p. 250.
[5] *The Kuwaiti-Iraqi Crisis*, op. cit., p. 4; Hewins, Ralph, *A Golden Dream: Miracle of Kuwait* (1963), p. 91. Here Mr Hewins rightly states that 'at no time the name

evidence the position is that the Ottoman Empire had never acquired a right of sovereignty over Kuwait, which was neither occupied nor conquered by the Turks. And since the allegation that 'Kuwait formed an integral part of the Ottoman Empire' has no historical or legal basis, it is, therefore, right to say that Ottoman Turkey had established no legal title to Kuwait whatsoever.[1] However, unlike Turkish sovereignty over Kuwait, which was non-existent, Turkish suzerainty over Kuwait in the past could not be easily dismissed. It seems undeniable that some vague form of Turkish suzerainty had existed in Kuwait during the last half of the nineteenth century, and, probably, during the first decade of the present century.[2] There is evidence to show that the rulers of Kuwait continued to accept the title of *Qaim Maqam* until 1896. When in that year Shaikh Mubarak Al-Sabah made himself the new ruler of Kuwait, the Turkish Government hastened to appoint him a *Qaim Maqam*, but he declined to accept the title. He also refused to accept a Turkish quarantine officer, and in May 1899, only four months after his conclusion of the 1899 Agreement with Britain, he imposed a customs duty of 5 per cent on Turkish goods.[3] Regarding the British Government, it had never attempted to dispute the assertion of Turkish suzerainty over Kuwait. This explains the reason for its conclusion of the 1899 Agreement with Shaikh Mubarak secretly and without the knowledge of the Turks.[4] Evidence of British recognition of Turkish suzerainty over Kuwait before the First World War can be found in the abortive Anglo-Turkish Convention of 1913, which formed the basis of Turkish recognition of the independent status of Kuwait.[5] Having now established that Kuwait was virtually a Turkish vassal enjoying a considerable measure of autonomy, the

---

Kuwait was understood on maps as part of the Ottoman Empire'. As regards the title of *Qaim Maqam*, conferred upon the Ruler of Kuwait, the Kuwaiti Government argued that it was no more than an 'honorific title' which did not, in any way, affect the separate entity of the Ruler.

[1] According to historical sources, the Shaikhs of Kuwait had 'owned no allegiance to the Turkish Sultans'. However, there is evidence that the Turkish Sultans had exercised a loose system of 'tutelage' over Kuwait during the nineteenth century. For Turkey's relationship with Kuwait, see the following: Lorimer, pp. 1008–12; United Kingdom, Admiralty, *A Handbook on Arabia*, I (1920), p. 29; United Kingdom, Foreign Office, *Peace Handbook: Turkey and Asia* (1920), p. 15; Grohmann, Adolf, *The Encyclopaedia of Islam*, II (Part 2) (1927), pp. 1172–5. Hewins, Ralph, op. cit., pp. 91–182.

[2] Aitchison, pp. 202–3; Grohmann, op. cit., pp. 1172–5; Hewins, op. cit., p. 182. And see Longrigg, S. H., 'Iraq's Claim to Kuwait', *Royal Central Asian Journal*, 48 (1961), pp. 309–11.

[3] Ibid.   [4] See above, Chapter 5.

[5] In the Convention of 1913, the territory of Kuwait, as delimited in Articles 5 and 7, was recognised as 'an autonomous kaza of the Ottoman Empire'. And Turkey recognised the 1899 Agreement between Kuwait and Britain as well as the autonomous status of the Shaikh. See Hurewitz, I, pp. 270–2. And see Grohmann, op. cit., pp. 1172–5.

question arises whether Iraq had a legal right to annex her on this ground? This will now be examined below.

Succession of Iraq to the rights of the Ottoman Empire in Kuwait

The Iraqi Government's argument was that the new State of Iraq had succeeded to the former Turkish provinces of Mesopotamia, including Kuwait which then formed a sub-province of the *Wilayat* of Basrah.[1] What is the truth behind this statement? As stated earlier, the Ottoman Empire had not acquired any territorial sovereignty in Kuwait.[2] But even if it is assumed, for the sake of argument only, that Turkey had possessed a sovereign right over Kuwait, does it follow that Iraq, as a successor to the former Turkish *Wilayat* of Basrah, had legally succeeded to such a right over Kuwait? It is clear that when Turkey went to war with Britain in 1913, the then Ruler of Kuwait had no hesitation in declaring himself on the British side and taking an active part in the hostilities against the Turks in Basrah. Having thus declared himself at war with Turkey, he received in 1914 Britain's recognition of his country as 'an independent Government under British protection'.[3] Subsequently, Kuwait continued to enjoy this status until June 1961 when she became a fully independent State. Concerning Iraq, which succeeded to the former Turkish provinces of Mosul, Baghdad and Basrah, she was declared a British mandate on 3 May 1920. On 20 June 1920 an Arab Government was formed in Iraq under British advice, and on 11 July 1921 King Faisal I was declared by a Council of State as the Hashemite King of Iraq. On 23 August 1921 a new civil ministerial government was appointed by the King.[4] Finally, the British mandate system was liquidated on 28 January 1932, when Britain recommended the admission of Iraq to the League of Nations. Having fulfilled the conditions of 'statehood', in accordance with Article 22 of the Covenant of the League,[5] Iraq was, therefore, admitted on 3 October 1932 to membership of the League of Nations.[6] Consequently, whether the State of Iraq was legally established in 1921, when a civil government was formed, or in 1932, as a result of Iraq's admission to the League of Nations, she could not have succeeded in international law to former Turkish possessions without the limitations imposed by the peace treaties of 1920 and 1923. What were those limitations?

---

[1] *The Truth About Kuwait*, op. cit., pp. 4–5, 24–5.

[2] See above, p. 253. And see Longrigg, S. H., *Iraq, 1900–1950* (1953), p. 68: 'Shaikh Mubarak at Kuwayt maintained his delicate triple position of nominal Qa'immaqam, treaty-bound British protégé, and effectively independent ruler.'

[3] See above, Chapter 5.

[4] Ireland, P. W., Article on 'Iraq', *Encyclopaedia Britannica*, 12th ed. (1963), pp. 589–90.

[5] Hurewitz, II, pp. 61–2; *U.K.T.S.*, No. 11 (1920), *Cmd.* 964.

[6] Ireland's article on Iraq, op. cit., pp. 589–90.

The abortive treaty of Sèvres of 1920, and the treaty of Lausanne of 1923: following her defeat in the First World War, Ottoman Turkey negotiated and signed the peace treaty of Sèvres on 10 August 1920.[1] By Article 94 of this treaty 'Mesopotamia' and Syria were recognised 'as independent States, subject to the rendering of administrative advice and assistance' under Article 22 of the League Covenant. It was also agreed that the boundaries of the former Turkish possessions were to be determined subsequently by the parties concerned. But the treaty made no mention of Kuwait as being one of those Turkish possessions. Although this treaty was not ratified, it could, nevertheless, be regarded as forming valuable evidence as to the actual status of the boundaries of the then newly born State of Iraq. At any rate, with the conclusion of the Treaty of Lausanne of 24 July 1923,[2] which was a ratified treaty, the renunciation clauses of the treaty of Sèvres were embodied, in a revised form, in the former treaty. By Article 16 of the Treaty of Lausanne, it is stated:

Turkey hereby renounces all rights and titles whatsoever over or respecting the territories situated outside the frontiers laid down in the present Treaty and the islands other than those over which her sovereignty is recognised by the said Treaty, the future of these territories and islands being settled or to be settled by the parties concerned.

The above Article clearly shows that Turkey had renounced her rights to all Turkish possessions lying outside the frontiers of modern Turkey. The renunciation applied to Kuwait as being part of the former Turkish *Wilayat* of Basrah. Accordingly, by the Treaty of Lausanne of 1923, 'Turkey clearly had renounced all title to territory south of that prospective boundary'.[3] Furthermore, Article 27 of the treaty embodied provisions similar to those of Article 139 of the abortive treaty of Sèvres respecting Turkey's renunciation of all 'rights of suzerainty or jurisdiction' over nationals of territories which later came under the sovereignty or the protection of the foreign Powers which signed the treaty with Turkey. Consequently, it seems unwarranted to invoke the principles of state succession in support of the Iraqi claim to the territory of Kuwait, since Iraq, as a successor to former Turkish territories, was legally bound by the limitations imposed upon Turkey by the Treaty of Lausanne. In other words, if it is assumed that Ottoman Turkey had a sovereign title to Kuwait, Iraq could not have succeeded to that title because it was already

---

[1] Hurewitz, II, pp. 81–2; *U.K.T.S.*, No. 11 (1920), *Cmd.* 964.

[2] Hurewitz, II, pp. 119–20; *U.K.T.S.*, No. 16 (1923), *Cmd.* 1929.

[3] Wright, Quincy, 'The Mosul Dispute', *A.J.I.L.*, 20 (1926), p. 455. As a result of the settlement of the Iraqi-Turkish dispute over Mosul, the northern and southern boundaries of the new State of Iraq were definitely settled. See *P.C.I.J.*, Ser. B, No. 12, 21 November 1925, and *U.K.T.S.*, Miscellaneous, No. 17 (1925), *Cmd.* 2562.

surrendered by Turkey, in accordance with the provisions of the Treaty of Lausanne of 1923. Moreover, it is evident that after the liquidation of the Turkish Empire Iraq became subject to the mandatory system, under Article 22 of the Covenant of the League of Nations, while Kuwait remained, as before, a distinct territory under British protection.[1]

Continued maintenance of the claim

In order to establish the validity of her claim to Kuwait, Iraq should also be able to prove that this claim was not subsequently lost as a result of Iraq's past conduct towards Kuwait which could be construed as an 'acquiescence in the continued existence of Kuwait as a separate entity'.[2] Furthermore, the independent State of Iraq had already recognised in 1932 the present boundary limits of Kuwait by virtue of the Exchange of Letters of 21 July and 10 August 1932 between the then Prime Minister of Iraq, Nuri Pasha al-Said, and the former Ruler of Kuwait, Shaikh Ahmad Al-Sabah, respectively.[3] This Exchange of Letters of 1932 had, in fact, reaffirmed 'the existing frontier between Iraq and Koweit', the definition of which was already embodied in a former Exchange of Letters, dated 4 April and 19 April 1923, between Shaikh Ahmad Al-Sabah and Sir Percy Cox, the then British High Commissioner for Iraq, respectively.[4] Although the Iraq-Kuwait

[1] See Pillai, R. V., and Kumar, Mahendra, 'The Political and Legal Status of Kuwait', *I.C.L.Q.*, II (1962), pp. 128 et seq.

[2] Ibid. Evidence of tacit recognition by Iraq of Kuwait as a separate entity can be found in a number of inter-governmental correspondence which took place in the past between Iraq and Kuwait in relation to various commercial, economic and security matters. See *The Kuwaiti-Iraqi Crisis* op. cit., pp. 15–32 for reproduction of the texts of such correspondence. See also ibid., p. 7, for the list of names of the International Organisations to the membership of which Kuwait was admitted with the Iraqi Government's consent. And in particular, Iraq had sponsored Kuwait's application to join the International Telecommunication Union and the International Labour Organisation. See Gott, Richard, 'The Kuwait Incident', *Survey of International Affairs* (1961), p. 525.

[3] Great Britain, *The Pink Volume* (Foreign Office Unpublished Records) Containing the *Collection of Treaties and Engagements Relating to the Persian Gulf Shaikhdoms and the Sultanate of Muscat and Oman in Force up to the End of 1953*.

[4] The Exchange of Letters of 1923 is published in Aitchison, Document No. XLIII, p. 266. The definition of the Iraq–Kuwait frontier in the 1932 Letters, which is similar to that of the 1923 Letters, states the frontier line as follows:

'From the intersection of the Wadi-el-Audja with the Batin and thence northwards along the Batin to a point just south of the latitude of Safwan; thence eastwards passing south of Safwan wells, Jebel Sanam and Umm Qasr leaving them to Iraq and so on to the junction of the Khor Zobeir with the Khor Abdulla. The islands of Warbah, Bubiyan, Maskan (or Mashjan), Failakah, Auhah, Kubbar, Qaru and Umm-el-Maradim appertain to Koweit.'

See *Pink Volume*, op. cit. Note, in this connection, that although the 1932 Letters form, in practice, the basis for the Iraq–Kuwait border, however between 1938–58, the Government of Iraq objected to demarcating the frontier on this basis. It

boundary has actually remained undemarcated, the definition of the boundary contained in the Exchange of Letters of 1932 cannot, in the absence of an express agreement to the contrary, be deprived of its binding force upon the two parties. Moreover, so far as Iraq is concerned, the 1932 concord constitutes a valid estoppel to her claim to Kuwait.[1]

Conclusion

The preceding examination of the Iraqi claim to Kuwait helps to show the frivolousness of the claim. It is abundantly clear from this examination that such a claim does not stand legal analysis, simply because it is not a legal claim to territory in the real sense of the word. Throughout the period during which this claim assumed its seriousness—a period extending between 19 June 1961 and 8 February 1963—the Iraqi Government had failed to convince the nations of the world that it had a legally valid claim to territory.[2] In fact, the Iraqi claim to Kuwait was 'essentially' based on 'political arguments' which should be differentiated from 'legal arguments touching title' to territory.[3] This political claim, which like similar claims cannot withstand legal reasoning, was motivated by the personal ambition of General ʿAbd al-Karim Qasim, who was then head of the Iraqi Government. The collapse of the Qasim regime and its replacement on 8 February

---

maintained, *inter alia*, that the date of Nuri al-Said's letter on 21 July 1932 preceded the date of Iraq's full independence which coincided with the date of her admission to the League of Nations on 3 October. After 1958, the new Government of ʿAbd al-Karim Qasim did not publicly state its attitude towards these Letters. It is believed that the decision of the late Ruler of Kuwait not to 're-affirm formally his adherence to the Agreement would not legally prejudice Kuwait's claim that it remains valid'. Recently, the Governments of Iraq and Kuwait have agreed to re-open the question of the permanent demarcation of their frontier. It is understood that the British Government has advised Kuwait to take the 1932 line as a basis for any future negotiations with Iraq on this matter.

It seems doubtful that Iraq could be induced to abide by the 1932 Concord, since it recognises Kuwait's sovereignty over the Warbah and Bubiyan islands over which Iraq has laid claims. As regards Kuwait, it would appear that her reluctance to re-affirm publicly her position on the 1932 Concord indicates that she equally does not wish to be bound by it.

[1] See Oppenheim, pp. 147–8: 'The only legitimate occasions for implying recognition are (*a*) the conclusion of a bilateral treaty. . . .'

[2] See Gott, Richard, op. cit., pp. 519 et seq. In fact, in his news conference on 28 June 1961, the Iraqi Permanent Representative at the U.N., Adnan Pachachi, referred to Iraq's 'historic title' to Kuwait, but he failed to substantiate the legal grounds of the claim. See ibid., p. 530.

[3] See Jennings, Professor R. Y., *The Acquisition of Territory in International Law* (1963), p. 77.

1963 by a new revolutionary government had paved the way for the final relinquishment of the claim. This was achieved on 4 October 1963, when Iraq extended her official recognition of the sovereign status of Kuwait.[1]

[1] See above, pp. 251–2.

PART FOUR

BOUNDARY PROBLEMS

16

Disputes over land boundaries

A significant feature of the geographical structure of the Arabian Gulf States abutting on the eastern coast of Arabia is that, with the exception of Kuwait whose land boundaries only have been delimited by an international agreement,[1] they do not have completely defined land or sea boundaries.[2] Although this caused little or no trouble in the past, today, as a result of the operation of oil companies within the territories of these States, the interested parties have become anxious to delimit these boundaries and to settle the disputes arising from the present state of affairs.

The unsettled boundary disputes

(a) *The dispute between Qatar and Abu Dhabi over the location of Khaur al-ʿUdaid boundary and the dispute between Saudi Arabia, Qatar and Abu Dhabi over the demarcation of their common frontiers.* These triangular disputes are dealt with together because they involve overlapping claims by three States over a common coastal area.

In the dispute involving Qatar and Abu Dhabi, each party contends that *Khaur al-ʿUdaid*, an uninhabited inlet near the base of Qatar peninsula, lies within its frontier. The historical basis of this dispute has been explained earlier.[3] It suffices to say here, however, that Abu Dhabi's claim to this inlet derives its historical basis from the settlement made by some of the Ruler's subjects at some uncertain date between 1869 and 1880. These subjects were known as Bani Yas who later deserted the place and returned to Abu Dhabi. In the years which followed, the inlet of *Khaur al-ʿUdaid* remained virtually under the influence of the Turks, who established themselves in Hasa in 1871, and of the Qatar Rulers. However, in 1872 the British Government of India approved a decision taken by their Political Resident in the Gulf, Colonel Pelly, to the effect that the territory of Abu Dhabi extended down on the coast as far as the vicinity of *Khaur al-ʿUdaid*. Subsequently, the British Government frustrated attempts made by the Ruler of Qatar in the years 1880 to 1886 to recover that place, over

---

[1] For the 1922 Convention between Kuwait and Saudi Arabia, see Appendix VIII.

[2] It is to be noted that Bahrain offshore boundaries with Saudi Arabia have been defined by the Agreement of 22 February 1958, reference to which is provided below. But Bahrain still shares undefined boundaries with Qatar. Moreover, in December 1965 Saudi Arabia signed agreements with Qatar and Iran in which she defined her boundaries with these countries, as will be seen later.

[3] See above, p. 224.

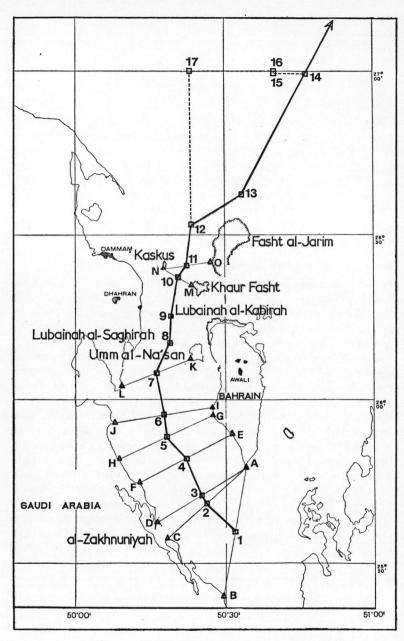

MAP 4: The Bahrain–Saudi Arabia boundary 1958

which Qatar has laid a claim.[1] The British Government has in the meantime made unsuccessful attempts to pave the way for a mutually agreed settlement of the Abu Dhabi–Qatar frontiers. It is assumed that the British Government would not object to 'the extension of the Qatar boundary south to the vicinity of al-ʿUdaid,' but without taking it in.[2]

As regards Saudi Arabia's boundary dispute with both Qatar and Abu Dhabi, the former 'claims the southern shore of the Arabian Gulf westerly from a point between al-Mughairah and al-Marfa on the coast of the Dhafrah to a point on the southeastern coast of the Qatar peninsula'.[3]

The British Government, acting on behalf of the Rulers of Abu Dhabi and Qatar, has contested this claim.[4] However, although the Qatar–Saudi Arabia boundary has been considered in dispute, recent reports indicate that an amicable settlement of the dispute has been reached by an agreement signed in December 1965, between the Crown Prince of Qatar, on behalf of the Government of Qatar, and the Saudi Minister of Petroleum, on behalf of the Saudi Government. The terms of the agreement have not been published, but they purport to delimit both the land and sea boundaries of the two countries. It is understood that the British Government—contrary to its usual practice in such matters affecting the foreign relations of one of its protected Rulers—did not apparently take part in the conclusion of this agreement.[5] It did, however, subsequently notify the Saudi Government that it does not recognise the validity of this agreement in so far as it affects the rights of a third party, namely, Abu Dhabi, over the territory demarcated.[6]

(b) *Boundary disputes of the Trucial Shaikhdoms:* These Shaikhdoms stretching eastwards from the base of the Qatar peninsula to the coast of the Gulf of Oman also have problems relating to their common frontiers. These problems are complicated by the fact that no recorded data exists about where the territory of each Shaikhdom begins and ends. Local investigation has been going on for some time by British experts with a view to the delimitation of the boundary of each Shaikhdom, but not much progress on this matter has so far been achieved.[7] Meanwhile, the Ruler of Abu Dhabi, for instance, claims

---

[1] Lorimer, pp. 766, 818–20; Hay, *The Persian Gulf States*, p. 107.

[2] Arabian American Oil Company, *Oman and the Southern Shore of the Persian Gulf* (1952) p. 185.

[3] Ibid. And see above, p. 200.   [4] Ibid. And see above, pp. 200–1.

[5] The agreement has not been published. For press reports, see *MEES*, No. 6, 10 December 1965.

[6] Information supplied to the author from a private source.

[7] Although tentative plans for the demarcation of the land and sea boundaries of the Trucial Shaikhdoms have been almost completed by the British Foreign

practically half of the present territory of neighbouring Dubai. Dubai, for her part, asserts ownership of part of the territory of Sharjah, her eastern neighbour.[1] But, according to Sir Rupert Hay, a former British Political Resident in the Gulf,

a substantial portion of the frontier between Abu Dhabi and Dubai has been defined, but the definition has only been accepted by one of the parties. The determination of the boundary between Dubai and Sharjah has also been taken in hand.[2]

The difficulties about determining the boundaries of these Shaikh-doms have been helpfully explained in the following statement:

For a long time the Foreign Office has been patiently trying to get them agreed, but the lines on the map remain tentatively dotted. No Ruler will make concessions when the pencil hovers over an area which he thinks might be the very spot to yield a millionaire's revenue.

Lately, a different approach has been made, rather more hopefully. Although the Shaikhs will not forego any of their claims against each other, it may be possible to persuade them to agree to disagree. Certain areas of the desert could then be marked as disputed, with the understanding that if oil were ever found there the revenue would be equally shared.[3]

The above description covers the principal boundary disputes among the Shaikhdoms stretching over the whole coast of eastern Arabia.[4]

The Kuwait–Saudi Arabia neutral zone as an example of interim settlement

Legal status

The status of the Kuwait–Saudi Arabia Neutral Zone is examined as an example of the way in which boundary problems have been settled without the drawing of a definitive frontier line.

The southern boundary of Kuwait with what was to become the Kingdom of Saudi Arabia was first demarcated by the Anglo-Turkish Convention of 29 July 1913,[5] but the outbreak of World War I prevented the ratification of this Convention. Subsequently, when the

---

Office, these boundaries still give rise to some concern, due to the rulers' indecision about the precise limits of their boundary claims.

[1] Hay, Sir R., 'The Persian Gulf States and their Boundary Problems', *Geographical Journal*, vol. 120 (1954), p. 439.   [2] Ibid.

[3] See *The Daily Telegraph*, 19 August 1954. The above-mentioned arrangement, if proved successful, contemplates the establishment of a number of neutral zones similar to that of Kuwait–Saudi Arabia.

[4] In addition, there are the boundaries between Muscat and the Trucial Coast on the north and Muscat and the Aden Protectorate on the extreme south. These boundaries still remain undefined. See Hay, op. cit., pp. 3–4 and art. cit., *Geographical Journal*, p. 440.   [5] See above, pp. 218–19.

British Government recognised Saudi Arabia in 1915, as an independent State, the problem of settling her boundaries arose again.
After negotiations by Sir Percy Cox, representing the British Government, with the late King ʿAbd al-ʿAziz ibn Saʿud a compromise settlement was reached by which a neutral zone of 2000 square miles was
established.[1] This settlement is incorporated in the ʿUqair Convention
of 2 December 1922. This convention provides as follows:

> The frontier between Najd and Kuwait begins in the West from the
> junction of the Wadi al Aujah (W. al Audja) with the Batin (El Batin),
> leaving Raqi (Rakai) to Najd, from this point it continues in a straight line
> until it joins latitude 29° and the red semi-circle referred to in Article 5 of
> the Anglo-Turkish Agreement of 29th July 1913. The line then follows the
> side of the red semi-circle until it reaches a point terminating (sic) on the
> coast south of Ras al-Qaliah (Ras el Kaliyah) and this is the indisputable
> southern frontier of Kuwait territory. The portion of territory bounded on
> the North by this line and which is bounded on the West by a low moun-
> tainous ridge called Shaq (Esh Shakk) and on the East by the sea and on
> the South by a line passing from West to East from Shaq (Esh Shakk) to
> Ain al Abd (Ain el Abd) and thence to the coast north of Ras al Mishab
> (Ras Mishaab), in this territory the Government of Najd and Kuwait will
> share equal rights until through the good offices of the Government of
> Great Britain a further agreement is made between Najd and Kuwait
> concerning it.[2]

It is noticeable that the above convention, by providing for 'a
further agreement' on the frontier, has in fact amounted to creating a
modus vivendi by which the parties concerned could exploit on an
equal basis the natural resources of the zone pending a permanent
settlement. This interpretation is evident not merely from the provisions of the convention itself, but also from the fact that the frontier
defined by the convention had not been demarcated on the ground.[3]

Meanwhile, this convention constitutes the only document which
defines the legal position of Kuwait and Saudi Arabia in the Neutral
Zone. It thus provides that

> . . . in this territory the Governments of Najd and Kuwait will share equal
> rights until through the good offices of the Government of Great Britain
> a further agreement is made between Najd and Kuwait concerning it.

---

[1] For a verbal account of the negotiations at the Conference of ʿUqair, see
Dickson, op. cit., pp. 274–7. And see Longrigg, op. cit., pp. 214–16.

[2] Aitchison, pp. 213–14. The convention was signed on behalf of Kuwait by the
British Political Agent of Kuwait. It is to be noted that the ʿUqair convention was
closely related to the Treaty of Muhammarah, dated 5 May 1922, between Saudi
Arabia and Iraq. The Protocol attached to this treaty, which bears the same date
as that of the ʿUqair convention, set up another Neutral Zone between Saudi Arabia
and Iraq on the same principles applied in drawing the Kuwait–Saudi Arabia
Neutral Zone boundaries. For the Treaty of Muhammarah and its Protocol, see
Aitchison, pp. 208–12 and Appendix VIII below.

[3] Hay, art. cit., *Geographical Journal*, p. 435.

The question arises whether the words 'in this territory the Governments of Najd and Kuwait will share equal rights' could be construed as meaning the establishment of co-sovereignty over the zone. The words are so general that they could in fact be interpreted as meaning that the two governments should 'share equal rights' not only in the ownership of the natural resources of the zone, but also in its administration. However, the convention itself does not provide for the establishment of a constitutional system or joint administration in the zone. Nor does there exist today any system of joint administration in the zone. This is, probably, because the zone has remained, at least before the inception of oil operations, an isolated and an uninhabited area.[1] Now that a number of oil companies are operating both on the land and the offshore of the zone, it should assume a greater importance than it used to have prior to the discovery of oil. It is therefore necessary to define more clearly the legal status of the zone.

The position of the Kuwait–Saudi Arabia Neutral Zone may be likened to that of a condominium arrangement[2] in which both Kuwait and Saudi Arabia enjoy an equal right of undivided sovereignty over the zone. Upon the manner in which this joint sovereignty is exercised, the Agreement of 1922, as explained above, does not shed any light. Moreover, until mid-1965, no attempt was made to establish a joint authority responsible for the administration of the zone. However, the great interest centred on the zone recently as a result of the growth of oil operations in the area, has given rise to some legal problems.

---

[1] See Longrigg, op. cit., pp. 214–16. According to the writer, even 'the definitions (of the Convention) leave much room for dispute'. But see below, p. 271, where for the first time in the history of the Zone a system of separate administration has been established.

[2] Dr Jessup defines a 'condominium' as a 'political device . . . used for sharing among two or three states the governing powers over a particular area.' See Jessup, P. C., and Taubenfeld, H. J., *Control for Outer Space and the Antarctic Analogy* (1959), p. 11.

It may be helpful to cite two examples of condominium arrangements, namely (a) the former Anglo-Egyptian Sudan, and (b) the New Hebrides. As to (a), the Anglo-Egyptian condominium over the Sudan derived its status from an Agreement dated 19 January 1899. This Agreement established joint Anglo-Egyptian military and civil command in the Sudan. (For the legal status of the Anglo-Egyptian Sudan before the declaration of the independence of the Sudan in January, 1956, see *British and Foreign State Papers*, vol. 91 (1898–9), pp. 19–22. And see O'Rourke, V. A., *The Juristic Status of Egypt and the Sudan* (1935), pp. 142–70. See also Jessup, op. cit., p. 20.)

As to (b), the condominium over the New Hebrides was established by an Agreement, dated 6 August 1914, concluded between Britain and France. This provided for joint sovereignty over the 'Group of the New Hebrides' and over the native population. It also provided for a separate jurisdiction to be exercised by each signatory Power over its own subjects. (For the legal status of the New Hebrides, see *Treaty Series*, No. 7 (1922), Cmd. 1681. And see Hackworth, vol. I op. cit., pp. 56–8; Oppenheim, pp. 452–4.)

Legal problems

(a) *The grant of oil concessions*

Practice has shown that the concession agreements concluded by Kuwait and Saudi Arabia, separately, with foreign oil companies in respect of their own territories did not include the Neutral Zone area.[1] Both Kuwait and Saudi Arabia granted separate concession agreements to oil companies in respect of their undivided half shares in the Zone. Thus, in June 1948, Kuwait signed an agreement with American Independent Oil Company, and in February 1949, Saudi Arabia signed an agreement with Pacific Western Corporation. These agreements covered the land territories of the Zone.[2] Similarly in 1957 and 1958, both Governments granted to the Japanese Arabian Oil Company separate concessions in respect of the offshore areas of the Zone.

It can be deduced from this practice that the conception of joint sovereignty over the Neutral Zone, as conceived in the Agreement of 1922, did not prevent either Kuwait or Saudi Arabia from granting separate concession agreements to different companies in respect of each country's undivided share in the Neutral Zone. In other words, it was not regarded as necessary for Kuwait and Saudi Arabia to conclude a joint concession agreement in respect of their 'equal rights' in the Zone.

A further implication of this practice seems to be that in a case where Saudi Arabia alone, for instance, grants a concession to a foreign company in respect of her own share in the Zone, the validity, or the operation, of this concession does not appear to be conditional on another agreement being concluded by Kuwait with the same, or a different, company. Thus the Saudi Arabian Japanese Offshore Agreement of 10 December 1957[3] came into effect from the date of its

---

[1] It is to be noted, as an exception to this practice, that in her Agreement of 1933 with Aramco, Saudi Arabia specifically mentioned, in Article 3 of the Agreement, the Neutral Zone as an area to which the preferential rights of exploitation of oil granted to the Company should apply. (See *Umm al-Qura* Semi-official gazette, 14 and 21 July 1933.) However, this right was abandoned by the Company in 1948, when the Shaikh of Kuwait secured more favourable terms by his Agreement of 1948 with American Independent Company, as will be explained below.

[2] See Shwadran, B., *The Middle East Oil and the Great Powers* (1956), p. 393. According to the writer, the two American companies 'worked out an agreement between them' for the joint exploitation of oil in the zone. And quoting from the *New York Times* of 6 August 1947 the writer says that 'early in August, 1947, it was reported that King Ibn Saud and the Shaikh of Kuwait had agreed to share the income from any oil discovered in the neutral zone'.

[3] For text, see *The Petroleum Times*, suppl. to vol. LXII, No. 1579, 14 February 1958.

publication in the Saudi Arabian gazette.[1] No reservation was made in the agreement that its coming into force was dependent on the signing by Kuwait of another agreement with the same, or a different, company. At the same time the agreement did provide for its implementation whether or not Kuwait concluded an agreement with the Japanese or any other company. For instance, article 28 provided for subscription by Saudi Arabia to 20 per cent of the shares of the company, in the case where the company did not acquire concessions from Kuwait in respect of her undivided share. The same article also provided that, in the absence of an agreement with the Shaikh of Kuwait in respect of his share, the 'Government shall be entitled to nominate one third of the board of directors'.

As a final word on the legal consequences of concluding an agreement by Saudi Arabia in respect of her share in the Neutral Zone, without a similar agreement being concluded with Kuwait, it may be useful to cite the following comment:

In theory and, indeed, legally, there seems nothing to prevent the Saudi Japanese Agreement from being fully implemented even if no parallel agreement with Kuwait is forthcoming. Several of its Articles, as may be seen, are drafted so as to make provision for that contingency. But nevertheless, if the Japan Petroleum Trading Co. Ltd. were to operate in respect of 'an undivided one-half interest in and to the offshore (outside territorial waters) of the Neutral Territory lying between Saudi Arabia and Kuwait' (Article 1) over which the Kingdom of Saudi Arabia has sovereignty, without any parallel agreement with Kuwait—which has exactly the same sovereignty over exactly the same area—the situation might prove very awkward in practice. For 'an undivided one-half interest' means precisely what it says. It is a half interest in the whole of an area not divided up into halves; it is a half interest in a whole, not a whole interest in a half. Imagine a situation in which Kuwait wanted submarine drilling to be conducted in exactly the same locality in which the Japan Petroleum Trading Co. was already drilling or about to drill—or drilling taking place there before it could do so, under an agreement concluded by Kuwait with some company other than the Japanese one. Both would be there by equal right. Co-sovereignty by States in undivided shares over land may differ in some respects from individuals' tenancy of land in undivided shares . . .[2]

The problems raised in this comment on the over-lapping of concession agreements in the Neutral Zone have now become hypothetical owing to the fact that the same Japanese Company—the Arabian Oil Company—has secured a similar Agreement dated 5 July 1958 with Kuwait in respect of her own undivided one-half share in the area.[3]

[1] The Petroleum Times, comment on the 'An Undivided One-half Share Interest', vol. LXII, No. 1579, 14 February 1958, p. 111.

[2] The Petroleum Times, op. cit., p. 111.

[3] For text, see Kuwait Al-Yawm (Government of Kuwait's official gazette), No. 181, 13 July 1958.

Recognition of joint sovereignty by Kuwait and Saudi Arabia over the Neutral Zone is clearly given in the Offshore Agreements of 1957 and 1958, in the following manner:

1. The preambles of both agreements provide that the agreements in question are concluded subject to the provisions of the Convention of 2 December 1922 providing for sovereignty by Kuwait and Saudi Arabia over equal shares in the Neutral Zone.

2. Article 4 of the Kuwait Agreement, dated 5 July 1958, provides for equal sharing in the profits of the Zone in the following terms:

One half of all Petroleum produced within the Concession Area shall be deemed to have been produced from the Shaikh's undivided one half share in the Petroleum resources in the said Area and one half shall be deemed to have been produced from the undivided one half share therein belonging to the Government of the Kingdom of Saudi Arabia.

3. Article 22 of the Kuwait agreement and Article 33 of the Saudi Arabian agreement provide for police protection and guards for the company, its employees, and its installations and property in the concession area. Such police protection is, however, not provided conjointly by the Governments of both Kuwait and Saudi Arabia.

4. Article 29B of the Kuwait agreement and Article 50 of the Saudi Arabian agreement provide for the hoisting of the flag of each respective country within the concessionary area.

5. Articles 24 and 25 of the Kuwait agreement and Article 56 of the Saudi Arabian agreement provide that upon the termination of the concessions all properties and installations within and without the concession area shall be owned or bought jointly by Kuwait and Saudi Arabia.

(b) *The conclusion of treaties*

There can be no real doubt that neither Kuwait nor Saudi Arabia can unilaterally bind the Neutral Zone by individual treaty action, though each State can of course conclude treaties which affect only its own rights there.[1] Treaties can apply to the Neutral Zone only with the consent and agreement of both Kuwait and Saudi Arabia. The case of the Neutral Zone in this respect may be compared to that of

[1] Practice has shown that treaties concluded by Saudi Arabia did not specifically refer to the Neutral Zone. E.g., see the Treaty of Jiddah, 20 May 1927. (Aitchison, p. 227.) As regards Kuwait, it may be interesting to ask whether the British Government's treaty of protection with Kuwait of 1899 applied to the Neutral Zone area which owed its existence to an agreement concluded in 1922? In view of the provisions of the Kuwait Orders in Council of 1925–59, which until 1961 applied to Kuwait, it seems that the British Government had actually assumed the right of protection over the area of the Neutral Zone in so far as this protection affected the rights, properties and nationals of the Shaikh of Kuwait in the Zone. (See *Persian Gulf Gazette*, suppl. no. 25, Aug. 1959.)

the Anglo-Egyptian Sudan, with the main exception that the latter had an autonomous government distinct from Egypt and Great Britain.[1] The Neutral Zone, on the other hand, has no separate government distinct from the Governments of Kuwait and Saudi Arabia. It forms an undivided part of the territories of both Governments.

Furthermore, it follows from the above principle regarding the application of treaties to the Neutral Zone, that treaties, even if concluded between the Governments of Kuwait and Saudi Arabia, do not apply to the said Zone, unless such intention is expressly provided for in these treaties. This contention may find support in the Agreement for Extradition of Offenders, concluded on 20 April 1942 between the Governments of Saudi Arabia and Kuwait.[2] Article 8 of this agreement expressly provides for its application to the Neutral Zone in these terms:

> The provisions of this Agreement shall apply to the area on the Nejd–Koweit Frontier hereinafter termed the Neutral Zone, whose limits were laid down in the Protocol of Uqair, dated the 2nd of December, 1922 . . .

As the provisions of the above agreement also have some bearing on the exercise of jurisdiction in the Neutral Zone, it will be more convenient to discuss them under the next heading.

(c) *The exercise of jurisdiction*

The above Extradition Agreement of 1942 sheds some light on the manner in which jurisdiction in the Neutral Zone may be exercised by both Kuwait and Saudi Arabia. This agreement provides that each country can exercise separate jurisdiction over its own nationals in the Neutral Zone without affecting the rights of the other country. (There seems to be no innovation in this arrangement, since the condominium Agreement of the New Hebrides of 1914 provided for a similar arrangement of separate jurisdiction.)[3] The relevant terms of the agreement, in so far as it affects jurisdiction over Kuwaiti and Saudi offenders fleeing from or into the Neutral Zone, are as follows:

> Art. 8 (1) Where an offence, as defined in Article 3 of this Agreement, has been committed in either of the two territories and the offender has fled to the Neutral Zone, the offender shall be deemed to be still within the territory in which the offence was committed, and may be arrested and tried by the Government thereof.
>
> (2) Where an offence, as defined in Article 3 of this Agreement, has been committed in the Neutral Zone and the offender escapes to the territory

---

[1] As a result of the Treaty of 1899, the Anglo-Egyptian Sudan became 'an autonomous government absolutely distinct from' the Governments of Britain and Egypt. Thus the power to conclude treaties for the Sudan was vested, solely, with the Governor-General of the Government of the Anglo-Egyptian Sudan. See O'Rourke, op. cit., pp. 155–7.

[2] For reference, see above, p. 103.   [3] See above, p. 266, n. 2.

of the Government of which he is a national, he shall be deemed to have committed the offence within the territory of his own Government and shall be liable to arrest and trial by that Government.

(3) Where an offence, as defined in Article 3 of this Agreement, has been committed in the Neutral Zone, and offender being a national of one of the two Governments, escapes into the territory of the other, he shall be deemed to have committed the offence within the territory of the Government of which he is a national, and shall be liable to extradition proceedings under this Agreement.

It is noteworthy that the above article of the agreement does not expressly provide for the application of the procedure in its paragraphs 2 and 3 to foreign nationals who commit non-political offences in the Neutral Zone. One way of solving this problem would be to subject such foreign nationals, for the purpose of article 8, to the jurisdiction of the country under whose auspices they had originally entered the Neutral Zone.[1]

Joint or separate administration

Problems relating to the administration of the Neutral Zone assumed greater importance after the granting of the offshore concessions of 1957–8 to the Japanese Arabian Oil Company. Consequently, as a result of the influx of workers and employees of the oil companies to the Neutral Zone, Kuwait and Saudi Arabia found it necessary to hold joint discussions aimed at finding a workable solution for the administration of the Zone. The two parties, therefore, held a series of negotiations encompassing the general legal status of the Neutral Zone and its offshore area. These negotiations were continued, intermittently, until July 1965 when the two parties finally concluded an agreement in which they agreed to partition the territory of the Neutral Zone into two equal parts, with each party annexing to its own territory one part of the partitioned Zone. The following is a general description of these developments.

The Period of Negotiations on the Status of the Zone: The first important round of negotiations on the general problems of the Neutral Zone took place in 1960, when at the end of that year the two Governments agreed on the following resolutions: That each country shall appoint an expert committee which shall draw tentative boundary lines for the Zone; that the Zone shall, in principle, be divided into two geographical parts so that one part can be annexed by Kuwait and the other by Saudi Arabia; and that the question relating to the ownership of the two islands of Qaru and Umm al-Maradim shall be temporarily set aside, pending the settlement of the onshore and offshore boundaries of the Zone. Then there was a break in the chain of

---

[1] But see below, p. 273, for the provisions of the 1965 Agreement.

negotiations.[1] During this period, the Kuwaiti authorities lodged complaints against the Saudis who were accused of an extensive control of administration in the Zone, to the detriment of the Kuwaiti right of equal share in such administration. According to some reports, the number of workers in the Zone in 1962 was estimated at 4000. The Saudis formed 55 per cent of this working force; other Arabs were 25 per cent and the rest were foreigners, while there was not a single Kuwaiti national working in the Zone. Kuwaiti authorities also complained that labour disputes were being settled in accordance with Saudi labour laws, irrespective of the nationalities of the workers or the country from which they originally entered the Zone. Moreover, they accused the Saudi authorities of sending directions to the oil companies in the Zone requiring that each company should employ not less than 75 per cent of Saudi workers. Consequently, the Kuwaitis took certain measures aimed at strengthening their administrative authority in the Zone, such as establishing new governmental offices in the Zone similar to those already established by the Saudis.[2] Such unilateral actions on both sides had naturally complicated the system of administration in the Zone. As Kuwait was also anxious to settle the question of the islands of Qaru and Umm al-Maradim, she therefore offered sometime in 1961 to share equally with Saudi Arabia any future oil proceeds accruing from the two islands, provided that Saudi Arabia conceded their ownership to Kuwait. The Saudi Government, however, preferred to defer this matter until the two parties reached a final settlement on the demarcation of both the land and sea boundaries of the Neutral Zone.[3]

As regards the land area of the Zone, it appears that at a conference held in Kuwait, the two parties agreed, in principle, on the manner of drawing the boundary line. It was also reported at the time that the Saudis submitted to their Kuwaiti counterparts a plan for establishing a system of joint administration in the Zone. This plan contemplated the establishment of an administrative council in the Zone, composed of two Saudis and two Kuwaitis who would be responsible directly to the Governments of Saudi Arabia and Kuwait, respectively. The administrative Council reserved governmental powers in all fields (i.e., security, justice, immigration, etc.). Further, the two Governments were to appoint an equal number of judges and officials in the Zone. In short, the plan purported to establish a real condominium system in the Zone. However, the Kuwaiti Government rejected the above Saudi plan as being complicated and impractical. It took the view that the Neutral Zone should be divided into two separate areas

---

[1] *MEES*, No. 17, 28 February and No. 19, 13 March 1964; *MEES*, 27 March 1964.

[2] The author's private notes. And see *MEES*, 28 February, 13 and 27 March 1964.   [3] *MEES*, No. 6, 13 September 1963.

and that each Government should administer one such area. After further discussions, the Saudis agreed to the Kuwaiti suggestion respecting the division of administration in the Zone and in August 1963 it was reported that the parties had reached agreement on the principle of the division of the Zone.[1] Further top level discussions were later held between the two parties on the problem of the division of the Neutral Zone and on other related problems, such as the demarcation of the Zone's offshore boundaries and the status of Qaru and Umm al-Maradim islands.[2] Following talks on these points, it was revealed that the two Governments initialled on 8 March 1964 an agreement by which the Neutral Zone was to be divided between them into two equal parts, for administrative purposes, without, however, affecting the existing arrangement under the ʿUqair Convention of 1922 respecting the equal participation of natural resources in the Zone.[3] This agreement did not cover the other two questions relating to the demarcation of the Zone's offshore and the status of the islands. These questions were regarded as 'purely legal questions' which should be studied by 'a conciliation commission of impartial legal experts which would be asked to recommend a suitable solution to the two governments'.[4]

The Kuwait-Saudi Arabia Agreement to partition the neutral zone, signed on 7 July 1965[5]

According to this agreement, the parties have agreed to put an end to the temporary state of affairs prevailing under the Convention of ʿUqair of 2 December 1922,

by means of partitioning that Zone into two sections, so that the one shall be annexed to the State of Kuwait and the other shall be annexed to the Kingdom of Saudi Arabia, provided that these equal rights of the two parties shall be preserved in full in the whole partitioned Zone as this had originally been decided by the Convention made at Al Uqair that it is shared between the two parties, and shall be safeguarded by the provisions of international responsibility. . . . (The Preamble)

---

[1] *MEES*, No. 44, 6 September 1963.

[2] MEES, No. 17, 28 February 1964.

[3] *MEES*, No. 22, 3 April 1964. And see ibid., 13 and 27 March 1964. The Neutral Zone Agreement of 8 March 1964 was ratified by the Saudi Arabian Council of Ministers on 1 April 1964, and by the Kuwaiti Council of Ministers on 23 March 1964.

[4] *MEES*, No. 19, 13 March 1964. For further useful information on these matters, see ibid., 28 February 1964.

[5] For the Arabic text of the agreement, see *Umm al-Qura*, No. 2132, dated 18 Rabi II 1386 (5 August 1966). And see Appendix XII for non-official translation supplied by Dr S. Hosni, a former legal adviser, Ministry of Foreign Affairs, Kuwait.

T

The relevant provisions of the agreement are:

The boundary line between the two sections of the Zone is to be the line which divides them into two equal parts and which begins from a point at the mid eastern shore on the low-tide line, and ends at the western boundary line of the Zone . . . (Art. I)

Without prejudice to the provisions of this agreement, the part lying to the north of the line dividing the Partitioned Zone into two equal parts shall be annexed to Kuwait as *an integral* part of its territory, and the part lying to the south of the line . . . shall be annexed to the Kingdom of Saudi Arabia . . . (Art. II)[1]

Each of the Contracting Parties shall exercise the rights of administration, legislation and defence over that part of the Partitioned Zone annexed to his territory in the same manner exercised in his territory of origin while observing other provisions of the agreement, and without prejudice to the rights of the contracting parties to natural resources in the whole of the Partitioned Zone. (Art. III)

The same rights exercised by each party over his annexed part of the Zone also apply to the territorial sea which adjoins that part. For the purpose of exploiting the natural resources in the Partitioned Zone, it is agreed that the territorial sea adjoining that Zone shall be fixed at 'six marine miles'.[2] It is also agreed that the boundary line separating the 'territorial waters' which adjoin the 'Partitioned Zone' shall be determined in future by agreement (Art. VII).

As regards the 'northern boundary' of the submarine areas adjacent to the Partitioned Zone, 'it shall be delineated as if the Zone has not been partitioned and without regard to the provisions of this agreement'. And, 'unless the two parties agree otherwise', they 'shall exercise their equal rights' in the exploitation of natural resources in these submarine areas beyond the six-mile limit (Art. VIII).

The agreement does not alter or affect, in any way, the status of the existing oil concessions in the Zone which shall continue in force (Art. XI). And it guarantees freedom of work to citizens of both parties in either part of the Partitioned Zone (Art. XV).

In order to safeguard the continued efforts of the two parties in exploiting the natural resources in the Partitioned Zone, 'a joint permanent Committee shall be set up . . .' to which shall be entrusted such functions. This Committee shall be composed of an equal number of Kuwaitis and Saudis (Arts XVII–XIX).

The question of amending oil concessions or granting new oil concessions in the Partitioned Zone, including its offshore area, shall be subject to a joint decision by the two competent Ministers of Petroleum (Art. XX).

---

[1] The Arabic text of the agreement does not contain the above italicised words.
[2] The adoption of the 6-mile limit for the zone is an exception to the official 12-mile limit adopted by Saudi Arabia for her own territorial sea; see below, p. 281.

The agreement also contains an arbitration clause and a provision for the reference of disputes arising from the parties' obligations under it to the International Court of Justice for examination and adjudication under the Court's procedure. The Court's judgment shall be binding upon the two parties (Art. XXII).

If either party refuses to implement the judgment made in accordance with the above article, the other party shall be relieved from its obligations under the agreement (Art. XXII).

Finally, the agreement shall enter into force on the date of the exchange of instruments of ratification (Art. XXIII).

The above agreement received constitutional sanction under the law of Saudi Arabia by virtue of the Royal Decree No. 3, dated 11 July 1965, and it was approved by the Kuwaiti National Assembly on 4 June 1966. In accordance with the provision of Article XXIII, Kuwaiti and Saudi representatives exchanged the instruments of ratification of the agreement at Jiddah on 25 July 1966.[1]

It is noteworthy that the above agreement contains a novel arrangement by virtue of which the Neutral Zone territory could be divided geographically into two equal parts, with each part being subject to one distinct sovereignty, while still retaining its condominium status under a joint sovereignty for the purpose of exploiting its natural resources.

It is clear from the provisions of this agreement that the parties to it were primarily concerned with finding a satisfactory and practical solution to the problems arising from the absence of a joint administrative machinery in the Zone that could, effectively and satisfactorily, represent the parties' equal rights and interests in the area. Consequently, the parties, having failed to agree upon a joint administrative system in the Zone (a kind of condominium) to represent their joint authority there, decided to divide the whole area of the Zone equally between them, with each party annexing as part of its own territory that equal portion of the Zone which is contiguous to its frontier.

Accordingly, the part of the partitioned Zone lying to the north of the dividing line became part of the original territory of the State of Kuwait and the part lying to the south of that line became part of the original territory of the Kingdom of Saudi Arabia (Art. II). Each State retains in the portion of the Zone attached to its original territory exclusive rights of 'administration, legislation and defence'. The exercise of these rights by either Party shall, however, not affect, in any manner, the 'equal rights' of both contracting parties in respect of the exploitation of natural resources (at present these are taken to mean oil) of the whole Zone, notwithstanding the partition (Art. III).

Measures for the exploitation of these natural resources from the whole Neutral Zone, including its territorial sea and the offshore area

[1] See *Umm al-Qura*, 5 August 1966, op. cit.

contiguous to it, shall be entrusted to 'a Joint Permanent Committee' to be formed from 'an equal number of representatives of the two contracting Parties' (Arts. XVII–XVIII).

While agreeing that the present oil concessions in respect of both the onshore and offshore areas of the Neutral Zone shall continue in full force, the position with regard to 'granting or amending any new concession relating to shared natural resources', in future, shall be subject to joint consultation by the two competent Ministers of Petroleum in both countries, who are authorised to take, through the medium of the 'Joint Permanent Committee' over which they preside, the appropriate measures in all such matters (Arts. XV–XX).

It may be submitted that the emphasis in the provisions of this agreement on the 'equal rights' of the contracting parties in the Neutral Zone as a whole clearly indicates that the legal status of this territory still continues, as in the past, to be based on the 1922 Convention; the 1965 Agreement has, it would seem, by no means affected the legal status of this territory as a separate entity subject to the joint sovereignty of both Kuwait and Saudi Arabia. Furthermore, although the agreement provides, under the provisions of Articles I and II, for the annexation of one part of the Zone to Kuwait and the other to Saudi Arabia, it is clear that the restrictions imposed by subsequent provisions of the agreement on the exercise of the sovereign rights attached to each section of the partitioned Zone have greatly diminished the legal effects of such annexation.[1] These restrictions are contained in Articles V and XXII of the agreement. According to Article V, either party 'shall be relieved of its obligations under this Agreement' in the case that the other party 'cedes or otherwise alienates all or part of the said equal rights ... which are exercised over any part of the partitioned Zone, to any other State. . . .' Also Article XXII, which deals with questions giving rise to arbitration and other related matters, states that 'if one of the parties refuses to abide by the judgment made against it, the other party shall be relieved from its obligations under this Agreement'. Consequently, should either of the contracting parties act contrary to the provisions of these two articles, the other party

[1] The arrangement made under the 1965 Agreement may be analogous to a cession of territory, or a piece of shared territory. The legal form in which a cession 'can be effected is an agreement embodied in a treaty between the ceding and the acquiring State.' (See Oppenheim, p. 548.) But the arrangement in respect of the Neutral Zone does not specifically fall within this concept, since 'the object of cession is sovereignty over such territory as has hitherto already belonged to another State.' (See Oppenheim, op. cit.) In the case of the Zone, the joint sovereignty attached to the territory has not been completely relinquished in respect of either part of the divided Zone. Therefore, it may be argued that what has been ceded in the case of the partitioned Zone is 'the exercise of sovereignty rather than sovereignty itself.' (See Oppenheim, p. 549, note 7, in reference to certain cases of 'leases'.)

would be entitled unilaterally to denounce the present agreement and the arrangements made under it. And once the 1965 Agreement falls to the ground, the annexation of the two parts of the Zone becomes null and void and the two parties would have to revert to the 1922 Convention.

At any rate, the 1965 Agreement has greatly alleviated the enormous administrative and jurisdictional difficulties which had, for many years past, hindered the co-Partners from exercising their sovereign rights in the Zone on an equal basis. Moreover, the significance of this agreement lies in the fact that it opens the door to a new era of full co-operation between the two neighbouring Arab States in matters relating to the future exploitation of natural resources in the Zone.

17

Disputes over the determination of submarine boundaries in the Arabian Gulf

The practice of the littoral Arab States of the Gulf: The Saudi Royal Pronouncement and the Proclamations of the Shaikhdoms respecting their offshore boundaries, 1949

Following President Truman's Proclamation of 1945,[1] each of Saudi Arabia and the nine Arab Shaikhdoms abutting on the Arabian Gulf issued proclamations in which they individually defined their future policies respecting the natural resources of the sea-bed and sub-soil of the offshore areas contiguous to their coasts. Saudi Arabia was the first Arab Kingdom which by the Royal Pronouncement of 28 May 1949[2] claimed that the sea-bed and sub-soil areas of the Gulf contiguous to her coasts are 'subject to her jurisdiction and control'. The boundaries of such areas, the Pronouncement continued, 'will be determined, in accordance with equitable principles, by our Government in agreement with other states having jurisdiction and control over the sub-soil and sea-bed of adjoining areas'.[3] Soon after the Saudi Pronouncement each of Bahrain, Kuwait, Qatar and six Shaikhdoms of the Trucial Coast issued proclamations in which they asserted their rights to the offshore areas contiguous to the coasts of their territories. These proclamations were all issued in June 1949,[4] in the following chronological order: Bahrain, 5 June; Qatar, 8 June; Abu Dhabi, 10 June; Kuwait, 12 June; Dubai, 14 June; Sharjah, 16 June; Ras al-Khaimah, 17 June; Ajman, 20 June; and Umm al-Qaiwain, June (no definite date).

[1] For United States' Proclamation of 28 September 1945, see *U.N.L.S.*, 1951, p. 39. In this Proclamation the United States Government declared that 'the natural resources of the subsoil and seabed of the continental shelf beneath the high seas but contiguous to the coasts of the United States' were to be considered as 'appertaining to the United States and subject to her jurisdiction and control'. For a legal analysis of the subject. see Young, R., 'The Legal Status of Submarine Areas Beneath the High Seas', *A.J.I.L.*, 45 (1951), p. 225.

[2] For the English text of the Pronouncement of 28 May 1949, see *A.J.I.L.*, Suppl., 43 (1949), p. 154. For a useful commentary on the Saudi Pronouncement, see Young, R., 'Saudi Arabian Offshore Legislation', *A.J.I.L.*, 43 (1949), p. 530. There the writer points out that unlike the United States' Proclamation, the Saudi Pronouncement declares 'the seabed and subsoil (and not merely the resources therein)' to be subject to Saudi Arabian jurisdiction and control. See n. 1 above.

[3] Ibid.

[4] For the English texts of the Proclamations of the Arabian Gulf Shaikhdoms, see *U.N.L.S.*, High Seas, vol. I (1951), pp. 22–30.

The proclamations issued by the Gulf Shaikhdoms, under British auspices, are all similar, if not identical. In issuing them, the Rulers were, no doubt, encouraged by the great hopes of the existence of great oil deposits beneath the high sea waters of the Gulf. In order to form a clear view about the main issues involved in these proclamations, the following operative paragraphs of the Bahrain Proclamation may be quoted, as an example:

... Whereas the right of any coastal government to exercise its sovereignty over the natural resources of the sea-bed and the sub-soil in the vicinity of its shores has been established by international practice through the action taken by other governments ...

We ... the Ruler of Bahrain hereby declare that the sea-bed and the sub-soil of the high seas of the Persian Gulf bordering on the territorial waters of Bahrain and extending seaward as far as limits that we, after consultation with neighbouring governments, shall determine more accurately in accordance with the principles of justice, when the occasion so requires, belong to the country of Bahrain and are subject to its absolute authority and jurisdiction.[1]

The above proclamations represented at the time a new development of claims to large portions of the sea-bed and sub-soil of the Arabian Gulf lying beyond the territorial seas of the countries concerned.[2]

(a) Common features of the Proclamations of 1949

The Proclamations of the Arabian Gulf States of 1949, have the following characteristics in common: (a) They all seem to avoid the use of the expression 'continental shelf' which does not *stricto sensu* exist in the Arabian Gulf which is a shallow sea of much less than 100 fathoms deep.[3] Accordingly, they uniformly regard the contiguity of the sea-bed and sub-soil of the high sea areas to the territorial seas of the littoral States concerned as the basis of the claims asserted.[4] In contrast, it should be noted that the Iranian draft legislation of 1949, which was passed as a law on 19 June 1955,[5] refers to the Persian

[1] For the English text of the Proclamation of Bahrain No. 37/1368, 5 June 1949, see *A.J.I.L.*, Suppl. 43 (1949), pp. 185-6. See also Appendix IX.

[2] See Young, R., 'Further Claims to Areas Beneath the High Seas', *A.J.I.L.*, 43 (1949), p. 790, where he maintains that the claims thus asserted 'represent a further development along somewhat divergent lines of the continental shelf doctrine enunciated by the United States in 1945'.

[3] See R. Young's commentary on 'Saudi Arabian Offshore Legislation', *A.J.I.L.* 43 (1949), p. 531.

[4] See Young, R., 'The Legal Status of Submarine Areas Beneath the High Seas', *A.J.I.L.*, 45 (1951), p. 239, where he states that 'it has been suggested that the most satisfactory basis for the claims is to regard submarine areas as appurtenant to the contiguous coastal state in a manner analogous to the appurtenance of territorial waters'.

[5] For the French text of the Iranian Law on the continental shelf, see *U.N.L.S.*, High Seas (1957) p. 25.

term 'Falat Gharreh' as conveying the same meaning as the English term 'continental shelf'. Although this reference to the continental shelf in the Arabian Gulf has been criticised as 'meaningless', the Iranian legislation is also applicable to the Gulf of Oman which does contain a continental shelf in the legal sense.[1] (b) They recognise the rights of the coastal States to control and to 'subject to their jurisdiction' certain undefined portions of the high sea outside their territorial seas, provided that these offshore areas claimed shall be delimited on 'equitable and just principles' by agreement with neighbouring States. According to Richard Young, this pattern adopted by the Arab States of the Gulf 'exemplifies one approach to the difficult problem of how to divide amicably submarine areas of narrow seas where the continental shelf doctrine is not applicable'.[2] However, the proclamations do not expressly utilise the median line as a basis for defining the common submarine boundaries of the States concerned. (c) They do not affect the international character of the superjacent waters of the high sea, the status of the air space above such waters or the traditional rights of fishing and pearling in them.[3]

(b) *Definition of the territorial sea*

The above-mentioned claims to the natural resources of the sea-bed and sub-soil of the high sea areas contiguous to the territorial seas of the Arabian Gulf States give rise to the question as to the limits of the territorial seas of these States. With respect to the Gulf Shaikhdoms, they have not issued proclamations on the definition of their territorial seas. However, it is assumed that the British sponsored customary rule of the three-mile limit from the low-water mark on

[1] See Young, R., 'The Legal Status . . .' op. cit., p. 236.

[2] Young, R., 'Saudi Arabian Offshore Legislation', *A.J.I.L.*, 43 (1949), p. 532. Similarly, see Padwa, D. J., 'Submarine Boundaries', *I.C.L.Q.*, 9 (1960), 630, where he states that these proclamations 'generate a fairly uniform affirmation of the comparatively modest proposition that submarine boundaries should be determined on an equitable basis, preferably by mutual agreement'. The principle of 'equity' is also accepted by Article 3 of the Iranian Law of 19 June 1955 as a basis for determining the offshore boundaries of Iran. See *U.N.L.S.* (1957) p. 25.

[3] See, e.g., the Proclamation of Bahrain, the relevant provisions of which are cited above. Similar provisions are contained in the proclamations of the other Shaikhdoms. As regards the Proclamation of Abu Dhabi, the assurance regarding the unchanged status of the air space above the high sea areas claimed was, probably, 'inadvertently' omitted. See Young, R., 'Further Claims to Areas Beneath the High Seas', *A.J.I.L.*, 43 (1949), pp. 790–2. Concerning rights of fishing and pearling in the Gulf, there exists no national legislation regulating them. 'The fisheries', says Auguste, 'which long antedate the growth of national states in the Gulf area, are governed by customs and usages of immemorial standing. Basic among these is the concept that pearl banks are open equally to all the peoples of the Gulf on the common understanding that methods and standards will be observed.' See Auguste, B.B.L., *The Continental Shelf: The Practice and Policy of the Latin American States* . . ., etc. (1960), pp. 68–9, note 148.

the coast would apply to them. In his Award in *Petroleum Development (Trucial Coast) Ltd* v. *Shaikh Abu Dhabi*, 1951,[1] Lord Asquith defined the territorial sea of Abu Dhabi, for the purpose of the oil concession agreement of 1939, as a belt of three miles in width.[2] But in recent oil concessions some Shaikhdoms have defined their territorial seas as extending to six nautical miles from their coasts.[3] And in the 1951 revised concession of the Kuwait Oil Company the territorial sea of Kuwait was fixed at six nautical miles.[4]

Both Iran and Saudi Arabia, the two principal coastal States on the Gulf, have passed legislation defining the breadth of their territorial seas. In the case of Iran, the first law of 19 July 1934[5] defined Iran's territorial sea as extending to six nautical miles from the low-water mark. But by a new law issued on 12 April 1959 Iran extended the breadth of her territorial sea to twelve nautical miles.[6] With respect to Saudi Arabia, the first official declaration on the breadth of the Saudi Arabian territorial sea was made by virtue of the Royal Decree issued on 28 May 1949,[7] which defined that sea as 'including a distance of six nautical miles from the coastal sea which lies outside the inland waters of the Kingdom'. But this decree was later repealed by the Royal Decree dated 16 February 1958.[8] Article 2 of this Decree claims a belt of internal waters between the coasts of the Kingdom and shoals or islands extending out to twelve nautical miles, while Article 4 of it claims a belt of territorial sea lying outside the inland waters of the Kingdom and extending seaward for a distance of twelve nautical miles. Article 5 contains a detailed system of 'base-lines' from which

[1] *I.C.L.Q.*, 1 (1952), p. 247.

[2] Ibid. But see Young, R., 'Lord Asquith and the Continental Shelf', *A.J.I.L.*, 45 (1951), p. 514, where he states that it is doubtful whether 'the Shaikh [of Abu Dhabi] is bound for any purpose, except the allocation of concession rights, to accept Lord Asquith's views'.

[3] See, e.g., the Shaikhdoms' offshore concessions, below, pp. 291, 300–1.

[4] *MEES*, No. 11, 18 January 1963. It is to be noted that by Article 1 of the AOC concession, the 'concession area' begins at the end of 'the distance of six nautical miles from the low water base or base points used on June 18, 1948, for delimiting the territorial waters of the Neutral Zone'. And by Article 1 of the Kuwait-Shell concession of 1961, 'the concession area', begins outside the distance of six nautical miles from 'the low water base or base points used on October 11, 1955, for delimiting the territorial waters of Kuwait'. For the Arabic and English texts of the AOC concession agreement of 1958, and the Kuwait-Shell concession agreement of 1961, respectively, see *Kuwait al-Yawm* (Special Issue), No. 181, 13 July 1958, and ibid., No. 311, 22 January 1961.

[5] *U.N.L.S.*, Territorial Seas (1957) p. 24.

[6] See Lauterpacht, E., 'Contemporary Practice of the United Kingdom in the Field of International Law', *I.C.L.Q.*, 9 (1960), p. 278.

[7] For English text, see *A.J.I.L.*, Suppl., 43 (1949), *Official Documents*, p. 154.

[8] For English text, see *MEES*, Suppl., No. 11, 18 January 1963. In this Royal Decree the expression 'territorial sea' is used instead of the old expression 'territorial waters'. This expression conforms to the expression used in the Geneva Convention on the Territorial Sea of 1958.

the territorial sea of the Kingdom is measured. Safeguards against overlapping of the territorial sea of the Kingdom by 'the waters of another State', are contained in Article 7 which states that in this case 'boundaries will be determined by our Government in agreement with that State in accordance with equitable principles'. This Article, which applies to narrow seas like the Gulf of Aqaba,[1] seems to comply with Article 12 of the Convention on the Territorial Sea of 1958,[2] which provides that the extension of the territorial sea between the coasts of two opposite or adjacent States is not valid, failing agreement to the contrary, beyond the median line. At the head of the Arabian Gulf, Iraq has also issued a decree, the Decree of 4 November 1958,[3] in which the territorial sea of Iraq has been fixed at twelve nautical miles from the coast. With respect to the Iraqi Government's right over the continental shelf, the decree states that it 'affects in no way the international right which Iraq holds over the two maritime zones called the contiguous zone and the continental shelf situated beyond the limits of the Iraqi territorial sea . . .'

It is clear from the above statements that while the Arab Shaikhdoms have adopted, for the purpose of oil concessions, a breadth of territorial sea which varies from three to six nautical miles, other littoral States, such as Iran, Iraq and Saudi Arabia, have made legislation extending their territorial seas to a distance of twelve nautical miles from their coasts. The question now arises, to what extent is such unilateral legislation internationally binding *vis-à-vis* other States? The territorial sea is defined as the 'belt of water running along the coast over which the coastal State exercises sovereignty, subject to certain limitations imposed by international law'.[4] As regards the customary evolution of the three-mile limit rule, M. W. Mouton states:

A certain rule has developed from vague principles, that a State has sovereignty rights in the adjacent sea to a distance of at least three miles from low water mark. Also a rather dominant State practice has evolved to the effect that the territorial waters belong to the territory of the littoral State.[5]

---

[1] See Young, R., 'Saudi Arabian Offshore Legislation', *A.J.I.L.*, 43 (1949), p. 531.

[2] Convention on the Territorial Sea and the Contiguous Zone, 27 April 1958, A/CONF. 13/L. 52. And see The Society of Comparative Legislation and International Law, London, *The Law of the Sea: The Final Act and Annexes of the United Nations Conference on the Law of the Sea*, Geneva, 1958, pp. 4–11.

[3] Quotations from the Iraqi decree are provided in Auguste, B. B. L., *The Continental Shelf: The Practice and Policy of the Latin American States*, etc. (1960), p. 81.

[4] Dean, A. H., 'The Geneva Conference on the Law of the Sea: What was Accomplished?', *A.J.I.L.*, 52 (1958), p. 610.

[5] Mouton, M. W., *The Continental Shelf* (1952), p. 215.

The fact that international law does not accept any unilateral extension of the territorial sea is confirmed by A. H. Dean who states:

Although, within the limits of international law, each State has a right to
legislate with respect to its own territory, a unilateral extension by municipal law of the limits of its territorial sea into the high seas . . . will not be
valid in international law unless and until it is recognised by other States.
. . . either by general custom and assent, or by a series of treaties or multilateral conventions.[1]

As a multilateral treaty, the Geneva Convention on the Territorial
Sea and the Contiguous Zone which was adopted on 27 April 1958[2]
fails to define a definite breadth of the territorial sea. The States parties
to the Convention disagreed on the adoption of one uniform definition
of the territorial sea.[3] In view of these uncertainties about the breadth
of the territorial sea, this aspect of the law of the sea may rightly be
described, in Professor Riesenfeld's words as 'one of the most unsatisfactory portions of international law'.[4]

In connection with the Arabian Gulf region, the non-agreement
among its littoral States upon a uniform definition of the breadth
of their territorial seas adds yet another obstacle in the way of reaching
agreement on the delimitation of their submarine boundaries. In the
case of the littoral States of Iran, Iraq and Saudi Arabia, they have
already uniformly extended their territorial seas to twelve miles. It
may be argued that as long as the extension by these States of their
territorial seas beyond the three-mile limit has not been recognised
by other maritime States or adopted in a multilateral convention, it
could be opposed by those maritime States which still conform to the
internationally accepted standard on the limit of the territorial sea.[5]

[1] Dean, A. H., 'The Second Conference on the Law of the Sea: The Fight for
Freedom of the Sea', *A.J.I.L.*, 54 (1960), p. 760.

[2] See above, p. 282, n. 2.

[3] During the discussions in the second Geneva Conference on the Territorial
Sea, the Afro-Asian countries submitted a proposal which stipulated that a State
'should have the right to fix the breadth of its territorial sea up to a limit of 12
miles'. But this proposal was defeated by 39 votes to 36 with 13 abstentions. It was
clear from the discussions of the Conferences on the Territorial Sea that major
maritime nations held to the 3-mile rule, while the smaller coastal nations sought
to extend their sovereignty seaward to 12 miles or more. At this second Conference held on 26 April 1960, the U.S.-Canadian proposal, claiming 'a six-mile
territorial sea and an additional six-mile fishing zone' failed, by one vote, 'to win
the two-thirds majority needed for its adoption'. For fuller reports on the 1960
Conference on the Law of the Sea, see *The Times*, 14, 20 April 1960; *Herald Tribune*,
N.Y., 5 May 1960; Dean, A. H., 'The Second Conference on the Law of the
Sea . . .', *A.J.I.L.*, 54 (1960), pp. 751–69.

[4] Quotation from Riesenfeld, S. A., *Protection of Coastal Fisheries Under International Law* (1942), p. ix, by Boggs, S. W., 'Delimitation of Seaward Areas Under
National Jurisdiction', *A.J.I.L.*, 45 (1951), p. 240.

[5] See Dean, A. H. 'The Second Geneva Conference on the Law of the Sea:
the Fight for Freedom of the Sea', *A.J.I.L.*, 54 (1960), p. 769.

Britain, the maritime State which is most involved in the Gulf,[1] has already challenged Iran's action in a note of protest which was delivered to the Iranian Foreign Minister on 12 October 1959. In that note, it was stated, *inter alia*, that 'Her Majesty's Government cannot recognise as valid under international law unilateral claims to a breadth of territorial sea greater than three miles.'[2]

(c) *Nature and legal effects of the Proclamations of 1949*

The question as to the legal effects of the Proclamations of 1949 arose in connection with Lord Asquith's Award in the case of *Petroleum Development (Trucial Coast) Ltd v. Shaikh Abu Dhabi, September 1951.*[3] It may be useful to explain in some detail the relevant issues involved in this Award and its general bearing on the Shaikhdoms' claims to the continental shelf in the Arabian Gulf. The facts of the Abu Dhabi case are:

On 11 January 1939 Shaikh Shakhbut of Abu Dhabi granted an oil concession agreement to Petroleum Development (Trucial Coast) Ltd, a British company. The concession included 'exclusive right' to drill for and win mineral oil within a certain area in Abu Dhabi.[4] On 10 June 1949 the Shaikh issued a proclamation which declared that 'the sea-bed and sub-soil lying beneath the high seas in the [Arabian] Gulf contiguous to the territorial waters of Abu Dhabi' was subject to the 'exclusive jurisdiction and control' of that country. The precise limits of the offshore areas claimed were to be determined by agreement with other littoral States.[5] The Shaikh also undertook in 1949, ten years after the conclusion of the 1939 concession agreement, to transfer his asserted rights with respect to the offshore areas of Abu Dhabi to Superior Oil Corporation, an American company. The British company, Petroleum Development, challenged the Shaikh's right to give away to another company the Abu Dhabi offshore areas which, it alleged, were already covered by the 1939 agreement. The Shaikh, on the other hand, took the view that the agreement of 1939 was restricted to the land territory of Abu Dhabi and it, therefore, covered neither the territorial waters nor the sea-bed and sub-soil of the offshore areas which were the subject of the Proclamation of 1949. The Arbitrator was asked to determine whether the Shaikh at the time of the agreement of 1939, or 'as a result of the Proclamation of 1949', had in fact acquired rights over the mineral resources of the submarine areas lying outside territorial waters. If

---

[1] Britain's involvement in the Gulf is due to her protectorate relationship with the Gulf Shaikhdoms.

[2] See Lauterpacht, E., *I.C.L.Q.*, op. cit., p. 279.

[3] For text of the Award, see *I.C.L.Q.*, 1 (1952), p. 247.   [4] Ibid.

[5] For the text of the Abu Dhabi Proclamation of June 1949, see *U.N.L.S.*, High Seas (1951) pp. 22–30.

so, was the effect of the 1939 agreement 'to transfer such original or acquired rights to the Claimant Company?'[1] In answer to these questions, Lord Asquith, who devoted part of his lengthy, but weighty, Award to an analytical discussion of the status of the continental shelf doctrine in international law, found as follows:

That the Claimants succeed as to the sub-soil of the territorial waters (including the territorial waters of islands) and the Shaikh succeeds as to the sub-soil of the Shelf; by which I mean in this connection the submarine area contiguous with Abu Dhabi outside the territorial zone; viz: the former is included in the Concession, and the latter is not; and I award and declare to that effect.[2]

In the course of interpreting the agreement of 1939, the Award dealt with two interesting points, namely,

(a) Whether the agreement was modified by the existence in international law of an established doctrine of the continental shelf so as to attribute to it (the agreement) an additional application to the subsoil of the submarine areas of Abu Dhabi; and (b) Whether the Proclamation of 10 June 1949 has the effect of establishing for the Shaikh such rights over the submarine areas as were already transferred to the Claimants by virtue of the terms of the contract signed in 1939. Lord Asquith's answer to these two propositions was in the negative. On the question of the continental shelf, he found that neither the practice of nations and the pronouncements of learned jurists nor the draft Articles of the International Law Commission could be regarded as establishing or even recording a settled doctrine in international law on the continental shelf. With regard to the legal effect of the Proclamation of 1949, Lord Asquith held that it could not have established for the Claimants any right respecting the submarine areas outside the territorial waters, since these areas did not, legally, fall within the provisions of the contract of 1939.[3] According to Lord Asquith, the proclamations issued by the Shaikhdoms in 1949 were not 'constitutive' of a new right or title but rather 'declaratory' of a pre-existing one.[4]

Generally, there appears to be no concurrence among writers[5] on the legal effects of claims to the continental shelf. According to one writer, B. B. L. Auguste, the 'practices of States have not revealed any uniformity' on this subject,[6] while L. C. Green is of the view that proclamations can amount to 'inchoate titles requiring some measures of

---

[1] *I.C.L.Q.* (1952), op. cit.   [2] Ibid.   [3] Ibid.   [4] Ibid.
[5] See Young, R., 'The Legal Status of Submarine Areas Beneath the High Seas', *A.J.I.L.*, 45 (1951), pp. 225–32; Mouton, M. W., 'The Continental Shelf', *The Hague Recueil Des Cours*, I (1954), p. 436; Auguste, B. B. L., *The Continental Shelf: The Practice and Policy of the Latin American States, etc.* (1960), p. 82.
[6] Auguste, op. cit., p. 82.

occupation or exploitation to perfect them'.[1] On the other hand, M. W. Mouton, disagreeing with Green, states that 'title to resources can only be obtained from a convention to be concluded'.[2] However, J. L. Kunz maintains that although the doctrine of the continental shelf 'is not yet a norm of general customary international law, but in view of the practice of a number of States, the lack of protests, and the general consent of writers, with the exception of Scelle . . . it can be considered as a new norm of general customary international law [and] there is a clear tendency toward the coming into existence of this new norm.'[3]

A similar view was also taken by the International Law Commission in the comments on its 1953 Report.[4] In the Arabian Gulf, the legal effects arising from the Rulers' proclamations of 1949 are, in the words of D. J. Padwa:

That each of the littoral States accepts the doctrine of the continental shelf and the necessary implication of exclusive use. In any controversy between two or more States accepting that principle, their public utterances can be asserted against them. One State having made a proclamation cannot with respect to another such State, allege that a particular submarine area may be freely exploited by either or both parties.[5]

(d) *Definition of the Arabian Gulf offshore areas on the basis of the principles of the Geneva Convention on the Continental Shelf, 1958*[6]

This is the first multilateral convention which embodies the continental shelf as a legal concept. It resulted from the Conference of the International Law of the Sea, held in Geneva from 24 February to 27 April. The Convention on the Continental Shelf, which comprises 15 Articles, was adopted by the States represented in the Conference on 26 April 1958.[7] Article 11 of the Convention provides that it 'shall come into force on the thirtieth day following the date of deposit of the twenty-second instrument of ratification or accession with the Secretary-General of the United Nations'. The convention has recently entered into force after receiving its 22nd ratification, following its ratification

[1] Mouton, M. W., *The Continental Shelf* (1952), p. 329, quoting L. C. Green from his article on the Continental Shelf in *Current Legal Problems* (1951), p. 79.

[2] Mouton's Book, op. cit., p. 329.

[3] Kunz, J. L., 'The Continental Shelf and International Law: Confusion and Abuse', *A.J.I.L.*, 50 (1956), p. 832.

[4] International Law Commission, Report of 1953, 5th Session, *U.N.G.A.*, *Official Records*, 8th Session, Suppl. No. 9 (A/2456), p. 73.

[5] Padwa, D. J., 'Submarine Boundaries', *I.C.L.Q.*, 9 (1960), p. 639.

[6] Convention on the Continental Shelf, 1958 (A/CONF. 13/L.55). And see The Society of Comparative Legislation and International Law, London, *The Law of the Sea: The Final Act and Annexes of the United Nations Conference on the Law of the Sea*, Geneva (1958) pp. 24–7.

[7] For a description of the proceedings of the Conference, see Auguste, op. cit., pp. 94–5.

by the United Kingdom on 10 June 1964. According to B. B. L. Auguste, the convention is 'both a law-making treaty and an instrument codifying existing law'. It is, he says, the first act of international legislation on the subject which 'marked the progressive development of international law'.[1] Richard Young describes it as representing 'a moderate approach'. It, he says, 'rejects the view that the doctrine justifies claims to vast offshore areas regardless of depth or exploitability, or that it entitles a coastal State to exercise unlimited jurisdiction over the waters above the shelf'.[2]

Although the Arabian Gulf, which has no 'sudden drop-off' on its sea-bed, cannot be regarded as 'shelf' in a legal sense, the definition of the continental shelf provided in Article 1 does, however, apply to the sea-bed of the Gulf. Under this Article the term 'continental shelf' refers:

(a) to the sea-bed and sub-soil of the submarine areas adjacent to the coast but outside the area of the territorial sea, to a depth 200 metres or, beyond that limit, to where the depth of the superjacent waters admits of the exploitation of the natural resources of the said areas; (b) to the sea-bed and sub-soil of similar submarine areas adjacent to the coasts of islands.

Under Article 2 of the Convention a coastal State exercises over the shelf 'sovereign rights for the purpose of exploring it and exploiting its natural resources'. This means that the coastal State's right over the shelf is vested in it *ipso jure*, and does no longer need be perfected by a formal claim embodied in a decree or a proclamation. Some writers have criticised this Article on the ground that it establishes the State's right over its offshore areas 'irrespective of actual activity or occupation'.[3]

The settlement of offshore boundary disputes in the Arabian Gulf cannot be considered without reference to the principles adopted in the 1958 Convention on the Continental Shelf. This Convention devises methods which have received general recognition for demarcating the continental shelf of two or more States which have been unable to reach mutual agreement in this respect. These methods are contained in Article 6 of the Convention which states:

1. Where the same continental shelf is adjacent to the territories of two or more States whose coasts are opposite each other, the boundary of the continental shelf appertaining to such States shall be determined by agreement between them. In the absence of agreement, and unless another

---

[1] Ibid., pp. 100–2.
[2] Young, R., 'The Geneva Convention on the Continental Shelf', *A.J.I.L.*, 52 (1958), p. 733.
[3] See ibid., pp. 733–8; Padwa, op. cit., pp. 633–46; Whiteman, M. M., 'Conference on the Law of the Sea: Convention on the Law of the Continental Shelf', *A.J.I.L.*, 52 (1958), pp. 651–9.

boundary line is justified by special circumstances, the boundary is the median line, every point of which is equidistant from the nearest points of the baselines from which the breadth of the territorial sea of each State is measured.

2. Where the same continental shelf is adjacent to the territories of two adjacent States, the boundary of the continental shelf shall be determined by agreement between them. In the absence of agreement, and unless another boundary line is justified by special circumstances, the boundary shall be determined by application of the principle of equidistance from the nearest points of the baselines from which the breadth of the territorial sea of each State is measured.

3. In delimiting the boundaries of the continental shelf, any lines which are drawn in accordance with the principles set out in paragraphs 1 and 2 of this article should be defined with reference to charts and geographical features as they exist at a particular date, and reference should be made to fixed permanent identifiable points on the land.

The principle of 'equidistance', as adopted in the above Article, is regarded as 'the most recent innovation' in the technique of demarcating the boundaries of two adjacent or opposite States situated on the same continental shelf.[1] Although States can, by agreement, utilise some other techniques in demarcating their submarine boundaries, the principle of equidistance is, however, 'distinguished for its convenience, wide-spread applicability and for the equitable result it generally yields'. According to D. J. Padwa, the line of equidistance— in other words the median line, consists of 'a locus of points, each equidistant from the nearest points on the baselines of adjacent or opposite States'.[2]

In the Arabian Gulf, where the littoral States share the same continental shelf, the proclamations issued by these States have expressed awareness of this fact by emphasising the need for reaching agreement among the littoral States on the basis of 'equitable principles'.[3] Consequently, it would seem that the median line is equitably the most applicable boundary line in the Gulf in all cases where there is failure to reach agreement 'and unless another boundary line is justified by special circumstances'.[4] It is, of course, questionable whether the Arabian Gulf littoral States are, necessarily, bound by the principles of the Geneva Convention of 1958, concerning the division of the continental shelf, since none of them has ratified or adhered to it.

[1] Padwa, op. cit., p. 628.

[2] Ibid., pp. 631-2. For the technique of drawing 'baselines', see Fitzmaurice, Sir Gerald, 'Some Results of the Geneva Conference on the Law of the Sea', *I.C.L.Q.*, 8 (1959), pp. 73-90.

[3] See above, p. 280 and Appendix IX.

[4] According to Padwa, D. J., op. cit., p. 644, the term 'special circumstances' lacks proper definition, since it 'can have reference to certain legal, political and economic considerations as well as geographic ones'. See also Young, R., 'The Geneva Convention on the Continental Shelf', *A.J.I.L.*, 52 (1958), p. 737.

(Iran alone has signed the Convention but has not yet ratified it.) At any rate, all these States have already accepted the codified rules of the Convention concerning the median line as valid expressions of international practice.

Baseline problems: The adoption of the median line principle as a basis for the division of the continental shelf in the Gulf raises the relative problem concerning the drawing of the baseline from which the breadth of the territorial sea or the median line could be measured. In accordance with the principles laid down in the 1958 Conventions on the Territorial Sea and on the Continental Shelf, 'the normal baseline for measuring the breadth of the territorial sea [or the median line] is the low-water line along the coast as marked on large-scale charts officially recognised by the coastal State'.[1] Moreover, under certain conditions the above principles permit the use of low-tide elevations and islands within the breadth of the territorial sea from the mainland as baselines for measuring the breadth of the territorial sea[2] or the median line. It is suggested by some authorities that the construction of median lines in narrow seas and gulfs, such as the Arabian Gulf, could give rise to the questions of 'special circumstances', referred to in Article 6 of the Continental Shelf Convention. Thus, in the Arabian Gulf, in particular, the principle of special circumstances could be invoked in disregarding the great number of small islands and shoals that are scattered in this Gulf for measuring the median line, since the use of these islands and shoals as baselines for constructing the median line could produce inequitable results, viz. large deflections of the line. These considerations have led some experts to recommend the construction of the median line directly from baselines fixed along the opposite coasts of the mainland, irrespective of islands.[3]

[1] Article 3 of the Convention on the Territorial Sea and the Contiguous Zone and Article 6 of the Convention on the Continental Shelf.

[2] Article 11 of the Convention on the Territorial Sea. However, it is provided by Article 4 (3) of this Convention that 'baselines shall not be drawn to and from low-tide elevations, unless lighthouses or similar installations which are permanently above sea level have been built on them'. For lawyers' comments on the 'controversial problems' of drawing baselines, see Dean, A. H., 'The Geneva Conference on the Law of the Sea: What was Accomplished', *A.J.I.L.*, 52 (1958), pp. 616–19; Fitzmaurice, Sir Gerald, 'Some Results of the Geneva Conference on the Law of the Sea', *I.C.L.Q.*, 8 (1959), 84–7.

[3] According to Padwa, op. cit., p. 649: 'The best rule would include only those islands which form an integral part of the coastal domain. This is determined on an objective basis by excluding all islands except those linked by straight baselines or those within the territorial sea of the coastal State as measured from the mainland. . . .' For a similar view, see Boggs, S. W., 'Delimitation of Seaward Areas under National Jurisdiction', *A.J.I.L.*, 45 (1951), p. 258. Here Boggs states his theory about the cases where an island could be treated as part of the mainland baseline. He says: 'The most reasonable and workable rule is believed to be to

U

However, in view of the differences of opinion among the Gulf littoral States on the use of islands and low-tide elevations as baselines for establishing the Gulf median line, it may be suggested that only those islands and elevations that are 'situated wholly or partly at a distance not exceeding the breadth of the territorial sea from the mainland or an island' could be used as baselines for measuring the median line for the demarcation of submarine areas in the Gulf.[1]

THE UNSETTLED BOUNDARY DISPUTES

1. *Boundary disputes in the Higher Gulf*

(a) *Definition of offshore areas over which concession rights are granted*

On the Persian side of the Gulf, the relevant concession agreements are:

(i) *Agreement between National Iranian Oil Company (NIOC) and Agip-Mineraria* (SIRIP), 24 August 1957[2]

Article 3 of this agreement defines the concession area as including:

(1) a zone of the continental shelf located in the northern part of the Persian Gulf measuring approximately 5,600 sq. kilometres.

(3) a zone along the coast of the Oman Sea extending up to the continental shelf, measuring approximately 6,000 sq. kilometres.

The limits of the above-mentioned zones are indicated respectively in Appendices 2, 3 and 4 of this agreement.

(ii) *Agreement between National Iranian Oil Company (NIOC) and Pan-American Petroleum Corporation* (IPAC), April 1958.[3]

The concession area of the Company is stated in Schedule I of the agreement as including:

Area I, to the north of SIRIP concession, approximately 1,000 sq. kilometres.

(This area was later relinquished by IPAC and it is now available for bidding after having been enlarged.)

Area II, to the south of SIRIP concession, approximately 15,000 sq. kilometres.

---

draw that pair of parallel lines tangent to opposite ends or sides of the island which encloses the least area of water between island and mainland. . . . Then, if the land area of the island . . . exceeds the water area bounded by the parallel lines, the island and the mainland, the island should be reckoned as if part of the mainland baseline, in laying down the median line . . .'

[1] Article 11 of the Convention on the Territorial Sea.

[2] For English text, see *The Petroleum Times*, Suppl., vol. LXI, No. 1572, 8 November 1957.

[3] Ibid., Suppl., vol. LXII, No. 1586, 23 May 1958.

This area which is still held by IPAC excludes the 'Islands of Kharg and Khargo and the three-mile territorial waters of each, which this described area surrounds.'

On the Arabian side of the Gulf, the relevant concession agreements are:

(i) *Agreement between the Government of Kuwait and Kuwait Shell Company, 15 January 1961*[1]

According to Article 1 of this agreement, the concession area includes:

(I) All the seabed and subsoil underlying the waters of the Arabian Gulf the subject of the Proclamation made by the then Ruler of Kuwait on 12th June, 1949, but excluding Concessionary Waters (as hereinafter defined).

(II) Any and all islands, islets, shoals . . . which fall within the jurisdiction of the Emir and lie within the boundaries of the area defined in (I) above but excluding certain islands defined under this section and their concessionary waters.

(ii) *Saudi Arabia-Kuwait Agreements of 1957 and 1958 with Arabian (Japanese) Oil Company (AOC) respecting the neutral zone offshore areas*[2]

By Article 2 of the AOC 1957 Agreement with Saudi Arabia, the concession area includes 'the Government's undivided share in all that offshore area outside the territorial waters limit of the Saudi Arab-Kuwait Neutral Zone over which the Government now has or may hereafter, during the period of this Agreement, have right, title and interest'.

And by Article 1 of the AOC 1958 Agreement with Kuwait, the concession area includes Kuwait's undivided half interest in 'the seabed and subsoil lying beneath the high seas of the Arabian Gulf contiguous to the territorial waters of the Neutral Zone . . . with the exception of the seabed and subsoil beneath the Concessionary Waters'.

(iii) *Agreement between the Government of Saudi Arabia and Arabian American Oil Company (ARAMCO), 10 October 1948*[3]

This Letter Agreement grants Aramco concession rights over the offshore areas of the Saudi Arabian northeastern coast on the Arabian Gulf which extends from the Neutral Zone southward.

[1] For Arabic and English texts, see *al-Kuwait al-Yawm*, No. 311, 22 January 1961.
[2] For the AOC Concession Agreement of 10 December 1957, see *The Petroleum Times*, Suppl., vol. LXII, No. 1579, 14 February 1958. For Arabic and English texts of the AOC Concession Agreement of 5 July 1958, see *al-Kuwait al-Yawm* (Special), No. 181, 13 July 1958.
[3] *MEES*, No. 33, 21 June 1963.

(b) Overlapping of concession areas

Disputes over the delimitation of the offshore boundaries in the higher Gulf arose as a result of the overlapping of oil concessions covering the various areas described above. These disputes became publicly known after the publication of the sets of concessions of 1957–8 which were granted by each of Iran, Saudi Arabia and Kuwait to various oil concerns. A further aggravation of these disputes occurred in 1961, as a result of the signing of Kuwait-Shell offshore agreement. However, it was not until 1963 that these claims to concessionary areas had actually assumed an international character. It may be desirable to explain briefly the development of these claims and counter-claims below:

(i) Pre-announcement of National Iranian Oil Company No. 228/15, 1 April 1963[1]

On 1 April 1963 NIOC published an Announcement in Platt's Oil-gram Service in which it declared open for international bidding, with effect from 1 July 1964, two areas of the continental shelf of the Arabian Gulf adjacent to the Iranian mainland: Area 1 of District I is located north of the two areas and it comprises the concession area which was originally held by IPAC, but with an additional area of 380 sq. miles. Area 2 of District I is located to the south of IPAC area but separated from it by a wedge of some 15,000 sq. kilometres.

(ii) Diplomatic protests by littoral Arab States against the Iranian pre-announcement of 1 April 1963

The Iranian Pre-announcement provoked diplomatic protests from Iraq, Kuwait and Saudi Arabia. Iraq was the first Arab country to deliver a strongly worded protest to Iran. In its statement dated 1 May 1963, the Iraqi Government stated, inter alia, that

... since most of the areas declared open (for bidding) are exclusively Iraqi territorial waters, it will not recognise, nor permit, any concession granted to any party whatsoever for oil exploration in these areas. . . . All the parties concerned must ascertain the ownership of these areas before seeking to grant or acquire any oil exploration concessions in them. . . .[2]

On 4 June 1963, the Kuwaiti Government followed the Iraqi Government's example by issuing a statement in which it condemned the action of National Iranian Oil Company as an infringement of its territorial sovereignty. The area declared open for concession, the statement continued, constituted 'an additional infringement on the continental shelf of Kuwait'.[3]

---

[1] MEES, No. 27, 10 May and No. 31, 7 June 1963.
[2] MEES, No. 27, 10 May 1963.
[3] MEES, No. 31, 7 June, and No. 32, 14 June 1963.

As regards the Government of Saudi Arabia, it objected in a statement issued on 15 June 1963, against 'Area 2, District I' of the Pre-announcement which lies to the south of IPAC concession area. It also objected to the concession area granted to IPAC on the ground that it constituted 'an infringement of the legitimate rights of Saudi Arabia in respect of the natural resources in the offshore area opposite Saudi Arabia's territorial waters or the territorial waters of the Saudi Arab–Kuwait Neutral Zone'.[1]

(c) *Definition of the overlapping areas*

The overlapping concession areas that have given rise to the above-mentioned claims and counter-claims may be described as follows:[2]

Iraq–Iran: The Iraqi Government claims that the Iranian Pre-announcement defining Area 1, District I constituted an infringement of the Iraqi territorial sea at the head of the Gulf. As stated earlier, the Iraqi Decree of 4 November 1958, created two maritime zones: the contiguous zone and the continental shelf zone, situated beyond the limits of the Iraqi territorial sea which was fixed at twelve nautical miles.

Kuwait–Iran: The Kuwaiti Government claims that IPAC concession area, Area 1, amounted to an infringement of its offshore concession area held by Kuwait-Shell. Iran, on the other hand, claims that Kuwait-Shell concession area has very greatly interfered with both SIRIP and IPAC concessions, granted in 1957 and 1958, respectively.[3]

Kuwait–Saudi Arab Neutral Zone–Iran: The Saudi Government claims that IPAC concession of 1958 has interfered with Japanese AOC concession of 1957, in respect of its undivided half interest in the Neutral Zone.

Saudi Arabia–Iran: The Saudi Government claims that both IPAC concession of 1958 and Area 2, District I of the Iranian Pre-announcement constituted an infringement of ARAMCO concession area of 1948.

---

[1] *MEES*, No. 33, 21 June 1963.

[2] For a description of these disputes, see *MEES*, No. 11, Suppl., 18 January, No. 31, 7 June, No. 32, Suppl., 14 June and No. 33, 21 June 1963.

[3] It is to be noted that Kuwait-Shell Company, which holds Kuwait's offshore concession, had informed Kuwait of its decision to suspend its drilling operations within the concession area pending the settlement of the Kuwaiti-Iranian dispute. The Company informed Kuwait that 'its best drilling prospect now lies in the south-eastern part of the concession area which is nearer to IPAC Cyrus field, but that drilling in this area will not be possible until some agreement on the delimitation of offshore boundaries between Kuwait and Iran is reached'. See *MEES*, No. 51, 25 October 1963.

Saudi Arabia–Kuwait (overlapping of the Neutral Zone and the Kuwait-Shell concessions): According to Saudi Arabia, this dispute concerns the overlapping of Kuwait-Shell concession area of 1961 with AOC 1957 concession area respecting her undivided half-share interest in the natural resources of the Neutral Zone offshore areas. The difference appears to have arisen from different definitions given for the offshore boundaries of the Neutral Zone by Kuwait and Saudi Arabia in their 1957–8 concessions with AOC. It is suggested that the definition of the concession area embodied in the Kuwaiti concession agreement with AOC is less extensive than the definition of such area in the Saudi concession agreement with the same company; the Saudi concession area granted to AOC extends further northward. According to the Saudi Minister of Petroleum, who commented recently on the situation, a seismic survey over the Neutral Zone concession area has revealed 'a structure with a large production potential' which would be covered by the definition of the concession area embodied in the AOC 1957 concession with Saudi Arabia but not by the definition contained in the AOC 1958 concession with Kuwait. This Saudi-Kuwaiti controversy, which primarily concerns the definition of the Neutral Zone northernmost boundary, has resulted from the Kuwait-Shell 1961 concession agreement. According to the Saudi Government, the 'structure' in question which is thereby allotted to the Kuwait-Shell concession area, constitutes an overlapping with the Neutral Zone 1957 concession area.[1]

(d) *The process of negotiations on the settlement of offshore boundary disputes*

A beginning in the way of seeking settlement of offshore boundary disputes in the Gulf was made in October 1963, when representatives from Iran, Iraq, Kuwait and Saudi Arabia, meeting in Geneva, all expressed their agreement on working together to reach equitable settlements of their disputes.[2] Soon after that an Iranian delegation arrived in Iraq in November 1963, where it held discussions with Iraqi authorities on the question of the delimitation of the offshore boundaries of the two countries. Consequently, it was announced that the two States agreed on 'a basis for joint exploitation of oil in the disputed areas whereby the interests of both parties would be observed'. Later, it was announced in April 1964, that Iran was to begin talks with both Kuwait and Saudi Arabia relating to the determination of her offshore boundaries with them. Subsequently, the Iranian Foreign Minister visited Kuwait, and after holding talks with his counterpart, the Kuwaiti Foreign Minister, the two Ministers issued a joint communiqué in which they announced their concurrence

[1] *MEES*, No. 21, 27 March 1964.   [2] *MEES*, No. 51, 25 October 1963.

to establish a joint 'committee of experts' whose task would be to study on an equitable basis the problems of the division of the continental shelf between the two States. Similarly, discussions were held in April between the Iranian Foreign Minister and Saudi Government officials. It was then understood that the two parties agreed to refer their dispute to a jointly appointed 'committee of experts' which should study it and recommend an equitable basis for resolving it.[1]

The negotiations on the definition of offshore boundaries have continued ever since between Iran, on the one side of the Gulf, and the Arab States, on the other side of it. The crucial problem in these negotiations is centred around the question of finding an equitable basis for constructing the Gulf median line which should thus separate, more accurately, the Persian claimed areas of natural resources from the Arabian claimed areas.[2] Once this goal is achieved, it would then be possible for Iran and each of the Arab States, on the other side of the Gulf, to reappraise and determine the boundaries of the concessionary areas of their respective oil companies, on both sides of the line, in accordance with the delineation settlements reached among them.

To the time of going to press, one offshore boundary agreement has been initialled, but not yet signed, in December 1965,[3] between Iran and Saudi Arabia. This agreement firstly, determines the sovereignty of Saudi Arabia and Iran, respectively, over the two offshore islands of al-Arabiya and Farsi, and secondly, divides the sea-bed and sub-soil areas of the continental shelf contiguous to the Saudi and Iranian coasts on the basis of the median line principle. The remaining offshore boundary disputes which have not yet been resolved concern the following:

Iran–Iraq: Negotiations regarding the demarcation of the sea-bed and sub-soil areas of the continental shelf between the two States have not developed beyond the proposal made in August 1963 to the effect that 'joint exploitation of oil resources located in the disputed offshore areas would be "in the interests of the two sides" '.[4]

Iran–Kuwait: With respect to the definition of the offshore boundaries between Iran and Kuwait proper, negotiations which have been in progress for some time have not yet produced an agreed solution.[5]

[1] *MEES*, No. 3, 22 November 1963, and No. 24, 17 April 1964.
[2] See above, pp. 286–9 for useful suggestions on how equitable settlements could be reached on the question.
[3] See below, p. 310.
[4] *MEES*, No. 46, 16 September 1966.
[5] One of the main obstacles in the negotiations between Iran and Kuwait in this matter appears to be 'Iran's insistence on using Kharg (Khark) island as the base point for determining the Gulf median line (on the ground that it is linked to the

Iran–Neutral Zone: In the summer of 1966, Iran, Kuwait and Saudi Arabia participated in discussions connected with the problem of demarcating the border of the continental shelf contiguous to the opposite coasts of the Kuwait–Saudi Arabia Neutral Zone and Iran. The discussions, which centred around the problem of measuring the median line dividing the Iranian offshore areas from the Neutral Zone offshore areas, proved to be inconclusive. The main obstacle in the way of measuring the Neutral Zone offshore median line is the interception of some offshore islands on both sides of the Gulf coasts. As a result, differences have arisen between the parties concerned on the extent to which these offshore islands could be considered for the purpose of fixing the baseline from which the Neutral Zone–Iran median line could be measured.[1]

Kuwait–Saudi Arabia: Neutral Zone Offshore Boundary: The problem of the delimitation of the 'north-eastern boundary separating the Neutral Zone offshore from that of Kuwait' remains to be solved.[2]

(e) *The problem of islands: the status of Kubr, Qaru and Umm al-Maradim*

The island of Kubr lies off the coast of Kuwait proper, while the islands of Qaru and Umm al-Maradim are situated off the coast of the Kuwait–Saudi Arabia Neutral Zone. Although there appears to be no dispute over Kuwaiti full sovereignty over the island of Kubr, the position with regard to the other two islands is somewhat different, since their status has been subject to a long-standing dispute between Kuwait and Saudi Arabia. Basically, Kuwait claims the islands to be 100 per cent Kuwaiti islands while Saudi Arabia considers them to be subject to the same co-sovereignty status of the Neutral Zone. In the past, the United Kingdom, which was until 1961 responsible for the conduct of the foreign relations of Kuwait, had entertained the view that the islands of Qaru and Umm al-Maradim did not form part of the Neutral Zone offshore on the ground that they were not subject

---

mainland by pipeline). In earlier talks the Kuwaitis were understood to have offered to accept this, provided that the Iranians agreed to acknowledge equivalent status for the island of Failaka off the Kuwait coast . . .' See *MEES*, No. 8, 24 December 1965; ibid., No. 20, 18 March, and No. 22, 1 April 1966. It is suggested above at p. 290 that islands lying within the limits of the territorial sea could be considered as base points for determining the Gulf median line. However, the problem becomes more difficult with Kuwait, since Iran and Kuwait do not adopt a uniform belt of territorial sea. See above, p. 281. In the Iran-Saudi Arabia agreement of 1965, the problem of 'Khark' has been solved by giving 'half-weight status' to the island. See below, p. 310.

[1] See *MEES*, No. 37, 15 July, No. 36, 8 July, and No. 26, 26 August 1966.
[2] *MEES*, No. 32, 10 June 1966.

to the dispute over 'pasture rights' which later determined the settlement involved in the creation of the Neutral Zone.[1]

Aminoil concession over the Islands: On 22 September 1949 the Ruler of Kuwait granted a subsidiary of Aminoil of the Neutral Zone, known as the American Oil Company of California, a concession covering 'the islands of Kubr, Qaru and Umm al-Maradim and their territorial waters'. The concession gave the company exclusive rights of exploration, production and ownership of all petroleum produced. The concession defined the territorial sea of the islands as 'three nautical miles from low-water mark' (Art. 1).

However, despite the above concession, no work or drilling had taken place until 1962, when a seismic survey was carried out by Aminoil. In his recently published book, the late E. Brown describes the Aminoil concession as being 'based on ludicrously cheap financial terms'. He also says that there 'was no down payment upon signature as in the case' of Aminoil's concession applying to the Neutral Zone.[2] Although Saudi Arabia had made no formal protest in the past against the above concession, there are, nevertheless, indications that she vigorously disputes the Kuwaiti claim to exclusive sovereignty over the two islands of Qaru and Umm al-Maradim which she regards as being part of the Neutral Zone offshore areas. According to E. Brown, there exists 'a separate confidential letter agreement' between Saudi Arabia and Arabian (Japanese) Oil Company which specifically refers to the two islands as falling within the offshore 'concession area' granted to the company by Saudi Arabia in respect of the latter's undivided half interest of the Neutral Zone. But, in the words of the author, this letter agreement states further that

since the two Governments of Saudi Arabia and Kuwait are contemplating discussions as to their territorial rights over these islands, they would not be mentioned in the concession agreement. However, if at a future time, it was determined that these islands belonged either to the Kingdom of Saudi Arabia or the Neutral Zone, they would become subject to the terms and conditions of the Japanese concession agreement.[3]

It is noteworthy that Kuwait has recently signed a new concession agreement with Aminoil. The new concession involves 'extensive revisions of the terms of the 1949 agreement' under which Aminoil obtained its original concession over the three islands. The purpose of the new agreement was to bring the financial terms of the original agreement into line with those of Aminoil's agreement pertaining to the Neutral Zone onshore.[4] Furthermore, recent developments of

[1] For background information on this subject, see *MEES*, No. 11, Suppl., 1 January 1963; ibid., No. 15, 14 February 1964. And see Brown, E. H., *The Saudi Arabia–Kuwait Neutral Zone* (1963), p. 107.
[2] Brown, op. cit., p. 107.   [3] Ibid., p. 108.
[4] *MEES*, No. 6, 13 September 1963; ibid., No. 15, 14 February 1964.

the dispute over the two islands of Qaru and Umm al-Maradim show that although Kuwait still insists on her full sovereignty over the islands, she, nevertheless, appears to be willing to concede to Saudi Arabia the half-share ownership of 'any income accruing from future oil discovered' from the two islands. On the other hand, the Saudi Minister of Petroleum was reported to have said recently that the islands in dispute constituted 'purely legal questions' and that his Government and Kuwait agreed to refer them to 'a conciliation commission of legal experts' for consideration on the basis of legal principles. When Kuwait and Saudi Arabia reached an agreement in July 1965, on the division of the Neutral Zone between them, their dispute over the two Neutral Zone islands was still awaiting settlement.[1]

(f) *The problem of capture*

The problem of capture adds yet further complications to the already tangled problems of the overlapping of offshore concession areas in the Gulf. According to some reports, this problem first arose in May 1963 between Aramco, the holder of Saudi Arabia's north-eastern offshore concession, and AOC, the holder of Saudi Arabia and Kuwait's offshore concessions of the Neutral Zone. The reports which referred to what was termed to be 'a silent war' between the two companies 'over the exploitation of their two adjoining fields', stated the problem as follows:

Aramco's Safaniya offshore field—the world's largest offshore reservoir —inclines towards the Japanese-held acreage in the Neutral Zone in a manner favouring the Japanese company. Consequently, Aramco has not only increased the producing capacity of its Safaniya field to 360,000 b/d (with plans for a further increase to 425,000 b/d in 1964), but also felt the urgent need to offset Japanese production next door which threatens to drain away Aramco's prize field at Safaniya.[2]

What is the solution to the above problem? It appears that neither customary international law nor, for that matter, the 1958 Geneva Convention on the Continental Shelf could provide, in terms of rigid legal principles, a satisfactory solution to the problem of capture. If guidance is sought from Article 6 of the Continental Shelf Convention, the problem could, most probably, be treated in the light of the principle of 'special circumstances', as embodied in this Article.[3] Consequently, it may be suggested that, in accordance with this principle, a boundary line could be drawn by agreement on a basis not corresponding to the line of equidistance, should such a line

[1] *MEES*, No. 19, 13 March 1964 and No. 6, 13 September 1963. See also above, p. 273

[2] *MEES*, No. 38, 26 July, and No. 32, 14 June 1963. The producing capacity of Safaniya field is today estimated to be more than 600,000 b/d.

[3] See above, p. 288.

prove to be more equitably applicable to the situation. Furthermore, guidance in this matter may be sought from the treatment of the problem by some writers. Thus, according to one writer, M. W. Mouton, where an oil pool might be divided by a line drawn in accordance with the principle of equidistance, 'account must be taken of the essential unity of a deposit'. In this writer's view, 'the strict application of the general rule (of equidistance) may involve the danger of an oil-pool being divided up among different countries'.[1] However, the writer agrees that this exceptional situation, which undoubtedly gives rise to the question of 'special circumstances', 'can only be solved by agreement . . . for which it would be difficult to lay down a general rule'.[2] The Memorandum on the Regime of the High Seas, prepared by the Secretariat of the United Nations in July 1950, foresaw the problem in the following statement:

. . . the same deposits will frequently be found on both sides of a proposed boundary line. The exploitation of a mineral deposit at any given spot will, at least as regards oil-bearing strata, undoubtedly react on other parts of the deposits.

In this case, the statement continued.

it is not possible . . . to fix an exact limit within which submarine drilling shall be permissible and beyond which it shall not. To allow drilling just outside the limit (by the other State) is quite unthinkable if such drilling is liable to react on the exploitation of substances within that limit.[3]

The solution of the above problem, it is suggested, lies in the adoption of 'the concept of a protective perimeter' which is regarded as 'an indispensable adjunct to the idea of a demarcation of the areas allotted to the States interested in the same shelf'.[4]

On the other hand, Padwa, who has discussed this problem, does not seem to agree with Mouton on the idea of 'the essential unity of a deposit'. The problem itself, says Padwa, is not within the meaning of special circumstances. 'The possibility that one party', he continues, 'might deplete such a divided reserve before the other commenced exploitation is not sufficient reason to justify a departure from the principle of equidistance. In such a case the parties must arrive at an accommodation between themselves.'[5] Similarly, another writer, Auguste, who admits the shortcomings of international law on providing a solution to the problem of directional drilling at the very

---

[1] Mouton, *The Hague Recueil*, op. cit., pp. 420–1. According to the writer, 'the danger . . . exists also on land and in granting concessions the principle is followed that two concessionaires should not tap the same pool or in a descriptive parable, never two straws in one glass'.   [2] Ibid.

[3] A/CN.4/32, 14 July 1950, as supplied by Mouton, *The Hague Recueil*, op. cit., pp. 420–1.

[4] Ibid.   [5] Padwa, op. cit., p. 645.

median line, suggests that the solution might, perhaps, lie in economic agreements and not in international law.[1]

It remains to be seen whether the above suggestions made by some experts in the field could in any way be useful in reaching an equitable solution to the problem of capture in the Arabian Gulf. It seems clear now that the tendency among some authorities is to consider the problem as forming a ground for departure from the application of the principle of equidistance.

2. Boundary disputes in the Middle and Lower Gulf

(a) *Definition of offshore areas over which concession rights are granted*

(i) *Bahrain concessionary areas:* According to supplemental concession contracts signed in 1940 and 1942, the Ruler of Bahrain extended the 'exclusive area' of the concession granted in 1934 to Bahrain Petroleum Company (Bapco) to 'all present and future land and marine territories under the sovereignty of the Shaikh'.[2] As a result, Bapco's concession was extended to the submarine areas claimed to belong to the Shaikh of Bahrain by the Proclamation of 5 June 1949.[3] However, at present, Bapco's offshore concession area does not include (*a*) the Abu Sa'fah field which is now being exploited by Aramco under the joint-sharing of profits arrangement of 1958,[4] between Bahrain and Saudi Arabia; and (*b*) the offshore concession area, covering 2500 sq. kilometres, which was granted on 20 September 1965 to a subsidiary of the Continental Oil Company. This latter concession area, which was relinquished by Bapco lately, lies northeast of the Island between Aramco's Abu Sa'fah field and the adjoining Qatar offshore acreage held by Continental Oil Company (Qatar). The acreage of Continental Oil Company (Bahrain) includes 'the Fasht-al-Jarim area north of Bahrain and the Huwar islands and their surrounding waters southeast of Bahrain'.[5]

[1] Auguste, op. cit., p. 95.

[2] See Ely, Northcutt, *Summary of Mining and Petroleum Laws of the World* (1961), Chapter 6 on Arabian Peninsula Countries.

[3] See Appendix IX.

[4] See below, p. 306. Oil in commercial quantities was discovered in Abu Sa'fah in 1965, and production at a rated capacity of 30,000 b/d was started by Aramco from December 1965. The Abu Sa'fah field has a complex legal and tax status; it lies on the Saudi Arabian side of the agreed offshore boundary with Bahrain. But for tax purposes, the field is treated as lying within 'a neutral zone, wherein 50 per cent of the net profit from production will be evenly split between Bahrain and Saudi Arabia. Aramco gets the other 50 per cent.' See *The Oil and Gas Journal*, 27 September and 4 October 1965, p. 99. See also Map 4.

[5] The 1965 Continental Oil Concession of Bahrain has been regarded as a modern agreement. It has been awarded for a forty-five-year period, and it provides, *inter alia*, for 50–50 profit sharing on a posted price basis, with provisions for expensing of royalties along the lines of the OPEC formula. The Company has already started seismic survey. See *The Oil and Gas Journal*, 27 September 1965;

(ii) *Qatar concessionary areas:* The Qatar offshore concession was obtained by Shell Overseas Exploration Company (later known as Shell Company of Qatar). The concession covers approximately 10,000 sq. miles of marine areas. In 1962–3, Shell relinquished about 60 per cent of its original area, 'including all acreage on the western side of the peninsula and nearly all to the north and off the east coast out to longitude 52 degrees'. Now Shell retains the area on the northeast corner of its original concession near 'Ras Rakan and the area round Halul island and including Idd el-Shargi field'. On 15 September 1963 the offshore acreage to the north and southeast of the peninsula was granted to Continental Oil Company.[1]

(iii) *The Trucial Shaikhdoms concessionary areas*:

Abu Dhabi: Offshore concession rights in Abu Dhabi are held by Abu Dhabi Marine Areas (ADMA). The company's rights are split: over two-thirds held by British Petroleum (BP) and one-third held by Compagnie française de Petroles (CFP). The present offshore oil-producing field is Umm Shaif which is located 60 miles off the coast of Abu Dhabi.[2]

Dubai: Dubai offshore concession is held by Dubai Marine Areas. The concession rights are divided as follows: BP holds two-thirds and CFP holds one-third. And in accordance with the provision of an agreement signed on 24 September 1963, Continental Oil now holds 50 per cent interest in an offshore joint venture with Dubai Marine Areas. The concession covers the continental shelf area outside Dubai's territorial waters.[3]

Sharjah: In August 1962, the Texas independent oil man, J. W. Mecom, was granted a concession in respect of the western part of Sharjah, including offshore. It was learned later that Mecom took Pure Oil as a partner in a joint venture. They drilled a wild-cat[4] in the Abu Musa island which is located 38 miles off the coast of Sharjah.

World Petroleum Report, 15 March 1966; *MEES*, No. 47, 24 September 1965. In this connection, it is interesting to note that NIOC (Iran) representative in Tehran was reported to have protested to the American ambassador in Tehran about the acceptance of an oil concession by Continental Oil Company from Bahrain authorities, since Iran allegedly considers Bahrain as its '31st unredeemed province'. See above, Chapter 12.

[1] Qatar-Shell Agreement of 1952; Ely, op. cit.; *MEES*, No. 46, 20 September 1963.

[2] Ely, op. cit.; *MEES*, No. 38, 27 July 1962; *Petroleum Press Service*, August 1962, p. 308. The field of Umm Shaif is connected with a terminal on Das Island which is 20 miles from the field.

[3] *MEES*, No. 45, 13 September 1963; ibid., No. 10, October 1963; *Petroleum Press Service*, No. 5, May 1963, p. 194.

[4] This expression relates to an oil or gas well drilled in a territory not known to be productive.

The concession extends offshore to a distance of about 100 kilometres, as far as the islands of Abu Nuʿayr and Abu Musa.[1]

Ras al-Khaimah: By an agreement signed on 3 March 1964 the Ruler of the Shaikhdom awarded to Union Oil of California and Southern Gas a concession covering his country's offshore areas.[2]

(b) *Disputes over the delimitation of offshore boundaries*

Although the dispute between Bahrain and Saudi Arabia over the delimitation of their offshore boundaries has already been settled by virtue of their 1958 agreement,[3] there are still some causes for serious disputes over the delimitation of offshore boundaries in this portion of the Gulf. Moreover, the potential causes for disputes arising from overlapping of newly granted oil concessions in this part should not be underestimated. The fact that offshore boundaries in this portion of the Gulf between Iran and the littoral Shaikhdoms, on the one hand, and between the littoral Shaikhdoms themselves, on the other, have not yet been delimited, would, undoubtedly, demonstrate the intricacy of the problems at issue. Apart from the Persian claim to Bahrain,[4] which would affect any settlement based on the drawing of the median line in the Gulf, there is the added problem of Bahrain's claim to certain rights over the village of Zubarah, on the northwestern coast of Qatar peninsula. The long-standing dispute between Bahrain and Qatar over Zubarah has been discussed in this work in connection with the problems of territorial claims.[5] But this Bahraini territorial claim to Zubarah, or to jurisdictional rights over it, seems to overshadow any future settlement of the Bahrain–Qatar submarine boundaries. The problem of the delimitation of submarine areas between Bahrain and Qatar has become more pressing at present, as a result of the acceleration in recent years of offshore oil operations.

It is understood that British Foreign Office experts have been for some years working on a practical plan for dividing the Bahrain–Qatar submarine areas on an equitable basis, while shelving for the time being the question of Bahraini claims to Zubarah. Consequently, the British Government presented a tentative plan to Bahrain for the demarcation of her boundaries with Qatar. After having studied this plan, the Bahrain Government was understood to have presented a counter plan which seemed to have claimed much more areas of the sea-bed than those embodied in the British plan. This Bahraini counter plan was later communicated to Qatar for consideration by the Ruler. The Ruler's reaction to the plan is not known. At any rate, it is understood that the question of the Bahrain–Qatar submarine boun-

---

[1] *MEES*, No. 38, 26 July 1963; ibid., No. 6, 13 September 1963.
[2] *Platt's Oilgram*, 14 March 1963; *MEES*, No. 20, 22 March 1963.
[3] See below, p. 306, and see Map 4 on p. 262.   [4] See Chapter 12.
[5] See Chapter 14, p. 247 and Map 1.

daries has become more complicated recently, due to differences over the ownership of some offshore islands and reefs that would naturally affect the construction of the median line of the sea between Bahrain and Qatar. Apparently, the only large island that forms an obstacle in the way of reaching a settlement on this matter is Huwar, the Bahraini ownership of which is disputed by Qatar. From the viewpoint of Qatar, Huwar, which has for a long time been recognised as belonging to Bahrain, is very close to the Qatar peninsula and it thus should be regarded as part of it. Besides, Qatar also objects to Bahraini ownership of certain reefs and sand islands; in particular, Qatar seems to question Bahraini right to attribute territorial seas to such tiny islands.[1]

With regard to the offshore boundaries of Qatar and the seven Trucial States, they still seem to be in dispute. Qatar shares undefined offshore boundaries with both Abu Dhabi and Saudi Arabia,[2] while Abu Dhabi shares undefined offshore boundaries with Dubai. The problem of delimiting the offshore boundaries of Trucial Shaikhdoms has assumed greater importance recently as a result of the claim which the Ruler of Abu Dhabi laid to an offshore area lying within the jurisdiction of neighbouring Dubai, where Continental Oil of Dubai recently spudded a wildcat well. The strip of territory concerned was 'apparently allotted to Dubai as a result of a settlement reached in 1965'. The well, 'located 100 kilometres offshore, in the northwest corner of Dubai concession area is close to the border of Abu Dhabi and not far from the median line with Iran'.[3]

(c) *The problem of islands: disputes over the ownership of Halul, Sir Abu Nuʿayr, Abu Musa, Tunb and other smaller islands*

Disputes over the ownership of offshore islands extending from west to east in the lower Gulf may be described in the following order:

Abu Dhabi–Qatar dispute over the ownership of Halul and other smaller islands: Halul, the largest of these islands, lies about 60 miles

---

[1] Information supplied to the author from a private source. See Map 4.

[2] See above, p. 263 where reference is made to the conclusion in December 1965 of an agreement defining both the onshore and offshore boundaries of Saudi Arabia with Qatar. It is reported that Saudi Arabia's boundaries with Qatar 'have not yet been demarcated'. Historically, Saudi Arabia has claimed 'about 23 miles of coast line southeast of Qatar, thus separating the latter from . . . Abu Dhabi. A concession granted by Qatar in 1963 to the Continental Oil Company covers, among other things, a 337-sq. mile strip in the extreme south of the Shaikhdom along the Saudi border in the disputed area.' See *MEES*, No. 6, 10 December 1965; *World Petroleum*, February 1966, p. 10.

[3] According to reports the then Ruler of Abu Dhabi, Shaikh Shakhbut, had questioned the validity of the boundary agreement he himself reached, through British mediation, with the Ruler of Abu Dubai. See *MEES*, No. 32, 10 June 1966; *The Oil and Gas Journal*, 13 June 1966.

off the coast of the Qatar peninsula. According to Sir Rupert Hay, in the past Halul 'has usually been regarded as belonging to Abu Dhabi but is also claimed by Qatar'.[1] Recently, as a result of offshore oil exploration in the vicinity of Halul, the two Shaikhdoms intensified their rivalry over the ownership of the island. Consequently, the British Government chose, with the approval of the two Shaikhdoms, two British 'experts' to whom it assigned the duty to examine the Shaikhdoms' rival claims to the islands. According to reports, in the spring of 1962, the two British experts, Mr Charles Goult, former British Political Agent in Bahrain, and Professor J. N. D. Anderson, Professor of Islamic Law in the University of London, reported to the British Government their findings on the issue. They found that 'the largest of the islands, Halul, should belong to Qatar and several smaller ones to Abu Dhabi'. However, it was then reported that the British experts left undecided the question of two of the islands 'over which the rival claims are judged to be equal'.[2] Having received the approval of the British Government, the decision of the British experts was communicated to the Rulers of the two Shaikhdoms. So far as Qatar is concerned, the Ruler issued on 10 March 1962 a decree in which he declared his concurrence with the decision of the British experts regarding the establishment of Qatari right of ownership over the island of Halul. The decree also noted the fact that the British Government 'has approved the extension of Qatar's sovereignty to this island'.[3]

By way of comment, it would be interesting to know the historical and legal basis upon which the two British arbitrators based their verdict. In particular, the question arises whether they, in the course of their consideration of the issue of ownership over the islands, applied, or sought guidance from, certain principles of customary international law relating to title to territory (i.e., the principles of 'contiguity' or 'historical continuity').[4] Having regard to the fact that one of the arbitrators is Professor of Islamic Law, there would, perhaps, be a basis for the belief that certain Muslim and Arabian customary principles relating to fishing and hunting activities on the islands were considered by the arbitrators in the course of their deliberations.

The status of Sir Abu Nuʿayr, Abu Musa, Sirri and Tunb: These islands, except Sir Abu Nuʿayr, are nearer the eastern side of the Gulf. They

[1] Hay, op cit., p. 118.

[2] A brief reference to the award was made in *The Daily Telegraph*, 26 April 1962. No mention was made of the names of the other two smaller islands. The British Government has not published the award.

[3] The Decree issued by the Ruler of Qatar was published in the Government's *Official Gazette*, No. 2, Shawwal 27/1381–2 April 1962.

[4] Jennings, R. Y., *The Acquisition of Territory in International Law* (1963), pp. 76–80.

have been subject to long-standing disputes between Iran and both Sharjah and Ras al-Khaimah. Although at present Ras al-Khaimah exercises jurisdiction over Tunb (or Tanb) islands, while Sharjah exercises jurisdiction over the rest (except Sirri), Iran has not yet relinquished her claim to these islands. Such unsettled claims could delay offshore boundary settlements. According to Sir Rupert Hay, the islands of Abu Musa and Abu Nu'ayr, lying 'about 45 and 65 miles from Sharjah respectively, are included in the Shaikhdom [of Sharjah]'. The Ruler of Sharjah, he says, granted a British Company concessions to exploit the 'deposits of red oxide' which the two islands contain. The former, he continues, 'has wells of potable water and a small settled population, and a brother of the Ruler sometimes resides on it as Governor'.[1] Concerning the island of Sirri, Lorimer states that as early as 1887 the Persians started flying their flag over it. Although the British Government, he continues, supported Sharjah's claim to the island at the time, it did not seem to pursue the claim after 1888. Subsequently, the Persians appear to have exercised various acts of jurisdiction over the island.[2]

In the summer of 1964, the island of Abu Musa was reported to have been occupied by Iran. But the reports about the latter's occupation of the island appear to have started 'when a Persian ship put a buoy near the island'. Although Iran subsequently denied the reports, it seems clear that she still maintains a claim to this as well as to Tunb islands.[3]

(d) *Negotiations on the settlement of the offshore boundaries between Iran and the Shaikhdoms of Bahrain, Qatar, Abu Dhabi, Dubai, Sharjah, Ajman, Umm al-Qaiwain and Ras al-Khaimah*[4]

Negotiations between Iran and the United Kingdom on the delimitation of the submarine boundaries between Iran, on the eastern side of the Gulf, and the Arab Shaikhdoms, on the western side of the Gulf, have been in progress for some time. It is reported that the negotiations are aimed at reaching an agreement on the principle of constructing the median line between Iran and these Shaikhdoms. According to recent reports, 'negotiations are being held in London between the British Foreign Office, which looks after the foreign relations of the Shaikhdoms, and an Iranian delegation headed by Amir Taimur, Political Director of the Iranian Foreign Ministry'. In view of the Iranian territorial claim to Bahrain, the latter is excluded from the negotiations for the time being. The agreement will probably

---

[1] Hay, op. cit., pp. 123–4.   [2] Lorimer, p. 2066.

[3] *MEES*, No. 14, 4 February 1966. And see Appendix IV for the undertaking by Sharjah respecting Tumb island.

[4] For first hand information on the progress of these negotiations, see *MEES*, No. 8, 24 December 1965 and No. 14, 4 February 1966. See Map 1.

incorporate the same principles upon which the Iran-Saudi Arabia offshore agreement was initialled on 13 December 1965. This latter agreement, as will be seen below, is based on the acceptance of the principle of fixing the baseline, from which the median line could be constructed between the two countries, from the low water, or 'the lowest low water' mark on both sides of the Arabian and Iranian coasts. One of the major problems facing the British Government in this matter is the question whether islands could be considered for the purpose of fixing the baseline. It is understood that the British Government has consistently taken the view that islands should, generally, be disregarded for the purpose of measuring the baseline. Iran, on the other hand, appears to insist on considering certain islands that are not located at a considerable distance from her main-land as part of her coastline. For that reason, she has regarded the large island of Qeshm—Jazireh-e Qeshm—as part of the Iranian coastline.[1] Concerning the Arabian side of the Gulf, the Ruler of Abu Dhabi is reported to have claimed the island of Bani Yas as part of the Shaikhdom's coastline. According to reports, 'he feels so strongly about this that he is willing to go to arbitration with the Persians on this matter'. Furthermore, there is the problem of deter-mining ownership of the islands of Abu Musa and Tunb, as part of the awaited settlement of the submarine boundaries in this sector of the Gulf.[2]

THE SETTLED BOUNDARY DISPUTES

(a) *The Offshore Boundary Agreement between Bahrain and Saudi Arabia, dated 22 February 1958*

This is the first formally concluded agreement concerning the delinea-tion of offshore boundaries in the Arabian Gulf. The agreement which was signed personally by the King of Saudi Arabia and the Ruler of Bahrain on 22 February 1958,[3] deals with the definition of the offshore boundaries between Saudi Arabia and Bahrain on the basis of 'the middle line', as drawn with reference to fixed geographical points on maps. By Article 1, paragraph 16, of the agreement, it is stated that

[1] It is learned that the Iranians had expressed the view that the baseline for measuring the median line in the Gulf should be fixed from the southern edge of the prominent island of Qeshm. This suggestion seems to favour the famous rule put forward by S. W. Boggs, the United States (Department of State) geographer. See above, p. 289 and n. 3.

[2] *MEES*, No. 14, 4 February 1966.

[3] The agreement was written and signed in Riyadh, in two original Arabic copies, on 4 Sha'ban 1377, corresponding to 22 February 1958. For the original Arabic text, see *Umm al-Qura* (Saudi Gazette), No. 1708, dated 17 Sha'ban 1377, corresponding to 7 March 1958. The above-mentioned quotations from the agree-ment are based upon an English translation of the agreement provided by the British Foreign Office and published in *I.C.L.Q.*, 7 (1958), pp. 519–21.

'everything that is situated to the left of the abovementioned line . . . belongs to the Kingdom of Saudi Arabia and everything to the right of that line to the Government of Bahrain, with the obligation of the two governments to accept what will subsequently appear' in the second Article. Article 2 refers to an irregular hexagonal zone (approximately double the size of Bahrain) situated north of Bahrain within six defined sides. The definition of this zone is made by reference to latitudes and longitudes. By this Article, it is stated that 'this area cited and defined above shall be in the part falling to the Kingdom of Saudi Arabia, in accordance with the wish of His Highness the Ruler of Bahrain and the agreement of the King of Saudi Arabia'. Concerning the exploitation of oil resources from the Abu Sa'fah field, lying within this hexagonal area, it is agreed that this 'will be carried out in the way chosen by His Majesty on the condition that he grants to the Government of Bahrain one half of the net revenue accruing to the Government of Saudi Arabia and arising from this exploitation, and on the understanding that this does not infringe the right of sovereignty of the Government of Saudi Arabia nor the right of administration over the above-mentioned area'.[1]

The significance of this agreement lies in the fact that it represents the first attempt made in the Arabian Gulf between States whose coasts are opposite each other to comply with the proposals of the International Law Commission on the Law of the Sea, later embodied in the Geneva Convention on the Continental Shelf of April 1958. Article 6 of this Convention provides that 'the boundary of the continental shelf appertaining to such States shall be determined by agreement between them'.[2] Moreover, it is suggested that the boundary line established by Article 1 of the agreement constitutes an approximate median line.[3] It is noteworthy that the conformity of this agreement with 'the principle of equidistance' is of special importance because its validity *vis-à-vis* third littoral States would have to be due 'either to the application of the principle of equidistance or to an

---

[1] Article 3 of the agreement provides: 'Two copies of a map shall be attached to this agreement, making as clear as possible the positions and points referred to in the foregoing subsections, subject to the map being made final by the expert knowledge of the committee defined in the fourth clause below. This map shall become final and an integral part of this agreement after approval and signature by the accredited representatives of the two governments on behalf of the two parties.' It is learned that the final maps of the agreement were approved under cover of a letter from the Ruler of Bahrain dated 21 April 1960. See Appendix X and Map 4.

[2] See above, p. 288.

[3] See Lauterpacht, E., 'Contemporary Practice of the United Kingdom in the Field of International Law', *I.C.L.Q.*, 7 (1958), p. 519. But see a contrary view by Padwa, op. cit., p. 630, where he maintains the view that the Bahrain-Saudi Arabia agreement does not 'utilise the principle of equidistance'. It is to be noted that the Arabic text of the agreement uses the expression 'al-Khat al-Wasat', the literal meaning of which is translated in the English text as 'the middle line'.

absence of protest and tacit acquiescence by such other States'[1].
As Iran was the only littoral State which protested to Saudi Arabia
against the conclusion of this offshore agreement, it may be presumed
that her protest was based on her claim to sovereignty over Bahrain
rather than on the non-utilisation of the line of equidistance in the
agreement.[2]

General observations: The above-mentioned Bahrain–Saudi Arabia
boundary agreement deserves the following observations.

It is clear from the general direction of the 'middle line' of the
agreement that after reaching Point 12 it deflects abruptly to Points
13 and 14 in a northeasterly direction in order to facilitate the shifting
of the whole of the 'hexagonal zone' (the subject of Article 2) which
contains the Abu Saʿfah oil field to the Saudi Arabian side of the
line. An examination of the records[3] of the negotiations between
Bahrain and Saudi Arabia over the delimitation of their offshore
boundaries reveals that 'Fasht Abu Saʿfah' (the Arabic name for the
hexagonal area which has been allocated to Saudi Arabia under this
agreement) was originally claimed to belong to Bahrain. In fact, the
former Ruler of Bahrain had for many years in the past laid a claim
to Fasht Abu Saʿfah and the two islands of Lubaynah al-Kabirah and
Lubaynah al-Saghirah. Accordingly, the Bahrain Petroleum Company
(Bapco) was granted in 1941 the right to carry out exploration and
drilling work on Fasht Abu Saʿfah. However, owing to the Saudi
Government's objection, the exploration work on the Fasht, which
was undertaken by Bapco following the end of the Second World
War, was suspended pending the settlement of the question of sover-
eignty over the Fasht. In the first major round of negotiations which
were held in London in 1951, the British delegation representing
Bahrain proposed that the Lubaynah islands should be recognised as
belonging to Bahrain and the Rennie shoal to Saudi Arabia. This
proposal was refused by the Saudi delegation who claimed that
Fasht Abu Saʿfah and Lubaynah al-Kabirah should belong to Saudi
Arabia. A few years later, the Ruler of Bahrain offered to cede
Lubaynah al-Kabirah to Saudi Arabia provided it carried with it no

---

[1] Padwa, op. cit., p. 630. And see McGibbon, I. C., 'The Scope of Acquiescence
in International Law', *B.Y.I.L.*, 31 (1954), p. 143.

[2] Press reports confirmed that Iran's objection to the conclusion of the boundary
agreement was based on her claim to sovereignty over Bahrain which she regards
as an 'integral part of Iran'. Iran was reported to have presented protest notes to
both Saudi Arabia and Britain in this regard. In addition, Dr A. Ardalan, the
then Foreign Minister of Iran, was reported to have said that Iran would consider
as 'an encroachment on her right' any move by any foreign country or oil company
to utilise the agreement. See *New York Times*, 11 March 1958; *United Press International* (Radio News), 4 March 1958.

[3] Government of Bahrain, The Secretariat, *File of Confidential Correspondence
regarding Bahrain–Saudi Arabia Boundaries*, 1959.

territorial waters. Concerning Fasht Abu Sa'fah, he proposed the division of the Fasht into two parts: a western part which should belong to Saudi Arabia and an eastern part which should belong to Bahrain. Following discussions in 1954, the Saudis agreed to the principle of dividing Fasht Abu Sa'fah. However, in a meeting which was held in Dammam (Saudi Arabia) there arose a difference of opinion on the principle of drawing the dividing line of the Fasht. Consequently, during the negotiations which followed the Dammam conference the idea of the equal sharing of oil exploited from the area of the Fasht, without attempting to make a geographical division, seemed to have appealed to both countries.

The above description sums up the status of the offshore boundary dispute between Bahrain and Saudi Arabia up to the end of 1957. This brings us to the final stage of the negotiations which in turn prepared the way for the conclusion of the boundary agreement of 1958. This new phase of the negotiations took place in February 1958, during an official visit by the Ruler of Bahrain to Saudi Arabia. During this visit the King of Saudi Arabia and the Ruler of Bahrain had a chance to hold talks on their boundary problems 'in an amicable and friendly spirit'.[1] Consequently, the two Heads of Governments reached an amicable settlement of their boundary dispute, in accordance with the terms of the Boundary Agreement of 22 February 1958. As is shown above, the Ruler of Bahrain has agreed by this agreement to relinquish his claim to sovereignty over Fasht Abu Sa'fah in return for the Saudi Government's obligation to grant to Bahrain 'one half of the net oil revenue' accruing to the Saudi Government from the Abu Sa'fah area which now lies exclusively within the Saudi Government's jurisdiction.

Concerning the two islands of Lubaynah al-Kabirah and Lubaynah al-Saghirah, the boundary agreement assigns the former to Saudi Arabia and the latter to Bahrain without, however, attributing a belt of territorial sea to either of them. This arrangement is consistent with the proposal which the late Ruler of Bahrain made to the Saudis during the early part of the negotiations. However, the arrangement to deprive the two islands from their natural territorial seas is not expressly provided in the agreement. It is noteworthy, in this connection, that according to generally accepted legal principles, an island, 'wherever it may be situated, and whatever (and however minimal) its area, . . . *must have* its own territorial sea'.[2]

---

[1] The preamble to the agreement.

[2] Fitzmaurice, Sir Gerald, 'Some Results of the Geneva Conference on the Law of the Seas', *I.C.L.Q.*, 8 (1959), p. 85. A territorial belt is thus regarded as an essential and 'inseparable appurtenance' of the land territory. See *Grisbadarna case*: Decision of the Tribunal of the Permanent Court of Arbitration, as quoted in Scott, *The Hague Court Reports*, p. 127. Naturally, the definition of an island must

(b) *The Offshore Boundary Agreement between Iran and Saudi Arabia, initialled on 13 December 1965*[1]

On 13 December 1965 the Government of Saudi Arabia, represented by Shaikh Ahmed Zaki Yamani, Minister of Petroleum and Mineral Resources, and the Government of Iran, represented by Mr Abbas Aram, Minister of Foreign Affairs, initialled an agreement relating to the definition of the 'boundary line separating the submarine areas which appertain to Saudi Arabia from the submarine areas which appertain to Iran'. The agreement, which has not yet been signed or ratified, purposely avoids mentioning the 'Gulf' under any description. Although neither Iran nor Saudi Arabia has yet acceded to the Geneva Convention on the Continental Shelf of 1958, the boundary agreement generally conforms to the principles adopted in that Convention. Accordingly, the preamble to the agreement provides that each party enjoys, in respect of the 'submarine areas' in the Gulf, the same 'sovereign rights' as those to which it is 'entitled by International Law'. Furthermore, the agreement resolves the long-standing dispute between the two countries over the ownership of the two islands of al-Arabiyah and al-Farisiyah (Farsi) by recognising Saudi sovereignty over the former and Iranian sovereignty over the latter. It also resolves Saudi-Iranian dispute over the overlapping of offshore concession areas resulting from the NIOC pre-announcement about the opening of acreage in Iran's District I in the Gulf.[2] Briefly, the provisions of the agreement are as follows:

Articles 2 and 3 provide that 'except in the vicinity of Al-ʿArabiyah and Farsi' islands, 'the boundary line separating the submarine areas which appertain to Saudi Arabia from the submarine areas which appertain to Iran' shall be determined by 'a straight line' drawn between geographical co-ordinates. By Article 3, the 'lowest low water' mark along the opposite coasts is recognised as the base point for the drawing of the median line. The islands lying not more than twelve nautical miles from the mainland are included within the division of the boundary line. However, in relation to Kharg island, which lies more than twelve nautical miles from the Iranian mainland, it is stated that two lines shall be laid out: 'one equidistant from the coastlines of Saudi Arabia and Iran and the other equidistant from the line of lowest low water on Kharg and the coastline of Saudi Arabia. The boundary line in this area shall be a line equidistant between the

---

conform to Article 10 of the Convention on the Law of the Sea, op. cit. Accordingly, an island 'is a naturally-formed area of land, surrounded by water, which is above water at high-tide'.

[1] The draft agreement has not been published.

[2] See above, p. 295

two lines thus described until this line intersects the line drawn from
point 5 to point P. described above.' Concerning the islands of al-
'Arabiyah and Farsi, each of which is assigned a 12-mile belt of
territorial sea, it is provided that 'where these belts overlap, a boundary
line separating the territorial seas of the two islands shall be drawn so
as to be equidistant throughout its length from the lowest low water
lines on each island' (Art. 1).

By Article 4, it is provided that 'within two months of the entry into
force of this agreement, there shall be established a joint technical
commission of four members . . . which shall be charged with defining the boundary herein agreed upon, in terms of a series of geographical co-ordinates. . . .' The line fixed by the joint commission
shall, if approved by the two Governments, 'constitute the final and
binding definition of the boundary, unless either Government makes
objection thereto within one month after its submission'.

APPENDIX I

Translation of Agreement signed by the Chief of Bahrain, dated 22 December 1880[1]

I, Isa bin Ali Al-Khalifeh, Chief of Bahrein, hereby bind myself and successors in the Government of Bahrein to the British Government to abstain from entering into negotiations or making treaties of any sort with any State or Government other than the British without the consent of the said British Government, and to refuse permission to any other Government than the British to establish diplomatic or consular agencies or coaling depots in our territory, unless with the consent of the British Government.

This engagement does not apply to or affect the customary friendly correspondence with the local authorities of neighbouring States on business of minor importance.

The above Agreement is subject to the approval and acceptance of His Excellency the Viceroy and Governor-General of India in Council.

ISA BIN ALI
AHMAD BIN ALI

Signed and sealed at Bahrein on the twenty-second day of December one thousand eight hundred and eighty in my presence.

E. C. ROSS, *Lieut.-Col.,*
Political Resident, Persian Gulf

The above Agreement was accepted and ratified by Her Britannic Majesty's Government in 1881.

E. C. ROSS, *Colonel,*
Political Resident, Persian Gulf

APPENDIX II

Exclusive Agreement of the Shaikh of Bahrain with the British Government dated 13 March 1892[2]

I Esau bin Ali, Chief of Bahrein, in the presence of Lieutenant-Colonel A. C. Talbot, C.I.E., Political Resident, Persian Gulf, do hereby solemnly bind myself and agree, on behalf of myself, my heirs and successors, to the following conditions, *viz.*:—

1st.—That I will on no account enter into any agreement or correspondence with any Power other than the British Government.

2nd.—That without the assent of the British Government, I will not

---

[1] Aitchison, p. 237.   [2] Ibid., p. 238.

consent to the residence within my territory of the agent of any other Government.

3rd.—That I will on no account cede, sell, mortgage or otherwise give for occupation any part of my territory save to the British Government.

Dated Bahrein, 13th March 1892, corresponding with 14th Shaaban 1309.

ESAU BIN ALI,
Chief of Bahrein

A. C. TALBOT, *Lieut.-Col.,*
Resident, Persian Gulf

LANSDOWNE,
Viceroy and Governor General of India

Ratified by His Excellency the Viceroy and Governor-General of India at Simla on the twelfth day of May 1892.

H. M. DURAND,
Secretary to the Government of India, Foreign Dept

APPENDIX III

Exclusive Agreement of the Chief of Abu Dhabi with the British Government, dated 6 March 1892[1]

I, Zaeed bin Khalifah, Chief of Abu Dhabi, in the presence of Lieutenant-Colonel A. C. Talbot, C.I.E., Political Resident in the Persian Gulf, do hereby solemnly bind myself and agree, on behalf of myself, my heirs and successors to the following conditions, *viz.*:—

1st.—That I will on no account enter into any agreement or correspondence with any Power other than the British Government.

2nd.—That without the assent of the British Government I will not consent to the residence within my territory of the agent of any other Government.

3rd.—That I will on no account cede, sell, mortgage or otherwise give for occupation any part of my territory, save to the British Government.

Dated Abu Dhabi, 6th March 1892, corresponding to 5th Shaaban 1309 Hijri.

SIGNATURE OF ZAEED BIN KHALIFA, CHIEF OF ABU DHABI
A. C. TALBOT, *Lieut.-Col.,*
Resident in the Persian Gulf

LANSDOWNE,
Viceroy and Governor-General of India

Ratified by His Excellency the Viceroy and Governor-General of India at Simla on the twelfth day of May 1892.

H. M. DURAND,
Secretary to the Govt. of India,
Foreign Dept

[1] Aitchison, p. 256.

(The agreements signed by the other Trucial Shaikhs, *viz.*, the Chiefs of Dabai, Ajman, Shargah, Ras-ul-Khima and Umm-ul-Gawain, the first three dated 7 and the last two 8 March 1892, are identical in form.)

APPENDIX IV

Undertaking by the Chief of Shargah, for the establish-ment of a lighthouse on the Island of Tamb—1912[1]

Dated 1st Zilkadah 1330 (= 13 October 1912).

From—SHAIKH SAGAR BIN KHALED, Chief of Shargah.,
To—LIEUTENANT-COLONEL SIR PERCY COX, K.C.I.E., C.S.I., Political Resident in the Persian Gulf.

After compliments and enquiries after your health—
I beg to state that our condition is good and the news is tranquil. Your esteemed letter dated the 16th Shawal (28th September) was received on the 1st Zilkadah (= 13th October 1912) and what you had stated was duly understood.

As regards our Island of Tamb and (the fact that) you have requested me for permission for the establishment of a lighthouse thereon for the guidance of steamers. All right; but we hope from you that there will be no interference with the Island beyond that. This is a condition from us and we trust that, God willing, we shall receive a letter from you to this effect. In regard to our representative there we shall, God willing, not neglect about him as stated by you. And I will esteem it an honour to carry on what you require of us.

APPENDIX V

The Treaty of Sib, 1920[2]

In the Name of God, the Compassionate, the Merciful

This is the peace agreed upon between the Government of the Sultan, Taimur ibn Faisal, and Shaikh Isa ibn Salih ibn Ali on behalf of the people of Oman whose names are signed hereto, through the mediation of Mr. Wingate, I.C.S., Political Agent and Consul for Great Britain in Muscat, who is empowered by his Government in this respect and to be an inter-mediary between them. Of the conditions set forth below, four pertain to

[1] Aitchison, p. 258.
[2] The Arab Information Centre, *The Status of Oman and the British Omanite Dispute*, New York, September 1957.

the Government of the Sultan and four pertain to the people of Oman. Those pertaining to the people of Oman are:

1. Not more than five per cent shall be taken from anyone, no matter what his race, coming from Oman to Muscat or Matrah or Sur or the rest of the towns of the coast.
2. All the people of Oman shall enjoy security and freedom in all the towns of the coast.
3. All restrictions upon everyone entering and leaving Muscat and Matrah and all the towns of the coast shall be removed.
4. The Government of the Sultan shall not grant asylum to any criminal fleeing from the justice of the people of Oman. It shall return him to them if they request it to do so. It shall not interfere in their internal affairs.

The four conditions pertaining to the Government of the Sultan are:

1. All the tribes and Shaikhs shall be at peace with the Sultan. They shall not attack the towns of the coast and shall not interfere in his Government.
2. All those going to Oman on lawful business and for commercial affairs shall be free. There shall be no restrictions on commerce, and they shall enjoy security.
3. They shall expel and grant no asylum to any wrongdoer or criminal fleeing to them.
4. The claims of merchants and others against the people of Oman shall be heard and decided on the basis of justice according to the law of Islam.

Written on 11 Muharram 1339, corresponding to 25 September 1920

APPENDIX VI

Undertaking by the Shaikh of Shargah, regarding oil—1922[1]

Letter from Sheikh Khaled ben Ahmed, Chief of Shargah, to the Hon'ble Lieutenant-Colonel A. P. Trevor, C.S.I., C.I.E., Political Resident, Persian Gulf, Bushire, dated 18th Jamadi-os-Sani, 1340 (= 17 February 1922).

After Compliments—

My object in writing this letter of friendship is to convey my compliments to you and to enquire after your health.

Secondly, let it not be hidden from you that I write this letter with my free will and give undertaking to Your Honour that if it is hoped that an oil mine will be found in my territory I will not give a concession for it to foreigners except to the person appointed by the High British Government.

This is what was necessary to be stated.

NOTE.—A similar undertaking was given by the Chief of Ras-al-Khaima, on the 22nd February 1922.

[1] Aitchison, p. 261.

APPENDIX VII

Undertaking by the Shaikh of Dibai, regarding oil—1922[1]

Letter from Sheikh Saeed ben Maktoom, Chief of Debai, to Lieutenant-Colonel A. P. Trevor, C.S.I., C.I.E., Political Resident, Persian Gulf, dated 4th Ramazan 1340 (= 2 May 1922).

After Compliments—
Let it not be hidden from you that we agree, if oil is expected to be found in our territory, not to grant any concession in this connection to any one except to the person appointed by the High British Government.

NOTE.—Undertakings similar in substance to the above were given by the following Shaikhs on the dates mentioned:—

Shaikh of Abu Dhabi .   .   .   .   . 3 May 1922.
Shaikh of Ajman   .   .   .   .   . 4 May 1922.
Shaikh of Umm-al-Qaiwain   .   .   . 8 May 1922.

APPENDIX VIII

Kuwait–Najd Boundary Convention—1922[2]

KUWAIT-NAJD BOUNDARY CONVENTION

In the Name of God, the Merciful, the Compassionate

The frontier between Najd and Kuwait begins in the West from junction of the Wadi al Aujah (W. al Audja) with the Batin (El Batin), leaving Raq'i (Rikai) to Najd, from this point it continues in a straight line until it joins latitude 29° and the red semi-circle referred to in Article 5 of the Anglo-Turkish Agreement of 29th July 1913. The line then follows the side of the red semi-circle until it reaches a point terminating (*sic*) on the coast south of Ras al-Qali'ah (Ras el Kaliyah) and this is the indisputable southern frontier of Kuwait territory. The portion of territory bounded on the North by this line and which is bounded on the West by a low mountainous ridge called Shaq (Esh Shakk) and on the East by the sea and on the South by a line passing from West to East from Shaq (Esh Shakk) to 'Ain al 'Abd (Ain el Abd) and thence to the coast north of Ras al Mish'ab (Ras Mishaab), in this territory the Governments of Najd and Kuwait will share equal rights until through the good offices of the Government of Great Britain a further agreement is made between Najd and Kuwait concerning it.

The map on which this boundary has been made is Asia 1-1,000,000, made by the Royal Geographical Society under the direction of the Geographical Section General Staff and printed at the War Office in the year 1918.

[1] Ibid.   [2] Ibid., pp. 213–14.

Written in the port of 'Uqair and signed by the representatives of both Governments on the Second day of December 1922 corresponding to 13th of Rabi'al Thani, 1341.

> ABDULLAH SA'ID DAMLUJI
> Representative of His
> Highness the Sultan of Najd
> J. C. MORE Major
> Political Agent, Kuwait.

I have agreed to the contents of this agreement.

> 'ABDUL 'AZIZ BIN 'ABDUL RAHMAN AS-SA'UD
> Sultan of Najd and its Dependencies

I have agreed to the contents of this agreement.

> AHMAD AL-JABIR AS-SUBAH
> Hakim of Kuwait

(*Translator's note.*—The spelling of place names in brackets is that used in the map referred to in the treaty.)

APPENDIX IX

Bahrain Government Proclamation No. 37/1368
5 June 1949[1]

TO WHOM IT MAY CONCERN:

Whereas it is desirable to encourage any efforts to facilitate the derivation of greater benefit from the natural resources of the earth, and

Whereas valuable resources exist beneath parts of the Persian Gulf near the shores of Bahrain, and it has become possible to derive increasing benefit from these submarine resources, and

Whereas it is desirable, for the purposes of conservation, preservation, and orderly development, that extraction of these resources shall be regulated as necessity dictates, and

Whereas it is just that the sea bed and subsoil extending a reasonable distance from the shore should belong to and be administered by the government of the adjacent coast, and

Whereas the right of any coastal government to exercise its sovereignty over the natural resources of the sea bed and the subsoil in the vicinity of its shores has been established by international practice through the action taken by other governments.

Accordingly, We, Salman Ibn Hamad Al Khalifah, Ruler of Bahrain, by virtue of the powers vested in us in this respect are pleased to issue hereby the following proclamation:

We, Salman Ibn Hamad Al Khalifah, Ruler of Bahrain hereby declare that the sea bed and the subsoil of the high seas of the Persian Gulf bordering on the territorial waters of Bahrain and extending seaward as far as

---

[1] *A.J.I.L.*, Vol. 43, Suppl. (1949), pp. 185–6. Translation from Arabic.

limits that we, after consultation with neighbouring governments, shall determine more accurately in accordance with the principles of justice, when the occasion so requires, belong to the country of Bahrain and are subject to its absolute authority and jurisdiction.

There is nothing in this proclamation that may be interpreted as affecting dominion over the islands or the status of the sea bed and the subsoil underlying any territorial waters.

There is nothing in this proclamation that may be interpreted as affecting the character of the high seas in the waters of the Persian Gulf overlying the sea bed and beyond the limits of the territorial waters, or the status of the air space above the waters of the Persian Gulf beyond the territorial waters, or fishing or the traditional rights of pearling in these waters.

SALMAN IBN HAMAD AL KHALIFAH
Ruler of Bahrain

8 Sha'ban 1368
(5 June 1949)

APPENDIX X

The Bahrain–Saudi Arabia Boundary Agreement dated 22 February 1958[1]

In the Name of God the Merciful, the Compassionate. Agreement between the Kingdom of Saudi Arabia and the Government of Bahrain

Whereas the regional waters between the Kingdom of Saudi Arabia and the Government of Bahrain meet together in many places overlooked by their respective coasts,

And in view of the royal proclamation issued by the Kingdom of Saudi Arabia on the 1st Sha'aban in the year 1368 (corresponding to 28th May 1949) and the ordinance issued by the Government of Bahrain on the 5th June 1949 about the exploitation of the sea bed,

And in view of the necessity for an agreement to define the under-water areas belonging to both countries,

And in view of the spirit of affection and mutual friendship and the desire of H.M. the King of Saudi Arabia to extend every possible assistance to the Government of Bahrain,

the following agreement has been made:

First Clause

1. The boundary line between the Kingdom of Saudi Arabia and the Bahrain Government will begin, on the basis of the middle line from point 1, which is situated at the mid-point of the line running between the tip of the Ras al Bar (A) at the southern extremity of Bahrain and Ras Muharra (B) on the coast of the Kingdom of Saudi Arabia.

2. Then the above-mentioned middle line will extend from point 1 to

[1] English text published in *I.C.L.Q.*, vol. 7 (1958), p. 518.

point 2 situated at the mid-point of the line running between Point (A) and the northern tip of the island of Zakhnuniya (C).

3. Then the line will extend from point 2 to point 3 situated at the mid-point of the line running between point A and the tip of Ras Saiya (D).

4. Then the line will extend from point 3 to point 4, which is defined on the attached map and which is situated at the mid-point of the line running between the two points E and F which are both defined on the map.

5. Then the line will extend from point 4 to point 5, which is defined on the map and which is situated at the point [sic] of the line running between the two points G and H which are defined on the map.

6. Then the line will extend from point 5 to point 6, which is defined on the map and which is situated at the mid-point of the line running between the two points I and J which are defined on the map.

7. Then the line will extend from point 6 to point 7 situated at the mid-point of the line running between the south-western tip of the island of Umm Nasan (K) and Ras Al Kureya (L).

8. Then the line will extend from point 7 to point 8 situated at the western extremity of the island Al Baina As Saghir, leaving the island to the Government of Bahrain.

9. Then the line will extend from point 8 to point 9 situated at the eastern extremity of the island Al Baina Al Kabir, leaving the island to the Kingdom of Saudi Arabia.

10. Then the line will extend from point 9 to point 10 situated at the mid-point of the line running between the north-western tip of Khor Fasht (M) and the southern end of the island of Chaschus (N).

11. Then the line will extend from point 10 to point 11 situated at the mid-point of the line running between point O situated at the western edge of Fasht Al Jarim and point N referred to in subsection 10 above.

12. Then the line will extend from point 11 to point 12 situated at latitude 26 degrees 31 minutes 48 seconds north and longitude 50 degrees 23 minutes 15 seconds east approximately.

13. Then the line will extend from point 12 to point 13 situated at latitude 26 degrees 37 minutes 15 seconds north and longitude 50 degrees 33 minutes 24 seconds east approximately.

14. Then the line will extend from point 13 to point 14 situated at latitude 26 degrees 59 minutes 30 seconds north and longitude 50 degrees 46 minutes 24 seconds east approximately, leaving the Rennie Shoals (known as Najwat Al Riqai and Fasht Al Anawiyah) to the Kingdom of Saudi Arabia.

15. Then the line will extend from point 14 in a north-easterly direction to the extent agreed upon in the royal proclamation issued on the 1st Sha'aban in the year 1368 (corresponding to 28th May, 1949) and in the ordinance issued by the Government of Bahrain on the 5th June, 1949.

16. Everything that is situated to the left of the above-mentioned line in the above subsections belongs to the Kingdom of Saudi Arabia and everything to the right of that line to the Government of Bahrain, with the obligation of the two governments to accept what will subsequently appear in the second clause below.

Second Clause

The area situated within the six defined sides is as follows:

1. A line beginning from a point situated at latitude 27 degrees north and longitude 50 degrees 23 minutes east approximately.

2. From there to a point situated at latitude 26 degrees 31 minutes 48 seconds north and longitude 50 degrees 23 minutes 15 seconds east approximately.

3. From there to a point situated at latitude 26 degrees 37 minutes north and longitude 50 degrees 33 minutes east approximately.

4. From there to a point situated at latitude 26 degrees 59 minutes 30 seconds north and longitude 50 degrees 46 minutes 24 seconds east approximately.

5. From there to a point situated at latitude 26 degrees 59 minutes 30 seconds north and longitude 50 degrees 40 minutes east.

6. From there to a point situated at latitude 27 degrees north and longitude 50 degrees 40 minutes east approximately.

7. From there to the starting point.

This area cited and defined above shall be in the part falling to the Kingdom of Saudi Arabia in accordance with the wish of H.H. the Ruler of Bahrain and the agreement of H.M. the King of Saudi Arabia. The exploitation of the oil resources in this area will be carried out in the way chosen by His Majesty on the condition that he grants to the Government of Bahrain one half of the net revenue accruing to the Government of Saudi Arabia and arising from this exploitation, and on the understanding that this does not infringe the right of sovereignty of the Government of Saudi Arabia nor the right of administration over this above-mentioned area.

Third Clause

Two copies of a map shall be attached to this agreement, making as clear as possible the positions and points referred to in the foregoing subsections, subject to the map being made final by the expert knowledge of the committee defined in the fourth clause below. This map shall become final and an integral part of this agreement after approval and signature by the accredited representatives of the two governments on behalf of the two parties.

Fourth Clause

The two parties shall choose a technical body to undertake the necessary measures to confirm the boundaries in accordance with the provisions of this agreement on the condition that this body shall complete its work two months at the most after the date of execution of this agreement.

Fifth Clause

After the committee referred to in the fourth clause has completed its work and the two parties agree on the final map which it will have prepared, a body of technical delegates from both sides shall undertake the placing of signs and the establishing of the boundaries in accordance with the detailed announcements made clear in the final map.

Y

Sixth Clause
    This agreement shall come into effect from the date on which it is signed by the two parties.
        Given in Riyadh in two original Arabic copies on the 4th of Sha'aban in the year 1377 corresponding to February 22nd in the year 1958.

APPENDIX XI

Exchange of Notes regarding relations between the United Kingdom of Great Britain and Northern Ireland and the State of Kuwait

Kuwait, 19 June 1961

No. 1

Note from Her Majesty's Political Resident in the Persian Gulf to His Highness the Ruler of Kuwait

Your Highness
Kuwait,
June 19, 1961.

    I have the honour to refer to the discussions which have recently taken place between Your Highness and my predecessor on behalf of Her Majesty's Government in the United Kingdom about the desirability of adapting the relationship of the United Kingdom of Great Britain and Northern Ireland and the State of Kuwait to take account of the fact that Your Highness' Government has the sole responsibility for the conduct of Kuwait's internal and external affairs.
    The following conclusions were reached in the course of these discussions:

(a) The Agreement of the 23rd of January, 1899,[1] shall be terminated as being inconsistent with the sovereignty and independence of Kuwait.

(b) The relations between the two countries shall continue to be governed by a spirit of close friendship.

(c) When appropriate the two Governments shall consult together on matters which concern them both.

(d) Nothing in these conclusions shall affect the readiness of Her Majesty's Government to assist the Government of Kuwait if the latter request such assistance.

    If the foregoing correctly represents the conclusions reached between Your Highness and Sir George Middleton I have the honour to suggest, on the instructions of Her Majesty's Principal Secretary of State for Foreign Affairs, that the present Note together with Your Highness' reply to that effect shall be regarded as constituting an Agreement between the United

[1] See Annex.

Kingdom and Kuwait in this matter which shall continue in force until either party gives the other at least three years' notice of their intention to terminate it, and that the Agreement of the 23rd of January, 1899, shall be regarded as terminated on this day's date

I have the honour to be,

With the highest consideration,

Your Highness' obedient servant,

W. H. LUCE

(Her Majesty's Political Resident).

No. 2

Note from His Highness the Ruler of Kuwait to Her Majesty's Political Resident in the Persian Gulf

(Translation)

Kuwait.

His Excellency,

Her Britannic Majesty's Political Resident in the Persian Gulf.

Greetings,

I have the honour to refer to Your Excellency's Note of to-day's date which reads as follows:

[As in No. 1]

I confirm that Your Excellency's Note correctly represents the conclusions reached by myself and Sir George Middleton and I agree that Your Excellency's Note and my reply shall be regarded as constituting an Agreement between Kuwait and the United Kingdom in this matter. With best regards.

ABDULLAH AL SALIM AL SABAH

June 19, 1961.

ANNEX

Agreement with the Sheikh of Koweit
23 January 1899

Translation from Arabic Bond

Praise be to God alone (lit. in the name of God Almighty) ('Bissim Illah Ta'alah Shanuho')—

The object of writing this lawful and honourable bond is that it is hereby covenanted and agreed between Lieutenant-Colonel Malcolm John Meade, I.S.C., Her Britannic Majesty's Political Resident, on behalf of the British Government on the one part, and Sheikh Mubarak-bin-Sheikh Subah, Sheikh of Koweit, on the other part, that the said Sheikh Mubarak-bin-Sheikh Subah of his own free will and desire does hereby pledge and bind himself, his heirs and successors not to receive the Agent or Representative of any Power or

Government at Koweit, or at any other place within the limits of his territory, without the previous sanction of the British Government; and he further binds himself, his heirs and successors not to cede, sell, lease, mortgage, or give for occupation or for any other purpose any portion of his territory to the Government or subjects of any other Power without the previous consent of Her Majesty's Government for these purposes. This engagement also to extend to any portion of the territory of the said Sheikh Mubarak, which may now be in the possession of the subjects of any other Government.

In token of the conclusion of this lawful and honourable bond, Lieutenant-Colonel Malcolm John Meade, I.S.C., Her Britannic Majesty's Political Resident in the Persian Gulf, and Sheikh Mubarak-bin-Sheikh Subah, the former on behalf of the British Government and the latter on behalf of himself, his heirs and successors do each, in the presence of witnesses, affix their signatures on this, the tenth day of Ramazan 1316, corresponding with the twenty-third day of January, 1899.

M. J. MEADE   MUBARAK-AL-SUBAH
Political Resident in
  the Persian Gulf

Witnesses:

E. WICKHAM HORE, Capt., I.M.S.   MUHAMMAD RAHIM BIN
T. CALCOTT GASKIN   ABDUL NEBI SAFFER

APPENDIX XII

Kuwait–Saudi Arabia Agreement to partition the Neutral Zone Signed at Al-Hadda, Saudi Arabia, 7 July 1965[1]

AGREEMENT BETWEEN THE STATE OF KUWAIT AND THE KINGDOM OF SAUDI ARABIA RELATING TO THE PARTITION OF THE NEUTRAL ZONE

In the Name of God the Compassionate, the Merciful.

Whereas the two Contracting Parties have equal rights in the shared Zone whose land boundaries are delineated in accordance with the boundary Convention made at Al Uqair in 13 Rabi, Thani, 1341 corresponding to 2nd December, 1922, and the agreed Minutes signed at Kuwait on 12 Shaual, 1380, corresponding to 21st March, 1961 (called hereinafter the 'Partitioned Zone'), and

Whereas the aforesaid Convention did not regulate the exercise of those rights, and as that state of affairs was of a provisional nature which entailed serious practical difficulties and

[1] *International Legal Materials*, vol. LV No. 6, November (1965), pp. 1134–7.

Whereas the two Contracting Parties, by an exchange of notes on 15/3/1383 corresponding to 5th August, 1963 (in regard to partitioning the Neutral Zone), have accepted to put an end to that temporary state of affairs by means of partitioning that Zone into two sections, so that the one shall be annexed to the State of Kuwait and the other shall be annexed to the Kingdom of Saudi Arabia, provided that these equal rights of the two Parties shall be preserved in full in the whole partitioned Zone as this had originally been decided by the Convention made at Al Uqair that it is shared between the two parties, and shall be safeguarded by the provisions of international responsibility. They therefore have agreed upon the following:—

Article I. The boundary line between the two sections of the Zone is to be the line which divides them into two equal parts and which begins from a point at the mid eastern shore on the low-tide line, and ends at the western boundary line of the Zone. That boundary line shall be demarcated in a natural manner by the Committee of Survey which is to determine that boundary line of the Neutral Zone and which is to be set up in the manner agreed upon in the protocol annexed to the notes exchanged between the two parties at Jeddha on 15/3/1383 corresponding to 5th August, 1963. This boundary line shall be approved by the two sides in an agreement they will conclude later on.

Article II. Without prejudice to the provisions of this agreement, the part lying to the north of the line dividing the Partitioned Zone into two equal parts shall be annexed to Kuwait as an integral part of its territory, and the part lying to the south of the line dividing the Partitioned Zone into two equal parts shall be annexed to the Kingdom of Saudi Arabia as an integral part of its territory.

Article III. Each of the Contracting Parties shall exercise the rights of administration, legislation and defence over that part of the Partitioned Zone annexed to his territory in the same manner exercised in his territory of origin while observing other provisions of the Agreement, and without prejudice to the rights of the contracting parties to natural resources in the whole of the Partitioned Zone.

Article IV. Each of the Contracting Parties shall respect the rights of the other Party to the shared natural resources either existing at present or that shall exist in future in that part of the Partitioned Zone which is annexed to his territory.

Article V. If one of the parties cedes or otherwise alienates all or part of those equal rights which are safeguarded by the provisions of this Agreement and which are exercised over any part of the Partitioned Zone to any other State, the other Party shall be relieved of his obligations under this Agreement.

Article VI. Each of the Contracting Parties shall be under obligation not to take any local or international measure or action which may result in whatsoever form in hindering the other party from exercising the rights which are safeguarded by this agreement, and he shall be under obligations to co-operate with the other Party fully to protect these rights.

Article VII. Each of the Contracting Parties shall exercise over the territorial waters which adjoin that part of the Partitioned Zone which will be annexed to its territory the same rights as those exercised over the part annexed to its territory; and the two Contracting Parties shall agree to determine the boundary line which divides the territorial waters which adjoin the Partitioned Zone.

For the purpose of exploiting the natural resources in the Partitioned Zone, not more than six marine miles of the sea-bed and sub-soil adjoining the Partitioned Zone shall be annexed to the principal land of that Partitioned Zone.

Article VIII. On determining the northern boundary of the submerged Zone adjoining the Partitioned Zone, it shall be delineated as if the Zone has not been partitioned and without regard to the provisions of this Agreement.

And, the two Contracting Parties shall exercise their equal rights in the submerged Zone beyond the aforesaid six miles limit mentioned in the previous Article, by means of shared exploitation unless the two Parties agree otherwise.

Article IX. Each of the Contracting Parties shall in the part annexed to the other party of the Partitioned Zone evacuate the establishments occupied by the government officials who perform administrative and legal work, and hand it over to the other party provided that such provisions shall not apply to establishments occupied by employees engaged in measuring oil, checking and auditing accounts, technical supervision and purchasing committees and such similar supervision work.

Article X. If one of the Contracting Parties entrusts the companies that have been granted a joint concession by the two parties, with the construction of establishments for judicial and administrative purposes in accordance with terms of the concession in that part of the Partitioned Zone to be annexed to his territory, the cost of establishing such constructions shall be deducted from the capital expenses of the concessionary companies, provided that such costs shall be limited to necessary and reasonable expenses.

Article XI. The present agreements of oil concessions shall remain in force and either Party pledges to respect their provisions and the amendments entered into in that half of the Partitioned Zone which shall be annexed to its territory. He shall also undertake such legislative and legal measures necessary for the continued exercise by the concessionary companies of their rights and discharge of their obligations.

Article XII. Each Contracting Party shall be responsible in that part of the Partitioned Zone which will be annexed to its territory for protection and security according to the obligations provided for in the present concession agreements in force.

Article XIII. To avoid double taxation, each Contracting Party shall undertake to enact legislative safeguards which ensure the non-imposition of taxation or custom duties or royalties on the companies that have been granted a concession, in the Partitioned Zone by the other Party.

Article XIV. Entry of citizens of the two contracting parties, and their moving about in the Partitioned Zone, who are working as officials, employees, labourers and contractors in establishments and firms engaged in the exploitation of natural resources according to concessions now in force and their subsidiaries shall be by valid passports issued by the other Party or by a card of special form to be issued by one of the Contracting Parties, and to be agreed upon, without the need for obtaining entry visas.

Article XV. Without prejudice to the concessionary oil agreements in force, each of the parties shall safeguard in that part of the Partitioned Zone annexed to his territory, freedom of work to the citizens of the other party and the right to practice any profession or occupation on equal levels with his citizens, concerning oil resources granted in the present concessions or in what may supersede them in future.

With regard to natural resources which may be discovered in future, the two parties shall agree on the rights of each other's citizens to work and to practice any occupation.

Article XVI. Each of the contracting parties shall respect the rights of the other party's citizens in the present establishments and constructions, existing in that part of the Partitioned Zone which shall be annexed to its territory.

Article XVII. To safeguard the continuance of the two Contracting Parties' efforts in exploiting natural resources in the Partitioned Zone, a joint permanent committee shall be set up and called hereinafter the 'Committee'.

Article XVIII. The Committee shall be composed of an equal number from the two Contracting Parties' representatives, and the two competent ministers for natural resources, in each of the Contracting Governments, shall agree upon the number of the Committee members, its rules of procedure and how to safeguard the necessary appropriations for it.

Article XIX. The Committee shall have the following powers:

(a) To facilitate passage of officials, employees of concessionary Companies and of ancillary companies and establishments in the Partitioned Zone, other than the citizens of the two Parties.
(b) Studies relative to projects of exploiting common natural resources.
(c) To study the new licences, contracts, and concessions relating to common natural resources and submit its recommendations to the two competent ministers as to what should be done in this respect.
(d) To discuss whatever the two competent ministers refer to it.

The Committee in performing its duties shall have the right to sign contracts, and shall submit its reports and recommendations directly to the two competent ministers.

Article XX. The two competent ministers shall consult together to grant or to amend any new concession relating to common natural resources and the party who does not agree with the other, shall send him a written notification giving the reasons, before granting or amending the new concession.

If any other establishment or company is allowed to replace any present establishment or company exploiting natural resources in the Partitioned Zone, this replacement shall not be considered as a new concession provided that the rights of the other Party shall remain intact.

Article XXI. The two Contracting Parties shall undertake to supply the

Committee with information, data and documents which are needed by it to facilitate its task.

Article XXII. If a dispute arises with regard to the interpretation or application of this agreement or the rights and obligations which it creates, the two Contracting Parties shall seek to settle such disputes by friendly means for the settlement of disputes which include having recourse to the Arab League.

If the aforesaid methods fail to settle the dispute, then it shall be submitted before the International Court of Justice.

The two Contracting Parties shall accept the compulsory jurisdiction of the International Court of Justice in this respect.

If one of the two Contracting Parties takes a measure which is objectionable to the other Party, the objecting Party may ask the International Court of Justice to indicate any provisional measures to be taken to suspend the measure which is objected to or allow its continuance pending the final decision.

If one of the Contracting Parties refuses to abide by the judgment made against it, then the other party shall be relieved from its obligations under this Agreement.

Article XXIII. This Agreement shall be subject to ratification by each Contracting Party in accordance with its constitutional procedures and shall come into force on the date of exchanging of instruments of ratification.

Done in two original texts in the Arabic Language and both of them are authentic.

For the State of Kuwait   For the Kingdom of Saudi Arabia

APPENDIX XIII

English version of the Agreement of
27 February 1968, forming the
'Federation of the Arab Amirates'

PREAMBLE

In view of the agreement signed by the Amirates of Abu Dhabi and Dubai on 20 Dhu al-Qaʿdah 1387, corresponding to 18 February 1968, to form a federation out of their desire to preserve stability in their countries and to realise a better future for their peoples; and

Because it is unanimously agreed that the formation of a federation to include all of the Arab Amirates in the Gulf, including the Amirates of Abu Dhabi and Dubai, is more satisfactory for the realisation of the purposes of these two Amirates and is wanted by the peoples of all the area; and

In order to support the strong fraternal bonds among all the Arab Amirates in the Arabian Gulf and to affirm the numerous strong ties among these Amirates; and

Because of a desire to direct all possible efforts of these Amirates toward their good and toward the security of their future and toward the good of all the Arab people; and

In response to the desire of the people of the area to strengthen the means of stability in their countries and to realise a collective defence of their existence, and to preserve their peace and security in accordance with the Charters of the U.N. and the Arab League,

The signatories of this agreement and their delegations met in Dubai between 26 Dhu al-Qa'dah 1387, corresponding to 25 February 1968, and 28 Dhu al-Qa'dah 1387, corresponding to 27 February 1968, and concluded an agreement and undertaking on the following:

CHAPTER I

ESTABLISHMENT OF A FEDERATION FOR ARAB AMIRATES

1. A federation known as 'The Federation of Arab Amirates' shall be formed of the contracting Amirates.

2. The purpose of the Federation is to strengthen the ties among member Amirates, to promote cooperation among them in all fields, to coordinate the plans of their development and welfare, to support respect for each other's independence and sovereignty, to unify their foreign policy, to regulate the collective defence of their countries in order to protect their people and to preserve their security, and to consider generally their mutual affairs and interests in a manner which guarantees their aspirations and realises the hopes of all the great Arab homeland.

CHAPTER II

AUTHORITY

3. The affairs of the Federation shall be supervised by a council, known as the Supreme Council, which shall be formed of the Rulers of these Amirates.

4. The Supreme Council shall draw up a complete and permanent charter of the Federation and formulate its high policy in international, political, defence, economic, cultural, and other matters related to the purposes of the Federation as prescribed in Article 2 of this agreement. The Council shall legislate federal laws required in this connection. The Council is the highest authority in defining jurisdictions. Its decisions shall be made unanimously.

5. The Rulers of member Amirates shall alternatively and annually preside over the meetings of the Supreme Council. The President shall represent the Federation internally and to foreign states.

6. The general federal budget shall be issued by a decision of the Supreme Council. Revenues of the budget and the share to be paid by each member Amirate shall be determined by a law.

7. The Supreme Council, in exercising its authorities, shall be assisted by a council known as the Federal Council.

8. The Federal Council shall be the executive body of the Federation. The Federal Council shall exercise its duties in accordance with the high policy decided by the Supreme Council and pursuant to the federal laws.

9. The manner in which the Federal Council shall be formed and its basic rules and system shall be determined by legislation.

10. The decisions of the Federal Council shall not be final until approved by the Supreme Council.

11. The councils and committees necessary to assist the Federal Council in discharging its duties shall be formed and organised by federal laws.

CHAPTER III

GENERAL RULES

12. In exercise of the right of legitimate individual and collective defence of their existence, the contracting Amirates shall cooperate with each other to support and strengthen their military capabilities. To do their joint duty in repelling any armed aggression committed against any of them, the contracting Amirates shall, according to the resources and requirements [of each], participate in the preparation of their individual and collective means of defence in order to fulfil such duty.

13. (a) The Federation shall have a supreme court known as The Supreme Federal Court.

(b) The law shall prescribe the manner in which the court shall be formed, its regulations, and its jurisdictions.

14. The permanent headquarters of the Federation of Arab Amirates shall be determined by a decision of the Supreme Council, which may meet in any other place specified.

15. The government of each Amirate shall manage its internal affairs which are not entrusted to the Federation under this agreement or which are not provided for by federal laws.

16. The Supreme Council of the Federation may, by a decision, amend this agreement—particularly if the amendment tends to make the ties among the member Amirates stronger and more firm. An amendment shall not be considered except in the session which follows the one in which the request for amendment is made.

17. This agreement shall be put into effect as of the beginning of the month of Muharram 1388, corresponding to 30 March 1968, pursuant to the regulations observed in each member Amirate and when a complete and permanent charter has been drawn up for the Federation.

This agreement is done in Dubai on 28 Dhu al-Qaʿdah 1387, corresponding to 27 February 1968, in nine copies, one of which has been delivered to each member Amirate.

SIGNATURES

'Isa ibn Salman Al Khalifah   Ruler of Bahrain
Zayid ibn Sultan Al Nuhayyan   Ruler of Abu Dhabi
Ahmad ibn ʿAli Al Thani   Ruler of Qatar
Rashid ibn Saʿid Al Maktum   Ruler of Dubai

Saqr ibn Muhammad al-Qasimi   Ruler of Ras al-Khaimah
Khalid ibn Muhammad al-Qasimi   Ruler of Sharjah
Ahmad ibn Rashid al-Muʿalla   Ruler of Umm al-Qaiwan
Rashid ibn Humayd an-Nuʿaymi   Ruler of Ajman
Muhammad ibn Hamad ash-Sharqi   Ruler of Fujairah

APPENDIX XIV

Land Boundaries of the Trucial States, 1968

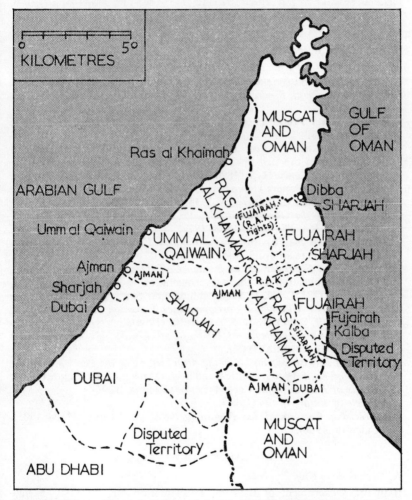

Reproduced from *Economic Report of the World Trade Information Service*, part
I, no. 61–21, U.S. Department of Commerce, 1961.

Select bibliography

I. ORIGINAL SOURCES

A. *Public Record Office* (The British Foreign Office Papers). Records relating to Persia from 1820 to 1869.

These are as follows:

F.O. 60/Nos 17, 21, 98, 102, 104, 112, 113, 118, 136, 143, 145, 157, 170, 176, 249.

F.O. 248/Nos 48, 251, 247, 249, 260.

B. *India Office Records*

AITCHISON, C. U., *A Collection of Treaties, Engagements and Sanads Relating to India and Neighbouring Countries*, vol. XI, Calcutta (1933).

I.O., Bombay Secret Proceedings, vol. 40, Secret Consultation, No 17, April 1819.

Bombay Secret Proceedings, vol. 41, Secret Consultation, Nos 20–1, 28, July 1819.

India, Foreign and Political Department, Treaties and Engagements in force between the British Government and the Arab Shaikhs of the Persian Gulf, Parts 1–5 (1820–1916). Texts in Arabic and English. (Kept in State Papers Department, British Museum.)

Persia and Persian Gulf Series, vol. 35, January 1823.

Proceedings of the Government of India, Foreign and Political Department, Nos 368, 370, 371, March 1872.

Selections from the Records of the Bombay Government, vol. 24, New Series, The Persian Gulf, Bombay (1856).

LORIMER, J. G., *Gazetteer of the Persian Gulf, Oman and Central Arabia*, Official Publication of the Government of India, Calcutta, vol. I, Historical (1915), vol. II, Geographical and Statistical (1908).

SALDANHA, J. A., *A Précis of Correspondence Regarding the Affairs of the Persian Gulf*, Secret (1801–53). Calcutta (1906).

A Précis of Correspondence of International Rivalry of the Persian Gulf (1872–1905). Calcutta (1906).

A Précis of Turkish Expansion on the Arab Littoral of the Persian Gulf, the Hasa and Katif Affairs, Political and Secret Department. Calcutta (1904).

A Précis of Bahrain Affairs (1854–1904). Calcutta (1906).

A Précis of Katar Affairs (1904).

A Précis of Correspondence Regarding the Trucial Chiefs (1854–1905). Calcutta (1906).

II. DOCUMENTARY MATERIAL

A. *The Arabian Gulf*

BAHRAIN, Government of Bahrain, Proclamation No. 37/1368, 5 June 1949, on claims to offshore areas (translation from Arabic), *A.J.I.L.*, Suppl. to vol. 43 (1949), p. 185.

Government of Bahrain, Secretariat, *File of Confidential Correspondence Regarding Bahrain–Saudi Arabia Boundaries* 1959.

Government of Bahrain, *Offshore Boundary Agreement Between Bahrain and Saudi Arabia*, 22 February 1958, *al-Jaridah al-Rasmiyah* (Bahrain official Gazette), 15 Sha'ban, 1377 (corresponding 6 March 1958). English text of the Agreement, *I.C.L.Q.*, vol. 7 (1958), p. 518.

British Political Residency, *The Persian Gulf Gazette*, Supplements Nos 1–52, Years 1952–66. H.M.S.O., London.

BURAIMI, Arbitration for the Settlement of the Territorial Dispute Between Muscat and Abu Dhabi on one Side and Saudi Arabia on the other, *Memorial of the Saudi Arabian Government* Submitted to the Arbitration Tribunal, Geneva, July 1955, 3 vols, Cairo (1955).

Arbitration Concerning Buraimi and the Common Frontier Between Abu Dhabi and Saudi Arabia, *Memorial Submitted by the Government of the United Kingdom of Great Britain and Northern Ireland*, 2 vols, July (1955).

Mimeographed Minutes of the Proceedings of the Buraimi Arbitration Tribunal (Complaint by the United Kingdom against Saudi Arabia), Sessions 11–15 September 1955, Geneva.

KUWAIT, Concession Agreement Between Kuwait Oil Company Ltd and His Excellency Shaikh Sir Ahmed al-Jabir as-Sabah, dated 23 December 1934. (Not published.)

Exchange of Notes Regarding Relations Between the United Kingdom of Great Britain and Northern Ireland and the State of Kuwait, 19 June 1961, *U.K.T.S.*, No. 1 (1961), *Cmnd.*, 1409.

MUSCAT, The Treaty of Sib, dated 11 Muharram 1339 (corresponding to 25 September 1920), the Arab information Centre, *The Status of Oman and the British Omanite Dispute*, New York, September (1957).

NEUTRAL ZONE (KUWAIT-SAUDI ARABIA), American Independent Oil Company (Aminoil) Concession over Kuwait Half of the Neutral Zone, dated 28 June 1948.

Offshore Concession Agreement Between the Government of Kuwait and Arabian Oil Co. Ltd, dated July 1958, *Kuwait al-Yawm*, No. 181, 13 July 1958.

Offshore Concession Agreement Between the Kingdom of Saudi Arabia and the Commercial Japanese Petroleum Company (Arabian Oil Co.), dated 10 December 1957, *The Petroleum Times*, Suppl. to vol. LXII, No. 1579, 14 February, 1958.

Agreement Between Kuwait and Saudi Arabia Relating to the Partition of the Neutral Zone, 7 July 1965, translation published by the American Society of International Law, *International Legal Materials*, vol. LV, No. 6, November, 1965, p. 1134. Arabic text of the Agreement in *Umm al-Qura* (Saudi Arabia), No. 2132, dated 18 Rabi' II, 1386 (5 August 1966).

QATAR, Concession Agreement Between the Ruler of the State of Qatar and Shell Overseas Exploration Co. Ltd, 29 November 1952.

B. *General*

Annual Digest and Reports of Public International Law Cases, Years 1919–1924. London.

GOOCH, G. P. AND TEMPERLEY, H., *British Documents on the Origins of the War*, 1898–1914, vol. 10. London (1938).

GREAT BRITAIN, *British and Foreign State Papers*, Years 1864–5, 1867, 1898–9, 1913, 1925, 1939, 1946, 1950.

Command Papers.

House of Commons Debates.

House of Lords Debates.

Report by the Resumed Nigeria Constitutional Conference, September–October 1958, *Cmnd*. 569, November 1958, Annex II.

Statutes, Statutory Instruments and Statutory Rules and Orders.

Treaty Series.

HACKWORTH, G. H., *Digest of International Law*, vols 1, 2, 5. Washington (1940–4).

HALSBURY, *Statutes of England*, 2nd ed., vol. 6. London (1948).

HARVARD LAW SCHOOL, Research in International Law, *Draft Convention on the Law of Responsibility of States for Damages Done in Their Territory to Person or Property of Foreigners, A.J.I.L.*, vol. 23 (1929), *Supplement*, p. 131.

HERTSLET, SIR E., *China Treaties* (1908).

The Map of Africa by Treaty (1909).

Treaties and Conventions between Great Britain and Foreign Powers so far as they relate to Commerce and Navigation. Years 1890, 1917, 1919.

HUDSON, M. O., *International Legislation*, vols 3, 5, 6, 7. Washington (1932–45).

HUREWITZ, J. C., *Diplomacy in the Near and Middle East, a documentary record*, 2 vols, Princeton (1956).

International Law Reports. Years 1950–58. London.

LEAGUE OF NATIONS, *Documents.*

Official Journal, Years 1925–34.

Third Committee of the Conference for the Codification of International Law (Doc. C.351 (c) M.145(c). 1930.V). The Hague (1930).

Report of the League of Nations Commission in the Mosul Dispute, 1925 (Doc. C.400.M.147. 1925. VII.)

MOORE, J. B., *A Digest of International Law*, vol. 2, Washington (1906).

NIELSEN, F. K., *American and British Claims Arbitration*. Report, 1926.

PEASLEE, A. J., *International Oganisations*, vol. 2, London (1956).

PERMANENT COURT OF INTERNATIONAL JUSTICE, *Publications.*

SCOTT, J. B., *The Hague Court Reports* (1916).

UNITED NATIONS, *Documents.*

Conference on International Organisation, Documents, vols 1, 3, 10, San Francisco (1945).

Conventions on the Law of the Sea, 1958: The Law of the Sea, The Final Act and Annexes of the United Nations Conference on the Law of the Sea, Geneva, 1958.

International Court of Justice, *Reports*. 1948–52.

Legislative Series, Laws and Regulations on the Regime of the High Seas, United Nations, New York, 1951.

Legislative Series, Laws and Practices Concerning the Conclusion of Treaties, United Nations, New York, 1953.

Legislative Series, Laws and Regulations on the Regime of the Territorial Seas, United Nations, New York, 1957.

Monthly Chronicle, 1961–6, United Nations, Office of Public Information, New York.

Non-Self-Governing Territories, Summaries and Analysis of Information Transmitted to the Secretary General (under Article 73 of the United Nations Charter). Years 1946–55.

Official Records of the Economic and Social Council, 1960.

Official Records of the General Assembly. Years 1946–53.

Official Records of the General Assembly. *The Question of Oman, Report of the Ad Hoc Committee on Oman*, 22 January 1965, by Mr Fernando Volio Jimenez (Document A/5846. English).

Official Records of the Security Council, Years 1947–8, 1957.

Treaty Series.

Yearbook. Years 1947–55, 1963–5.

UNITED STATES, Treaties and Other International Agreements of the United States, in Force on 1 January 1966, Compiled by the Treaty Affairs Staff, Department of State, U.S.A.

III. LEGAL BOOKS AND ARTICLES

ADAMIYAT, F., *Bahrein Islands, a legal and diplomatic study of the British-Iranian controversy*, New York (1955).

ALLEN, E. W., *The Position of Foreign States before National Courts, chiefly in Continental Europe*, New York (1933).

ASBECK, F. M. VON, 'International Law and Colonial Administration', *Transactions of the Grotius Society*, vol. 39 (1953), p. 5.

AUGUSTE, B. B. L., *The Continental Shelf: The Practice and Policy of the Latin American States, etc.*, Geneva (1960).

BAGGE, A., 'Intervention on the Ground of Damage caused to Nationals, with Particular Reference to Exhaustion of Local Remedies and the Rights of Shareholders', *B.Y.I.L.*, vol. 34 (1958), p. 162.

BATY, T., *The Canons of International Law*, London (1930).

'Protectorates and Mandates', *B.Y.I.L.*, vol. 1 (1921–2), p. 109.

BENTWICH, N., 'The End of the Capitulatory System', *B.Y.I.L.*, vol. 14 (1933), p. 89.

BOGGS, S. W., 'Delimitation of Seaward Areas under National Jurisdiction', *A.J.I.L.*, 45 (1951), p. 240.

BORCHARD, E. M., *Diplomatic Protection of Citizens Abroad*, New York (1916).

BRANDON, M., 'The Validity of Non-Registered Treaties', *B.Y.I.L.*, vol. 29 (1952), p. 156.

BRIERLY, J. L., *The Law of Nations*, 5th Ed., Oxford (1955).

'International Law and Resort to Armed Force', *Cambridge Law Journal*, vol. 4 (1932), p. 308.

Third Report on the Law of Treaties, International Law Commission (U.N. Doc. A/CN. 4/54, 10 April 1952).

BRIGGS, H. W., '*Rebus sic stantibus* before the Security Council; The Anglo-Egyptian Question', *A.J.I.L.*, vol. 43 (1949), p. 762.

'Jurisdiction Over the Sea Bed and Sub-Soil Beyond Territorial Waters', *A.J.I.L.*, vol. 45 (1951), p. 338.

The Law of Nations, Cases, Documents and Notes, 2nd ed., New York (1952).

BRINTON, J. Y., 'The Arabian Peninsula, The Protectorates and Shaikhdoms', *Revue Egyptienne de Droit International*, vol. 3 (1947), p. 5.

BROWN, D. J. L., 'The Ethiopia–Somaliland Frontier Dispute', *I.C.L.Q.*, vol. 5 (1956), p. 249.

BROWN, E. H., *The Saudi Arabia–Kuwait Neutral Zone*, Beirut (1963).

CAVARÉ, L., *Le droit international public positif*, vol. 1, Paris (1951).

CHEN, TI-CHIANG, *The International Law of Recognition*, London (1951).

DEAN, A. H., 'The Geneva Conference on the Law of the Sea. What Was accomplished?', *A.J.I.L.*, vol. 52 (1958), p. 607.

'The Second Geneva Conference on the Law of the Sea: The Fight for Freedom of the Sea', *A.J.I.L.*, vol. 54 (1960), p. 751.

DICEY, A. V., *Conflict of Laws*, 7th ed., London (1958).

DUNN, F. S., *The Protection of Nationals: a study in the application of international law*, Baltimore (1932).

EAGLETON, C., *The Responsibility of States in International Law*, New York (1928).

EDITORIAL NOTE, 'British Intervention in Oman', *Revue Egyptienne de Droit International*, vol. 13 (1957), p. 114.

ELY, N., *Summary of Mining and Petroleum Laws of the World*, New York (1961).

ESMAILI, M. *Le golfe persique et les îles de Bahrein*, Paris (1938).

FAWCETT, J. E. S., 'Treaty-Relations of British Overseas Territories', *B.Y.I.L.*, vol. 26 (1949), p. 86.

The British Commonwealth in International Law, London (1963).

FELLER, A. H., 'Procedure in Cases Involving Immunity of Foreign States in United States Courts', *A.J.I.L.*, vol. 25 (1931), p. 83.

FENWICK, C. G., *International Law*, London (1924).

FITZMAURICE, Sir G., 'The Law and Procedure of the International Court of Justice: International Organizations and Tribunals,' *B.Y.I.L.*, vol. 29 (1952), p. 1.

'The Law and Procedure of the International Court of Justice', *B.Y.I.L.*, vol. 30 (1953), p. 4.

'The Law and Procedure of the International Court of Justice: Points of Substantive Law, Part II', *B.Y.I.L.*, vol. 32 (1955-6), p. 20.

'The Law and Procedure of the International Court of Justice, 1951–1954', *B.Y.I.L.*, vol. 33 (1957), p. 203.

'Some Results of the Geneva Conference on the Law of the Sea', *I.C.L.Q.*, vol. 8 (1959), p. 73.

FREEMAN, A. V., *The International Responsibility of States for Denial of Justice*, London, New York (1938).

GARCIA AMADOR, F. V., 'Report on State Responsibility', *Yearbook of the International Law Commission*, II (1956), p. 173.

GOODRICH, L. AND HAMBRO, E., *The Charter of the United Nations*, 2nd ed., Boston (1949).

GOY, R., 'L'Affaire de l'Oasis de Buraimi', *Annuaire français de Droit international* (1957), p. 188.

GREEN, L. C., 'Membership of the United Nations', *Current Legal Problems*, vol. 2 (1949), p. 258.

International Law Through the Cases, 2nd ed., London (1959).

GUTTERIDGE, J. A. C., 'The Geneva Convention of 1949', *B.Y.I.L.*, vol. 26 (1949), p. 294.

HALL, W. E., *A Treatise on the Foreign Powers and the Jurisdiction of the British Crown*, Oxford (1894).

A Treatise on International Law, 8th ed., by A. P. Higgins, Oxford (1924).

HAMSON, C. J., 'Immunity of Foreign States, the Practice of the French Courts', *B.Y.I.L.*, vol. 27 (1950), p. 293.

HILL, N., *Claims to Territory in International Law and Relations*, New York (1945).

HOLLAND, SIR T. E., *Lectures on International Law*, London (1933).

HUMBER, P. O., 'Admission to the United Nations', *B.Y.I.L.*, vol. 24 (1947), p. 90.

HUREWITZ, J. C., 'The British Imperial System', *International Conciliation*, No. 481 (1952), p. 217.

HURST, CECIL J. B., 'State Succession in Matters of Tort', *B.Y.I.L.*, vol. 5 (1924), p. 163.

'Nationality of Claims', *B.Y.I.L.*, vol. 7 (1926), p. 163.

HYDE, C. C., *International Law Chiefly as Interpreted and Applied by the United States*, 3 vols., 2nd rev. ed., Boston (1945).

JENKS, C. W., 'State Succession in Respect of Law-Making Treaties', *B.Y.I.L.*, vol. 29 (1952), p. 105.

JENNINGS, R. Y., *The Acquisition of Territory in International Law*, Manchester (1963).

JESSUP, P. C., 'The Palmas Island Arbitration', *A.J.I.L.*, vol. 22 (1928), p. 735.

JESSUP, P. C., AND TAUBENFELD, H. J., *Controls for Outer Space and the Antarctic Analogy*, New York (1959).

JOHNSON, D. H. N., 'Acquisitive Prescription in International Law', *B.Y.I.L.*, vol. 27 (1950), p. 332.

'Artificial Islands', *International Law Quarterly*, vol. 4 (1951), p. 203.

'Decisions of English Courts during 1951–1952 involving Questions of Public or Private International Law, *A*. Public International Law', *B.Y.I.L.*, vol. 29 (1952), p. 455.

JONES, J. M., 'Who are British Protected Persons?', *B.Y.I.L.*, vol. 22 (1945), p. 122.

'State succession in the Matter of Treaties', *B.Y.I.L.*, vol. 24 (1947), p. 360.

'British Nationality Act, 1948', *B.Y.I.L.*, vol. 25 (1948), p. 158.

British Nationality Law, rev. ed., Oxford (1956).

KEITH, A. B., *The Theory of State Succession with Special Reference to English and Colonial Law*, London (1907).

'Notes on Imperial Constitutional Law: Jurisdiction in Respect of Sovereign States Under British Protection', *Journal of Comparative Legislation and International Law*, vol. 5 (1923), p. 120.

Constitutional Law, 7th ed., London (1935).

z

The Governments of the British Empire, London (1935).

The Dominions as Sovereign States, London (1938).

KELSEN, H., *The Law of the United Nations*, London (1950).

KELLER, A. S., *et al.*, *Creation of Rights of Sovereignty through Symbolic Acts*; (1400–1800), Columbia University Press (1938).

KHADDURI, M., 'Iran's Claim to the Sovereignty of Bahrayn', *A.J.I.L.*, vol. 45 (1951), p. 631.

KUNZ, J. L., 'The Continental Shelf and International Law: confusion and abuse', *A.J.I.L.*, vol. 50 (1956), p. 828.

LAUTERPACHT, E., 'The Contemporary Practice of the United Kingdom in the Field of International Law', *I.C.L.Q.*, vol. 5 (1956), p. 405.

'The Contemporary Practice of the United Kingdom in the Field of International Law, II, III, IV', *I.C.L.Q.*, vol. 6 (1957), pp. 126, 301, 506.

'The Contemporary Practice of the United Kingdom in the Field of International Law: Survey and Comment', *I.C.L.Q.*, vol. 7 (1958), pp. 92, 514.

'The Contemporary Practice of the United Kingdom in the Field of International Law, VII', *I.C.L.Q.*, vol. 8 (1959), p. 146.

'The Contemporary Practice of the United Kingdom in the Field of International Law, Survey and Comment, VIII', *I.C.L.Q.*, vol. 9 (1960), p. 253.

'Intervention by Invitation', *The Times* (London), 24 August 1960.

LAUTERPACHT, H., *Recognition in International Law*, Cambridge (1947).

Report on the Law of Treaties, International Law Commission (U.N. Doc. A/CN.4/63 March 24, 1953).

LEE-WARNER, Sir W., *The Native States of India* (1910).

LEWIS, M. M., 'The International Status of the British Self-Governing Dominions', *B.Y.I.L.*, vol. 3 (1922–3), p. 21.

LIEBESNY, H. J., 'International Relations of Arabia; the dependent areas', *The Middle East Journal*, vol. 1 (1947), p. 148.

'Legislation on the Sea Bed and Territorial Waters of the Persian Gulf', *Middle East Journal*, vol. 4 (1950), p. 94.

'Administration and Legal Development in Arabia: Aden Colony and Protectorate', *Middle East Journal*, vol. 9 (1955), p. 385.

'Administration and Legal Development in Arabia: The Persian Gulf Principalities', *Middle East Journal*, vol. 10 (1956), p. 33.

LINDLEY, M. F., *The Acquisition and Government of Backward Territory in International Law*, London (1926).

LOEWENFELD, E. H., 'Protectorates', *Encyclopaedia Britannica*, vol. 18 (ed. 1957), p. 608.

LYONS, A. B., 'The Conclusiveness of the "suggestion" and Certificate of the American State Department', *B.Y.I.L.*, vol. 24 (1947), p. 116.

'The Conclusiveness of the Statements of the Executive: Continental and Latin-American Practice', *B.Y.I.L.*, vol. 25 (1948), p. 180.

MACGIBBON, I. C., 'Some Observations on the Part of Protest in International Law', *B.Y.I.L.*, vol. 30 (1953), p. 293.

'The Scope of Acquiescence in International Law', *B.Y.I.L.* vol. 31 (1954), p. 143.

MANN, F. A., 'The Proper Law of Contracts Concluded by International Persons', *B.Y.I.L.*, vol. 35 (1959), p. 34.

McNair, Lord, *The Law of Treaties, British Practice and Opinions*, Oxford (1938).

International Law Opinions, 3 vols, Cambridge (1956).

'The General Principles of Law Recognized by Civilized Nations', *B.Y.I.L.*, vol. 33 (1957), p. 1.

Meron, T. 'The Incidence of the Rule of Exhaustion of Local Remedies', *B.Y.I.L.*, vol. 35 (1959), p. 100.

Mouton, M. W., *The Continental Shelf*, The Hague (1952).

'The Continental Shelf' *The Hague Recueil Des Cours*, I (1954), p. 347.

Muralt, R. W. G., De, *The Problem of State Succession With Regard to Treaties*, The Hague (1954).

Myers, D. P., 'Contemporary Practice of the United States Relating to International Law', *A.J.I.L.*, vol. 54 (1960), p. 632.

Noel-Baker, P. J., *The Present Juridical Status of the British Dominions in International Law*, London (1939).

O'Connell, D. P., *The Law of State Succession*, Cambridge (1956).

Oppenheim, L., *International Law*, vol. 2, 7th ed. by Sir H. Lauterpacht, London (1952).

International Law, vol. 1, 8th ed., by Sir H. Lauterpacht. London, (1955).

O'Rourke, V. A., *The Juristic Status of Egypt and the Sudan*, Johns Hopkins Press, (1935).

Padwa, D. J., 'Submarine Boundaries', *I.C.L.Q.*, vol. 9 (1960), p. 628.

Parry, C., *Nationality and Citizenship Laws of the Commonwealth and of the Republic of Ireland*, London (1957).

Phillips, O. H., *The Constitutional Law of Great Britain and the Commonwealth*, 2nd ed., London (1957).

Pillai, R. V., and Kumar, M., 'The Political and Legal Status of Kuwait', *I.C.L.Q.*, vol. 11 (1962), p. 108.

Ridges, E. W., *Constitutional Law*, 8th ed. by G. A. Forrest, London (1950).

Robbin, R., 'The Legal Status of Aden Colony and Aden Protectorate', *A.J.I.L.*, vol. 33 (1939), p. 700.

Rosenne, Shabtai, *The International Court of Justice*, Leyden (1957).

Ross, A., *A Text-Book of International Law*, London (1947).

Russell, R. B., *The History of the United Nations*, New York (1958).

Rutherford, J. W., 'Spheres of Influence', *A.J.I.L.*, vol. 20 (1926), p. 300.

Schwarzenberger, G., *International Law: International Court*, vol. 1, 3rd ed., London (1957).

A Manual of International Law, 2 vols, 4th ed., London (1960).

Sinclair, I. M., 'Nationality of Claims: British practice', *B.Y.I.L.*, vol. 27 (1950), p. 129.

'Decisions of English Courts During 1951–1952 Involving Questions of Public or Private International Law, *B*. Private International Law', *B.Y.I.L.*, vol. 29 (1952), p. 476.

Smith, H. A., *Great Britain and the Law of Nations: a selection of documents*, 2 vols, London (1932–1935).

Snow, A. H., *The Question of Aborigines in the Law and Practice of Nations*, New York (1919).

Somervell, D. B., 'The Indian States', *B.Y.I.L.*, vol. 11 (1930), p. 55.

STARKE, J. G., 'Imputability in International Delinquencies', *B.Y.I.L.*, vol. 19 (1938), p. 104.

STEWART, R. B., 'Treaty Making Procedure in the British Dominion', *A.J.I.L.*, vol. 32 (1938), p. 467.
Treaty Relations of the British Commonwealth of Nations, New York (1939).

SUCHARITKUL, SOMPONG, *State Immunities and Trading Activities*, London (1959).

SVARLIEN, O., *An Introduction to the Law of Nations*, New York (1955).

TOUSSAINT, C. E., 'The Colonial Controversy in the United Nations', *The Yearbook of World Affairs*, vol. 10 (1956), p. 170.

UHLER, O. A., COURSIER, H., *et al*, *The Geneva Conventions of August 12, 1949, Commentary IV*, Geneva (1949). English translation by R. Griffin and C. W. Dumbleton.

WADE, E. C. S., 'Acts of State in English Law: its relations with international Law', *B.Y.I.L.*, vol. 15 (1934), p. 98.

WADE, E. C. S., AND PHILLIPS, G. G., *Constitutional Law*, 6th ed., London (1960).

WALDOCK, C. H. M., 'Disputed Sovereignty in the Falkland Island Dependencies', *B.Y.I.L.*, vol. 25 (1948), p. 311.

WALTON, F. P., 'States Immunity in the Laws of England, France, Italy and Belgium', *Journal of Comparative Legislation and International Law*, vol. 2 (1920), p. 252.

WATERFIELD, G., 'Trouble in the Horn of Africa: The British Somali Case', *International Affairs*, vol. 32 (1956), p. 52.

WESTLAKE, J., *International Law*, 2 vols. 2nd ed. Cambridge, (1910–1913).
The Collected Papers of John Westlake on Public International Law, by L. Oppenheim, Cambridge (1914).
'The Nature and Extent of the Title of Conquest', *Law Quarterly Review*, vol. 17 (1901), p. 392.

WHEATON, H., *Elements of International Law*, 6th ed., by A. B. Keith, London, (1929).

WHITEMAN, M. M., 'Conference on the Law of the Sea: Convention on the Continental Shelf', *A.J.I.L.*, vol. 52 (1958), p. 629.

WILKINSON, H. A., 'The American Doctrine of State Succession', *The Hopkins University Studies*, Ser. 52, No. 40 (1934), p. 17.

WILLIAMS, J. F., 'Sovereignty, Seisin and the League', *B.Y.I.L.*, vol. 7 (1926), p. 24.
'Recognition', *Transactions of the Grotius Society*, vol. XV (1930), p. 53.
'The New Doctrine of Recognition', *Transactions of the Grotius Society*, vol. 18 (1933), p. 109.

WILLOUGHBY, W. W., *Fundamental Concepts of Public Law*, New York (1924).

WILSON, R. R., 'Legal Relations Between Commonwealth Members', *A.J.I.L.*, vol. 51 (1957), p. 611.

WRIGHT, Q., 'The Mosul Dispute', *A.J.I.L.*, vol. 20 (1926), p. 455.
Legal Problems in the Far Eastern Conflict, New York (1941).
'The Prevention of Aggression', *A.J.I.L.*, vol. 50 (1956), p. 514.
'U.S. Intervention in the Lebanon', *A.J.I.L.*, vol. 53 (1959), p. 112.
'Subversive Intervention', *A.J.I.L.*, vol. 54 (1960), p. 521.

Young, R., 'Recent Development with Respect to the Continental Shelf', *A.J.I.L.*, vol. 42 (1948), p. 849.

'Saudi Arabian Offshore Legislation', *A.J.I.L.*, vol. 43 (1949), p. 530.

'Further Claims to Areas Beneath the High Seas', *A.J.I.L.*, vol. 43 (1949), p. 790.

'The Legal Status of Submarine Areas', *A.J.I.L.*, vol. 45 (1951), p. 225.

'Lord Asquith and the Continental Shelf', *A.J.I.L.*, vol. 45 (1951), p. 512.

'The United Kingdom-Muscat Treaty of 1951', *A.J.I.L.*, vol. 46 (1952), p. 704.

'The Geneva Convention on the Continental Shelf', *A.J.I.L.*, vol. 52 (1958), p. 733.

IV. ARTICLES, BOOKS AND REPORTS RELATING TO THE HISTORICAL AND ECONOMIC AFFAIRS OF THE ARABIAN GULF

Abu Hakima, A. M., *History of Eastern Arabia, 1750–1800, The Rise and Development of Bahrain and Kuwait*, Beirut (1965).

Al-Baker, A. R., *Min al-Bahrain Ela al-Manfa* (From Bahrain to Exile), Beirut (1965).

Al-Nabhani, M. K., *Tarikh al-Jazira al-'Arabiyya*, vol. I, *Tarikh al-Bahrain*, Cairo, 1342/1923.

Al-Rihani, *Tarikh Najd al-Hadith*, 2nd ed. (1954).

Arab Observer, The Middle East News Magazine, Cairo, 26 February 1961.

Arabian American Oil Company, Research Division, *Oman and the Southern Shore of the Persian Gulf*, Cairo (1952).

Badger, G. P., *History of the Imams and Seyyids of Oman* by Ibn Ruzaiq, English Translation and Introduction (1871).

Belgrave, Sir C., *Personal Column: autobiography*, London (1960).

Belgrave, J. H. D., *Welcome to Bahrain*, 5th ed., London (1965).

Bent, T., 'The Bahrain Islands in the Persian Gulf', *Proceedings of Royal Geographical Society*, vol., 12 (1810), p. 1.

Berreby, Jean-Jaques, *Le Golfe persique; mer de légende réservoir de pétrole*, Paris (1959).

Bulletin of International News, *British Interests in the Persian Gulf*, vol. 28, No. 19, 20 September (1914), p. 1193.

Buss, K. C., 'Persian Gulf', *Encyclopaedia Britannica*, vol. 17, ed. (1963), p. 595.

Cox, Sir P., 'Some Excursions in Oman', *Geographical Journal*, vol. 66 (1925), p. 207.

Curzon, G. N., *Persia and the Persian Question*, 2 vols, London (1892).

Daily Telegraph, The, 19 August 1954, 26 April 1962.

Dickson, H. R. P., *Kuwait and Her Neighbours*, London (1956).

Eccles, G. J., 'The Sultanate of Muscat and Oman', *Journal of Central Asian Society*, vol. 14 (1927), p. 19.

Economist, The, 28 March 1955, 21 January 1967.

Economist Intelligence Unit, The, *Quarterly Economic Review*, No. 22, July 1965.

Quarterly Economic Review, Middle East Oil and the Arabian Peninsula, Annual Supplement (1966).

EUROPA PUBLICATIONS, *The Middle East and North Africa*, 1966–7, 13th ed., London (1966).

Financial Times, The, 15 October 1960, 30 January 1961.

FRASER, L., *India Under Curzon and After* (1911).

GOTT, R., 'The Kuwait Incident', The Royal Institute of International Affairs, *Survey of International Affairs* (1961), p. 519.

GOVERNMENT OF BAHRAIN, *Annual Reports*, Years 1926–65.

Al-Jaridah al-Rasmiyah, Years 1957–61.

Majmu'at al-Qawanin Wal E'lanaat (Collection of Laws and Notices), Bahrain, 1377 (corresponding to 1958).

The 4th Census of Population, Department of Finance, Bahrain (1965).

GOVERNMENT OF BRITISH INDIA, *Annual Report of the Persian Gulf Residency and Muscat Political Agency* (1878–9).

GOVERNMENT OF KUWAIT, *Al-Kuwait al-Yawm* (Official Gazette), Years 1957–60.

The Kuwait-Iraqi Crisis, Government's Printing and Publishing Department (1961).

GOVERNMENT OF QATAR, *Laws and Regulations File*, Qatar (1951).

Official Gazette (Arabic), April 1962.

GREAT BRITAIN, Admiralty, *A Handbook of Arabia*, vol. I (1916).

Foreign Office, Historical Section, *Peace Handbook*, No. 76 (1920).

Central Office of Information, *The Arab States of the Persian Gulf*, August (1956).

Gulf Daily Times (Bahrain), 1958–9.

HAY, SIR R., 'The Persian Gulf States and their Boundary Problems', *Geographical Journal*, vol. 120 (1954), p. 431.

The Persian Gulf States, Washington (1959).

Herald Tribune, The, New York, 5 May 1960.

INTERNATIONAL BANK OF RECONSTRUCTION AND DEVELOPMENT, THE, *The Economic Development of Kuwait* (Report of Missions Organised by the Bank), Baltimore (1965).

IRELAND, P. W., 'Iraq', *Encyclopaedia Britannica*, vol. 12, ed. (1963), p. 589.

JOHNSON, P., *Journey Into Chaos*, London (1958).

KELLY, J. B., 'The Buraimi Oasis Dispute', *International Affairs*, vol. 32 (1956), p. 318.

'The Persian Claim to Bahrain', *International Affairs*, vol. 33 (1957), p. 51.

'Sovereignty and Jurisdiction in Eastern Arabia', *International Affairs*, vol. 34 (1958), p. 16.

Eastern Arabian Frontiers, New York (1964).

'The Future in Arabia', *International Affairs*, vol. 42 (1966), p. 633.

KUWAIT, BRITISH POLITICAL AGENCY, *Administrative Report for the Year 1921*, by Major J. C. More, Political Agent, Baghdad (1922).

LENCZOWSKI, G., *Oil and State in the Middle East*, New York (1960).

LONGRIGG, S. H., *Iraq 1900–1950*, Oxford (1953).

Oil in the Middle East, London (1954).

'Iraq's Claim to Kuwait', *Royal Asian Journal*, vol. 48 (1961), p. 309.

MAHAN, A. T., 'The Persian Gulf and International Relations', *The National Review*, vol. 6, Sept.–Feb. (1902–3), p. 27.

Manchester Guardian (*Guardian*), *The*, Years 1957, 1959, 1961.

MANN, C., *Abu Dhabi: Birth of an Oil Shaikhdom*, Beirut (1964).

MARLOWE, J., *The Persian Gulf in the Twentieth Century*, London (1962).

MEZERIK, A. G., *The Kuwait-Iraq Dispute*, New York (1961).

Middle East Economic Survey (A Weekly Review of News and Views on Middle East Oil), Published by the Middle East Research and Publishing Centre, Beirut, Years 1960–6.

Middle East Journal, vol. 14 (1960), p. 449.

MILES, S. B., *The Countries and Tribes of the Persian Gulf*, 2 vols, London (1919).

MORRIS, J., *Sultan of Oman: Venture Into the Middle East*, London (1957).

New York Times, The, 11 March 1958, 28 August 1960.

Observer, The, London, 18 June 1961, 14 August 1966.

OESTRUP, J., 'Al-Bahrain', *Encyclopaedia of Islam*, vol. 2 (1913), p. 584.

Oil and Gas Journal, The, 27 September, 4 October 1965, 13 June 1966.

OWEN, R., *The Golden Bubble*, London (1957).

Petroleum Press Service, London, August 1962, May 1963.

PHILBY, H. St J. B., *Report on the Operations of the Najd Mission*, 29 October 1917 to 1 November 1918, Baghdad, Government Press (1918).

    The Empty Quarter, London (1933).

    'Arabia Today', *International Affairs*, vol. 14 (1935), p. 619.

    Arabian Jubilee, London (1952).

    Saudi Arabia, London (1955).

Platt's Oilgram, 14 March 1963.

REPUBLIC OF IRAQ, THE, Ministry of Foreign Affairs, *The Truth About Kuwait*, July (1961).

ROYAL INSTITUTE OF INTERNATIONAL AFFAIRS, Survey of International Affairs: *The Dispute between Persia and Great Britain over Bahrayn, 1927–1934*, by A. Toynbee (1934), p. 221.

    The Middle East, A Political and Economic Survey, 2nd ed., by Sir R. Bullard, Oxford (1951).

SCHWADRAN, B., *The Middle East Oil and the Great Powers*, London (1956).

Spectator, The, London, 1 July 1960, 17 February, 16 June 1961.

Statesman's Year-Book, 103rd ed., 1966–7, London (1966).

THESIGER, W., 'Desert Borderlands of Oman', *Geographical Journal*, vol. 116 (1950), p. 151.

THOMAS, B., *Alarms and Excursions in Arabia*, London (1931).

    Arab Rule Under the Al Bu Said Dynasty of Oman, 1741–1937, London (1938).

THORNBURG, M. W., *People and Policy in the Middle East*, New York (1964).

Times, The, London, Years 1914, 1939, 1954–61, 1965–6.

WILKINSON, J. C., 'A Sketch of the Historical Geography of the Trucial Oman Down to the Beginning of the Sixteenth Century', *Geographical Journal*, vol. 130, Part 3, September (1964), p. 338.

WILSON, Sir A. T., *The Persian Gulf*, Oxford (1928), reprinted in 1954.

WINGATE, SIR R., *Not in the Limelight*, London (1959).

ZWEMER, S. M., 'Three Journeys in Northern Oman', *Geographical Journal*, vol. 19 (1902), p. 63.

Index

'Abbas Aram, 310
'Abd al-'Aziz, Amir, 210
'Abd al-'Aziz ibn Sa'ud, King, 196n, 217, 265
of Kuwait, 40, 250
'Abd Allah ibn Ahmad, Shaikh of Bahrain, 31
'Abd Allah ibn Jasim Al-Thani, 4
'Abd Allah ibn Faisal, Amir, 211 f
'Abd al-Rahman ibn Faisal, Amir, 196, 217
'Abd al-Razzaq al-Sanhuri, Dr, 21
Aberdeen, Lord, 170
Abu Dhabi: oil production, 17; Finance Department, 18n; claim to Buraimi, 215–17, 222–4, 237 f; boundary disputes with Qatar and Saudi Arabia, 261–3, with Dubai, 264; territorial sea, 281, 284–6; Petroleum Development (Trucial Coast) Ltd case, 284–6; offshore concessions, 301; offshore boundaries, 303; ownership of Halul, 304; Exclusive Agreement, 1892, 314
Abu Musa, 301, 305 f
Abu Nu'ayr, 302, 305
Abu Sa'fah oilfield, 300, 307 f
acknowledged war, 26
acquisition of territory, by occupation, 177–8; by conquest, 178–9, 220; by prescription, 184–6, 191–2, 220, 223
Adamiyat, Dr F, 195
Aden Protectorate, 82, 83n, 96–7, 227; boundary problems, 196, 219
Ahmad Al-Sabah, Shaikh of Kuwait, 256
Ahmad ibn Ali Al-Thani, Shaikh of Qatar, 11
Ahmed Zaki Yamani, Shaikh, 310
al-Arabiya, 295, 310
Al Bu Shamis tribe, 208, 211, 217
Al Bu Sa'id dynasty, 2–3, 239
Al-Jalahimah Arabs, 3 f, 36
Al-Khalifah dynasty, 3 f, 31, 36, 167, 182
al-Manasir tribe, 201
al-Marfa, 263
al-Mughairah, 263
Al-Murrah tribe, 201
al-Rashid, House of, 196n, 217

Al-Sabah dynasty, 3
Al-Thani dynasty, 4
al-'Utub, 3
Amador, Garcia, 129
American Independent Oil Company, 267, 297
Anderson, J. N. D., 304
Anglo-Egyptian Sudan, 266n, 270
Anglo-Egyptian treaty 1936, 94
Anglo-French controversy over Muscat and Oman, 47, 49 ff
Anglo-Persian dispute over Bahrain, 167–95
Anglo-Saudi Treaty 1915, 232, 235
Anglo-Saudi controversy over Qatar, 75–6; Buraimi, 196–238
Anglo-Turkish (Draft) Convention 1913, 34n, 45, 68, 198, 218–19, 226–227, 248, 253, 264 f
Anglo-Turkish Convention 1914, 198, 207, 219–20, 227–8; recognition by Saudi Arabia, 231–2
annexation by discoverers, 72–3
Aqaba, Gulf of, 282
Arab Amirates, Federation of, 7, 328–330
Arab League, 77, 95, 245, 250 f
Arab Nationalist Movement, 20 f
Arab Oil Conferences, 77n
Arab Social Experts Conference 1956, 77n
Arabian American Oil Company (ARAMCO), 200, 267n, 291, 298, 300
Arabian Gulf, 1; states (map), xvi, 2; Portuguese influence, 5; British influence, 5–7; Political British Resident, 9; sea bed and geography, 287–9; median line, 295
Arabian (Japanese) Oil Company (AOC), 267 ff, 291, 293 f, 297 f.
Argyll, Duke of, 174 f, 188
arms trade agreements, 30, 35, 38, 44
Asquith, Lord, 16n, 281, 284 f
Auguste, B. B. L., 285, 287

Baghdad Railway project, 43
Bahrain: conquest by Al-Khalifah, 4; Political British Resident, 9; administrative system, 12–13; judicial system, 14–15; constitutional reform,

Bahrain—*contd.*
14n; British government relations, 31 ff; assoc. membership of international organisations, 76, 113n; Arab League, 77; treaty-making capacity, 102 ff; transit dues agreement with Saudi Arabia, 102–3; nationality laws, 124 f; Persian claim to sovereignty, 167–95; tribute paid to Wahhabi rulers, 169, 172, 190, to Persia, 190–1; assertion of independence, 182–4, 194; population census 1965, 195; Turkish interest in, 219; Zubarah dispute, 247–9; offshore areas and boundary, 262, 278, 302–3, 318–19; concessionary areas, 300;
—Treaties:
Draft Treaty of Friendship (Britain) 1816, 31
Treaty of Peace 1820, 31, 194
Agreement concerning suppression of slave trade 1856, 31
Friendly Convention 1861, 4, 31 ff
Agreements with Britain 1880 and 1892, 34–5, 74, 313–14
Subsidiary agreements with Britain 1898–1914, 35
Offshore Boundary Agreement with Saudi Arabia 1958, 104–6, 306–11, 319–22
Bahrain Petroleum Company (Bapco), 300, 308
Bani 'Utbah settlement at Qatar, 3, 36
Bani Yas tribe, 201, 208, 215, 261
Bani Yas island, 306
Basrah, Wilayat of, 252, 254 f
Baty, T., 61
Belgium, 183
Belgrave, Sir Charles, 12n, 249
Benenson, P., 246
Blue line (Saudi Arabian boundary), 199, 201, 207, 219 f, 227, 228n, 230n, 232, 237
Borchard, E. M., 136
boundaries, land: controversies, 216–277; eastern Saudi Arabia, 196 ff, 207, 219; Iraq-Kuwait, 256 f, 261; interim settlement ('neutral zone'), 264–6; neutral zone partition, 274
boundaries, submarine, 274, 278–311
Brierly, J., 86, 184
Britain: influence in Arabian Gulf, 5–6, 9; courts in Gulf States, 14–15, 17, 19; international representation of Trucial Shaikhdoms, 30, 74, of

Muscat, 67–8; protection for Gulf States, 38, 45, 254, 256; regular officers seconded to Muscat armed forces, 54, 205, 218, 238; suppression of Omani revolt, 54, 157, 244; sovereignty over shaikhdom rights, 73–4, 79; constitutional law, 80
British Government of India, 8
British Nationality Act 1948, 122
British Petroleum, 301
British Protected States, 78; forces in, 97, 117; withdrawal of forces, 7; position before British courts, 145–8, before foreign courts, 148–9
British protectorates, 41, 80 ff
British Protectorates, Protected States and Protected Persons Order in Council 1949, 82, 122–3
Brown, D. J. L., 88
Brown, E. H., 297
Bruce, Captain William, 31, 168, 186 f; Bruce Agreement, 186–7
Bullard, Sir Reader, 203 ff
Buraimi: sovereignty dispute, 196–238; boundary lines (map), 197; oasis and villages, 200 f, 202 f, 208; Arbitration Agreement on boundaries 1954, 203 f, 208; occupied by Trucial Oman Levies (Scouts), 206, 218, 238; Wahhabi control, 208, 220–1; Saudi tax collection, 201, 207, 217–18, 226; Omani occupation, 212; 'annexation' by Abu Dhabi, 213, 222; control by Muscat, 214–15, by Abu Dhabi, 215–17, by Saudi Arabia, 217–18; historical title to, 220–6
Bushire Residency, 5, 9

cable landing rights, Qatar, 38
Cadogan, Sir Alexander, 94
Canning, Lord, 49
Cavaré, L., 64
Chamberlain, Sir Austen, 71n, 176, 179 f, 187, 190 f
Clarendon, Lord, 174 f, 186 ff
Clarendon Note, 176, 187 f
coalfield in Oman, 48, 69, 240
Codrai, R. A., 215
'colonial clause', 106–7
colonial protectorates, 80
Compagnie française de Petroles, 301
concession agreements in disputed boundary areas, 290–1, 300–2
condominium arrangement, Kuwait-Saudi Arabia, 266, 272, 275

Conference on Law of the Sea 1960, 238n
consuls, reciprocal appointing rights, 52, 55, 57
Continental Oil Company, 300 f; of Dubai, 303
continental shelf, 278n, 279–80, 285, 286 ff
contractual obligations, violation, 135 ff
Cox, Sir Percy, 216, 256, 265
Crimean War, 117
Currie, P., 41
Curzon, Lord, 6, 33n, 48

Dammam Conference 1952, 198, 201
Danzig, 85
Dean, A. H., 283
De Muralt, R. W. G., 229
de Ribbing, Herbert, 159 f, 206–7
De Visscher, Charles, 203
Dhawahir tribe, 208, 211, 215
Dicey, A. V., on jurisdictional immunity, 146–7
Dihgo, Dr Ernesto, 204
domestic jurisdiction principle, 157, 159
Dubai: administration, 16–17; Boat incident, 30; boundary disputes, 264; offshore boundaries and concessions, 301, 303; undertaking regarding oil, 317

Eagleton, C., 129
East India Company: expedition against Shaikhdoms, 5; Residency at Bushire, 5; General Treaty of Peace, 1820, 5 f, 26; treaties with Gulf States, 8; agreement with Sultan ibn Saqr, 25; and Persian claim to Bahrain, 171
Eccles, Capt. G. J., 214, 217
Egypt, 65, 94
Elphinstone, Mountstuart, 168
equidistance, principle of, 288, 307
Ethiopia: treaties with Britain, 87 f
Exclusive Agreement Britain-Trucial Shaikhdoms, 1892, 5, 29
exhaustion of local remedies, 137
extra-territorial jurisdiction, British, in Gulf States, 10, 15, 17, 22; in Bahrain, 33; in Kuwait, 22; in Muscat, 52–3, 55 f
extra-territorial seas, 280
extradition of criminals, Turkey-

Bahrain, 74–5; Kuwait-Saudi Arabia, 270–1

Faisal I, of Iraq, 254
Faisal ibn Turki, Amir, 172, 210
'Falat Gharreh', 280
Fars, 168, 170 f, 186–7
Farsi, 295, 310
Fasht Abu Sa'fah, 308 f
Fasht-al-Jarim, 300
Fawcett, J. E. S., 90, 106
Fenwick, C. G., 64
Fez, Treaty of, 1912, 66, 84
Fitzmaurice, Sir Gerald, 65
fishing rights, 280
Ford, Sir C., 41
fortifications, construction of, 28 f
France, 157; activities in Muscat, 48; treaty with Muscat, 50, 51–2; extra-territorial jurisdiction in Muscat, 55; and international responsibility, 131
Fraser, Lovat, 214
Fuad Bey Hamzah, 198, 230n, 231
Fuad's line (Saudi Arabian boundary), 198 f, 201
Fujairah, 5, 78n

General Agreement of Tariff and Trade (GATT), 110
General Treaty of Peace 1820, 5 f, 26–29, 31
Geneva Arbitration on Saudi Arabian boundaries 1955, 203 f, 231–2, 237
Geneva Convention on Territorial Sea 1958, 282 f; application to Gulf States, 286–90, 298, 307, 310
Geneva Conventions 1949 and 1956, 111, 121–2
Goult, Charles, 304
Greece, 183
Green, L. C., 285
Grey, Sir Edward, 218
Grotius, 186
Gulf States: as British Protected States, 82; treaty making capacity, 98–112; and international organisations, 106–114; nationals and diplomatic protection, 126–8, 140; nationals and claims, 141–2; and international responsibility, 131–6; and jurisdictional immunity before British courts, 145–8; eligibility for U.N. membership, 151–6, 161–4; disputes with Britain, 156–61

Gutteridge, J. A. C., 121

Halul island, 301, 303–4
Haji Meerza Aghassi, 169 ff, 193
Hall, W. E., 92, 100
Hamerton, Capt. Atkins, 210
Hasan, Mahmoud, 203
Hay, Sir Rupert, 8 f, 19, 202, 264, 304
Hennal, Lieut S., 210
Hennell, Captain, 169
Hill, Norman, 178, 193 f
Hood Philips, O., 83
Huber, Max, 64, 88n, 181, 185, 220
Humaid ibn Ruzaiq, 210, 212 f
Humphreys, D., 16n
Hurewitz, J. C., 79
Hurst, Sir Cecil, 141, 181
Huwar island, 300, 303
Hyde, C. C., 99 ff, 246
Hyderabad, 157

Ibrahim Hakki Pasha, 218
immunities of protected states, 145 ff, 149–50
India, 157; treaty with Muscat, 55; Princely States, 82; treaties with Britain, 84
Indian States Committee Report 1928–1929, 82
Indonesia, 157
International Bank for Reconstruction and Development Agreement (IBRD) and International Monetary Fund (IMF), 109
International Convention on Arms and Ammunition Trade 1919, 108
International Court of Justice: decisions on protectorates, 65–6; interpretation of treaties, 96; claims of nationals of Gulf States, 142
international delinquency: responsibility of protecting States, 129 f
international law and nature of treaties between protected and protecting states, 84 ff, 90 f; and immunity of protected states, 149–50; and acquisition of territory, 181–95 passim; and prescription, 185; and territorial seas, 282–3; and continental shelf doctrine, 285 f
International Law Commission on continental shelf doctrine, 286; on Law of the Sea, 307
international organisations, Gulf States and, 106–14

international personality, 73–80, 107, 130
International Sanitary Convention 1917, 108
international status of treaties between Gulf States and Britain, 84 ff, 90 f, 93
international treaties, 72 f
International Wheat Agreement 1949, 109
intervention by invitation, 246
Ionian Islands, 62; Ships case, 117–118
Iran, 167, see Persia
Iraq: sovereignty over Kuwait, 250–7; succession to Turkish suzerainty in Kuwait, 252, 254; British Mandate, 254; territorial sea, 282;
Iraq Petroleum Company, 215, 243
Isa ibn Salman Al-Khalifah, Shaikh, 10, 34
Islam: Ibadi sect, 2, 18; Empire, 167
islands, 291, 295; as baselines, 289, 296–8, 303, 306; disputed ownership, 303–6
Israel Boycott Committee, 77n, 139 f

Japanese Arabian Oil Company; see Arabian Oil Company
Jiddah, Treaty of, 1927, 68, 75 f, 176, 269n
Johnson, D. H. N., 185, 191
Johore, 82, 98, 131
judicial decisions on international responsibility, 131
jurisdiction, claim to, 249; in neutral zone, 270 f

Kamel, Dr Hassan, 12, 16n
Kay, L. J., 98
Keir, W. Grant, 26n, 27 f
Keith, A. B., 81, 229
Kemball, Lieut A. B., 210 f
Khadduri, Majid, 178
Kharg and Khargo, 291, 305n, 310
Khaur al'Udaid, 199 f, 202, 224, 261, 263
Kubr, 296 f
Kuwait: independence, 2, 40 f, 45, 78, 251 ff; administrative system, 19–20; judicial system, 21–2; Constitution of November 1962, 22; British government relations, 40 ff; tribute paid to Turkey, 41; oil resources, 45; participation in international organ-

Kuwait—*contd.*
isations, 76, 112–14, in Arab League, 77, 95n, 250 f, in OPEC, 77, in GATT, 110–11; treaty making capacity, 99n; nationality laws, 125–6; Israel Boycott Office, 140; boundaries, 219; Turkish and Iraqi sovereignty, 250–7; financial agreement with Iraq, 252; offshore areas, 278; territorial sea, 281;
—Treaties:
Agreement with Britain 1899, 3, 40, 42, 74, 250, 253, 323–4
Agreements on arms trade 1900, 44
Agreements on post office establishment 1904, and installation of telegraph 1912, 44
Kuwait Najd Boundary (Uqair) Convention 1922, 265 f, 273, 317–318
Exchange of Letters with Britain 1923, 256
Exchange of Letters with Iraq 1932, 256
Treaties of Friendship, Trade and Extradition with Saudi Arabia 1942, 103–4, 270
Exchange of Notes with Britain, on independence 1961, 40, 250, 322–323
Kuwait-Saudi Arabia Agreement on Neutral Zone partition 1965, 273–277, 324–8
Kuwait-Saudi Arabia Neutral Zone, 264–77; natural resources exploitation, 266 ff, 274 f, 277, 294, 296; conclusion of individual treaties, 269 f; jurisdiction, 270, administration, 271–3; division, 273
Kuwait Oil Company, 281
Kuwait Shell Company, 291

Lahej dispute, 96–7, 98; Treaty with Britain, 93, 97
Lansdowne, Lord, 6
Lausanne, Treaty of, 1923, 255
Lauterpacht, E., 246
Lauterpacht, H., 85, 101, 183, 185, 192
League of Nations: registration of treaties, 87; Persian protest over Bahrain, 192; admission of Iraq, 254
Liebesny, H. J., 91
Lloyd, Selwyn, 245
London Conference of 1951, 198, 201

Longrigg, S. H., 215
Lubainah islands, 308 f
Luce, Sir William, 250
Lushington, Dr, 117–18

MacGibbon, I. C., 192
Majlis al-Tijahar, 16
Malay, Federated and unfederated states of, 63, 82, 118
Maritime Truce of 1835, 26n, 36, 38
McNair, Lord, 86, 93 f, 100 f, 118, 145
Meade, M. J., 42 f
Mecom, J. W., 301
Mervyn Jones, H., 127
Mesopotamia, 255, *see* Iraq
Miles, Col., 214
mineral concessions, 73
Morocco, 63, 65 f, 77, 79n, 84 f, 131, 157
Mouton, M. W., 282 f, 286, 299
Mubarak ibn Sabah Al-Sabah, Shaikh, 3, 41–2, 250, 253
Muhammad Al-Khalifah, Shaikh, 33, 34n, 169, 171 ff, 174
Muhammad ibn Thani, Shaikh, 36
Muhammarah, Treaty of, 1922, 265n
Muscat: political evolution, 2 f; government and judicial systems, 18–19; Arms Warehouse, 38; British government relations, 47 ff, 67–8; non-alienation of territory, 48, 50; dhows conflict, 51; independent status, 67–70; treaty making capacity, 98; right to declare war, 119; passports, 128; international responsibility, 132; extra-territorial jurisdiction in, 134; dispute with Oman, 157, 160; membership of U.N., 162; concessions to Iraq Petroleum Co., 196; Buraimi Oasis dispute, 207, 214–15, 221, 237 f; British obligations to Sultan, 244 ff
—Treaties:
Treaty of Friendship with Britain 1798, 47
Agreements of 1822 and 1845 on suppression of slave trade, 47, 68
Treaty of Commerce 1839, 115
Treaty of Commerce (with France) 1844, 50, 51–2, 55
Anglo-French Declaration on independence of Muscat and Zanzibar 1862, 49 ff, 67
Declaration for Development of Commercial Relations with Netherlands 1877, 55

Muscat—*contd.*
Agreement on non-alienation of territory 1891, 48, 50, 69, 98
Agreement on coalfield concessions 1902, 48, 69
Treaty of Sib 1920, 158, 241–4, 315–316
Agreement on oil concessions 1923, 49, 69, 70
Treaty of Friendship . . . with Britain 1951, 47, 52–3, 84, 115
Treaty of Friendship . . . with India 1953, 55
Exchange of Letters concerning Muscat armed forces 1958, 54
Treaty of Amity . . . with U.S.A. 1958, 56

Nasser, President, 96
National Iranian Oil Company (NIOC), 290, 292
nationality of protected persons, 65 f, 140–1; of inhabitants of Gulf States, 122 ff; and Persian claim to Bahrain, 195
natural resources, 44, 62, 278 ff, 287
Netherlands, 55, 157
neutral zone: *see* Kuwait-Saudi Arabia Neutral Zone
New Hebrides, 266n, 270
Nu'aim tribe, 208, 211, 214 ff, 217, 221, 248
Nuri Pasha al-Said, 256

offshore boundaries, 288; median line, 306 f; baselines, 288–90, 306; equidistance, 288
Offshore Boundary Agreement, Bahrain-Saudi Arabia, 1958, 306–11
Offshore Boundary Agreement, Iran-Saudi Arabia 1965, 310–11
oil companies and delimitation of state boundaries, 261
oil concessions, 196, 243, 267–70, 274, 294, 296 ff; overlapping, 268, 292 f, 302, 310; negotiation on disputes, 294–5, 305–6
oilfields: problem of capture, 298–300
Oil Rivers Chiefs, Nigeria, 89
Oman: Imamate, 2, 158, 239; coal deposits, 48, 69, 240; sovereignty dispute, 157–61, 239–47; promontory, 208; independence of Inner, 242–3; British armed intervention in,

244–7; Ad Hoc Committee on, *see* United Nations
Omani Revolt, 157
Oppenheim, L., 63 f, 92 f, 99, 120, 140, 179 f, 227
optional clause in favour of Shaikhdoms, 142 f
Organisation of Petroleum Exporting Countries (OPEC), 77
Ormsby Gore, 189

Pacific Western Corporation, 267
Padwa, D. J., 286, 288, 299
Pan-American Petroleum Corporation 290
paramountcy, 82
passports, 127–8
Peace, G. L., 16n
pearling, 26, 30, 280; Qatar, 37 f; Kuwait, 44; Bahrain, 167
Pelly, C. J., 248
Pelly, Col Lewis, 36, 173n, 174, 224n, 261
Perpetual Treaty of Peace 1853, 5, 26n, 78
Persia, 33; title to Bahrain, 34, 167–95; protest on Treaty of Jiddah, 176; offshore area and territorial sea, 279–281; claim to islands, 305; Offshore Boundary Agreement with Saudi Arabia 1965, 310–11
Petroleum Development (Trucial Coast) Ltd, 284
Philby, H. St J. B., 218, 234 f
piracy, suppression of, 5, 25–32 *passim*, 38, 71
Poland, 85
Portuguese influence in Arabian Gulf, 5; government of Bahrain, 167
post office installation, 35, 39, 44
prescription, 184–6, 191–2, 220, 223
protected states, 81, 89, 99 ff, 145 ff, 149–50, 156–61
protectorates, 7, 61–5, 107

Qaru, 271 ff, 296 ff
Qatar: Turkish suzerainty, 4; administration and judicial systems, 12–15; British government relations, 36 ff; independence, 36; membership of international organisations, 76, of Arab League, 77, of OPEC, 77n; nationality laws, 125; oil concessions, 196, 301; boundary problems, 196, 219, 261–3, 302–3; Zubarah

Qatar—*contd.*
dispute, 247–9; offshore areas, 278; ownership of Halul, 304
—Treaties:
Agreement of peace with Britain 1868, 36
Agreement with Britain 1916, 4, 38
Qawasim tribe, 25
Qeshm, 306

Ras al Khaimah, 5, 147–8, 302, 305
Rashid ibn Sa'id al-Maktum, Ruler of Dubai, 11n
Ras Rakan concession, 301
Rawlinson, Sir Henry, 173 f
Rendel, Mr, 233n
Rennie shoal, 308
Rhodesia and Nyasaland, Federation, 107
Riesenfeld, S. A., 283
Riyadh, 196n; line, 199, 205, 224, 237; see Ryan's line
Robbins, R., 81–2
Rosenne, Shabtai, 142
Ross, A., 229–30
rulership, succession to, 10–11
Russian intrusion in Kuwait, threat of, 42
Ryan, Sir Andrew, 198, 230n, 231
Ryan's line, 199, 207, 224; see Riyadh line

Safaniya offshore oilfield, 298
Sa'id ibn Ahmad, Sultan of Muscat, 239
Saqr ibn Sultan, Ruler of Sharjah, 11n
Saudi Arabia: dispute with Britain over Qatar, 75–6; treaty relations with Gulf States, 102–6; boundary disputes, 196, 261–3, 302; Buraimi oases dispute, 196–238; succession to Turkish possessions, 228–31, 233–4; Treaty with Turkey 1914, 233, with Iraq, 265n; offshore areas, 278, 281–282; Offshore Boundary Agreements with Bahrain 1958, 306–9, with Iran 1965, 310–11; Neutral Zone with Kuwait, see Kuwait
Sayyid Sa'id ibn Taimur, Sultan of Muscat, 19, 49, 52
Schwarzenberger, G., 90
self-government and U.N. Charter, 151–6
Sèvres, Treaty of, 1920, 255
Shaikhdoms: internal independence, 83; international personality and

sovereignty, 91; treaty making capacity, 99–102; declaration of war, 116–18, 120–2; U.N. membership, 163; offshore areas, 278
Shakhbut ibn Sultan, 11n, 18n, 284
Shakespeare, W. H. I., 44, 234
Shari'ah law, 16 ff, 20, 21n, 22
Sharjah, 5, 264, 301, 305, 315, 316
Shawcross, Lord, 246
Sheil, Lt-Col, 170
Shell Company of Qatar, 301
shoals as baselines, 289
Sib, Treaty of, 1920, 158, 241–4, 315–16
Singapore, 107
Sirri, 305
slave trade, suppression, of, 27–32 *passim*, 38, 47, 68, 71, 111
Somaliland Protectorate dispute, 87 f
South Africa, 100 f
sovereignty, 222, 225, 252–3; joint, 266, 269, 275
Spain, 183
sphere of influence concept, 61
sponge concessions, 30, 45
Standstill Agreement (Saudi Arabian boundary) 1952, 202
Starke, J. G., 138
Studer, Adolph G. case, 131, 133, 137
Superior Oil Corporation, 284
Sur, 48, 240
suzerainty, 61, 237, 252–3

Tanb (Tunb), 305
telegraph installations, 35, 39, 44
'territorial application clause', 109
territorial seas, 280–4
Thesiger, W. P., 215 f, 218
Thomas, Bertram, 217
treaties between Gulf States and Britain: nature of, 71–2, 76, 78; justiciability, 84–91, 92 f; unilateral abrogation, 91–5; breaches of obligations, 95–8; bilateral, 102; multilateral, 106–14
treaties: state succession to, 228, 252
tribute, 36, 71; 215; see zakah
Trucial Shaikhdoms: administration and jurisdiction, 16–17; status prior to British protection, 70–3; status under British protection, 73–80; boundary disputes, 196, 263–4, 303; off-shore concessions, 301
—Treaties:
Agreement of Peace (East India Co.) 1806, 25

Trucial Shaikhdoms—*contd*.
General Treaty of Peace 1820, 5 f, 26
Perpetual Treaty of Peace 1853, 5, 26n
Exclusive Agreement 1892, 5, 29, 314
Agreement on arms trade suppression 1902, 30
Agreement on pearling and sponge concessions 1911, 30
Undertaking concerning oil exploitation 1922, 30
Trucial States Council, and Development Office, 17
Tunisia, 63, 65, 77, 85, 131, 157
Turkey, 33, 45; claims in Bahrain, 34, 172 f, in Qatar, 37, in Kuwait, 41, 43, 250, 252–3; control over Hasa, 212, 217; *see* Anglo-Turkish Conventions
Turki ibn 'Utaishan, Amir, 202, 221

Umm al-Maradim, 271 ff, 296 ff
Umm Shaif oilfield, 301
Union Oil of California and Southern Gas, 302
United Arab Republic, 96
United Nations: membership of Gulf States, 41, 151–6, 161–4, 251; Ad Hoc Committee on Oman, 54, 67n, 68n, 69 f, 158n, 159n, 160 f, 245n, 247; registration of treaties, 86; settlement of disputes between Gulf States and Britain, 156–61; fact-finding mission in Buraimi, 206–7;

and Iraqi threat to Kuwait, 251; Memorandum on Regime of High Seas, 299
United States of America: treaty with Muscat, 56 f; consulate in Kuwait, 77; independence, 183; proclamation on offshore areas, 278
'Uqair Convention 1922, 265 f, 273, 317–18
'Utubi Arabs, 36, 167, 182

Violet line, 199, 201, 220, 228n, 237

Wade, E. C. S., 81
Wahhabi Arabs, 25, 36, 71; House of Sa'ud, 196n; collection of tribute, 211
Waldock, C. H. M., 222 f, 225
Waterfield, Gordon, 88
Westlake, J., 61, 63 f, 181
Wheaton, E., 95
Williams, Sir John Fischer, 181
Wright, Quincy, 246

Yemen, 219, 227
Young, Richard, 204n, 280, 287
Yusuf Yasin, Shaikh, 203, 205, 233n

zakah, 201, 207, 217, 223, 226
Zanzibar, 49, 55, 82
Zayid ibn Sultan, Shaikh of Abu Dhabi, 18n
Zubarah, 3 f, 36 f, 167, 182, 247–9, 302
Zwemer, Samuel, 214